Migrant Cartographies

Migrant Cartographies

New Cultural and Literary Spaces in Post-Colonial Europe

Edited by
Sandra Ponzanesi and
Daniela Merolla

LEXINGTON BOOKS

A Division of
ROWMAN & LITTLEFIELD PUBLISHERS, INC.
Lanham • *Boulder* • *New York* • *Toronto* • *Oxford*

We gratefully acknowledge permission to reprint the following material. Chapter 1, Robert Fraser, "Mapping the Mind: Borders, Migration, and Myth," originally appeared in *Wasafiri* 39 (Summer 2003). Reprinted by permission of author and publisher. Chapter 4, Graham Huggan, "Virtual Multiculturalism: The Case of Contemporary Britain," originally appeared in *Britain at the Turn of the Twenty-First Century*, ed. Susan Bassnett and Ulrich Broich (Amsterdam/New York: Rodopi, 2001). Reprinted by permission of author and publisher. Chapter 11, Ena Jansen, "'The Risks Migrating Words Take': Some Thoughts on the Afrikaans Poetry of Elisabeth Eybers in a Context of Transmigration," originally appeared on pp. 141–62 in *Literature and Migration: South Africa*, ed. Catharina Loader and Helmuth A. Niederle (Vienna: Edition Praesens, 2004). Reprinted by permission of author and publisher.

LEXINGTON BOOKS

A division of Rowman & Littlefield Publishers, Inc.
A wholly owned subsidary of The Rowman & Littlefield Publishing Group, Inc.
4501 Forbes Boulevard, Suite 200
Lanham, MD 20706

PO Box 317
Oxford
OX2 9RU, UK

Copyright © 2005 by Lexington Books

British Library Cataloguing in Publication Information Available

Library of Congress Cataloging-in-Publication Data

Migrant cartographies : new cultural and literary spaces in post-colonial Europe / edited by Sandra Ponzanesi and Daniela Merolla.
   p. cm.
  Includes bibliographical references and index.
  ISBN 0-7391-0754-2 (cloth : alk. paper) — ISBN 0-7391-0755-0 (pbk. : alk. paper)
  1. Europe—Emigration and immigration—Social aspects. 2. Pluralism (Social sciences)—Europe. 3. Ethnicity—Europe. 4. Political geography—Europe. 5. Europe—Civilization—20th century. 6. Emigration and immigration in literature. 7. Emigration and immigration in motion pictures. I. Ponzanesi, Sandra, 1967– II. Merolla, Daniela, 1960– III. Series.
JV7590.M484 2005
304.8'4—dc22   2004025464

Printed in the United States of America

∞™ The paper used in this publication meets the minimum requirements of American National Standard for Information Sciences—Permanence of Paper for Printed Library Materials, ANSI/NISO Z39.48-1992.

Contents

Preface

The completion of *Migrant Cartographies* has been the result of a long and complex synergy between prominent international scholars, different academic institutions, and many geographical locations. Before reaching its final outline the text itself underwent a myriad of reconfigurations, incorporating all the cartographic migrations professed in its critical approach.

This project stemmed from a very successful international conference "Writing Europe 2001: Migrant Cartographies, Cultural Travelers, and New Literature" that was held March 22–24, 2001, at the University of Leiden and at the University of Amsterdam, The Netherlands. Speakers from all over the world contributed to an intellectual brainstorming on the necessity and difficulty of developing new critical tools for assessing the rapidly changing panorama of migration in Europe. This has inspired and stimulated us to organize a book reflecting not only the state of the art on migration literatures and cultures in Europe at the beginning of the new millennium, but as well views and ideas concerning some of the infinite future trajectories.

We are very pleased this volume works as a "text of transit." It does not claim to have reached its final destination, but offers instead a systematic and yet creative mapping of the many possible roots to be accounted for and routes to be undertaken. Though this is the first volume that attempts such a comprehensive and wide-ranging approach to migrant writings and cultures within postcolonial Europe we are very well aware of its "transitory" nature. Migrations to and within Europe are ever-changing phenomena and can hardly be constrained by conceiving Europe as a clear unchanging spatial container or temporal marker.

Preface

Cultural productions and artifacts keep reshaping the landscape of post-colonial Europe on a daily basis: many of the authors dealt with in these essays will have published new texts or have disappeared; new generations of migrant writers will have emerged and be into new forms of publication; a new wave of artists and filmmakers will have managed to have found their audiences; new bits of legislation and current affairs will have made it to the newspaper headlines and the EU will redraft its borders, expanding its membership and barricading its frontiers at the same time.

We hope the present reader will find some guidance here for further research, and some serious disorientation when the need to fix, codify, and determine migration cultures in postcolonial Europe will emerge. Postcolonial Europe is *not* just another arbitrary label. To the contrary, it is a critical term that reassesses Europe not only in its past imperial pluralities and contemporary divergent multicultural scenarios, but as well in its rearticulation of migration as an integral part of its territorial indeterminacy. Between the poles of geography and genealogy we have attempted to unpack the dynamics of identity and belonging by contesting the dominant discourses around homelands, nationality, and citizenship. Unpacking Europe as much as unpacking identity has been the main drive of this adventure. We hope to have charted some of the possible alternative representations and modes of thinking and writing.

We would like to thank for their financial support the Netherlands Organisation for Scientific Research, the Royal Netherlands Academy of Arts and Sciences, the Research School CNWS, School of Asian, African, and Amerindian Studies at Leiden, the University of Amsterdam, and Utrecht University.

Sandra Ponzanesi and Daniela Merolla

Amsterdam
April 2005

Introduction

Daniela Merolla and Sandra Ponzanesi

CULTURAL TRAVELERS AND NEW LITERATURES

Migration is a one-way trip. (Stuart Hall, *Minimal Selves*, 1996)

This book focuses upon the role migration plays in reshaping European identities. The wide-ranging articles gathered here adopt an interdisciplinary and comparative approach in which the literary and cultural representations of the migrant experience are interrogated across boundaries, languages, and identities. The increased significance of the migrant condition in contemporary society is, in fact, demonstrated not only by the exponential growth of texts produced by artists operating beyond national parameters but also by the flourishing of tropes of dislocation as necessary to capture the fleeting momentum of the urban experience.

It can therefore be said that grand historical narratives of former European metropolitan centers are being interrupted and de-centered by people shifting among multiple locations whose diasporic sensibilities refashion traditional definitions of literary canons, identities, and genres. But it can also be said that the settled experience has changed its connotations, from being related to origin, centrality, and authenticity to an increased awareness of its endless iteration and transformation.

Migration as a key moment in historical awareness breaks down the persisting force of oppositional discourses that strategically places white Western

1

Europe as the sovereign subject by marking the "rest" as excessive, disturbing, and strongly secluded. As Stuart Hall so poignantly has written:

> Identity is formed at the unstable point where the "unspeakable" stories of subjectivity meet the narratives of history, of a culture. And since he/she is positioned in relation to cultural narratives which have been profoundly expropriated, the colonized subject is always "somewhere else": doubly marginalized, displaced, always other than where he/she is, or is able to speak from.[1]

Playing Out Definitions

Migrations to and within Europe continue to be interpreted as relating to people from less affluent countries such as former colonial outposts or new destitute areas. It refers to disenfranchised people venturing toward the wealthier European metropolises that—as central locations of culture and rationality—are thus opposed to the migrants' lands of origin, seen as multiple peripheral arteries that depend upon the center for their definition. However, the question of migrant intelligentsia (cosmopolitan jet-setters and nomadic globe-trotters), which is quite central to the literary debate, risks turning the notion of migration into a "culturalism": an isolated emphasis upon the discursive aspects of representation, identity, and cultural hybridity would entirely miss those material and social implications of migrancy relating to issues of gender, ethnicity, class, and nationality.

Migration as a demographic phenomenon is far from being a contemporary and homogeneous movement that concerns Europe as the main recipient of global relocations of cultures and resources. Migrations have always been part of human civilization from ancient times to our days, and have been characterized by multiple articulations of difference. It has often concerned human migrations to and from regions, such as in the Arabic regions or the Far East, that were barely aware of Europe as a future hegemonic bulwark. Yet, the advent of European colonialism marked a turning point in the mapping of Europe as a self-contained entity, progressively defined through its opposition to the many ends of its empires. The colonies were, in fact, separated at political, geographical, and racial levels. This implied that the dislocation of white settlers and rulers to the colonies was reconfigured as a form of internal movement, and not as migration, since the hegemonic relationship guaranteed territorial continuity for the rulers well beyond their metropolitan centers. It was in fact during the colonial expansion that racial taxonomies were invented and deployed to secure the cultural supremacy of the West upon the natives. The need for an ideologically informed and scientifically motivated racial hierarchy was caused by the menacing proximity of the colonizers and the natives in the Tropics. This urge to justify the colonial exploitation as a civilizing mission (the white man's burden) rested heavily on the original implementation of racial disparity and continued to symbolically demarcate the center/periphery divide regardless of specific geographical locations.[2] This legacy was protracted far beyond the demise of Western empires and is still nowadays at the source of contemporary racism and xenophobia within Europe, sentiments that are often coupled with and played out against questions of migration and the redefinition of citizenship.

The changed nature of migration in the twenty-first century has resuscitated the phantom of the other in new fashions. The irreversible process of globalization—facilitated by new means of transportation, telecommunications, and internationalization of the labor force—has rendered national boundaries highly porous. Paradoxically, rather than being dissolved, the necessity to re-imagine and re-construct notions of political belonging along ethnic and religious identifications has become even more heightened. Migration has therefore come to signify all possible processes of identification and dis-identification relating to the trespassing of borders and of "off limits" territories—both material and symbolic. It is an almost utopian notion that is highly charged with the legacy of the past and promises of the future.

Hence migration becomes a literal and metaphorical transition in space but also a translation in time. It refers to a past and a present whose territorial boundaries do not overlap anymore. As Salman Rushdie has written, "The Past is a country from which we have all migrated."[3] It refers to a notion of home that becomes an abstraction, a desire for a lost origin, an ideal setting for nostalgia and memory, whereas migrancy becomes a new location to be inhabited, a new form of self-writing and imagining. Much of postcolonial theorizing has reified the category of migration as the leading metaphor—along with others such as diaspora, exile, expatriation, and cosmopolitanism. This is meant to express the reopened traffic between center and periphery, to contest those frontiers that cut across languages, cultures, and religions in hegemonic ways, and to convey the space where multiple selves, origins, and belongings can be articulated and jostled.

European Visions

As Marc Augé wrote, the "acceleration of history" and "the excess of space" is correlative with the shrinking of the planet.[4] It is, therefore, necessary to address the experience of migration both in terms of its traditional reference to human movements and as a signifier for the condition of "supermodernity" in which we all negotiate our networked self. In order to expose the conundrum of these world articulations this volume focuses on the relationship between migration, literature, and culture.

The development of migrant literatures in the European languages reveals indeed that not only people but also ideas have been traveling, transcending, and interconnecting apparently separate colonial legacies. This is happening at a moment when Europe is changing institutionally, and is renegotiating belongings, communities, and borders.[5]

Within the European scenario it is high time to ask when an idea of European literature will supersede the national literatures, or when migrant literature will be an object of comparison without having to pass via the national canon. What are the implications of globalization for literature? Does it reinforce the "re-location" of literature by rekindling regional literatures? Is Europe really moving toward a European literature that also reflects new migrant writings? To which audience is migrant literature directed? Does the migrant label enhance the visibility of writers shifting between languages and cultures, or does it simply relegate them to a luxury ghetto?

These questions relate to the difficulties we encountered while discussing how to define the "migrant" and subsequently the "migrant writer and artist." The major thorny question was whether such a notion would not be ethnocentric, by assuming that the migrant is not just a traveler, a wanderer, but implicitly the person who reproduces the colonial divide in new global terms. Indeed, very often the label of "migrant" is imposed upon exoticism and ethnic difference in order to mark "otherness," even in literary terms. So far migrant literature as a category has been relegated to the realm of social studies: therefore it is time to search for new paradigms of interpretation that can assess the value of a literature of migration in its own terms. However, it is difficult not to fall into the pitfall of historical demarcation. When does a migrant stop being a migrant? Often second or third generation immigrants are still strategically enclosed within the tradition of migrant literature, risking therefore their ghettoization from the mainstream canon, be it of the home or hosting nation. Within the international scenario the question of canon has become rather debatable since migrant or transnational writers are better equipped to evoke a new global poetics that cuts across literary compartments based on political boundaries and untenable cultural essentialisms. If we appeal to a new global aesthetics, in which both themes of dislocation and styles of hybridization are taken as indicators of the new contemporary intellectual experience, the category of "migrant literature" becomes redundant. The label is in fact used to mark writers who are at home in the world—though linked to a familiar genealogy of migration—and invalidate the notion of literary appropriation.

The only clear connection is that these are writers and artists who address and investigate issues of home and abroad, identity and language, private and public domains, in more acute forms. They often posit questions of cultural affiliation in terms of the way the inherited legacy of migration impinges upon integration and belonging in the country of destination—or better, in the country of new belonging. This creates a hiatus between the transformative force of migration and its positive metabolization of differences, and the conservative aspect of migration, which reinforces communal and ethnic enclaves in order to safeguard the identity of the guests vis-à-vis the omnivorous assimilationist force of the host country.

The much-celebrated cultural fusion has, in fact, its global backlash. This refers to claims made by religious fundamentalism or resurgent "ethnic" literatures or artistic enclaves to the right of engaging in authentic celebrations of the self that are often dissonant with the spirit of migration as a renovating and challenging force. By exploring the intersections between migration, literature, and culture, the dual goal of this book can be summarized: First, we aim to upgrade migration from its natural association with the myth of origin and authenticity in sociological and anthropological terms. Second, we aim to show the processes by which the writing of literature can be interpreted as a form of migration in itself, as a journey of the mind and as an itinerary of discovery. This is achieved by emphasizing the very migrant nature of creative writing, as exploration of the self, both as a process of identity formation and of critical investigation.

According to this interpretation Trinh T. Minh-ha's definition of the voyage as a re-siting of boundaries can be very useful. She writes that

> The traveling self is here both the self that moves physically from one place to another, following "public routes" and "beaten track" within a mapped movement, and the self that embarks on an undetermined journeying practice, having constantly to negotiate between home and abroad, native culture and adopted culture, or more creatively speaking, between a here, a there, *and* an elsewhere.[6]

Therefore migration implies both movements within and without, a becoming a "stranger in a strange land" (Minh-ha, 1994, p. 9) but also a form of undoing the self, what Gilles Deleuze and Félix Guattari have defined as "deterritorialization," a process by which one becomes "minor" in one's own country, language, and culture. To be a migrant becomes therefore an imperative, an injunction against the reproduction of hegemonic discourses, but also a way of keeping that double insight, that sharpness of critical experience that is based on the tingling feeling of unbelonging, of yet but not quite, of comforting un-homeliness.

The experience of migration, of what it means to be a migrant—in between spaces, identifications, and forms of expression—becomes lionized as the new existential condition that is based on the re-siting of imposed boundaries, undermining of codified cultural outings, and negotiation of multiple sites of differentiations.[7] This jargon has become common practice even in literary theory, where the legacy of postmodern thinking meets postcolonial critique imposing new explorations of "culturally different texts." The issue of positionality, of who is writing for whom, and of interpretation, who is "competent" to translate culturally different texts for whom, remains at the source of the multicultural scenario.

However unsatisfactory the term multiculturalism might be, and however contested it might be because of its implied leveling and essentializing of differences as cookie-cutter categories, one fits all, it remains an inevitably controversial arena. Stemming from differently articulated European public policies, multiculturalism remains useful to expose the limits and drawbacks of identity politics as much as the merits and potentiality of a common ground for alternative practices.

Theoretical Background

In order to explore the impact of migration on Western hegemonic cultures and on the definition of the nation-state, the various papers gathered in this collection question the very notion of Europe as an imaginary community. This is meant to undermine what Edward Said has defined as Orientalism—a Western projection of the other for the mere purpose of identifying the self as superior, unified, universal, and unassailable. The European borderline is now being redefined by voices which once were excluded or marginalized from its main body. Europe is, therefore, discussed as a terrain interlocking past legacies of empire and new global push and pull factors, and as the privileged site for investigating questions of migration both in their material and historical development and in their symbolic and creative overtones.

For that purpose this book focuses on questions of migration and their relation to artistic productions, in specific literary texts and cultural productions. Migrant literature has still the function of negotiation between the legacy of the past and the accelerated momentum of the present. The compression of space and time is already an integral part of being a migrant. By contributing to a form of particularization migrant literature resists global warming, literally meaning the panic of a world which is not one but is ruled as one.

However, this reading of migrant literature creates some critical questions. Does this migrant literature negotiate a space in-between or move further toward the creation of a third space, which is neither the local nor the global but something hovering between the two? Is hybridity a sufficient term to express the restlessness of literature and of literary affiliations? To explore the condition of migration as hybridizing force means to recognize the transformative effects of modernity and imperialism for both indigenous and metropolitan culture. It is based on the assumption that, unlike the old definition of the nation-state, all cultures are, in actual practice, heterogeneous, unmonolithic, mobile formations, as Edward Said,[8] among others, has argued. For Bhabha, the hybridity bound up with empire is not a simple mix, but a way of living and narrating unequal and antagonistic cultural encounters that disrupt and disturb the authoritative gaze of the oppressor and the discourse of colonial hegemony. Here it is a recognition of the disjunctive temporalities and cultural spaces that form the life-world where tradition, modernity, and community unevenly coexist or combine. In contemporary culture, one could conceptualize hybridity in relation to the emergence of a "third space," a space of transgression and subversion, the place whence "newness enters the world." Hybridity in this sense participates in a counter-hegemonic move.

More recently, a variety of insightful explorations such as in the work of Stuart Hall,[9] Paul Gilroy,[10] Cornell West,[11] or Anthony Appiah[12] have established the extent to which the polarities inscribed in the notion of the West and its "others" misunderstand and distort the complexities of the identities forged in the long time of living with racism and making one's own a critical modernity. Paul Gilroy has strategically focused on the importance of seeing whiteness and Europeanness not only as one of the many pieces of the mosaic, but as being racialized from within, as being formed and based on its very articulation of otherness. The history of Western modernity is in fact not based on the opposition between a Europe and its colonial liminality, but constructed upon and generated by that very "alterity" that operates from within. The empire was not something out there but inherent to the construction of the Western metropolitan self, as inherently and implicitly racialized, not existing without the other. Thereby all cultures are inherently diasporic, rhizomatic, and contaminated. To uphold authenticity and purity as a crucial aspect of minority cultures automatically reignites the Eurocentric discourse that migrant literature tries to undermine. Therefore, though the term is useful to identify shifts in global relations and in tracing the hybridization of cultural aesthetics, it should not be used as a dogma, but only deployed as a critical term, with more careful discrimination and need for specificity.

Female critics like Spivak,[13] hooks,[14] and Minh-ha,[15] among others, add the factor of gender to the overriding questions of subjectivity, questioning the new position of women within the new world relocation of multinational capital. The feminization of migration is one of the most remarkable features of recent movements due to the increased numbers of women requested in the West to work in the housekeeping sector. The domestic tasks have often not been redistributed between the partners, and Western women are increasingly engaged in a work career outside their home. Consequently, the private chores are left vacant, open to be filled up by a new migrant labor force, generally female and very often from the Philippines and Cape Verde. Other migrant women are involved in the new sweatshop industries, multinational garment factories that are based not only in Asian countries such as Bangladesh and India, but often within the heart of European metropolitan cities. Furthermore, migrant women from Eastern Europe are often the main target of sex trafficking within Europe, but this occurs significantly also from Latin America and Nigeria. Despite the policy of legalization of prostitution

embarked upon by the Dutch state, there remains a host of problems centered around the exploitation of illegal migrant women who are not accepted
or protected by the law remain. This vulnerable category of migrant women
is often helped in its migration to Europe by human smugglers under false
pretenses. Allured by the possibilities of attractive jobs, they land in the prostitution circuit in which they remain enslaved. It must be said, however, that
many migrant women intentionally and freely enter the profession as a temporary business, either to save enough money to support their family at home
or to initiate an economic activity in their homelands on their return.

Directions

So what next? How is this kind of hybridity as transition reflected in recent
cultural productions, and for this specific purpose in migrant literature and
culture? What is what Gilroy frames as the "rhizomorphic, fractal structure of
the transcultural"?[16] What then is beyond hybridity and syncretism in literature? What new identities? These are questions that resist neat solutions, not
least because they resist the problem of subjectification, metropolitan versus
migrant, and resist the normalization and re-appropriations to which the machinery of otherness is prone.

As a consequence, literature and art cannot be framed anymore within national canons, due to the global relocation of people and cultures: now every
attempt to grapple with questions of origin and belonging becomes tainted by
further questions of hybridity, syncretism, in-betweenness, interculturality,
multiculturalism, transformativity, cosmopolitanism. However, there is still
the need to classify, categorize, and find common parameters to define new
literary texts as part of world production. New cultural dimensions opened up
by migration are re-shaping the spaces of identification. Migration—often in
the form of the return of the repressed, and relating to people at the outposts
of the empire now coming to share the old metropolitan center—forces an
operation of hybridization not only of the metropolitan culture and of the literary representations of cultural difference, but also of the urban landscape
and media culture at large.

This book, through an interdisciplinary and comparative approach that
cuts across boundaries, languages, and identities, aims to highlight and rec-
tify many of the fateful myths around migration and ethnic absolutism. It further aims to shed a new light on the potential of migrant literatures as a form
of metropolitan transformation and new cosmopolitan humanism.

The various strands of literary and artistic productions within Europe are
explored, addressed, and questioned in the various essays here gathered.
They investigate the changed nature of migration and its impact on cultural
representations within Europe as connected to wider transnational and trans-
historical phenomena. However, these explorations concern not only litera-

ture and the arts in the traditional sense but also other cultural expressions as reflections of the lived experience. Migrants outside and around the literary representations are here, the last part of the book being devoted to the arts and mass culture in general.

The first part, "Mapping Europe: Theoretical Interventions," offers a critical view of the state of the art in theories of migration, on concepts of dislocation and their role in reshaping categories of thought and in visualizing new existential conditions.

In his opening article "Mapping the Mind: Borders, Migration, and Myth" Robert Fraser makes a major historical intervention by mapping the contribution made by migrancy to European national formations and the cartography of segregations. The incursion of the "other" as the dissident, diseased, or exotic nomad, has permeated European perception and definition of the self from the origin of Christendom to the contemporary digital traveler.

He examines in particular two dissenting societies that have marked the thinking around the previous fin-de-siècle: gypsies and bohemians. By means of this equation, the bohemian figure—artist, thinker, or revolutionary— becomes a paradigm of the alien within, the settled nomad, and the stranger with Eastern affinities whose very presence threatens the status quo. This leads the author to analyze within contemporary culture the way in which the concern with migration still feeds the vision and connotations of disjunctive grouping such as "counter-cultures," "alternative societies," and "new age travelers."

Following on Fraser's historical footpath, Tabish Khair argues in his essay "The Politics of the Perception of Human Movement" that travel writing and migration are not a specificity of European culture. In medieval times, for example, travelers within Asia and the Arabic world were hardly aware of Europe as such. Khair sketches three phases within the history of human movements. First, prior to the fifteenth century human movement appears to have been largely a random phenomenon—all communities and cultures could be just as mobile or as static depending on various material and symbolic factors (along with Marco Polo there was a very rich tradition of non-European travel writing ranging from Ash-Sharif al-Idrisi, 1100–1166, to Ibn Battuta, 1304–1369). Second, during the early Renaissance from the sixteenth century onward the visibility of travel writing and the related texts from outside Europe start to become invisible. Finally, only on the wake of European colonial conquest do Western tales completely overwrite the narrative of travel to Europe by non-Western travelers.

In short, even though Asians and Africans continued to "travel" during and after the sixteenth century, their movement appears to grow progressively less visible until the nineteenth and early twentieth centuries. With the demise of European empires however, non-Western travelers to Europe become magnified as the new migrants, the postcolonial refugees who came to occupy the former imperial centers. This new direction in human movements to Europe clearly brings with itself the racial connotations established in the outpost of empires by the European supremacy. Khair not only challenges the asymmetrical report and ideological claims about the visibility of these movements, but contests the very notion that European modernity was constructed in the pure outward mobility of Western travelers.

This contested synonymy of Europe with whiteness is strongly criticized by Paul Gilroy in his essay, "A Cat in a Kipper Box, or The Confessions of a 'Second Generation Immigrant.'" Gilroy adds a different slant to the theoretical debate by claiming that there cannot be a discourse on migration without addressing the historical source of current racism in contemporary Europe. The exploration of racial taxonomies created at the other end of the empire needs to be addressed and contested within the cultural contexts of Western metropolitan culture in order to understand how race thinking is intrinsic and not external to the European project of modernity. All across Europe, Gilroy argues, national identities are articulated with the language of absolute ethnicity and racialized difference. Gilroy nudges us to rethink the origin of racism, back to imperial and colonial domination, in order to understand contemporary nationalism and patriotism that often turns bad in racist, ultra-nationalist, and neo-fascist movements. To do away with race would be Gilroy's theoretical solution since, as he writes, "exposure to otherness always promotes ontological jeopardy." However, the abolition of the category of race does not mean the elimination of racism, and in order to fight totalitarianism the conflation between cultural terms and politics should be kept under strict scrutiny.

Paul Gilroy is troubled by the very notion of migration, regardless of its creative or sociological component. Migration to Europe implies the vision of a "white Europe" engrossed in its postcolonial melancholia, an essence in itself that reactively works against those "racialized" groups that are already within, and not at the other end of history. Migration functions as one more dangerous tool of multicultural myopia, an instrument that makes of diversity a "culturalism" and erases the still dominant political and economic materiality of racism and prejudicial representations.

On the wave of Gilroy, Graham Huggan questions the idea of Britain as a truly multicultural society. He explores and questions the insidious nature of the multicultural terminology and ideology within the British contexts. He surveys the literary, cultural, and sociological "unlikability" of "real" equality in a condition of "virtual" pluralism. In his essay, "Virtual Multiculturalism: The Case of Contemporary Britain," he argues that the term *multiculturalism*, as currently recycled by New Labour, is part of the clash between two apparently incompatible discourses: the modernization one, according to which all different ethnic communities are part of Britain, and the integrationist one, which stands for the notion of unity-in-diversity, with its racialist undertone. Huggan is particularly fascinated by the idea of "media spin" through which New Labour managed to create an idea of *virtual community*, linked by technology across race, class, and gender barriers. The question remains, in any case, as to whether multicultural policies are able to counteract systemic racial discrimination and interethnic violence in any effective way. Certainly in Britain, the recent evidence suggests that multiculturalism is trapped in a state of multiply encoded *virtuality*—"virtual" both in the sense of being part of an unfinished, perhaps unfinishable, social project and in the sense of being apparently condemned to exist—in effect not fact, theory not practice—at the level of the hyperreal.

Graham Huggan repeated his important statement that migrant literature is often accused of, or at least labeled as, being "sociologically overdetermined and aesthetically underrated," thereby reinforcing or reinventing the binarism between life and art, history and fiction, truth claims and arbitrariness that is not any longer tenable. This is the case nowadays not only in the realm of cultural studies but as well in more strict literary practices (postcolonialism, postmodernism, new historicism) and sociological practices (oral histories, gender studies, multiculturalism), which are at the crossroads with each other and in constant dialogue.

The first part on theoretical interventions is closed by Mineke Schipper with her essay "One Bangle Does Not Jingle: Cultures, Literatures, and Migration in a Globalizing World." Schipper asks the important question: what does this flow of intellectuals, writers, and artists to Europe mean in their respective countries of origin? The author emphasizes investigating the negative impact of the brain drain from the African academy and scientific world and the continuous production and reproduction of Africa's marginalization from the centers of economic and discursive power. The colonial paradigm of the West going to Africa in search of raw material seems to repeat itself within the new global system of corporate multinationals digging for resources at both the material, intellectual, and spiritual levels. In analyzing the nature of migration to Europe, Schipper points out the importance of focusing on historical and geo-political differences but also the importance of finding similarities, in an attempt to sketch a sort of humanism and common ground that are spread with globalization. This invocation to situate differences within similarities is further articulated in the next cluster.

The second part, "Writing across the Borders: New Literatures in Europe," goes more into the emergence of migrant literatures within the various national literary traditions and the way in which they are absorbed, rejected, or marginalized in the various national discourses.

In his essay "Stranger in a Strange Land: Jamal Mahjoub's *The Carrier*" Theo D'haen analyzes the past representations of Europe's other through the novel of Jamal Mahjoub, published in 1998 but set, in one of its narrative frames, in the dark days of medieval Europe, when the Arab world was at its

peak politically, scientifically, and culturally. *The Carrier* also "ethnographically" represents to us Europe as seen by its "others," upending most clichés
the West holds with regard to itself as well as to Islam. What is at stake in *The
Carrier* is obviously the relationship between East and West, between Christianity, or Europe, and Islam.

D'haen defines *The Carrier* as an example of "counter-postmodernism,"
that is, a fiction that avails itself of all the trappings of the postmodern paradigm not simply to undermine the certainties of Western civilization from the
inside, but rather to provide a corrective from the margins of that civilization.
D'haen goes on to further analyze the relationship between postmodernism
and postcolonial theorizing, and he quotes Stephen Slemon, who proclaims
the value of "rewriting the canonical 'master texts' of Europe," with the difference that "whereas a post-modernist criticism would want to argue that literary practices such as these expose the constructedness of *all* textuality, . . .
an *interested* postcolonial critical practice would want to allow for the positive production of oppositional truth-claims in these texts."[17] Instead of defining the relationship between postmodernism and postcolonialism as antagonistic, D'haen prefers to see it as complementary or "supplemental."

In "From Guest Worker to Hybrid Immigrant: Changing Themes of Ger-
man-Turkish Literature," Meyda Yegenoglu continues the analysis of the
other as religiously differentiated and orientalized in her essay on Turkish
migrant communities living in Germany. By departing from the reiterated
claim that "Germany is not a country of immigration," Yegenoglu goes on to
discuss the legal and epistemological status of more than twenty million immigrants living in Germany who are labeled as "guest workers," therefore
temporarily present and meant to return to their respective homelands. The
author focuses on the presence of Turkish immigrant communities who from
the beginning have written about their experiences in their new environment. From a first phase when immigrants longed to return home, glorifying
the notion of origin, a shift has occurred for the second generation, which
appears to have become hyphenated, Turkish-German, moving in and out of
cultures. The language used seems to reflect this hybrid identity and double
affiliation. By rejecting the label of "guest workers" as well as the role of
spokesperson for their particular ethnic group and cultural tradition, this
new generation of immigrants corrodes the divide between a no longer tenable notion of pure German society and the guests. By making a sophisticated intervention into the notion of the other as guest, using Derrida's argument about hospitality, Yegenoglu highlights the inherent paradox in the
conditional *and* lawful welcoming of the other as guest: since it can also be
productively understood as conforming to "the structure of exception," it is
thereby just a realignment of sovereignty.

Like Yegenoglu, Angelika Bammer also refers to the Turkish-German
writer Emine Sevgi Özdamar, whose novel *Mother Tongue* (1994) represents

a milestone for the study of crossing boundaries, generations, and identities through language itself, by contaminating and reinventing the grammar of migration. In her essay, "'Between Foreign and Floating Signs': The Language of Migrant Subjects," Angelika Bammer focuses on the notion of the migrant as seen from a position that has been officially declared vacant. Bammer's question is, then: What is the language of such a subject? How does a signifying absence speak? Bammer explores the possibilities of a language which is in between that of domination, the hegemonic Self, and that of resistance, the marginalized other. That space in-between is recognized by Bammer as a strategic play with silence, a silence that lets the body speak. Bammer goes on to apply her reading in two texts: the first one by the Franco-Moroccan writer and literary scholar Abdelfattah Kilito, "Les mots canins" ("Dog Words," 1985), and the second one by a Korean-American writer and video and performance artist, Theresa Hak Kyung Cha, *Dictée* (1982). Through the analysis of these two texts Bammer explores how silence and the articulating body are means by which available notions of self-identity can be questioned and resituated. Bammer proceeds to apply the theoretical framework elaborated by exploring the place of silence and its strategic use in relation to identity categories in the work of other contemporary immigrant European writers (Emine Sevgi Özdamar, Assia Djebar, Herta Müller).

Lourdes López-Ropero engages in the broader theme of migration from a diasporic perspective in her "Roots and Routes: Diaspora, Travel Writing, and Caryl Phillips's Sounding of the Black Atlantic." By connecting the reading of Caryl Phillips's travelogue *The Atlantic Sound* with Paul Gilroy's influential work *The Black Atlantic,* Lopez-Ropero investigates the resonances among these two projects that focus on the transcendence of "ethnic absolutism" and the relocation of the fluid network of black diasporic movements across historical, national, and cultural divides. Phillips charts in his fiction what Gilroy has defined as the black Atlantic world, "one single and complex unit." By discussing the black diaspora without relying on the paradigm of race Gilroy offers a response to the essentialist excesses of contemporary black cultural studies and politics. According to the author, Caryl Phillips is an exemplary writer of the new migrant Europe since his travelogue is a mature statement of the author's black identity politics that allows him to transcend the "watery boundaries of Gilroy's black Atlantic and explore new sites."

The exploration of new sites is central to Rosemarie Buikema's essay, "A Poetics of Home: On Narrative Voice and the Deconstruction of Home in Migrant Literature." She explores the role of the migrant author as a relatively new phenomenon in the Dutch literary industry. However, this sudden interest in the "migrant author," at least in the press, runs the risk of categorizing these authors only in sociological and biographical terms. The lack of literary analytical principle, Buikema warns us, can reignite orientalizing discourses according to which migrant authors are slotted in uncomfortable and discrediting literary niches. By exploring the work of bicultural authors in the Netherlands, such as the prize winning Dutch-Moroccan Abdelkader Benali, Buikema explores the new literary interventions through which these authors engage with style, themes, and genre and create new identities through new modulations in the use of the Dutch language. By showing the intersection between postcolonial and postmodern strategies the author elaborates on the complex ways of envisaging the concept of home in the context of migration.

Language and migration is also very central for Ena Jansen, who in her essay "'The Risks Migrating Words Take': Some Thoughts on the Afrikaans Poetry of Elisabeth Eybers in a Context of Transmigration" explores the important tradition of Afrikaans literature at a linguistic and cultural crossroads between South Africa and the Netherlands. Through the analysis of Elisabeth Eybers, a South African poet currently living in the Netherlands, Jansen voices the theoretical complexities of the discourse on transmigration and the unique position Eybers takes within it. The author proposes a reading according to which writing in exile does not mean loss and fragmentation but rather active negotiations along borderlines by forging alternative poetic spaces in which two or more languages, cultures, and countries can be expressed. Through a close reading of Eybers's poems Jansen outlines the personal and poetic trajectory of a unique poet who has chosen never to settle down in one specific home, identity, and accent.

The third part, "Mind the Gap! Cultural Trans/formations," investigates a range of cases where migration has an impact on the reinvention of public space and public memory in several art forms, such as cinema, cultural manifestations, visual arts, music, and urban culture.

Alec Hargreaves focuses in his essay "Street Culture: Dead End or Global Highway?" on the locus of the street as a site of cultural production and consumption. Seen both as a peripheral sub-culture and as part of wider global interaction, the street culture of the French *banlieues* both circumvents national boundaries and qualifies global pulls. Alec Hargreaves emphasizes the importance of "alternative voices," *beurs* or writing of other descent in France, as a necessary stage to problematize the French assimilationist policy, based on the Enlightenment model of "equality," for failing to take into account the different articulations required by non-Western histories and different collective identifications. Migrant identifications, or postcolonial discourses, have therefore an important role to fulfill in order to contest from within the ethnocentric assumption hidden behind a supposedly progressive agenda.

The next chapter, "'Migrant Websites,' WebArt, and Digital Imagination" by Daniela Moerolla echoes Hargreaves's interest in the technological revolution that has changed the relationship between spaces of migration and communities of belonging, but from a different angle. Given the proliferation of "migrant websites" on the World Wide Web, Merolla explores the redefinition of European identity and multiculturalism through new media, such as the Internet and the World Wide Web, which allows and encourages the reframing of group identities despite their global displacements. Merolla explores the values of these virtual communities not only for their rearticulation of belonging but also for their artistic output. So far, the author argues, the interaction between online and offline migrant productions has not received sufficient attention. Her chapter implies that new parameters must be developed to get a handle of new artistic innovations made possible by new technologies and the reformulation of forms and genres from various media. By addressing new digital imaginations as emerging from migrant websites, in this case the Netherlands, Merolla explores new artistic forms through which migrant communities reinforce local group identification as well as aspire to transnational recognition on the other. The question for Merolla is whether these migrant websites are pioneering in the creation of new forms of visual art.

John McLeod focuses in his "'London-stylee!': Recent Representations of Postcolonial London" on the literary images of multicultural and multiracial London as emerging from the representations of Caribbean writers such as Fred D'Aguiar and Bernardine Evaristo. Both writers resident in London inflect their imaginative endeavors with a politics of transfiguration. As the author highlights, this is achieved through innovative modes of representation that intertwine social consciousness with playful modes of resistance. In this way previous anti-racist discourses are transposed into new witty and poetic imageries that are clearly celebratory of a new appropriation of the city from its very .heart. By discarding oppositional politics and tales of victimhood these black migrant writers defamiliarize racist violence by adding unexpected registers and metaphors, such as the "red rose" to express the bruises of police beatings. Through their new language D'Aguiar and Evaristo, as examples of a new generation writing on the city, resist the representations of social marginality imposed on them and reimagine a space, both in the language of memory and in the political future, where London becomes part of a wider transcultural web. Much in line with Gilroy's black Atlantic, these writers reconceptualize themselves in the city of London by recurring to a transcultural consciousness.

In her essay "The Colonial Past in the Postcolonial Present: Cultural Memory, Gender, and Race in Dutch Cinema" Pamela Pattynama analyzes how the Dutch colonial past comes to haunt Holland through a powerful medium, the cinema. By analyzing a movie set in the Dutch East Indies, *Oeroeg* (1993), the author explores cultural interchanges, in the form of friendship, which get undone with the advent of nationalism and decolonization. The film is treated as a reconstruction of the colonial past, which has been so far locked up in traumatic memories, repression, and displacement. Such movies offer therefore a way of understanding the Dutch multicultural present though an account of collective, national memory. However, as Pattynama warns us, films are concrete manifestations of ideological constructions, and therefore her analysis takes into account the discursive formations around gender and ethnicity.

Stephen Gundle opens up a new cultural discourse by analyzing ethnic identity and nationality within Italy's mass media. In his essay "Miss Italia in Black and White: Feminine Beauty and Ethnic Identity in Modern Italy" he explores the phenomenon of a specific beauty contest. In 1996 a great national commotion was stirred when a black woman, Denny Mendez, originally from the Dominican Republic and resident in Italy, won the Miss Italy competition. This unleashed a wave of widespread and heated media discussion about the nature of Italian identity, and more specifically, of feminine beauty. By making a historical overview Gundle explores how the ideal of Italian female beauty developed through the ages, from Dante to Botticelli to the nineteenth century, and how this served to create a sense of national belonging. The author argues that this idea of blondeness and whiteness has been subject to various crises and challenges derived from mass communication, globalization, and female emancipation. Blondeness and whiteness were emphasized in the late nineteenth century to counteract racial theorists who sought to identify the Italians with darkness and primitivism. With the advent of mass communication, dark hair and Mediterranean bodily characteristics were reevaluated, exemplified in the Hollywood allure of the so-called typically Italian stars such as Sophia Loren and Gina Lollobrigida. However, the ambivalence between "olive skin" and darkness has retained a kind of symbolic significance for the Italian national identity, and was expressed in the strong reaction provoked by Mendez's candidature and election.

Questions of racism and national identity are also central to Sandra Ponzanesi's essay "Outlandish Cinema: Screening the Other in Italy." By accounting for the fundamental and strategic role that Italian cinema played in the construction of the national identity, both in Italy and abroad through the history of the diaspora, the author makes an intervention into recent cinematic traditions that combines aesthetic merits with new pressing societal issues, such as immigration. The author focuses in particular on the representation of immigration in the Italian cinema of the 1990s and more specifically in three films that focus on different historical and geo-political fluxes of migration: the Roma; the recent labour immigration from Africa; and that connected to sex trafficking and prostitution. According to the author, "outlandish cinema," a concept specifically developed here, is a cinema that reflects on the political power of imagination by making outlandish (migrant, foreign, exotic, nomadic, transgender) characters central

to the narrative structure, thereby steering away from biased representations of the "other" as menacing and outsider. It enacts therefore the transformation of the idea of centrality, normality, and sedentariness through the
encounter between different cultures and identities. The author explores
how outlandish cinema weaves traditional narrative forms with new stylistic tools such as intertextuality, voice-over, architectural relocations, multilingualism, and sensorial details. This poses at the same time new requirements on the audiences, who need to develop new sets of viewing skills.
Outlandishness becomes therefore a concept that re-orients both the discourse on integration and assimilation and the spectator's identification
with the status quo.

MIGRATIONS IN A HISTORICAL PERSPECTIVE

Migration has come to signify all possible processes of identification and dis-
affiliation evident in such material and symbolic phenomena as the trespassing of borders and labeling of certain territories as "off limits." Accordingly it
is an almost utopian notion, one highly charged with the legacy of the past
and promises of the future. It goes without saying that creative traditions and
literary genealogies have been revived by postcolonial criticism, slanted narrowly in the main along language groups and national boundaries aligned
with the major colonial axis. What is remarkable is that while the situation is
slowly evolving, within critical theory itself these remain almost separate
worlds. Their narrow focus is either on the English empire *writing back*
(clustered around the former notion of Commonwealth literature) or with
the world of *Francophonie* (although constantly questioned about its implication in the colonial past).

Since the 1980s this tendency has been progressively muddied because
there are innumerable "second generation" migrant writers who live and
work in Britain or France.[18] The recent appearance of a comparatively large
volume of studies and collections in Dutch, German, Portuguese, and Italian
testifies to how literary productions can become "cross-overs" when new interest emerges in those linked to other European colonial expansions, and to
migrant traditions expressed in languages that play a minor role in cultural
globalization. The new audience for these works encourages us to reevalu-
ate the relevant universe of discourse in the ongoing critique of migration,
multiculturalism, and literatures in English and in French.[19]

Despite the linguistic and national divide, the flourishing of these recent
studies offers new opportunities to chart contemporary literary productions
as historically linked to different migration flows from, to, and within Europe. Although we know a brief historical resume risks recreating and legitimizing further rigidification of the very borders of nation, language, gender,

and ethnicity this book invites you to leave behind, the value of rethinking the passages and denouements of the various European literatures as they have grown is nevertheless clear.[20] How else will we make visible how these have been modified and changed in relation to the multiple voices and writings which are constituted today—as much as in the past—by migration?

The symbolic date of 1492 signals the progressive intensification of global displacements caused by European expansion. In the next two centuries empires built by Britain, France, Spain, Portugal, and the Netherlands trampled the populations and cultures in the Americas and Indonesia, which laid the groundwork for further expansion in Africa, Asia, Australia, and New Zealand. In the ferocious competition for supremacy, Britain and France progressively imposed their respective economic and political colonial interests worldwide, annexing areas that were previously subject to other colonial powers. In the eighteenth century they indeed succeeded in limiting and outplaying the empires of Portugal, the Netherlands, and Spain. It was human forces and resources from their colonies that largely paid for the military and economic conflicts generated by their rivalry for colonial leadership. Without question this expansion marginalized the Mediterranean area in the European economy, a state of affairs exploited by the entrenched Ottoman Empire and the Arabic sultanates.

Late in the eighteenth century revolts in South and North America began, marking the historic shift from empires to nations. Benedict Anderson has underlined[21] the fact that this transition not only signified the emergence of new nationalisms within Europe and of new colonial ambitions, but also set the model for future anticolonial struggles across the world.

Europe consolidated itself into different nations in the second half of the nineteenth century. The expansion fostered by the "industrial revolution" determined the need for new markets, which motivated the creation and expansion of European empires, which flourished at the expense of people and properties in Africa and Asia.

Britain and France occupied immense territories, while Spain, Portugal, Germany, Italy, and Belgium directed their expansionistic drives toward Africa.[22] Early in the twentieth century a variety of different nationalistic ideologies and movements emerged, beginning an anticolonial struggle for independence. These nationalist movements for self-determination tended to unify and absorb the internal oppositions and religious rivalries, often appearing as socialist and communist waves. After long and bitter fighting, the independence of India in 1947 and Algeria in 1962 marked the dissolution of the British and French empires and symbolically the end of European colonialism, a process lasting till the late 1970s that culminated in the breakup of the Soviet empire a decade later.

This is not the place for a detailed comparison of the different colonial histories and systems or their devastating impact on indigenous populations.

But it is important to note that the reference to some European empires as "minor" in a few of this book's articles is intended to indicate they were marginal only with respect to the longer duration and scope of British and French colonial supremacy. This of course does not mean they were experienced as minor by those who were subject to this domination. There is extensive documentation of the massacre of Indians and their cultures by Portugal and Spain in Central and South America in early colonization, and the later brutal occupation of present-day Congo (Belgium); Libya, Somalia, Eritrea, and Ethiopia (Italy); Angola and Mozambique (Portugal); North Morocco and South Eastern Sahara (Spain); and Togo, Cameroon, Tanzania, and Namibia (Germany).

A major direction of migration was the forced displacement of millions from Africa to the Americas in the profitable slave trade. These flows of goods and wealth contributed to Europe's relative affluence and higher living standards in the eighteenth century. Subsequently the situation changed with the destabilizing effect of the industrial revolution, which condemned the European urban lower classes to extreme poverty, famines, and eventual displacement. The major solution involved new colonial settling policies[23] and mass migration from Europe to North and South America between 1850 and 1930.[24] While migration flows from and within Europe for religious and economic reasons had occurred in the previous centuries and never really stopped, the intercontinental migration waves at the start of the nineteenth century were of a magnitude unknown before and even now.[25] The subsequent depopulation coupled with economic improvement created a niche for new arrivals in Europe.[26] As Portes states:

> Contrary to widespread perceptions, immigrants come to wealthier nations less because they want to than because they are needed. A combination of social and historical forces has led to acute labor scarcities in these economies. In some instances, these are real absolute scarcities. . . . In other instances, . . . the scarcity stems from the culturally conditioned resistance of native-born workers to accept low-paid menial jobs commonly performed by their ancestors.[27]

In the colonized countries, on the other hand, social destabilization and poverty were increased by the cumulative effect of political and military domination, land expropriation, and industrial modernization. The European urban centers together with North America became the most attractive destinations.

After World War I, impoverished people from Algeria, and later from Morocco and Tunisia, started to cross the Mediterranean Sea in search of work in France. Immigrants from India came to Britain en masse after the creation of Pakistan in 1947—created through a partition of India—and from the West Indies and Africa after the 1950s. During this period migration flows from the former Soviet Union also increased. During the interwar period, and increasingly after World War II, the British and French colonial school systems very often redirected colonial students and intellectuals toward Europe. The assignment of grants and scholarships to "ex-colonized subjects" to study at the "centers" of science and knowledge continued in the postcolonial period. In the 1960s recruitment toward Germany, Belgium, and the Netherlands was initially directed to Italy, Spain, and Portugal, and later to Morocco and Turkey. The last decades of the twentieth century saw southern European countries experience a dramatic shift from being net sources of emigration to become net targets of immigration, an overall intensification of previous migration flows, and growing immigration from Sub-Saharan Africa.[28]

The extent to which the converging in Europe of wealth, ideas, and techniques accumulated from across the world supported the affluence of the colonizers, and the flourishing of sciences, technologies, philosophies, and literatures, is still under investigation.[29] But what is patently certain already is that the colonial expansion strongly contributed to the forging of the unitarian notion of Europe.

Recent reflections in all disciplines—from legal studies to history, from biology to cultural anthropology, from geography to philosophy—have shown[30] that racial taxonomies were created to demarcate the cultural supremacy of the colonial center upon the created peripheries, of the dominant majorities upon the internal minorities. The contemporary configuration of the twenty-five-member European Union was founded on the erasure of old economic borders and differentiations. In the process new barriers were raised against the migrants, who, while participating in the army, industry, schools, and farms, were still reified and racialized, and were refused the recognition of their founding intellectual and human contribution. The book before you tells one story—how in the last century the draining of human forces and imaginative powers by European colonization and economic-political hegemony has found expression in literary creations that put key aspects of canonical cultural, national, and artistic identities into question.

New Literary Spaces

Britain

While the presence of the colonized other intervenes in British literature from Shakespeare to the colonial literature of the twentieth century,[31] the other as subjective voice starts to make him- or herself heard only from the end of the eighteenth century. Except for the newly resuscitated text *Ooronoko: or the Royal Slave* (1688) by Aphra Ben, the first woman in England to make her living by writing (1640–1689), there are no early examples of colonial awareness in British literature. Aphra Ben's text is set in Suriname. It is not only an emancipatory text that precedes by a hundred years the first anti-slavery narratives, and written in a voice proudly feminine, it is also the very first modern English novel.[32]

However, it has been demonstrated (against the assumption that British society was exclusively white until the contemporary era) that a conspicuous community of twenty to thirty thousand black people was already present in London in the eighteenth and nineteenth centuries. As David Theo Goldberg wrote in his article "Heterogeneity and Hybridity: Colonial Legacy, Postcolonial Heresy":

> The heterogeneous mix of population making up the capitals of colonial empires has largely been downplayed, and indeed until quite recently all but ignored. Second, relatedly but more deeply, the occlusion of blacks from the representational historical record of this urban diversity indicates by extension that blacks for the most part were rendered invisible in the daily political life of those cities. This can be seen in sharp contrast to the persistent, one might say insistent, concern with colonized black people deemed administratively problematic by the colonizer.[33]

The view of Britain from the "outsider's" perspective therefore starts already around the concomitant arrivals of these first black—often forced—visitors. A somewhat limited range of writing, the so-called autobiographical slave narratives of Africans and Caribbeans,[34] characterized this early period. A major moment of production of migrant literature in Britain occurred later, signaled by the growing publication of poems, short stories, and novels by West Indian writers who converged on London after World War II.[35] This was also in the aftermath of the Nationality Act of 1948, designed to encourage immigration from Britain's colonies and former colonies.

However, prior to the demise of the British Empire, there were always regular exchanges between the British metropolitan centers and its colonial outposts. It has been widely studied and theorized about—how people from India regularly visited Britain (Gandhi visited London many times, and he, Nehru, and Jinnah studied law in England, just to mention the most famous). Various people from India came to the heart of the empire during the Victorian era, creating the first visible instances of racial encounter and further mobilizing the rigid divide between center and periphery, as demonstrated in the accounts of Pandita Ramabai, Cornelia Sorabi, and Behramji Malabari.[36]

Apparently black people who arrived in London before the end of the empire were not exposed to the same racial hatred as other immigrants of the 1950s, who reminded the colonizers not only of their lost empire but also of their socio-political responsibilities. Those migrants came in fact to stay and were not just passing through. The arrival of the first postwar/postcolonial immigrants in significant numbers marked the transition between exotic indifference to fierce intolerance. For this generation of immigrants London was a big disappointment. The glorious center of the empire, perceived as the model of civilization and grandeur, came to be experienced by migrants in the 1950s and 1960s only in terms of greyness and squalor, decadent suburbs, and cramped bedsits. The dreams of a better "home" turned into disillusionment with the metropolitan center, as narrated in Samuel Selvon's *The Lonely Londoners* (1956) and George Lamming's *The Immigrants* (1954). Instead of constructing an unexplored but wildly imagined territory, Britain came to symbolize the shattering of dreams, both of the empire and of future life in the metropolitan center. However, this disillusionment with the metropolitan center proved to be a necessary stage in the process of decolonization and demythologization of the colonial center.

Other representatives of a later immigration from the Caribbean are writers such as Jean Rhys (1890–1979), alias Ella Gwendoline Rees Williams, Andrew Salkey (1928–1995), and V. S. Naipaul (1932–), whose works were eagerly and enthusiastically received and won important literary prizes. While Naipaul, awarded the Nobel Prize for literature in 2001, remained in Britain, Selvon and many others returned to the West Indian islands—where the changed political situation at the end of the 1970s powerfully contributed to the development of Caribbean postcolonial literatures. Such (at least) double directional migrations signal a manifold series of connections and linkages between those influences of writing in and out of Britain.

Interconnections indeed also characterize the production of African and South Asian writers who spent a period of their life working or studying in Britain and then went on to assume cultural and political positions in their homelands. These include writers such as Tsitsi Dangaremba (1959–), Alex La Guma (1925–1985), Dambudzo Marechera (1952–1987), and the renowned writers Ngugi wa Thiong'o (1938–) and Wole Soyinka (1934–), and from India, Toru Dutt (1856-1877), Mulk Raj Anand (1905–2004), Sarojini Naidu (1879–1949), and Raja Rao (1908–), whose works constitute a crucial reference in postcolonial African and Indian literature. Likewise, intersections and interconnections mark the production of those who settled in Europe, as in the famous cases of Kamala Markandaya (1924–2004), Nirad C. Chaudhuri (1897–1999), and Attia Hosain (1913–1998) (as a consequence of Partition). In the 1970s, with the war in Bangladesh, a new flux of diasporic South Asian people arrived in London, adding to the already stabilized group of Asians who had arrived with the partition of Pakistan in 1947. This new ethnic stream within the country faced an apex of intolerance which crystalized in Enoch Powell's infamous Rivers of Blood speech, which categorically denied immigrants any legitimate claim to British identity.

In the 1980s and 1990s people born in Britain or of mixed parentage created a new shift in the notion of London as metropolitan center, bringing to the fore all the submerged ethnicities, and creating a discrepancy between the proposed model of national cohesion and the new diversification from within. As Paul Gilroy wrote in his influential *"There Ain't No Black in the*

Union Jack": The Cultural Politics of Race and Nation (1987), the notions of British identity and of blackness were considered to be mutually exclusive. Britain had built its fortune on the divide and rule principle, which allowed it to keep half the world under one crown. However, with the end of the empire several divisions had come to coexist in a relatively small territory, crammed into the same urban space—which reflected the colonial legacy and yet the separation from it—and the empire became split from within. Most of the African, Caribbean, and South Asian migrants recreated their diasporic space within the British urban spaces, transforming the heart of the empire into their new homeland. They had to fight rejection, racism, and exclusionary policies in order to transform the notion of Britain as a sovereign state still based on imperial dichotomies.

Writers such as Buchi Emecheta (1944–) and Ben Okri (1959–) from Nigeria, Okot p'Bitek (1931–) from Uganda, Salman Rushdie (1947–) and Amit Chaudhuri (1962–) from India, and Abdulrazak Gurnah (1948–) from Tanzania became prominent writers in Britain and most influential in the literary world of their respective lands of origin, transforming both the canon of British literature and shaping new cultural dimensions for world literatures. By the 1980s other extremely productive streams, again highly variegated in style, voices, and perspectives, were raised in Britain. We refer to the writings of the so-called second (and third, and so forth) generation, implying writers such as Hanif Kureishi (1954–),[37] Leena Dhingra (1942–), Ravinder Randhawa (1953–), Sunetra Gupta (1965–), Aamer Hussein (1955–), Atima Srivastava (1961–), Meera Syal (1963–), Zadie Smith (1975–), and Caryl Phillips (1958–) who were born or arrived at a young age in Britain when their parents had migrated from ex-colonial territories or from depauperated and politically risky areas.[38] Some of them live permanently in Britain, contributing to re-map London and re-design British identification. Others have migrated again together with their families or moved away when adults, as in the case of Mahjoub Jamal (1960–), presently living and working in Spain after several years in Denmark, whose works assemble and relocate East and West, Christianity and Islam.[39] Since the 1980s the visibility of migrant writing has grown and enlarged to include works by writers from other geo-cultural areas such as Japan, Hong Kong, and China in the respective cases of Kazuo Ishiguro (1954–), Timothy Mo (1950–), and Jung Chang (1952–).

This growing literature and the related questions of definitions and analysis and the present (re)construction of British literature progressively interacted with the discourse of multiculturalism in Britain.[40]

France

Migration literature in France is strongly marked by the history of colonization and decolonization of Algeria, Morocco, and Tunisia and by the long-term migration flows from these Maghrebian lands to France. Colonial literature and the arts created and invested the Maghreb with the imagery of the French Near Orient. In the 1950s student and intellectual migration from Algeria, Morocco, and Tunisia developed in a spectacular production that— not without difficulty and ambiguous paternalism—started to mark the literary world of Paris. The writers who settled in France, such as Assia Djebar (1936–), Driss Chraibi (1926–) and Albert Memmi (1920–), and those who went back to the Maghreb after the end of French colonization, such as Kateb Yacine (1929–1983), Ahmed Sefrioui (1915–2004), Mohamed Dib (1920–2003), and Mohamed Khair-Eddine (1941–1995), have left their imprint on the literary production in France and in the Maghreb. Writers working in the Maghrebian lands often established or maintained long-term relationships with France because of national political censure, as in the case of Mouloud Mammeri (1917–1991), who lived and worked in Algiers but, because of his outspoken minority belonging (Kabyle Berber) and his antitotalitarian position, could not publish his works in independent Algeria.[41] These writers of the 1950s have published extensively and some of them are still active.

Maghrebian writers were not, however, the first to be engaged with displacing spaces and languages in France. At the beginning of the 1930s, Paris was indeed the center of the stream lately known as "négritude" stemming from the works of the Martinican André Césaire (1913–), the Guyanese Leon Gontran Damas (1912–1978), and the Senegalese Léopold Senghor (1906–2001) and pivoting on the journal *L'Etudiant Noir*. Their works, reflecting on literary assertions and cultural propositions of both Surrealism and the American Harlem Renaissance,[42] contributed to form a transnational movement of black intellectuals.[43] Likewise, this current became influential in the Maghreb, as it is shown by the poems singing Africanity and "Berberitude" of Jean Amrouche (1906–1962), and later on in the literary works of Albert Memmi and in the political essays of Martinican Franz Fanon (1925–1961). Négritude was a literary and political stream, as signalled by the exemplary trajectories of Césaire and Senghor, who left France and became outstanding figures in the political life of Martinique and Senegal, respectively.

In the 1950s several writers from Africa and the Caribbean, such as Camara Laye (1928–1980), Edouard Glissant (1928–), and René Depestre (1926–), worked in Paris, but most of them went back to their respective homelands. In the following decades new impressive writers emerged. Their works and lives reveal the dialectical relationship of going to and fro between France and their homelands, the Maghreb for a majority of writers. But there were also other lands, as in the case of the Egyptian-born Andrée Chedid (1920–); the most famous Caribbean authors, Maryse Condé (1937–),[44] Raphaël Confiant (1951–), and Patrick Chamoiseau (1953–); the Lebanese Amin Maalouf (1946–); and the Cameroonian Calixtha Beyala (1961–). Outstanding writers from the Maghreb had also settled in France, such as Tahar Ben Jelloun (1944–), Hélé Béji (1948–), Nabile Farès (1940–), and Leila Sebbar (1940–), while others decided to live in the Maghreb, such as Abdelkebir Khatibi. In the 1990s several writers, Rachid Boudjedra (1941–) and Rachid Mimouni (1945–1995) among others, were compelled to leave Algeria because civil war erupted after the halt of the election with the rebellion of Islamic groups. Tahar Djaout (1954–1993), a writer and journalist was killed in an attack in Algiers.

The "second generation" writing made its first appearance in France with the novel *L'amour quand même* of Hocine Touabti (1949–), published in 1981. Since then the publication of works by authors issuing from the Maghrebian communities in France and in Belgium continues to grow, and is also evident in other fields, such as film and theater, sometimes trespassing genre borderlines.[45] The new stream is again largely but not exclusively Maghrebian. In the 1990s we also find novels by "second generation" writers from the Sub-Saharan African immigration, such as Marie Ndiaye (1967–), who actually always lived in Normandy and never met her possible Senegalese father, and from Asian immigration, such as the Vietnamese Linda Lê (1963–).

Critics and publishers labeled the writings by authors of Maghrebian origin, such as Mehdi Charef (1952–), Azouz Begag (1957–), Farida Belghoul (1958–), Sakinna Boukhedenna (1959–), Tassadit Imache (1958–), Arriz Tamza (pseud. Messaoud Bousselmania, 1957–), as "beur" literature, a term initially used by Maghrebian street children and youth to name themselves, but this term was rapidly discarded. Most writers refused it as a form of ghettoization. Opting instead for "literature" as such, they refused to be marginalized by being cast with references to geo-cultural origins. The opportunity and relevance of the definition "migrant literature"—or of other labels— applied to the works of writers whose "homeland" is France, likewise in the case of authors born and/or raised in Britain, is indeed under fire in literary and public debates. The question is about whether or not "migrant" is assumed as a metaphor for what Michel Laronde calls the "para-doxical" position of such writing within the dominant cultural and literary paradigm:

> Cette présence est para-doxale puisqu'elle donne lieu à des découpages et des regroupements d'éléments hétérogènes de la littérature française qui éclatent (transitivement) l'unicité de cette littérature. . . . De par leur position d'intériorité à la culture française, les discours des immigrations décalent encore le discours post-colonial vers d'autres horizons.[46]

Anew we find open questions about the parameters of national belonging and literary canonization, about inclusion or exclusion of works and writers. Likewise critical interrogations concern literary and social significance of these streams and further related literary developments and directions.[47]

Germany

In the last two decades new European migrant literatures have appeared. Works by new writers—migrant themselves or from immigrant communities—gained wide recognition in Germany and in the Netherlands. They also started to attract the interest of readers and critics in Italy and Portugal.

"Germany is a reluctant land of immigration," Philip Martin writes,[48] although in time it has become one of the first countries to receive immigrants and refugees in Europe; there are about 7.5 million newcomers living in Germany at the beginning of the twenty-first century.

After World War II, the Federal Republic of Germany professed early on the "postmodern" idea of a flexible labor market that considered immigrants as a temporary presence, *gastarbeiters* or "guest" workers who had "to go back" when German industrial and agricultural sectors did not need them anymore. On the other hand, East Germany received students and workers from communist and socialist countries, but without granting them lasting permits or citizenship. These policies, linked to the national identity myth of blood rights to citizenship, led to the perception of immigrants as lasting "foreigners" and to the refusal of thinking of Germany in terms of multiculturalism. However, already in 1920 immigrant laborers from Eastern Europe and Italy had started to arrive and settle in Germany, not to mention the forced laborers enslaved during World War II. After the war, the international recruitment agreements with Italy, Spain, Greece, Turkey, Morocco, Tunisia, and the former Yugoslavia brought thousands of immigrants who, in the 1970s, were joined by their families. To these flows should be added the immigration of German descendants who received the right to "re-enter" from Eastern Europe, and refugees from all over the world, since the Federal Republic of Germany—in memory of the tragedy of the Jews—adopted an open policy toward asylum seekers. Immigration from the few former colonies has been slight because German colonization lasted less than forty years and colonial policy did not stimulate African workers or intellectuals to move to—let alone to stay in—Germany.[49] A specific history of marginalization, however, is that of the children of Afro-German unions—which mainly occurred during the respective French and U.S. army occupations after World War I and World War II—who were regarded as "foreigners" in their own land at least until the 1980s.[50]

Although migrant writings were published as early as the 1950s and the 1960s,[51] the first large wave of production appears at the end of the 1970s and beginning of the 1980s with the works of Franco Biondi (1947–) and the poet and scholar Gino Chiellino (1946–), who had both immigrated from Italy. In the 1980s there was indeed the outbreak. Currently well-known authors started to publish in this period, such as Kemal Kurt (1946–2002) from Turkey, Libuse Moníková (1945–) from the former Czechoslovakia, the poet György Dalos (1943–) from Hungary, Natascha Wodin (1945–), born in a

Ukrainian family who immigrated to Fürth, Rafik Schami (1946–) from Iraq, Suleman Taufiq (1953–) from Syria, Dante Andrea Franzetti (1959–) from Switzerland, and the poet José Oliver (1961–), son of a Spanish family in Hausach. Almost one-third of the new writers had immigrated from Turkey, with outstanding authors such as the poets Aras Ören (1939–), Zehra Çirak (1960–), Zafer Senocak (1961–), and Hasan Özdemir (1963–) and the novelist Alev Tekinay (1951–).[52]

In the 1990s the writings of Emine Sevgi Özdamar (1946–), born in Istanbul, won multiple prizes, while works by Ilija Trojanow (1965–) from Bulgaria and Yoko Tawada (1960–) from Japan have also received an enthusiastic reception. On the other hand, the "street" novels by Feridun Zeimoglu (1964–), who emigrated with his family to Germany when he was four, have raised interest in and discussion of language use and related themes, as in the case of other street novels in France and the Netherlands, for example, those by Mehdi Charef and Hans Sahar, respectively.

The literary flourishing of the two last decades has been signaled by the institution of the Adelbert of Chamisso[53] prize in 1984, an award created for "foreigners" or "authors of not-German native language for the enriching and development of German literature." Assigned to many of the above-mentioned writers, the Chamisso prize has given them public acclaim and recognition. At the same time the apparently unforgettable extraneousness of such authors was clear when Emine Sevgi Özdamar said once (ironically) that they were accepted as "guest-writers," the intellectual counterpart of the *gastarbeiders*. The discussion about and within migrant literature as a production constitutive of a renewed German literature is nowadays in full swing.[54]

The Netherlands

The new stream of the 1990s corresponds to relatively new migration flows in the Netherlands. However, colonial history also determined the presence of different—in time and geo-cultural origins—migrant writings. The peculiar position of the Republic of the Netherlands in a Europe of empires and kingdoms (16th–18th centuries) and its tradition of domestic tolerance led to multiple strands of immigration flows throughout the modern and contemporary periods. Religious tolerance was the reason for Jews to immigrate to the Netherlands from Spain and Portugal in the 16th century,[55] and from Germany and the rest of Europe during the 20th-century interwar period. This European role of the Netherlands as a progressive, democratic, and tolerant country is strongly in contrast with its aggressive foreign policy in the far-off worlds of the colonial frontier, first with the Dutch mercantile expansion during the Golden Age[56] and later with the institutionalized colonial rule in what is present-day Indonesia, Suriname, and Antilles.[57]

Since the sixteenth century different immigrant flows have thus contributed to create Dutch culture. This finds expression in the writings of several writers born in refugee families and integrated in the national canon.[58] Moreover, Dutch colonial expansion stimulated the growth of a literature written by colonizers and administrators, in particular in and from Indonesia, the former Netherlands East Indies.[59] A strikingly high number of works by Dutch-Indonesian writers still mark and inform the contemporary national literature.[60]

On the other hand, Dutch colonialism determined the development of literary productions in Dutch written by Caribbean authors who eventually spent a period of their life in the Netherlands but mostly worked in their homelands, such as Tip Marugg (1923–), Frank Martinus Arion (1936–), and Cola Debrot (1902–1981).[61] These writers' works did not, or only with much difficulty, enter the Dutch literary canon.

The settlements of Dutch colonizers in South Africa likewise determined the growth of literary productions in Afrikaans (Dutch-African), but the separate historical developments determined a certain marginality of this literature in the Dutch canon, lately modified for the works critically treating the apartheid system, such as the novels of André Brink (1935–) and Breyten Breytenbach (1939–),[62] or at least marking the distance from such a system as do the poems of Ingrid Jonker (1936–1967) and of Elisabeth Eybers (1915–), who moved to Amsterdam in 1961.[63] A fresh interest in "Afrikaans" literature has developed in these last years, as shown in recent debates, conferences, and academic courses.

As in France and Britain, the process of migration from the ex-colonies to the Netherlands intensified after World War II and in the decolonizing period. It concerned different social classes of migrants or repatriates, and among them a number of writers who maintained interests in and communication with the respective migrant communities and homelands, such as Talje Robinson (1911–1974) and Rob Nieuwenhuys (1908–1999) from the former Indonesia, Frans Lopulalan (1953–) and Eddy Supusepa (1950–) from the Molukken, and Astrid Romer (1947–), Ellen Ombre (1948–), and Edgar Cairo (1948–2000) from Suriname.

Successive streams of migrants and refugees came from the former Eastern European block or escaped from totalitarian regimes in South America and in the Middle East. In the 1980s the refugees were largely from Sri Lanka, Ghana, and Somalia, and in the 1990s from the former Yugoslavia. The Netherlands was in need of workers because of market expansion and thanks to recruitment agreements between states.[64] Since the mid-1960s labor migrants arrived from southern Europe, leaving space for immigration from the rest of the Mediterranean basin, particularly Turkey and Morocco. Other minor migration flows arrived from Pakistan and from China. New immigrants and refugees have encountered restrictive domestic policies, also in contradiction to the Dutch liberal tradition, cosmopolitan cultural habitat, and professed progressive multicultural policy. The presence of immigrants is acknowledged differently from Germany. The Dutch system of "pillarization"[65] leads to both recognition and creation of ethnic and/or religious minorities and "their" rights "in" Dutch society.

Since the 1980s new migrant literature began to be published.[66] Yet it is in the 1990s that the explosive growth of publications occured, strongly sustained by the publishers' policy, including both writers who immigrated as adults and the so-called second generation that issued from immigrant families.[67] There is wide recognition by the public and critics of the works by, among others, Kader Abdollah (1954–), who arrived as a political refugee from Iran; Lu Wang (1960–), who emigrated from China; Moses Isegawa (1963–) from Uganda; Vamba Sherif (1973–), coming via Syria from Liberia;[68] Fouad Laroui (1958–) from Morocco;[69] Ramsey Nasr, born in a Dutch-Palestinian family in 1974, who has already had an impressive career as actor for theater and films; and Yasmine Allas (1967–), from Somalia, who also worked as an actress.[70] Indeed the outbreak of literary talent in the 1990s has also marked artistic fields such as films, theater, and the visual arts.[71] The works by Klark Accord (1961–), Antoine de Kom (1956–), and Alfred Birney (1951–) have further enriched the already highly productive streams of Caribbean and Indonesian Dutch writing.[72]

The "second generation" writers have had a prominent position in the new production since the 1990s. The immigrant community from Morocco indeed nurtured a strikingly high number of young and successful writers. Two of the most appreciated writers, already translated into several languages, are Hafid Bouazza (1970–) and Abdelkader Benali (1975–),[73] whose works won important literary prizes in the Netherlands and in Belgium in 1996, 1997, and 2003. Well known to the public and critics are also the works by the poet Mohamed Stitou (1974–), the youth book writer Naima El Bezaz (1974–), the novelist Hans Sahar (1974–), and more recently Said El Haji (1976–) and Khalid Boudou (1974–), who have successively obtained the yearly El Hizjra prize.

As in other European countries, the attribution of definitions and labels in critiques and the publishers' marketing—such as "Allochthonous literature" and "Allochthonous writers" or even "Dutch-Moroccan writers"—has been at the center of polemics and adamant refusal by numerous writers and artists. Such labels, attracting the social interest of the public and institutions, have initially sustained the publication of new texts, but they risk becoming a hindrance to freedom and creativity. These terms presuppose agreement about migrant themes and languages, and then impose them as if they were the only way to knowledge and literature for those who biographically have experienced immigration or are immigrants' children.[74] Alternative vision is searched for and created by writers and artists, as well as by the critics.[75]

Portugal and Spain

Marginalized empires, self-enclosed under dictatorship, Portugal[76] and Spain[77] exported laborers and imposed economic and cultural dependency on their colonies up until the 1970s. At the end of Salazar's and Franco's fascist regimes, African colonies obtained their independence and Portugal and Spain, re-admitted into the European Community, started their progressive economic growth. In the last decades, the economic improvement led to decreasing emigration toward northern Europe and increasing immigration from South America, North Africa, former sub-Saharan Portuguese colonies, and Eastern Europe.[78] This relocation in the migration flow reopened and revitalized questions about cultural and national identification already debated in the fight against Portuguese colonization in Africa, and in the controversial conflicts around minority languages and rights in Spain. However, recent immigration has not found voice in literary writings in Portuguese, or such writings have not found a way to publishers. In Spain, recent immigrant conditions are mainly "spoken about" in literary and film productions by Basque writers and directors. Artistic exchanges and reciprocal influence between the Iberian Peninsula and North Africa, notwithstanding their historical importance and richness, are accorded little attention. This is shown by the absence of institutional support for artistic and literary developments by Berber artists either in Spanish or in Tamazight in Melilla, the important Spanish outpost in Morocco.[79]

While Portugal and Spain only in recent decades have become receivers of immigrants and refugees, the colonial past has still caused linguistic and cultural dissemination and reciprocal influence—even when not wanted or even recognized—between former colonizers and colonized.[80] When literary criticism started to question colonization and decolonization and the role of writing in Portuguese and in Spanish, it was addressing sophisticated forms of literary relocation and shifting of the self. These of course encompassed a multitude of languages and cultures, and the interaction between writing and oral literature that had developed in Central and South American literatures. This is not surprising, since such literatures have not only retained international appreciation, but have also been highly influential for literary developments in Spain and in Portugal.

On the other hand, interest began later in African Lusophone literatures, or African literatures in Portuguese, and has slowly increased since the 1980s.[81] Artistic and literary productions from Africa were denied recognition in the Portuguese literary and artistic canon until the end of Salazar's regime—and the subsequent end of colonization in Angola, Mozambique, São Tomé, Cape Verde, and Guinea-Bissau. Nunes (1987, p. 63) mentions Amilcar Cabral, who accused the Portuguese of ignoring—at the same time a lack of knowledge and a gesture of arrogance—all cultures and peoples of

Africa.[82] Moreover, the mystifying self-image of a Portuguese cultural colonization leading to creolization and to a pan-Lusitanian society, covered up—in Portugal—the reality of harsh colonial exploitation and racialization, which were militarized by Salazar's fascist New State. Another aspect of the marginalized position of African Lusophone literatures was the difficulty of writing and publishing. Economic underdevelopment and poor investment in education restrained Lusophone literary creation in Africa. However, in 1936 a small number of intellectuals and writers gathered around the journal *Claridade,* which was founded by Manuel Lopes (1907–2005) and Baltasar Lopes (1907–1989). They were the initiators of Cape Verdean neorealism in literature, under the influence of American and Brazilian authors such as Ernest Hemingway and Jorge Amado.[83] The presence of a few well-known writers and poets who moved from Portugal to Cape Verde and Mozambique, such as Manuel Ferreira (1917–) and Glória de Sant'Anna (1925–), also contributed to stimulate African Lusophone literary creation.[84]

After World War II the increasing settling policy enforced by Salazar's New State caused a deep economic crisis in Angola and Mozambique and an intensified racialization of these societies. However, the Portuguese immigration was connected to a relative increase in schooling and strengthening of the local press. It was also the backdrop to the interaction of political dissidents who moved to Angola and Mozambique with members of the African nationalist movements in the fight against fascism and colonialism. In this period and until independence a most important trend in African Lusophone literature was the "revolutionary poems" of authors such as Alvos Preto (alias Tomás Medeiros, 1931–) from São Tomé, Osvaldo Osório (1937–), and later Sukre d'Sal (1951–). Among famous writers who were politically committed in their writings and in their lives we find the Angolans Agostinho Neto (1922–1979) and Pepetela (alias Artur Carlos M. Pestana, 1941–) and the Mozambican Luís Bernardo Honwana (1942–). An important development was the experimentation with African languages carried out in Angola by Luandino Vieira (1936–) and Uanhenga Xitu (1924–), who were also politically engaged and suffered many years' imprisonment.[85] The production of Lusophone African writers has slowly increased and in the 1980s new outstanding works were published, for example, the novels and short stories of the Cape Verdean Germano Almeida (1945–), the Angolan Manuel Rui (1941–), and the Mozambicans Mia Couto (1955–) and Suleiman Cassamo (1962–).

Writers also traveled to Portugal to study or work. Some went back to Africa, such as the already mentioned Luís Bernardo Honwana, Baltasar Lopez, Alvos Preto, and Agostinho Neto.[86] Others settled in Portugal, such as Manuel Lopes, and sometimes moved on to—and back from—France, Brazil, or the United States. These include writers such as Francisco José de Vasques

Tenreiro (1921–1963) from São Tomé; Nóema de Sousa (1926–2002), the first woman poet from Mozambique; and in the following decades the writer and singer Amélia Muge (1952–); later Paulo Teixeira (1962–) from Mozambique, Germano Almeida from Cape Verde, and Wanda Ramos (1948–1998); and most recently José Eduard Agualusa (1961–) and Paula Tavares (1952–) from Angola. Lusophone writings address identification and displacement in a high poetical style challenging geopolitical borders and temporal distinctions.

Italy

Besides a national history marked by dictatorship, Italy shares with Spain, Portugal, and Germany some recent migration patterns. As in the case of Portugal and Spain, Italy changed from an emigration to an immigration country only in the last two decades.[87] As in the case of Germany, the relative brevity of the colonial expansion (from 1880 to 1941) stimulated neither immigration from the African former colonies or the development of an African literature in Italian.[88] Furthermore, schooling in Italian was hardly encouraged during the colonial overture. In contrast to Britain and France, Italy did not invest in a "civilizing" mission via education. To the contrary, it was forbidden for native pupils to attend the Italian schools after the fifth grade. Therefore, until the last decades contemporary migrant literature largely concerned the writings of Italian immigrants in Germany, Belgium, Canada, and the United States. Displacement is indeed central to the productions of re-immigrants, such as Ungaretti's poems, which are marked by the colors, sea, and desert of his birthplace Alexandria and by what he called the impossibility of "accasarsi," that is, to find somewhere a stable anchor, home, and family.[89]

The limited colonial experience did not hinder the development of a colonial literature[90] that mystified Africa and the Orient, revitalizing and manipulating symbols and clichés present in Italian literature since its beginnings. The brief duration of Italian colonialism, however, has been considered the principal cause for the absence of a literary stream based on that event. After World War II, there was indeed a striking reticence to reflect on Italian colonialism. Along with its short duration, other factors concurred to narrow the Italian role in Africa and make it seem less stretched out. The association of the colonial enterprise with the defeated fascist regime[91] and the national self-vision of the Italians as "good people" and of Italian colonialism as "poor man's imperialism" worked together to increase the national desire to forget the past (and related responsibilities) for good.

Few are the examples of a reflective gaze on the colonial encounter, such as the ambiguous *Tempo di uccidere* [Time to Kill] (1947) by Ennio Flaiano (1910–1972) or the frankly sarcastic Mario Tobino's *Il deserto della Libia* [The Desert of Libya] (1952) and Enrico Emmanuelli's *Settimana Nera* [Black

Week] (1966). Other texts propose a mystifying vision of Africa, as in Alberto Moravia's short stories and essays published in the 1970s[92] and in his last novel *La donna leopardo* [The Leopard Woman] (1991), in which Africa becomes the locus of self-investigation and self-understanding for the (European) traveler.

Between 1970 and 1990, the post-colonial reflection on colonialism and self-identification coincides with the works by Alessandro Spina, who after World War II had spent several years in Africa, and by two outstanding women writers, Erminia dell'Oro (1938–), a daughter of Italian colonizers in Eritrea, and Maria Abbebù Viarengo (1949–), a daughter of an Piedmontese-Oromo marriage.[93] Whereas Erminia dell'Oro is a Jewish Italian citizen who emigrated to Eritrea to escape fascist persecution, Maria Abbebù Viarengo embodies the generation of métisse children, born to an Italian father and a native mother.[94] The fear of miscegenation in the colonies was strongly regimented with the introduction of apartheid laws in 1938, which created a sharp racial divide.

In the 1990s, the first publications by writers who had immigrated to Italy in the preceding decades appeared, such as those of Ndjock Ngana (1952–),[95] Salah Methnani,[96] Pap Khouma (1957–),[97] Sira Hassan (1962–),[98] and many others.[99] Other collective works, mostly poems and short novels, were published thanks to politically engaged associations, such as the volumes *Le voci dell'arcobaleno* (1995), *Mosaici d'inchiostro* (1996), *Memorie in valigia* (1997), *Destini sospesi di volti in cammino* (1998), and *Parole oltre i confini* (1999), edited by Alessandro Ramberti and Roberta Sangiorgi. They all derived critical attention by virtue of their selection for the prize Eks&Tra, which is awarded for poetry, literature, and essays by migrant writers.[100]

The collaboration between the author and an Italian editor characterizes many of the above-mentioned texts. It implies not only "split authorship" but also "split authority" since the interference by the Italian academics or journalists into the "immigrant grammar" often involved serious manipulation. This shows the difficulties encountered by immigrant writers in mastering Italian as literary language—often mediated not only by their mother tongues but also by French or Portuguese in the case of writers emigrated from Africa. It also shows, however, the difficulties immigrant writers encountered in working within the stifling Italian publishing system that takes no risks in promoting "alternative texts" in which the use of transgressive grammar exemplifies the ongoing contamination between Italian traditional literature and new voices.

However, against the conservatism of the established publishing houses, a flourishing of electronic journals online, specializing in migrant writing, has appeared in Italy during the last decade. These journals, such as *Sagarana* (www.sagarana.net), edited by the writer of Brazilian origin Julio Monteiro Martins, and *El Ghibli* (www.el-ghibli.provincia.bologna.it), edited by the

Senegalese Pap Khouma, are a testimony to the vitality and maturity reached by these new literary productions. Furthermore the University of Rome maintains a database on migrant writers active in Italy that goes under the name Basili (www.disp.let.uniroma1.it/basili.html). This is also connected to another online journal, *Kúmá: creolizzare l'Europa*, which, like *Sagarana* and *El-Ghibli*, explores and accounts for the emerging multicultural space within the Italian society and its interactions with Europe and the rest. These coordinated activities highlight not only the pervasiveness of migrant literature in Italy but also how against all odds, rather than vanishing, it has achieved a certain level of institutionalization and canonization.

Nevertheless, while it is clear new Italian writings have so far achieved far less media and public recognition than their German or Dutch counterparts, they have significantly begun to attract scholarly attention.[101] Several studies are informed by the discourses and theories developed within the postcolonial debates, while others focus on interviews with the authors or on newspaper articles that use those polarizing definitions (immigrant writers, migrant literature, and so forth). It shows the irreversible process of Italian culture coming to terms with new ethnicities, voices, and styles—a nation opening up from its southern location the gateway to a new Europe.

NOTES

1. Hall 1996, p. 115.
2. Stoler 1995; Gilman 1992, pp. 171–197.
3. Rushdie 1991, p. 12.
4. Augé 1995, p. 26 and p. 31.
5. Brinkler-Gabler and Smith 1997.
6. Minh-ha 1994, pp. 9–26, 9.
7. See Ponzanesi 2002.
8. Said 1993.
9. Hall 1997.
10. Gilroy 1993.
11. West 1994.
12. Appiah 1993.
13. Spivak 1998.
14. hooks 1990.
15. Min-Ha 1989.
16. Gilroy 1993, p. 4.
17. Slemon 1991, p. 5.
18. For example, Ashcroft et al. 1989; Gontard and Bray 1996; Dejeux 1993, 1994; Dennis and Naseem 2000; Ibnlfassi and Hitchcott 1996; Jack 1996; Green et al. 1996. The focus on different geo-cultural partitions may overcome language differences, as in a number of studies of Caribbean and African literatures. See the site Contemporary Postcolonial and Postimperial Literatures in English (G. P. Landow, Brown Uni-

versity). Likewise, the focus on gender allows for an enlargement of the comparison in the collection edited by Brinkler-Gabler and Smith (1997). Also, Bonn 1995 includes articles concerning migrant literatures in different European languages.

19. Boehmer 1995; Hargreaves 1991; Laronde 1993.

20. Adelson 1990; Allen and Russo 1997; Chabal 1996; Fachinger 2001; Leijnse and van Kempen 2001; Nunes, 1987; Parati 1999.

21. Anderson 1983.

22. Japan's invasion of Manchuria led to a massive administrative partitioning of its emerging Asian empire.

23. For example, in Algeria, Congo, and Angola.

24. About fifty million Europeans emigrated to North and South America between about 1850 and 1920 to escape religious and political persecution, extreme poverty linked to industrialization, and violent reorganization of the rural world.

25. Because of religious persecutions, there were large Jewish migration flows, and after 1922 there was political emigration from Spain, Portugal, and Italy directed toward Britain, the Netherlands, and France. Huge Chinese migrations toward Indonesia, Malaysia, and the Philippines also occurred before the nineteenth century, while Japanese emigration toward Asia mainly took place in the first half of the twentieth century.

26. Large groups migrating toward Europe are from South and South East Asia (from India, Pakistan, Sri Lanka, the Philippines, Indonesia, and Thailand); North Africa and the Middle East (from the Maghreb mainly toward France, Spain, Belgium, and Italy; from Turkey toward Germany and from the Netherlands; and from Egypt, Lebanon, Iraq, and Jordan toward Britain); and less extensively Sub-Saharan Africa (typically toward France, Belgium, and Britain but more recently to Italy, the Netherlands, and Portugal).

27. Portes 1995, p. 10.

28. The socio-economic divide underlying present migration flows is roughly indicated by two macroeconomic facts: about one seventh of the global population uses four-fifths of global resources; and one-third of the Mediterranean population produces nine-tenths of the National Bruto Production in the area.

29. Harding 1998 (in particular chapter 2); Hess 1995 (in particular chapter 3); Needham 1978.

30. See in this book the discussion carried out in the papers by Fraser, Khair, and Gilroy.

31. See the so-often cited *Othello* (1604) and *The Tempest* (1612) by William Shakespeare, *The Life and Adventures of Robinson Crusoe* by Daniel Defoe (1719), *The Jungle Book* (1894) by Rudyard Kipling, and *Heart of Darkness* (1902) by Joseph Conrad. Cf. Brantlinger 1988.

32. See Azim 1993.

33. Goldberg 2000, p. 77.

34. For example, see the works by Quobna Ottabah Cugoano (1787), Olaudah Equiano (1789), Ignatius Sancho (1782), Mary Prins (1831), and Mary Seacole (1800). The presence of African, Caribbean, and Asian slave servants in Britain slowly grew in the sixteenth and seventeenth centuries. See Phillips 1997.

35. Dabydeen 1991.

36. See Visram 1986; Burton 1998; Grewal 1996; and Nasta 2001.

37. His novel *The Buddha of Suburbia* was transformed into a TV series, and both *My Beautiful Launderette & Others* and *Sammy and Rosie Get Laid* were successful movies worldwide.

38. See in this book the chapters by McLeod, López-Ropero, and D'haen.

39. This new flourishing has involved different media and artistic fields. An example is Hanif Kureishi, who began his artistic career as screenplay writer and film director and whose novels have been adapted for theater and film.

40. See in this book the way Huggan frames this debate.

41. On the Berber presence in French literature see Merolla 1995.

42. See the role of the American Josephine Baker within the French artistic world of the 1930s. See also Archer-Straw 2000.

43. Successively, however, the "négritude" stream was criticized because its fundamentally essentialist and masculine assumption of a natural opposition between black man and white man entirely failed to perceive, or grasp the meaning of, the underlying complicity with the colonial and European vision of the other/black.

44. She began to publish in the 1970s and then international fame came with her historical novel *Segou*.

45. See the essay by Hargreaves in this book.

46. Laronde 1997, p. 38.

47. See in this book the essays by Schipper, Hargreaves, and Bammer.

48. Martin 1998.

49. The geo-temporal limitation of the German colonial empire is related to the late period of German unification as a nation (in 1870).

50. See Campt 2003; Lusane 2002; and articles by B. Cooper in Encarta Africana, www.africana.com. The activities of the association Initiative Schwarze Deutsche (Black German Initiative) started in the late 1980s.

51. See the works by Cyrus Atabay (1929–1996) and Bahman Nirumand (1963–)—who both immigrated to Germany from Teheran. They have published in German, respectively, since 1956 and since 1967. See also the works by Elazar Benyoëtz (who was born in Austria, emigrated as child to Israel and then to Germany in 1964, and has published in German since 1969).

52. See Rösch 1991, Adelson 1990.

53. Award of the "German as foreign language" institute at the University of Munich in cooperation with the Bavarian Arts Academy.

54. See the essay by Yegenoglu in this book.

55. Sephardic Jews were banished from Spain after 1492, and a significant number of exiles came to Holland, where they made a huge contribution to the Dutch secular culture. The influential philosopher Spinoza was the son of Jewish-immigrant parents.

56. More precisely the expansion of the VOC (Verenigde Oost-Indische Compagnie) and WIC (West-Indische Compagnie).

57. Gouda 1995.

58. See the philosopher Baruch Spinoza (1632–1677) and later the writers Isaac da Costa (1798–1860), Jacob Israël De Haan (1881–1924), and Israël Querido (1872–1932), of Jewish families that emigrated early to the Netherlands. More recently, there is the internationally famous Anne Frank, child of a German Jewish family that fled to the Netherlands before World War II.

59. Such as Multatuli (alias Eduard Douwes Dekker, 1820–1887), Augusta de Witt (1864–1939), and Edgar du Perron (1899–1940). Although laden with ambiguities, this literature is often critical of the colonial condition.

60. See, for example, Marion Bloem (1952–), Adrian van Dis (1946–), and Hella S. Hasse (1918–). Cf. Nieuwenhuis 1972, 1988; Birney 1998; Baay and van Zonneveld 1988; Francken and van Zonneveld 1995. See also Speestra 2001; Buikema and Meijer 2003.

61. In Indonesia Dutch was not officially endorsed and most writers continued to write in Indonesian. Only a few writers such as Karini and Soewarsih Djojopoespito adopted the language of the colonizers. A famous example is Pramoedya Ananta Toer.

62. These writers also write novels and essays in English.

63. See in this book the essay by Jansen.

64. Dutch agencies in Morocco and in Turkey had the task of recruiting workers for Dutch industries and agriculture.

65. Different communities, traditionally Protestant, Catholic, and Jewish, had rights to autonomous religious organization, schooling, unions, and so forth.

66. See, for example, Sera and Milo Anstadt (from Poland), the poet Leo Serano (from Chile), Ana Sébastán (from Argentina), and Ahmed Sefa and A. Pooyan (respectively from Christian and Kurdish minorities in Turkey). Dimitri Sideri (from Greece) belongs to the migration of the 1950s and her autobiographical novel *Vaderlanden* was published in 1992.

67. Merolla 2002.

68. Isegawa and Sherif actually wrote their novels in English, but they are published in Dutch translation. Likewise Snezana Bukal and Nasim Khaksar write respectively in Serbo-Croatian and in Farsi and publish Dutch translations, while Mimoun El Walid, Ahmed Essadki, and Ahmed Ziani publish bilingual editions of Berber poems with Dutch translation.

69. Laroui published in French extensively before writing for the first time in Dutch in 2001.

70. She was in her teens when she arrived in Belgium, and then she moved to the Netherlands. Allas played in *Idil, een meisje* [Idil, a Girl], a film based on her first novel and adapted by Karim Traïda, an Algerian director and writer who has produced films in French and in Dutch. See also Sevtap Baycili, from Istanbul, working in the Netherlands as a theater actress and columnist since 1991, who published her first novel in Dutch in 1999. Likewise Nilgün Yerli, who arrived in the Netherlands when she was ten years old, works as columnist and theater actress, and had her first novel published in 2001.

71. See in this book the essay by Pattynama. On the interaction between theater, films, and the Internet, see Merolla 2002 on Amazigh/Berber authors.

72. Birney and De Kom were born in The Hague, respectively in 1951 and 1956.

73. On migrant themes in their works, see Merolla 1998, 2002, and 2004.

74. This discourse was particularly explicit in Bouazza's unpublished lecture on literary influences, 27 November 2001, Leiden.

75. Bouazza 2001; Kuitert 2001; *TLC* 2001; Literatuur 1999; Merolla 2002. See in this book the essay by Buikema.

76. The expansion of Portugal began in 1415 with the conquest of Ceuta in North Africa, and continued in the sixteenth century with the acquisition of ports and markets

and the establishing of alliances in Sub-Saharan Africa (present-day Angola, Cape Verde, Mozambique, Guinea-Bissau, and São Tomé and Príncipe), Asia (India's coasts, Malacca, and Ceylon, and a few port rights in China and Japan), and South America (coast settlements in Brazil). Between 1578 and 1640, Portugal was subjected to Spanish hegemony, while the Netherlands acquired economic rights in Asian areas of previous Portuguese expansion. After 1703 Britain imposed its economic and political hegemony. In the early nineteenth century the Portuguese court escaped Napoleon's occupation and moved to Brazil, which became the administration post of Portugal, inverting the previous hegemonic relation. Brazil acquired independence in 1822. In Portugal the republic established in 1910 lasted only seven years. Then a first period of dictatorship started, and continued under the infamous Salazar regime until the Carnation Revolution in 1974 (Nunes 1987, pp. 1–18).

77. In the sixteenth century Spain colonized vast areas roughly corresponding to the present-day Spanish-speaking South and Central American countries. The destruction of the Spanish Armada and the subsequent loss of naval supremacy sunk Spain into decadence and opened the way to British supremacy. The Spanish empire in Europe (Belgium, Luxembourg, Milan, Sardinia, and Naples) was lost, while Britain gained the colonies of Gibraltar and Minorca. After the Napoleonic invasion, the Spanish colonies in America started wars of independence (a famous independence leader was Simon Bolivar). Venezuela gained independence in 1821 and the other lands followed (Colombia, Ecuador, Peru, Bolivia). The Cuban Revolution of 1895 was the beginning of the Spanish-American War. In 1898 the United States annexed the Spanish colonies of Cuba, Puerto Rico, Guam, and the Philippines. At the turn of the century Spain enlarged its colonized territories in northern Morocco and in Western Sahara. Morocco was finally freed in 1956, but Western Sahara remained under Spanish colonial mandate until 1974, just one year before the death of the dictator Francisco Franco, who took power in 1938 after a long and cruel civil war. Spain maintains two ancient posts in northern Morocco, the cities of Ceuta and Melilla. After the retreat of Spain the Western Sahara was partly annexed by Morocco against the will of the local Fronte Polisario, and the conflict is still going on.

78. The actual population in Portugal is about 10 million. Official data count about 200,000 legal foreign residents, while estimates of "illegal" immigrants range from 35,000 (official) to 150,000 (unions' account). Immigrants in Portugal come from Cape Verde, Brazil, Angola, Guinea-Bissau, Mozambique, São Tomé and Príncipe, and East Timor, and increasingly from Eastern Europe. The number of immigrants in Spain is estimated to be about one-fifth of the population (about 600,000 people), and an estimated 15 percent of the immigrants come from Morocco. See discussions in Della Piana 2000; Migrance 1999, p. 15 (on Portugal); and Torregrosa and El Gheryb 1994 (on Spain).

79. Melilla, geographically in northern Morocco, is Spanish but obtained Autonomous City Status in 1995. There are 65,000 inhabitants—Christian, Muslim, Jewish, and a small Hindu community, and several languages are spoken: Spanish, Arabic and Berber/Tamazight. The productions by Berber writers either in Spanish or in Amazigh are still very limited, but recently music and songs by Berber artists from this area have received some attention in Spain. See Toufali 1999.

80. Since the 1980s, several postcolonial literary studies on Lusophone (Portuguese language) literatures have appeared, such as Nunes 1987 and Chabal 1996.

See also Moser and Ferreira 1993. Previous pioneering works were Hamilton 1975, Ferreira 1977, and a number of anthologies (de Andrade 1958; César 1969; Ferreira 1975).

81. Since about 1850 a local colonial literature developed, mainly characterized by exoticism toward the local aspects and following the models for language and style from the "center."

82. Amílcar Cabral, assassinated in 1973, was an important leader of the African Party for Independence of Guinea and Cape Verde.

83. The literature from Brazil has historically played a particularly influential role on Lusophone literatures in Africa. Among the first attempts of colonial literature concerning the Portuguese colonies in Africa were the writings of Brazilian intellectuals deported to Angola, such as Grégorio de Matos, and to Mozambique, such as Tomás Antônio Gonzaga a century later (Moser and Ferreira 1993, p. 20).

84. Moser and Ferreira 1993 pp. 21–22; Peres 1997, pp. 7–15.

85. These writers renewed a trend already started with Nho Eugênio Tavares (1867–1930) writing in Crioulo, the language of Cape Verde. Also, Manuel Ferreira interspersed his texts with Criuolo.

86. Pepetela, on the other hand, was exiled to Paris and to Algeria for his political activity.

87. Before Mussolini's fascist policy closed the way to Italian emigration in the 1920s, about a third of the population, largely from southern Italy, emigrated toward the Americas. In the 1950s, there were more limited migrant flows to Italy (about 150,000 immigrants) largely arriving from European countries. In the 1970s the number of immigrants doubled. In the 1980s, the presence of immigrants became more visible, reaching about 750,000 (about half were illegally staying in the country). In 2000, immigration reached about 1,500,000 people (of whom the arrivals from outside the European Union were about 42 percent), representing about 2.5 percent of the Italian population. In the European Union, immigrants today are about 5 percent of the whole population. Immigration statistics are difficult to read since they classify varying populations whose definition alters over time (for example, data on immigration flows may or may not include temporary immigrants, children of immigrants, persons who acquired citizenship but were born abroad, and so forth).

88. Italian expansionism resembled Portuguese colonialism, which, coupling demographic growth with poor economic development, could reassure the national pride suffering from the otherwise "low" international political and military position. However, French colonialism—and not the German or the Portuguese—was the explicit model for Italian colonial expansion.

89. See *Ungaretti commenta Ungaretti* and Zingone 1993, pp. 62–73. This attitude is echoed by Italo Calvino in a short autobiographical text ("I was born when my parents were about to come home after years spent in the Caribbean; hence the geographical instability that makes me forever long for somewhere else") although it did not explicitly mark his literary production. Calvino was born in Santiago de Las Vegas, Cuba, in 1923. His Italian parents re-emigrated to San Remo (Italy) in 1925.

90. Including works by well-known authors such as Gabriele D'Annunzio and the founder of Futurism, Filippo Tommaso Marinetti. See Manaconda 1993; Ponzanesi 2004; Tomasello 1984.

91. Italian colonialism started well before fascism, but it ended with the defeat of fascist Italy in World War II.

92. Alberto Moravia (1907–1990), pseudonym for Alberto Pincherle, *A quale tribù appartieni?* [To What Tribe Do You Belong?] (1972), *Lettera dal Sahara* [Letter from Sahara] (1982), *Passeggiate Africane* [African Walks] (1987).

93. Alessandro Spina: *Il giovane maronita* [The Young Maronite] (1971), *Le nozze di Omar* (1973), *Il visitatore notturno* (1970), *Storie di ufficiali* (1967), *La commedia mentale* (1992), *La riva della vita minore* (1997). Erminia Dell'Oro: *Asmara Addio* (1988), *L'Abbandono, Una Storia Eritrea* (1991), *Il Fiore di Merara* (1994). Maria Abbebù Viarengo, "Scirscir 'n demna (Andiamo a Spasso)," *Linea D'Ombra* (1990).

94. See also Ponzanesi 2000.

95. Ndjock Ngana comes from Cameroon (Basaa language).

96. Salah Methnani emigrated from Tunisia in the mid-1980s and works in Rome as translator and writer.

97. The Senegalese writer Pap Khouma went first to the Ivory Coast, then to France. He later went to Italy, where he works as journalist.

98. Sirad Hassan, born in Mogadiscio, was brought up and educated in the United States. She lives in Italy and in the United States. See Ponzanesi 2000 ("Writing against the Grain").

99. See also the following writers: Mohamed Bouchane, who arrived in Italy from Morocco in the 1980s; Saidou Moussa Ba, who arrived in Italy from Dakar in 1988; Mohsen Melliti, who arrived in Italy from Tunis, where he had studied at and graduated from the Faculty of Arts, and who volunteered as a social worker for illegal immigrants at the decaying Pantanella building in Rome; Nassera Chohra, who arrived in Italy from France at the end of the 1980s and who was born in Marseilles, in an Algerian family from the southern Sahara; Shirin Ramzanali Fazel, who was born in a Somali-Pakistani family and arrived in Italy from Somalia in the 1970s; Kpan Teagbeu Simplice, who arrived in Italy from Abidjan, graduated in Rome, where he also volunteered as a social worker with legal and illegal immigrants, and lives in Palermo; Mohamed Ghonim, who has lived in Italy since the 1980s and who emigrated from Egypt, where he had published poems and theater texts; the journalist Maria De Lourdes Jesus, from Cape Verde, who presented *Non solo nero* [Not Only Black] (1988), one of the first television programs on immigration in Italy; Ribka Sibhatu, who escaped from the war in Eritrea in the mid-1980s and lives in Rome, where she graduated from the Faculty of Modern Languages; and Younis Tawfik, who was born in Iraq, has lived in Italy since 1979, and works as journalist and translator.

100. Dadina and N'Diaye 1994. On the Senegalese-Romagnol theater of Ravenna Teatro, see Picarazzi 1995; on the African theater groups Le Albe and Maschere Nere, see Moussa Ba 1995.

101. Gnisci 1992, 1995, 1998; Parati 1993, 1995, 1997; Ponzanesi 1999; and articles by Matteo, Parati, and Picarazzi in *Italian Studies in Southern Africa,* 1995.

WORKS CITED

Adelson L., Migrants' Literature or German Literature, *German Quarterly* 63.3–4 (1990): 382–90.

Allen B. and M. Russo (Eds.), *Revisioning Italy: National Identity and Global Culture*, Minneapolis: University of Minnesota Press, 1997.

Anderson B., *Imagined Communities: Reflections on the Origin and Spread of Nationalism*, London, Verso, 1983.

Andrade M. de (Ed.), *Antologia da Poesia Negra de Expressao Portuguese, Precedida de Cultura Negro-Africana e Assimilacao*, Germantown, NY, Periodicals Service Company, 1958.

Appiah A., *In My Father's House: Africa in the Philosophy of Culture*, Oxford, Oxford University Press, 1993.

Archer-Straw P., *Negrophilia, Avant Garde Paris and Black Culture in the 1920's*, London, Thames and Hudson, 2000.

Ashcroft B., G. Griffith, and H. Tiffin, *The Empire Writes Back*, London, Routledge, 1989.

Augé M., *Non-Places: Introduction to an Anthropology of Supermodernity*, London, Verso, 1995.

Azim F., *The Colonial Rise of the Novel*. London and New York, Routledge, 1993.

Baay R., and P. van Zonneveld, *Indisch-Nederlandse literatuur*, Utrecht, Hes-Uitgevers, 1988.

Bhabha, H. (Ed.), *Nation and Narration*. London and New York, Routledge, 1990.

Birney A. (Ed.), *Oost-Indische ink*, Amsterdam and Antwerpen, Contact, 1998.

Boehmer E., *Colonial and Postcolonial Literature: Migrant Metaphors*, Oxford, Oxford University Press, 1995.

Bonn C. (Ed.), *Littératures des immigrations: un espace littéraire émergent*, Vol. 2, Paris, L'Harmattan, 1995.

Bouazza H., *Een beer in bontjas*, CPNB, Amsterdam, Prometheus, 2001.

Braidotti R., *Nomadic Subjects: Embodiment and Sexual Difference in Contemporary Feminist Theory*. New York, Columbia University Press, 1994.

Brantlinger P., *Rule of Darkness: British Literature and Imperialism*, Ithaca, NY, Cornell University Press, 1988.

Brinkler-Gabler G., and S. Smith, *Writing New Identities: Gender, Nation and Immigration in the New Europe*, Minneapolis, University of Minnesota Press, 1997.

Buikema R., and M. Meijer (Eds.), *Kunsten in beveging 1900–1980*, Cultuur en Migratie in Nederland, den Haag, Sdu, 2003.

Burton A., *At the Heart of the Empire: Indians and the Colonial Encounter in Late-Victorian Britain*. Berkeley: University of California Press, 1998.

Campt T., *Other Germans: Black Germans and the Politics of Race, Gender, and Memory in the Third Reich*, Ann Arbor, University of Michigan Press, 2003.

César A. (Ed.), *Contos Portugueses do Ultramar, Vol. 2: Cabo Verde, Guiné e São Tomé e Príncipe*, Porto, Portucalense Editora, 1969.

Chabal P., *The Post-colonial Literature of Lusophone Africa*, Evanston, IL, Northwestern University Press, 1996.

Chambers I., *Migrancy, Culture and Identity*. New York and London, Routledge, 1994.

Dabydeen D., West Indian Writers in Britain, *Black Writers in Britain 1760–1890*, P. Edwards and D. Dabydeen (Eds.), Edinburgh, Edinburgh University Press, 1991.

Dadina L., and M. N'Diaye, *Griot Fulêr*, Rimini, 1994.

Dejeux J., *Maghreb: litteratures de langue francaise*, Paris, Arcantère, 1993.

Dejeux J., *La Littérature féminine de langue française au Maghreb*, Paris, Karthala, 1994.

Deleure, G. and F. Guattari, *Kafka: Toward a Minor Literatue*, trans. D. Polan, Minneapolis, University of Minnesota Press, 1986.

Dennis P. and K. Naseem (Eds.), *Voices of Crossing: The impact of Britain on Writers from Asia, the Caribbean and Africa*, London, Serpent's Tail, 2000.

Fachinger P., *Rewriting Germany from the Margins: "Other" German Literature of the 1980s and 1990s*, Montreal, Canada, McGill-Queen's University Press, 2001.

Ferreira M., *Literaturas Africanas de Expressao Portuguesa*, Vol. I, Lisboa, Instituto de Cultura e Lingua Portuguesa, 1977.

Ferreira M. (Ed.), *No Reino de Caliban, Vol. 1: Cabo Verde e Guiné-Bissau*, Lisboa, Seara Nova, 1975.

Francken E., and P. van Zonneveld, *Van Oost to West, koloniale en postkoloniale literatuur in het nederlands*, 1995.

Gilman S., Black Bodies, White Bodies: Towards an Iconography of Female Sexuality in Late Nineteenth-Century Art, Medicine and Literature, *'Race,' Culture and Difference*, J. Donald and A. Rattansi (Eds.), London, Sage Publications, 1992, pp. 171–97.

Gilroy P., *The Black Atlantic: Modernity and Double Consciousness*, London, Verso, 1993.

Gilroy P., *"There Ain't No Black in the Union Jack": The Cultural Politics of Race and Nation*, London, Hutchinson, 1987.

Gnisci A., *La letteratura italiana della Migrazione*, Roma, Lilith Edizioni, 1998.

Gnisci, A., *Noialtri Europei*, Roma, Bulzoni, 1995.

Gnisci A., *Il rovescio del gioco*, Roma, Carucci, 1992.

Goldberg D. T., Heterogeneity and Hybridity: Colonial Legacy, Postcolonial Heresy, *A Companion to Post-colonial Studies,* H. Schwarz and S. Ray (Eds.), Oxford, Blackwell, 2000, pp. 72–86.

Gontard M., and M. Bray (Eds.), *Regards sur la Francophonie*, Rennes, Presses Universitaires de Rennes, 1996.

Gouda F., *Dutch Culture Overseas: Colonial Practice in the Netherlands Indies, 1900–1942*, Amsterdam, Amsterdam University Press, 1995.

Green M. J. (et al.), *Postcolonial Subjects: Francophone Women Writers*, Minneapolis, University of Minnesota Press, 1996.

Grewal I., *Home and Harem: Nation, Gender, Empire, and the Cultures of Travel*, Durham, NC, Duke University Press, 1996.

Hall S., *Representation: Cultural Representations and Signifying Practices*, London, Sage, 1997.

Hall S., Minimal Selves, *Black British Cultural Studies: A Reader*. A. Houston Jr., Manthia Diawara Barker, and Ruth H. Lindeborg (Eds.). Chicago: University of Chicago Press, 1996, pp. 114–19.

Hamilton R. G., *Voices from an Empire*, Minneapolis, University of Minnesota Press, 1975.

Harding S., *Is Science Multicultural? Postcolonialisms, Feminisms, and Epistemologies*, Bloomington and Indianapolis, Indiana University Press, 1998.

Hargreaves A. G., *Voices from the North African Immigrant Community in France*, New York, Oxford, 1991.

Hess D. J., *Science and Technology in a Multicultural World: The Cultural Politics of Facts and Artifacts*, New York, Columbia University Press, 1995.

hooks b., *Yearning: Race, Gender, and Cultural Politics*, New York, South End Press, 1990.

Ibnlfassi L., and N. Hitchcott (Eds.), *African Francophone Writing*, Oxford and Washington, DC, Berg, 1996.

Jack B., *Francophone Literatures: An Introductory Survey*, New York, Oxford University Press, 1996.

Kuitert L., *Vleugelspelers, Uitgevers tussen twee culturen*, Utrecht, Forum, 2001.

Laronde M., Les littératures des immigrations en France. Question de nomenclature et directions de recherche, *Le Maghreb littéraire* 1.2 (1997): 25–44.

Laronde M., *Autour du roman beur, immigration et identité*, Paris, L'Harmattan, 1993.

Leijnse E., and M. van Kempen, *Schrijvers tussen de culturen*, Amsterdam, Het Spinhuis, 2001.

Literatuur, Themanummer literaturen in het Nederlands, 16 (1999): 99–6.

Lusane C., *Hitler's Black Victims: The Historical Experience of Afro-Germans, European Blacks, African and African Americans in the Nazi Era*, New York and London, Routledge, 2002.

Manaconda G., Le guerre italiane in Africa e la letteratura, *Studi di italianistica nell'africa australe, Special issue*, part 2, 6.1 (1993): 37–61.

Martin P. L., *Germany: Reluctant Land of Immigration*, Washington, DC, American Institute for Contemporary German Studies, 1998.

Matteo S., Blood and Memes on the Marciapiede: Memetics and Migration, *Italian Studies in Southern Africa, Special Issue, Margins at the Centre: African Italian Voices* 8.2 (1995): 67–81.

Merolla D., Poétique de la migration et renouvellement littéraire aux Pays-Bas, *Les identités néerlandaises et la Germanité*, P. Duval et T. Beaufils (Eds.), Strasbourg and Metz, conference, 2004.

Merolla D., Deceitful Origins and Dogget Roots: Dutch Literary Space and Moroccan Immigration, *Forging New European Frontiers: Transnational Families and Their Global Networks*, D. Bryceson and U. Vuorela (Eds.), Oxford and New York, Berg, 2002, pp. 103–23.

Merolla D., Digital Imagination and the "Landscapes of Group Identities": Berber Diaspora and the Flourishing of Theatre, Video's, and Amazigh-Net, *The Journal of North African Studies* 7.4, (Winter 2002): 122–31.

Merolla D., Un espace littéraire kabyle, *Etudes et Documents Berbères*, No. 13 (1995): 5–25.

Merolla D., and H. Bouazza, De voeten van Abdullah (Les pieds d'Abdullah), Lecture, *Le Maghreb Littéraire* 2.3 (1998): 117–21.

Minh-ha T. T., Other Than Myself/My Other Self, *Travellers' Tales: Narrative of Home and Displacement,* G. Robertson, M. Mash, L. Tickner, J. Bird, B. Curtis and T. Putnam (Eds.), London and New York: Routledge, 1994, pp. 9–26.

Min-Ha T. T., *Woman, Native, Other: Writing Postcoloniality and Feminism*, Minneapolis, Indiana University Press, 1989.

Moser G., and M. Ferreira, *A New Bibliography of the Lusophone Literatures of Africa/Nova Bibliografia das Literaturas Africanas de Expresso Portuguesa,* London, Zell, 1993.

Moussa Ba S., Uno 'straniero' fa teatro, *Italian Studies in Southern Africa, Special Issue, Margins at the Centre: African Italian Voices* 8.2 (1995): 100–103.

Nasta S., *Home Truths: Fiction of the South Asian Diaspora in Britain*, London, Palgrave, 2001.

Needham J., The *Shorter Science and Civilisation in China* [abridged by C. A. Ronan], Cambridge, Cambridge University Press, 1978.

Nieuwenhuis R. (Ed.), *Oost-Ondische Spiegel*, Amsterdam, Querido, 1972.

Nieuwenhuis R. (Ed.), *Mirror of the Indies: A History of Dutch Colonial Literature*, English trans., Amherst, University of Massachusetts Press, 1988.

Nunes M. L., *Becoming True to Ourselves: Cultural Decolonization and National Identity in the Literature of the Portuguese-speaking World*, New York, Greenwood Press, 1987.

Parati G. (Ed.), *Mediterranean Crossroads: Migration Literature in Italy*, Madison, NJ, Fairleigh Dickinson University Press, 1999.

Parati G., Looking through Non-western Eyes, *Writing New Identities: Gender, Nation and Immigration in the New Europe*, G. Briker-Gabler and S. Smith (Eds.), Minneapolis, University of Minnesota Press, 1997, pp. 119–42.

Parati G., Italophone Voices, *Italian Studies in Southern Africa, Special Issue, Margins at the Centre: African Italian Voices* 8.2 (1995): 1–15.

Parati, G., "When the 'Other' is Black: Portraits of Africans by Contemporary Italian Writers," *Romance Language Annual*, 1993, 272–77.

Phillips C., *Extravagant Strangers. A Literature of Belonging*, London and Boston, Faber & Faber, 1997.

Piana L. della, "Choose Your World": Race in Portugal and the New Europe, *ColorLines* 2.4 (Winter 1999–2000).

Picarazzi T., Griot Fulër: Performing National Identities, *Italian Studies in Southern Africa, Special Issue, Margins at the Centre: African Italian Voices* 8.2 (1995): 83–99.

Ponzanesi S., *Paradoxes of Post-colonial Culture: Contemporary Women Writers of the Indian and Afro-Italian Diaspora*, Albany, State University of New York Press, 2004.

Ponzanesi S., Diasporic Subjects and Migration, *Advanced Text Book on European Women's Studies*, R. Braidotti and G. Griffin (Eds.), London, Sage, 2002, 205–20.

Ponzanesi S., The Past Holds No Terror? Colonial Memories and Afro-Italian Narratives, *Wasafiri, Special Issue on Migrant Writings in Europe* 31 (Spring 2000): 16–22.

Ponzanesi S., Writing against the Grain. African Women's Texts on Female Infibulation as Literature of Resistance, *Indian Journal of Gender Studies, Special Issue on Feminism and the Politics of Resistance* 7.2 (2000): 303–18.

Ponzanesi S., Postcolonial Women's Writing in Italian: The Case Study of the Eritrean Ribka Sibhatu, *Northeast African Studies* 5.3 (New Series) (1998): 97–115.

Portes A., *Transnational Communities: Their Emergence and Significance in the Contemporary World System*, Working Paper 16, Program in Comparative International Development, Department of Sociology, The Johns Hopkins University, Baltimore, 1995.

Rösch, H., *Migrationsliteratur im Interkulturellen Kontext*, Frankfurt/M., Iko-Verlag für Interkulturelle Kommunikation, 1992.

Rushdie S., *Imaginary Homelands: Essays and Criticism 1991–1991*, London, Granta Books, 1991.

Said E., *Culture and Imperialism*, London, Vintage, 1993.

Slemon, S., Modernism's Last Post, *Past the Last Post: Theorizing Post-Colonialism and Post-Modernism*, I. Adam and Helen Tiffin (Eds.), London, Harvester / Wheatsheaf, 1991, pp. 1–11.

Speestra U., *Representaties van culturele identiteit in migrantenliteratuur. De Indiase diaspora als case studie,* (diss.), Leiden, 2001.

Spivak G., *In Other Worlds: Essays in Cultural Politics*, London, Routledge, 1998.

Stoler L. A., *Race and the Education of Desire: Foucault's History of Sexuality and Colonial Order.* Durham, NC, Duke University Press, 1995.

Tetu M., L. Senghor, and J.-M. Leger (Eds.), *La Francophonie: histoire, problématique et perspectives*, Paris, Hachette, 1988.

TLC, The Low Countries, Arts and Society in Flanders and the Netherlands, Special number *Low Countries, Host Countries?* Belgium, Stichting Ons Erfdeel, 2001.

Tomasello G., *La letteratura coloniale italiana dalle avanguardie al fascismo*, Palermo, Sellerio, 1984.

Torregrosa P. M., and M. El Gheryb, *Dormir Al Raso*, Madrid, Ediciones Vosa, 1994.

Toufali M., Literatura Rifeño-Andaluza...? (Reflexiones sobre la existencia de una literatura rifeña de expresión castellana), *Volubilis, revista de Pensamiento* .7 (March 1999).

Visram R., *Ayas, Lascars and Princes: The History of Indian in Britain, 1700–1947*, London, Pluto Press, 1986.

West C., *Race Matters*, London, Vintage Books, 1994.

Zingone A., Ungaretti. La culla araba, il miraggio d'Alessandria, *Italian Studies in Southern Africa, Special Issue, Margins at the Centre: African Italian Voices* 6.1 (1993): 62–73.

WRITERS AND WORKS MENTIONED

Britain

Anand Mulk Raj (1905–2004), *Untouchable*, 1935, *Coolie*, 1936.

Aphra Ben (1640–1689), *Ooronoko: Or the Royal Slave*, 1688.

Chang Jung (1952–), *Wild Swans*, 1993.

Chaudhuri Amit (1962–), *A Strange and Sublime Address*, 1991, *Afternoon Raag*, 1993, *Freedom Song*, 1998.

Chaudhuri Nirad C. (1897–1999), *The Autobiography of an Unknown Indian*, 1951.

Dangaremba Tsitsi (1959–), *Nervous Conditions*, 1984.

Dhingra Leena (1942–), *Amritvela* (1988).

Dutt Toru (1856–1877), *A Sheaf Gleaned in French Fields*, 1875, *Ancient Ballads and Legends of Hindustan*, 1882.

Emecheta Buchi (1944–) *Second Class Citizen* 1974, *The Rape of Shavi*, 1983, *Gwendolen*, 1989.

Gupta Sunetra (1965–), *Memories of Rain*, 1992, *Moonlight into Marzipan*, 1995, *Sins of Colours*, 1999.

Gurnah Abdulrazak (1948–), *Paradise*, 1995, *Admiring Silence*, 1996, *By the Sea*, 2001.

Hosain Attia (1913–1998), *Phoenix Fled*, 1951, *Sunlight on a Broken Column*, 1961.

Hussein Aamer (1955–), *Mirror to the Sun*, 1993, *This Other Salt Stories*, 1999.

Ishiguro Kazuo (1954–), *A Pale View of Hills*, 1982, *The Remains of the Day*, 1990, *When We Were Orphans*, 2000, *An Artist of the Floating World*, 2001.

Jamal Mahjoub (1960–), *Navigation of a Rainmaker*, 1995, *In the Hour of the Signs*, 1996, *The Carrier*, 1999.

Kureishi Hanif (1954–), *The Buddha of Suburbia* 1990, *The Black Album*, 1996, *My Son the Fanatic*, 1998, *Intimacy*, 1999, *Gabriel's Gift*, 2001. Among his theater pieces: "The King and Me," "Outskirts," "Borderline," "Birds of Passage."

La Guma Alex (1925–1985), *Walk in the Night*, 1962, *The Stone Country*, 1967, *Time of the Butcherbird*, 1979.

Lamming George (1927–), *The Immigrants*, 1954.

Marechere Dambudzo (1952–1987), *Black Sunlight*, 1980, *House of Hunger: Short Stories*, 1982.

Markandaya Kamala (1924–2004), *Nectar in a Sieve*, 1955, *A Handful of Rice*, 1966.

Mo Timothy (1950–), *Sour Sweet*, 1982, *Monkey King*, 1984.

Naidu Sarojini (1879–1949), *The Bird of Time: Songs of Life, Death and Spring*, 1912, *The Sceptred Flute: Songs of India*, 1928.

Naipaul V.S. (1932–), *A House for Mr. Biswas*, 1961, *An Area of Dark*ness, 1964, *The Enigma of the Arrival*, 1987, *Among the Believers: An Islamic Journey*, 1982.

Okri Ben (1959–), *The Famished Road*, 1992, *Songs of Enchantment*, 1994, *African Elegy*, 1997.

p'Bitek Okot (1931–), *Song of Lawino*, 1984, *White Teeth*, 1989.

Phillips Caryl (1958–), *The Final Passage*, 1985, *Cambridge*, 1993, *Crossing the River*, 1995, *The Nature of Blood*, 1998, *The Atlantic Sound*, 2000.

Randhawa Ravinder (1953–), *A Wicked Old Woman*, 1987, *Coral Strand*, 2001.

Rao Raja (1908–), *The Serpent and the Rope*, 1960.

Rhys Jean (1890–1979), alias Ella Gwendoline Rees Williams, *Wide Sargasso Sea*, 1966.

Roy Arundhati (1959–), *The God of Small Things*, 1997.

Rushdie Salman (1947–), *The Satanic Verses*, 1988, *East, West*, 1994, *The Moor's Last Sight*, 1996, *Fury*, 2001.

Salkey Andrew (1928–1995), *A Quality of Violence*, 1959, *The Adventures of Cactus Kelly*, 1969, *The River That Disappeared*, 1980.

Selvon Samuel (1923–1994), *The Lonely Londoners*, 1956, *Moses Ascending*, 1975, *Moses Migrating*, 1983.

Smith Zadie (1975–), *White Teeth*, 2000.

Soyinka Wole (1934–), *A Dance of the Forest*, 1963, *The Man Died*, 1972, *Death and the King's Horseman*, 1975.

Srivastava Atima (1961–), *Transmission*, 1992, *Looking for Maya*, 1999.

Syal Meera (1963–), *Anita & Me*, 1999, *Life Isn't All Ha Ha Hee Hee*, 2000.

wa Thiong'o Ngugi (1938–), *Weep Not Child*, 1964, *A Grain of Wheat*, 1967, *Petals of Blood*, 1977, *Decolonizing the Mind: The Politics of Language in African Literature*, 1986, *Moving the Centre: The Struggle for Cultural Freedom*, 1993.

France

Amrouche Jean (1906–1962), *Chants de Kabylie*, 1939.

Begag Azouz (1957–), *Le Gone du Chaâba*, 1986, *Quand on est mort c'est pour toute la vie*, 1994, *Zenzela*, 1997.

Béji, Hélé (1948–), *Le Désenchantement national*, 1982, *L'itinéraire de Paris à Tunis*, 1992, *L'imposture culturelle*, 1997.

Belghoul Farida (1958–), *Georgette!*, 1986.

Ben Jelloun Tahar (1944–), *L'écrivain public*, 1985, *L'enfant de sable*, 1989, *Une journée de silence à Tanger*, 1995.

Beyala Calixtha (1961–), *C'est le soleil qui m'a brûlée*, 1987, *Le Petit prince de Belleville*, 1992, *Les Honneurs perdus*, 1996.

Boudjedra Rachid (1941–), *La Répudiation*, 1969, *L'Escargot entêté*, 1977, *Le désordre des choses*, 1991, *Timimoum*, 1994.

Boukhedenna Sakinna (1959–), *Journal. Nationalité: immigré(e)*, 1987.

Césaire André (1913–), *Cahier d'un retour au pays natal*, 1956, *Une Saison au Congo*, 1966, *Une Tempête*, 1974, *Moi, laminaire*, 1982.

Chamoiseau, Patrick (1953–), *Éloge de la créolité*, 1989, *Texaco*, 1992.

Charef Mehdi (1952–), *Le thé au harem d'Archi Ahmed*, 1983, *Le Harki de Mériem*, 1989, *La Maison d'Alexina*, 1999.

Chedid Andrée (1920–), *Visage Premier*, 1972, *Cavernes et Soleils*, 1979, *7 Textes pour un Chant*, 1986.

Chraibi Driss (1926–), *Le passé simple*, 1954, *La civilisation, ma Mère!*, 1972, *Une enquête au pays*, 1981, *L'inspecteur Ali*, 1991.

Condé Maryse (1937–), *Segou* (vol. I and II) 1984–1986, *Desirada*, 1997, *Histoire de la femme cannibale*, 2003.

Confiant, Raphaël (1951–), *Éloge de la créolité*, (with J. Bernabé and P. Chamoiseau), 1989, *Jou Baré*, 1981, *Le Nègre at l'Amiral*, 1993.

Damas Leon Gontran (1912–1978), *Veillées noires*, 1943, *Graffiti*, 1952, *Black Label*, 1956, *Névralgies*, 1966.

Depestre, René (1926–), *Étincelles*, 1965, *Au matin de la negritude*, 1990, *Encore une mer à traverser*, 2005.

Dib Mohamed (1920–2003), *La grande Maison*, 1952, *L'Incendie*, 1954, *Le Talisman*, 1966, *Habel*, 1977.

Djaout Tahar (1954–1993), *L'exproprié*, 1981, *Les chercheurs d'os*, 1984.

Djebar Assia (1936–), alias Fatima-Zohra Imalayen, *La Soif*, 1957, *Les Enfants du Nouveau Monde*, 1962, *Femmes d'Alger dans leur appartement*, 1980, *Ombre sultane*, 1987.

Fanon Franz (1925–1961), *Peau noir, masque blancs*, 1952, *L'an cinq de la revolution algérienne*, 1959, *Les damnés de la terre*, 1961.

Farès Nabile (1940–), *Yahia, pas de chance*, 1970, *Mémoire de l'Absent*, 1974.

Glissant Edouard (1928–), *Le Discours Antillais*, 1997.

Imache Tassadit (1958–), *Une fille sans histoire*, 1989, *Le Dromadaire de Bonaparte*, 1995.

Kateb Yacine (1929–1983), *Nedjma*, 1957, *Le polygone étoilé*, 1966, *Mohammed, prends ta valise* (theater), 1971.

Khair-Eddine Mohamed (1941–1995), *Agadir*, 1967, *Ce Maroc!*, 1975, *Légende et vie d'Agoun'chich*, 1984.

Khatibi Abdelkebir (1938–), *La Mémoire tatouée*, 1972, *Le Prophète voile*, 1979, *Un été à Stockholm: roman*, 1990.

Laye Camara (1928–1980), *L'Enfant noir*, 1953, *Le regard du roi*, 1954, *Maître de la parole. Kuma lafolo kuma*, 1980.

Lê Linda (1963–), *Les trois Parques*, 1997.

Maalouf Amin (1946–), *Léon l'Africain*, 1986, *Les Croisades vues par les arabes* (essay), 1986, *Le Rocher de Tanios*, 1993, *L'Amour de loin*, 2001.

Memmi Albert (1920–), *La Statue de Sel*, 1953, *Portrait du colonisé* (essay), 1957, *Le Scorpion*, 1969, *Le Pharaon*, 1989.

Mimouni Rachid (1945–1995), *Le Fleuve détourné*, 1982, *La Malédiction*, 1993.

Ndiaye Marie (1967–), *Quant au riche avenir,* 1985.

Sebbar, Leila (1940–), *Le Chinois vert d'Afrique*, 1984, *Marguerite*, 2002.

Sefrioui Ahmed (1915–2004), *Le Chapelet d'ambre*, 1949, *La Boîte à merveilles*, 1954, *La Maison de servitude*, 2001.

Senghor Leopold (1906–2001), *Chants d'ombre* (poetry), 1945, *Ethiopiques* (poetry), 1956, *Lettres d'hivernage* (poetry), 1973, *Liberté 3: Négritude et civilisation de l'universel* (essay), 1977.

Tamza Arriz (1957–), pseud. Messaoud Bousselmania, *Ombres*, 1989.

Touabti Hocine (1949–), *L'amour quand même*, 1981.

Germany

Biondi Franco (1947–), *Nicht nur Gastarbeiterdeutsch* (poems), 1979, *Abschied der zerschellten Jahre* (novella), 1984, *Der Stau*, 2001.

Chiellino Gino (1946–), *Mein fremder Alltag* (poems), 1984, *Sich die Fremde nehmen* (poems), 1992.

Çirak Zehra (1960–), *Vogel auf dem Rücken eines Elefanten* (poems), *Leibesübungen*, 2000.

Dalos György (1943–), *Meine Lage in der Lage. Gedichte und Geschichten* (poems), 1979, *Der Versteckspieler. Gesellschaftsroman* (from Ungarian by György Dalos and Elsbeth Zylla), 1994, *Der Gottsucher* (from Ungarian by György Dalos and Elsbeth Zylla), 1999.

Franzetti Dante Andrea (1959–) *Der Großvater*, 1985, *Das Funkhaus*, 1993, *Curriculum eines Grabräubers*, 2000.

Kurt Kemal (1946–2002), *Weil wir Türken sind / Türk oldugumuz için*, 1981, *Ja, sagt Molly*, 1998, *Eine echt verrückte Nacht*, 2001.

Moníková Libuse (1945–), *Eine Schädigung*, 1981, *Die Fassade. Ein kollektiver Schelmenroman*, 1987, *Treibeis*, 1992, *Das Taumel*, 2000.

Oliver José (1961–), *Heimat und andere fossile Träume* (poems), 1989, *Gastling* (poems), 1993, *Duende* (poems), 1997.

Ören Aras (1939–), *Terkedilmislerin Aksami. Siir* (poems), 1960, *Privatexil* (poems), 1977, *Eine verspätete Abrechnung oder Der Aufstieg der Gündogdus* (trans. from Turkish), 1988, *Berlin-Savignyplatz* (trans. from Turkish), 1993, *Privatexil. Ein Programm?*, 1999.

Özdamar Emine Sevgi (1946–), *Mutterzunge*, 1990, *Die Brücke vom goldenen Horn*, 1998, *Der Hof im Spiegel*, 2001.

Özdemir Hasan (1963–), *Was soll es sein?*, 1989, *Das trockene Wasser*, 1998.

Schami Rafik (1946–), *Das Schaf im Wolfspelz*. *Märchen und Fabeln*, 1982, *Der Fliegenmelker und andere Erzählungen aus Damaskus*, 1986, *Zeiten des Erzählens*, 1994, *Die Sehnsucht der Schwalbe*, 2000.

Senocak Zafer (1961–), *Elektrisches Blau* (poems), 1983, *Das senkrechte Meer* (poems), 1991, *Die Prärie*, 1997.

Taufiq Suleman (1953–), *Dies ist nicht die Welt, die wir suchen*, 1983, *Im Schatten der Gasse*, 1992, *Spiegel des Anblicks* (poems), 1993.

Tawada Yoko (1960–), *Das Bad. Ein kurzer Roman*, 1989, *Ein Gast*, 1993, *Orpheus und Izanagi*, 1998, *The Bridegroom Was a Dog*, 1998.

Tekinay Alev (1951–), *Über alle Grenzen*, 1986, *Der weinende Granatapfel*, 1990, *Nur der Hauch vom Paradies*, 1993.

Trojanow Ilija (1965–), *Die Welt ist groß und Rettung lauert überall : Roman*, 1996.

Wodin Natascha (1945–), *Die gläserne Stadt*, 1983 and 1994, *Einmal lebt ich*, 1989, *Das Singen der Fische*, 2001.

Zeimoglu Feridun (1964–), *Kanak Sprak*, 2000.

The Netherlands

Abdollah Kader (1954–), *De meisjes en de partizanen*, 1995, *De reis van de lege flessen*, 1997, *Spijkerschrift*, 2000.

Accord Klark (1961–), *De koning van Paramaribo* [The Queen of Paramaribo], 1999.

Allas Yasmine (1967–), *Idil, een meisje*, 1998.

Arion Frank Martinus (1936–), pseudonym Frank Efraim Martinus, *Dubbelspel*, 1973, *Nobele wilden*, 1979, *De laatste vrijheid*, 1995.

Benali Abdelkader (1975–), *Bruiloft aan zee*, 1996 (English trans. 1999), *De ongelukkige* (theater), 1999, *Berichten uit Maanzaad Stad*, 2001, *De langverwachte*, 2002.

Birney Alfred (1951–), *Tamara's lunapark* (1987), *Sonatine voor zes vrouwen*, 1996, *Fantasia*, 1999.

Bouazza Hafid (1970–), *De voeten van Abdullah*, 1996 (English trans. *Abdullah's Feet*, 2000), *Momo*, 1998, *Salomon*, 2001, *Paravion* 2003.

Boudou Khalid (1974–), *Het schnitzel-paradijs*, 2001.

Breytenbach Breyten (1939–), *Katastrofes*, 1964, *Voetskrif*, 1976.

Brink André (1935–), *Lobola vir die lewe*, 1962, *Houd-den-bek*, 1982, *Duiwelskloof*, 1998, *Anderkant die stilte*, 2002.

Cairo Edgar (1948–2000), *Ik ga dood om jullie hoofd*, 1980, *Temekoe*, 1979, *Kopzorg: het verhaal van vader en zoon*, 1988.

Debrot Cola (1902–1981), pseudonym Nicolaas Debrot, *Mijn zuster de negerin*, 1935, *Navrante zomer* (poems), 1945, *Bewolkt bestaan*, 1948.

de Kom Antoine, (1956–), *Tropen* [Tropics], 1991, *De kilte in Brasilia* [Cold in Brasilia], 1995.

Du Perron E., (1899–1940), *Het land van herkomst*, 1935.

El Bezaz Naima (1974–), *De weg naar het noorden*, 1995.

El Haji Said (1976–), *De dagen van Sjaitan*, 2000.

Eybers Elisabeth (1915–), *Belydenis in die skemering*, 1936, *Versamelde gedigte*, 1957, *Versamelde gedigte*, 1990, *Winter-surplus*, 1999.

Haasse Hella S., (1918–), *Oeroeg*, 1948, *Heren van de thee*, 1992.

Isegawa Moses (1963–), *Abbesijnse kronieken*, 1998, *Slangenkuil*, 1999, *Twee chimpanzees*, 2001.

Jonker Ingrid (1936–1967), *Onvlugting* (poems), 1956, *Rook en Oker* (poems), 1963.

Laroui Fouad (1958–), *Les dents du topographe*, 1996, *Verbannen woorden* (poems), 2002.

Lopulalan Frans (1953–), *Onder de sneeuw een Indisch graf*, 1985, *Dakloze herinneringen*, 1994.

Marugg Tip (1923–), Silvio Alberto Marugg, *Afschuw van licht* (poems), 1946–1951, *Weekendpelgrimage*, 1957, *De morgen loeit weer aan*, 1988.

Multatuli (1820–1887), pseudonym for Eduard Douwes Dekker, *Max Havelaar*, 1860.

Nasr Ramsey (1974–), *De doorspeler* (monologue), 1995, *Kapitein Zeiksnor & Twee culturen*, 2001.

Nieuwenhuys Rob (1908–1999), *Vergeelde portretten*, 1954.

Ombre Ellen (1948–), *Maalstroom*, 1992, *Wie goed bedoelt*, 1996, *Valse Verlangens*, 2000.

Robinson Talje (1911–1974), pseudonym for Jan Johannes Theodorus Boon, *Piekerans van een straatslijper*, 1955, *Piekerans bij een voorplaat*, 1976, *Didi in Holland*, 1992.

Romer Astrid (1947–), *Over de gekke van een vrouw*, 1979, *Noordzeeblues* (poems), 1985, *Lijken op liefde*, 1997.

Sahar Hans (1974–), *Hoezo Bloedmooi*, 1995, id. *De heimwee-karavaan*, 2000.

Sherif Vamba (1973–), *Het land van de vaders*, 1999, *Het koningrijk van Sebah*, 2003.

Stitou Mohamed (1974–), *Mijn vormen* (poems), 1994.

Supusepa Eddy (1950–), *Yang tak terbungkamkan*, 1990 (subtitle in Dutch: Poems against the Fascist Dictatorship in Indonesia), *Amlan . . . Carpen*, 1999 (in Saparuan).

Van Dis Adriaan (1946–), *Indische duinen*, 1994.

Wang Lu (1960–), *Het lelietheater*, 1997, *Het tedere kind*, 1999.

Portugal

Agualusa José Eduardo (1960–), *A Conjura*, 1989, *Lisboa Africana*, 1993, *Nação Crioula*, 1997.

Almeida Germano (1945–), *O Testamento do Sr. Napumoceno da Silva Araújo*, 1989, *O Meu Poeta*, 1990, *A Família Trago*, 1998.

Cassamo Suleiman (1962–), *O Regresso do Morto*, 1989, *Palestra para Um Morto*, 1999.

Couto Mia (1955–), *Vozes Anoitecidas*, 1986, *Terra Sonâmbula*, 1992, *A Varanda de Frangipani*, 1996.

d'Sal Sukre (1951–), *Amdjers*, 1997.

de Sant'Anna Glória (1925–), *Distância* (poems), 1951, *Desde que o Mundo* (poems), 1972, *Do Tempo Inútil*, 1975.

de Sousa Nóema (1926–2002), *Poemas*, 1951.

de Vasques Tenreiro Francisco José (1921–1963), 1950, *Acerca da Casa e do Povoamento da Guiné O Rapaz Doente*, 1963, *Coração em África*, 1977.

Ferreira Manuel (1917–1992), *A Aventura Crioula*, 1973, *Terra Trazida*, 1972.

Honwana Luís Bernardo (1942–), *Nós Matámos o Cão Tinhoso*, 1964.

Lopes Manuel (1907–2005), *Chuva Braba*, 1956, *Crioulo e Outros Poemas* (poems), 1964.

Lopes Baltasar (1907–1989), *Chiquinho*, 1947, *Os Trabalhos e os Dias*, 1987.

Muge Amélia (1952–), *O Girasol* (poems), 1983, *Viagem ao meio das nuvens* (children's stories), 1983.

Neto Agostinho (1922–1979), *Quatro Poemas de Agostinho Neto*, (poems), 1957, *Sagrada Esperança* (poems), 1974, *Renúncia Impossível* (poems), 1987.

Osório Osvaldo (1937–), pseudonym for Osvaldo Alcântara Medina Custódio, *Caboverdeamadamente Construção Meu Amor*, 1975, *O Cântico do Habitante*, 1977.

Pepetela (1941–), alias Artur Carlos M. Pestana, *Muana Puó*, 1978, *Luandando*, 1990, *O Segredo de Kianda*, 1995.

Preto Alvos (1931–), alias Tomás Medeiros, *Um homem igual a tantos*, 1959.

Ramos Wanda (1948–1998), *Percursos (do luachimo ao lueno)*, 1981, *Litoral* 1991.

Rui Manuel (1941–), *Memória de Mar*, 1980, *Mortos & os vivos*, 1993.

Tavares Paula (1952–), *Ritos de passagem* (poetry), 1985, *O Lago da Lua* (poetry), 1999, *Dizes-me coisas amargas como os frutos* (poetry), 2001.

Teixeira Paulo (1962–), *As Imaginaçoes da verdade* (poems), 1985, *O Rapto de Europa* (poems), 1994, *As Esperas e outros poemas* (poems), 1997.

Vieira Luandino (1936–), *Luanda*, 1965, *Vidas Novas*, 1975, *Laurentino Dona Antônia de Sousa Neto e eu*, 1981.

Xitu Uanhenga (1924–), *Manana*, 1974, *Os Discursos do "Mestre" Tamoda*, 1984, *O Ministro*, 1990.

Italy

Abbebù Viarengo Maria (1949–), "Scirscir 'n demna (Andiamo a Spasso)," *Linea D'Ombra*, 1990.

Bouchane Mohamed (1964–), with Carla de Girolamo and Daniele Miccione, *Chiamatemi Alì* [Call me Ali], 1990.

Chohra Nassera (1963–), *Volevo diventare bianca* [I wanted to become white], 1993.

Da Costa Rosana Crispina, *Il mio corpo traduce molte lingue*, 1998.

De Lourdes Jesus Maria (1955–), *Racordai. Vengo da un'isola di Capo Verde* [Remembered: I Come from an Island of Cape Verde], 1996.

Dell'Oro Erminia (1938–), *Asmara Addio*, 1988, *L'Abbandono, Una Storia Eritrea*, 1991, *Il Fiore di Merara*, 1994.

Emmanuelli Enrico (1909–1967), *Settimana Nera* [Black Week], 1961, *La congiura dei sentimenti*, 1943, *La Cina è vicina*, 1957.

Fazel Shirin Ramzanali, *Lontano da Mogadiscio* [Away from Mogadiscio], 1994.

Flaiano Ennio (1910–1972), *Tempo di uccidere* [Time to Kill], 1947.

Ganabo Jadelin M. (1976–), *Verso la notte Bakonga*, 2001, *Rometta e Giulieo*, 2001.

Ghonim Mohamed (1958–), *Il segreto di Barhume* [Barhume's Secret], 1994 (re-edited 1997), *Quando cade la maschera* [When the Mask Falls], 1995.

Hassan Sirad Salad (1962–), *Sette Gocce di Sangue. Due donne somale* [Seven Drops of Blood: Two Somali Women], 1996.

Khouma Pap (1957–), with Oreste Pivetta, *Io, venditore di elefanti. Una vita per forza tra Dakar, Parigi e Milano* [I, the Elephant Seller: A Forced Life between Dakar, Paris, and Milan], 1990.

Kubati Ron (1971–), *Venti di libertà e gemiti di dolore*, 1991, *Va e non torna*, 2000, *M.*, 2002.

Melliti Mohsen (1967–), *Pantanella. Canto lungo la strada* [Pantanella: Song on the Road], 1992, *I bambini delle rose* [Rose's Children], 1995.

Methnani Salah (?), with Mario Fortunato, *Immigrato* [Immigrant], 1990.

Monteiro Martins Guido (1955–), *Racconti Italiani* [Italian Tales], 2000, *La Passione del Vuoto* [The Passion for Emptiness], 2003.

Moravia Alberto (1907–1990), pseudonym for Alberto Pincherle, *A quale tribù appartieni?* [To What Tribe Do You Belong?], 1972, *Lettera dal Sahara* [Letter from Sahara], 1982, *Passeggiate Africane* [African Walks], 1987, *La donna leopardo* [The Leopard Woman], 1991.

Moussa Ba Saidou (1964–), with P. A. Micheletti, *La promessa di Hamadi* [Hamadi's Promise], 1991, *La memoria di A.* [A.'s Memory], 1995.

Ngana Ndjock: (1952–), *Foglie vive calpestate. Riflessioni sotto il baobab*, 1989, *Nhindô Nero* [Black Nhindô], 1994 (bilingual edition).

Okayová Jarmila (1955–), *L'essenziale è invisibile agli occhi*, 1997, *Verrà la vita e avrà i tuoi occhi*, 1997, *Requiem per i padri*, 1998.

Sibhatu Ribka (1962–), *Aulò, Canto-poesia dall'Eritrea* [Aulò: Song-poem from Eritrea], 1998 (bilingual [Italian-Tigré] text).

Spina Alessandro (pseud.), *Il giovane maronita* [The Young Maronite], 1971, *Le nozze di Omar*, 1973, *Il visitatore notturno*, 1970, *Storie di ufficiali*, 1967, *La commedia mentale*, 1992, *La riva della vita minore*, 1997.

Tawfik Younif (1957–), *La straniera* [The Foreigner Woman], 1999.

Teagbeu Kpan Simplice (1952–), *Il condottiero*, 1996.

Tobino Mario (1910–?), *Il deserto della Libia* [The Desert of Libya], 1952.

Ungaretti, Giuseppe (1888–1970), *Allegria di naufragi*, 1919, *Le terra promessa*, 1950, *Il deserto e dopo*, 1961.

Zagbla Tano Emmanuel (1961–), *Il grido dell'AlterNativo, esperienze di un immigrato ivoriano*, 1998.

I

MAPPING EUROPE: THEORETICAL INTERVENTIONS

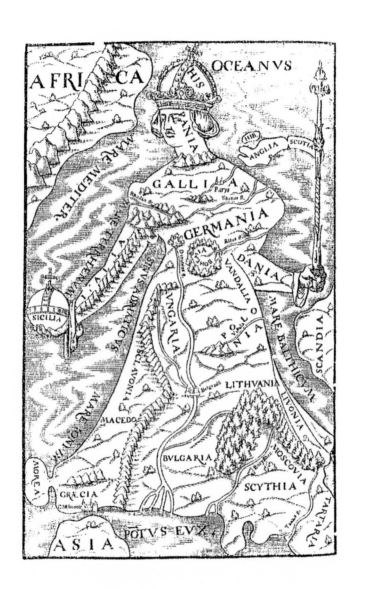

1

Mapping the Mind:
Borders, Migration, and Myth

Robert Fraser

This article is about traveling, and the various sorts of people who undertake it. I thought therefore that I would begin and end in one of those sedentary and routine-bound rolling conveyances: a suburban London railway carriage. My first wagon is attached to the 10:15 to Victoria, leaving and arriving during my preparation for this essay. It contains my commuting self, appreciatively immersed in Paul Gilroy's book *Between Two Camps*.[1] Pausing, I glance to my right, my attention briefly distracted by the woman seated beside me. She is absorbed in the monosyllabic Briton's verbal and pictorial breakfast, the *Sun* newspaper. This morning its cover displays a map of the United Kingdom with intrusive arrows converging from every direction. "LUNATIC ASYLUM!" shrieks the headline, amplifying this witticism with the observation that every day 3,500 human beings arrive seeking sanctuary in the United Kingdom, while a mere twelve are returned to their proper—or improper—places of habitation.[2] My neighbor turns the page. Inside, there is a photograph of a glum and wasted looking mother with her contrite-looking daughter, both white. "How could she let her child marry one of them?" the accompanying leader demands. At lunchtime, taking a break from the library, I try to acquire this journalistic rant to illustrate part of my argument. Every copy within a mile of St. Pancras has been sold. Instead I concentrate on this latest national obsession with asylum seekers caught in crouching postures in the lights of advancing Eurostars, hiding in concealed compartments beneath 186-mile-per-hour trains,[3] or arriving deep-frozen in the backs of lorries to thaw out illegally in Dover. In national and international debate, as Gilroy argues, the ubiquitous topic of "race" is forever being translated into new terms, inviting and taunting the decoder. We are used to some of these ciphers: developed/ underdeveloped, north/south, inner and outer city. This latest xenophobic seizure adds an appoggiatura to a very jaded tune. In that hastily snapped up issue of the *Sun*, the relevant codes had concerned maps and mental hygiene. The angle looked brash but it played on several time-worn idioms. Xenophobia itself may be a relatively modern disease, but the questions of where we are positioned in space, where we fit into the larger cosmogony, and who or what constitutes the healthy mind and body are many centuries old. If they stem from any one historic period of European history, it is surely from the Renaissance.

All maps, of course, are mental as well as physical projections. Look at the woodcut of "Queen Europa" featured in Sebastian Münster's *Cosmographia*, first published in Basel in 1540 and re-issued in 1588, the year of the Spanish Armada.[4] It features an upended topographical design with the shorelines distorted into the figure of a well-proportioned monarch and the compass bearings re-jigged to place Spain, then at the height of its imperial success, as the crowned head. In her right hand she holds the orb of Sicily, and in her left—itself composed of Denmark—a scepter, from which flutters a pennant made up of Scotland, England, and Ireland. France composes her upper chest, and Germany her stately bosom. The rest of her limbs languish in cartographic uncertainty caused by an absence of national boundaries, not to feature on any map of Europe until 1607. What look like borders in Münster's projection turn out, on closer inspection, to be rivers, each representing an artery feeding Europe's generous body: the Seine her rib cage, the Danube her calves, the Volga her left thigh. The most precious artery of all, the Upper Rhine, springs from her heart, made up of the enclosed grove of Bohemia.

I want us to think about two related consequences stemming from the upright carriage of this figure and the arrangement of her inner organs. Because of her orientation, it is very difficult to form a sense of an East-West axis and, even if there is a compensating North-South fulcrum, it is not where we would put it. Forty years before William Harvey's *De Motu Cordis* (1628), moreover, there is in this analogical body no sense of circulation of the blood. Instead there is a one-way outward flow quite consistent with Tudor notions of the arteries as conduits carrying the vital or intellectual spirits to each and every part. The source of the continuous flux on Münster's chart is the sylvan heart of Bohemia. This is remarkable in itself, since topographical ideas as to the whereabouts and extent of Bohemia were notoriously vague at the time. The most celebrated culprit in this respect was Shakespeare, who set Act Four of *The Winter's Tale* there, but managed in the process to equip Bohemia with a seashore. "Shakespeare in a play," crowed his friend and rival Ben Jonson, "brought in a number of men, saying that they had suffered ship-wreck in Bohemia, where there is no sea near by 100 miles."[5]

Over one fact, however, the Elizabethans were consistent. Bohemia—
wherever that was—was the immediate, though not the original, home of a
people who had first appeared on the highways of western Europe in the fifteenth century, and in the rural lanes and city streets of England and Scotland
from about 1507: the Roma, or as they were then—and are still—commonly
called, the gypsies.[6]

On why the Roma had come to be associated in the public mind with Bohemia, again our best informant is Münster, who had met a troupe of them
in Eberach near Heidelberg.[7] When he asked them how they traveled so
freely, they showed him a document of safe-conduct from the former Holy
Roman Emperor, King Zigmund of Bohemia. As it happens, a copy of this
document has survived. Signed at Spissky [Spisska Bela] Castle in what is
now the Slovak Republic on April 17, 1423, it enjoins all it may concern to
treat "Ladislav, Duke of his Gypsy People" and his followers with courtesy:
"We recommend that you show him the loyalty which you would show to
Us. Protect them so that Duke Ladislaw and his people may live without prejudice within your walls."[8] Believing the Roma's own explanation that they
were Egyptians on a seven-year pilgrimage of penance for having rejected
Christ, Zigmund had clearly taken on himself a role as their protector. Indeed, it was on account of this tale of origin, adopted to appeal to late medieval Catholic sympathies, that the Roma were already—and confusingly—
known as "gypsies." Sceptical as always, Münster asked his Heidelberg
friends where their homeland was, and was told it lay beyond the Holy Land,
beyond even Babylon. He learnedly replied, "Then your Lesser Egypt is not
Africa near the Nile but in Asia along the Ganges or the Indus." The gypsies,
who had long forgotten their place of ultimate origin, dissolved into mirth.

It is clear from these accounts that, wherever they wandered, the uncertainty of their place of origin, and the bizarre and eclectic nature of their language, colored the way the gypsies were received. All that anybody could
agree on was that they came from the East. This very indeterminacy, on
which the Roma themselves could shed little light, proved intriguing as well
as worrying. It was in the Dutch city and university of Leiden that the mists
at last began to clear. In the 1590s a Leiden professor called Joseph Scaliger
took to hanging around local taverns, chatting to gypsies in the only language they had in common: French. His methods of research were haphaz-
ard. One evening he approached a carousing Roma and inquired through the
hubbub, "How do you say in your language 'Qu'est-ce que *tu bois?*'" (What
are you drinking?). But the night was far spent, and the customers were rau-
cous. The gypsy tippler thought the Dutchman had asked him, "Qu'est-ce
que *du bois?*" and supplied him with *kascht*, the Romany noun for firewood.[9]
This error duly appeared under "bibere"—to drink—in the seventy-one-word
Romany-Latin lexicon contributed by Scaliger to Bonaventura Vulcanius's *De
literis et lingue sive Gothorum*, published in Leiden in 1597. On the basis of

such misinformation, and of the prevailing myth of gypsy origin, Scaliger concluded that Romany was a branch of Nubian. The truth had to wait until 1763, and another conversation in a Leiden pub. In that year a theology student from the Komorn region of Hungary, István Váli, fell into conversation with three Leiden undergraduates from the Malabar coast of southwest India, and asked them for snippets of their mother tongue. He was instantly struck by the similarity of certain words to the vocabulary of gypsies he had chatted to at home in Gyor.[10] Váli's inference that Romany was a distant dialect of Malabari was reported in the journal *Wiener Anzeigen* in 1776, though the 1,000 items listed there are closer to Malayalam than to the Indo-Aryan group to which he ascribed them. At last, however, the link with India—first casually proposed by Münster two centuries before—existed on an albeit unsteady philological footing.

We must dwell awhile in the immediate pre- and post-revolutionary period, because it is at this moment of the creation of the modern world and the slow consolidation of what were to become Europe's nation-states that the Roma enter European literature as a fully-fledged *topos*. There are references before, of course—in Ben Jonson's masks[11] and in Bunyan[12]—but the general impression of exoticism, skill, and spasmodic persecution is as yet unmatched by any commanding allure or threat. A change of attitude is already perceptible in a series of decrees passed by the Empress Maria Theresa of Austria between 1758 and 1773. She offered Hungarian Roma full citizenship provided they paid taxes and settled in one place; they were to give up their wagons and horses and their children for adoption.[13] The policy of enforced integration enjoyed very limited success. Behind it, however, we can discern a drift toward a more constrained, nation-bound notion of belonging. In 1815 the Treaty of Vienna consolidated this presumption by defining Europe's borders in a far more systematic way than ever before. Though Germany and Italy were still to be created as sovereign nations, the principle behind the 1815 settlement was clear: demarcated and rigorously policed borders, a bureaucratic infrastructure capable of interrogating all comers. As Jeremy Black observes in his book *Maps and Politics*, all charts "reflect a society that both seeks to understand and that can create, construct and control"; maps are "instruments of power."[14] On this analogy the European map of 1815 reflected a society that sought to understand culture as a static expression of place. Under this new dispensation all migrants posed a problem. In the legal as well as geographic sense, there was no room for the Roma, or indeed for roaming.

It was against this background that in that year of revolutions, 1830, Victor Hugo composed the first of the great nineteenth-century fables of Romany attraction and menace. *Notre Dame de Paris* is a historic romance that projects onto the fifteenth century—the period when the Roma first entered France—the political and cartographic anxieties of the new proto-nationalist age. In it Paris serves as a metonym for the French nation, the Ile de la Cité as a metonym for the city, and, within that citadel, the cathedral as the repository of France's memory: its proud but compassionate soul. On this pattern of symbols a concentric series of maps is superimposed: the street plan of Paris acts as a miniature of the nation while—on a smaller but still magnificent scale—the architecture of the church becomes a microcosm of both city and state. On the outskirts of the town—and hence of the nation—dwell a criminal underclass: the Truands under their leader, the Duke of Egypt and Bohemia. The relationship of this Romany rabble to the rest of society is manifest in a climactic scene in Book Ten when they attempt to rescue the gypsy dancer La Esmeralda from the cathedral, where Quasimodo is guarding her as a fugitive from French justice. As the hunchback stares from the great western towers, the darkness of the unlit quais beneath him heaves: it is the Romany mob, who then attempt to batter down the door. The outrage is possible because, as Hugo is obliged to pause in his narrative to explain, late medieval Paris has no police force. When the royal troops arrive, the crowd is dispersed and La Esmeralda arrested and hung. A fourth topography is then carefully laid onto these culminating events: a map both ethical and ethnic. Hugo reserves his moral approbation for those capable of a noble, self-sacrificing love. La Esmeralda is as capable of this feeling as is Quasimodo, whom she spurns. However, the narrative builds up to the moment when it is predictably revealed that the beautiful street performer is not a gypsy at all, but Agnes, lost daughter of the French recluse La Sachette. *Notre Dame de Paris* is perhaps the first nineteenth-century novel to depend upon that territorial phobia: the kidnapping and spiriting away of the community's children. Agnes's true identity is revealed just before she swings on the rope, at which point Hugo is free to compare her to the Angel of Humility from Dante's *Purgatorio*: "La Creature Bella Bianco Vestita."[15] The girl, the church, and the city are one.

In *Notre Dame de Paris* Europe, once seen by Münster as one large and confident body, is envisaged as a cluster of cells, such as had been observed by Hugo's fellow liberal, the hygienist and revolutionary Francois Vincent Raspail, who described them in the very year of the novel's composition in his *Essai de chimie microscopique*. During the following decade the physiological metaphor was explored in greater detail by the Prussian polymath and radical Rudolf Virchow. Virchow was a doctor, an energetic research scientist, and a political liberal who had experience fighting on one particular frontier, the Silesian border of Prussia, during the uprising of '48. A close associate of the archaeologist Schliemann, he also had a strong amateur interest in anthropology, a study that he did much to encourage in Germany. He was also in his later years a member of the Prussian diet, where he argued strongly against emerging German nationalism.[16]

As a physiologist Virchow concentrated on the structure of and interrelationship between cells, compared by him to the individuals composing a nation, or the nations that make up a continent. The body, he wrote, was itself "a republic of cells, each one living its own life." He was in strong agreement with the view earlier stated in Latin by Raspail: "omnis cellula ex cellula" (every cell originates in another cell). Virchow attributed this independence both to sound and to diseased organisms. Correspondingly, as an anthropological amateur, Virchow believed all cultural manifestations to be the products of movement and borrowing. Politically, he was a potential federalist who thought the newly clarified borders of Europe to be not merely permeable, but doomed. Doomed too was any attempt by a nation-state to enforce discipline and ethnic uniformity within its geographical boundaries. In an article written in 1847, a year before he served in Silesia, Virchow used ethnic cleansing as a metaphor for a reactionary and anachronistic pathology. Outbreaks of xenophobic zeal were like pus; like pus, moreover, they were powerless to ensure health. "Pus formation," he wrote, "is no longer the struggle of the organism to heal itself, by filling up this or that hole; the corpuscles are no longer the *gendarmes* whom the police state orders to escort over the border this or that foreigner who has entered without a passport; scar tissue no longer holds an imprisoning wall, in which such a prisoner is enclosed, when it pleases the Police-Organism."[17]

This insistence on the pointlessness of population control exasperated Bismarck, the architect of the new Germany, who once challenged Virchow to a duel. But the questions raised by the medical argument became central to Europe's evolving view of itself. If boundaries are analogous to membranes separating cells, how permeable are these walls, and what happens when they are breached? In the 1840s these worries were given memorable expression in the second of our nineteenth-century parables about the gypsy presence: Prosper Mérimée's misogynistic novella *Carmen* (1845).[18] Mérimée's tale is of special interest because this professional archaeologist and amateur writer had some knowledge of the Spanish gypsies, whom he had observed during a tour in 1830.[19] In 1847 he added an extra chapter to the book, summarizing his research. Two salient characteristics of the Roma, he stated, were "patriotism"—by which he meant loyalty to their kind—and absolute marital fidelity. His story demonstrates the very opposite. A sort of emotional vagrant, Carmen destroys the peace of the workplace, the lives of lovers and friends. After she has cathartically played out the reader's fantasies of masochistic freedom, her Basque lover Don José brutally stabs her. In Bizet's opera of 1875, she lies crumpled and humiliated on the stage before an audience whom she has musically and sexually excited for three hours. They are rid of her, and can safely go back home.

These stories by Hugo and Mérimée are not usually branded as racist, yet racialism is strongly encoded into each. The reason has, I believe, less to do with the dilutions of popular culture than with a phenomenon integral to the original texts. In these books a remarkable transformation is occurring before our very eyes: the myth of the vagrant gypsy is being annexed by the cult of the vagabond artist. The clearest evidence of this change at the time is the appropriation of the term *Bohemian* to cover dissident behavior by impoverished, and normally young, poets, painters, and musicians. The initiation of this neologism is easy to date since it occurs in Henry Murger's portrait of Left Bank Parisian life, *Scènes de la Bohème* (Scenes from Bohemia) of 1850, later to form the basis of a famous opera by Puccini. In his preface, written in May 1850, Murger stresses the novelty of his coinage. He is equally at pains to stress that the borrowing entails no cultural obligation or debt. Though the dissident artist may now be considered a Bohemian, he is free from infection by—and from occupations traditionally associated with—the Roma. "The bohemians I am dealing with here," Murger begins, "have nothing to do with those bohemians who serve in popular drama as synonyms for rogues and murderers. You will not find them amongst bear-leading gypsies, sword-sharpeners, vendors of safety-chains, practitioners of the quick buck, black market racketeers, and a thousand other suspect and ill-defined professions whose principal purpose is their apparent dereliction and willingness to do anything as long as it's up to no good." Murger's subjects are not nomads; they are settled. Turning Hugo's townscape inside out, he places his new bohemians in the Quartier Latin, in the very shadow of Notre Dame. By the end of Murger's humorous preface the appropriation and relocation are complete: "Bohemia," he announces with deliberate half-irony, "only exists—indeed is only conceivable—in Paris."[20]

The isolationism, and severance from suspect foreign connections, implied by this careful paradox were in step with the cultural ambience of the closing decades of the nineteenth century, during which a renewed imperial impulse on the part of the chief European powers went along with intensified nationalism at home. Cartographically and anatomically too, the relative openness to extraneous influence implied by Virchow's cellular structures with their semiporous walls gradually gave way to the régime of medical and political thought associated in Germany with Virchow's arch-enemy, the bacteriologist and political reactionary Robert Koch.[21] The driving force behind this change was disease. The cholera epidemics of 1832, 1849, and 1853 had concentrated medical inquiry on the problem of diffusion. Previously assumed to be the result of contiguous unhealthy environments, from the 1860s such outbreaks were increasingly attributed to micro-organisms that could be carried across borders. It was Koch who identified the tuberculosis bacillus in 1882; in 1883 he traced cholera back to India, from where it had advanced along an itinerary coinciding with that attributed to the gypsies. The prophylactic measures Koch proposed—in Europe, an increased emphasis on documentation, medical screening, and quarantine, and the establishment of *cordons sanitaires* between indigenous and settler communities overseas—reinforced the dividing lines between ethnic and social groupings. Already pestilence was commonly employed as a journalistic metaphor for unwelcome migration or revolution. The year after Koch published his findings on cholera, the British-held Sudan suffered the Mahdist rising, widely interpreted as an outbreak of religious dementia. A right-wing French satirist caught the mood of the moment when he compared the rising to a plague, the need to suppress which spelled the end of Virchow's liberal republic of permeable and mutually supportive units. He continued, "Cellular pathology has had its day. Our body is no longer that 'republic of cells' each leading its healthy life . . . so dear to the German professor Virchow. Dethroned is your cellular republic, Grand Master. . . . Down with cells, long live independent beings, infinitesimal but prolific . . . coming from outside, penetrating the organism like Sudanese, ravaging it by right of invasion and conquest."[22]

Inevitably the new dispensation impacted backward on historical readings of culture. Virchow's insistence on the interdependence of all civilizations gave way to a vision of each society as the unique expression of local conditions within a homeland or fatherland. Advanced nations, it came to be argued, were end results of the supplanting of hunter-gatherer societies by agrarian and then industrialized communities. Increasingly culture came to be defined as a condition of settling down. Adopted by German ethnology, this orthodoxy was eventually to become the cornerstone of Nazi anthropology. Its corollary was a view of all mobile groups as regressive, degraded, or deviant. In 1936, Martin Block, a leading German authority on the Roma— and a relatively sympathetic observer of them—wrote: "Gypsies are different from us. One realises that as soon as one meets them."[23] The incorrigible indifference toward sedentary life displayed by his subjects intrigued and exasperated Block. "It may be," he rhetorically observed, "that they are stronger than civilisation. But even if they are, why do they exercise that strength so relentlessly, rejecting all attempts to change them?"[24]

The incomprehension, sentimentalizing, and plain prejudice that mark attitudes toward the Roma in the late nineteenth and early twentieth centuries are exactly contemporaneous with the enshrining of Bohemianism as a defining feature of artistic life in the West. Puccini's *La Bohème* epitomizes a cult growing ever more tenacious and alluring as Romanticism reaches its decadent late phase. Interestingly, the most moving moment in the opera is Mimi's death from tuberculosis, the less virulent of the two diseases identified by Koch, already softened by fin-de-siècle myth into "consumption." In 1894 George du Maurier's novel *Trilby* glamorizes the casual and transgressive life of the "bohemian" Left Bank in much the same terms as Murger, adding an acceptable frisson of mesmerism and sex. In 1908 Augustus John, *enfant terrible* of British painters, portrays his wife in a Roma-style dress, starting a vogue for gypsy accessories that grips European capitals even as the models for the fashion are limited to—or expelled from—their margins.[25] As Block memorably puts it, "the carts move on."

What I seem provocatively to be proposing is that there exists, not simply a logical connection between the cult of the bohemian artist and the persecution of the Roma, but a causal link as well. The implications are disturbing. The myth of Bohemia, for example, is now the birthright, not simply of Western artists, but of a range of alternative and radical social groupings.[26] It has also provided a role model for generations of students and dropouts. Over the same post-war period, the map of Europe has been re-drawn twice: at the post-war settlement of 1945 and after the collapse of the Warsaw Pact in 1989. At much the same time, migration of various kinds and from various sources has become a dynamic feature of the European scene. Have these new realities done anything to relieve the Roma from their historic burden of glorification and denigration? How much light is shed on Europe's oldest society of travelers by our postcolonial understanding of the world, our new emphasis on hybridity and the migrant nature of cultures?

One clue is provided by a key migrant novel: *Le thé au harem d'Archi Ahmed* (1983), Mehdi Charef's affectionate and humorous study of young North African migrants and their friends set on a high-rise housing estate near Paris. In one scene the gang saunters past an encampment of Spanish gypsies. Majid, a second-generation Algerian settler, stands entranced:

> Majid can't take his eyes off the gypsy women. He thinks they're amazing, the way they're always dressed in technicolour like an arrangement of Japanese flowers. They wear long-brightly coloured skirts—a blinding yellow with bright pink roses. . . . [H]e wonders how on earth such beautiful women can have ended up here in the middle of nowhere, surrounded by filthy pots and pans. If he had his way, he'd haul them off to a fancy patisserie, and he'd make them a bed among the coloured candies—the round white ones, the blue oval ones and the red flat ones that he remembers from when he was a kid with his mouth watering at the shop window.[27]

Charef's novel is an expression of the migrant gaze as it re-interprets the city, a perspective present here in Majid's memory of himself as a poor child staring wistfully at the delicacies inside a Paris cake shop. In this passage, however, we also encounter another, far more unsettling gaze: the migrant staring upon the vagrant. The resulting perception of Romany life—beauty amid filthy pans—is indistinguishable from the centuries-old desire and contempt we have been describing.

So much for the glorification. To observe the denigration, I enter my second railway carriage. This one is attached to a late evening shuttle from Victoria. I am on my way home after watching a revival of Jonathon Miller's production of *Carmen* at the English National Opera.[28] My neighbor, I gather from the program he is reading, has been enjoying *Notre Dame de Paris* at the Dominion Theatre, with Danii Minogue as a scantily-clad La Esmeralda. We are approaching Gipsy Hill, a suburban station named after a Roma encampment cleared in 1866 to make way for a church.[29] As we draw level with Romany Avenue, the door at the end of the carriage slides open. Down the aisle an East European Roma slowly advances with a baby on her shoulder. One hand holds a piece of cardboard with an appeal in blue Biro; the other is cupped and imploring. As this real-life Carmen reaches us, the courting couple opposite me stiffen. The boy's face has hardened: he is repeating in a manic undertone, "I hate them. I hate them. I hate them." A Lonely Londoner of the Windrush generation then rises to his feet. His trilby hat trembling with indignation, he harangues us. "It is," he enjoins, "important that we British do not give to these people."

He has, of course, spoken for most people in the carriage, and for many in the nation. The British social historian Raphael Samuel once called the Roma "those age-old pariahs of British society."[30] But, of course, the taboo was and is Europe-wide; indeed, after this last illustration of history or hysteria one is entitled to ask whether, hounded by skinheads in the Czech Republic and Tory politicians in London, these peripatetic folk are any better understood than they were in the sixteenth century. All the evidence suggests that they were more hospitably received in the fifteenth. There is, however, an important theoretical issue. Over recent years postcolonial theory has added a different kind of map to those found in the conventional cartographies, whether in Sebastian Münster's *Cosmographia* or the latest *Times Atlas*: a chart drawn by the memories of peoples as they criss-cross continents and oceans. Paul Gilroy's reading of the Atlantic as a kinetic cultural space has provided one such reshaping.[31] The challenge of Europe's ancient travelers to all of us is this: to re-draw our continental map in such a way as to reflect their point of view. It is the perspective of those who, questioned at border posts now as always, have for centuries interrogated those very divisions with their own *perpetuum mobile*. In 2004, as Heathcliff squats in a disused garage in Holloway, and as army barracks in Oxfordshire are converted to hold a new generation of Carmens, the time is surely ripe.

NOTES

1. Paul Gilroy, *Between Two Camps: Race, Identity and Nationalism at the End of the Colour Line* (London: Allen Lane, 2000).

2. "Lunatic Asylum," *The Sun*, 14 February 2001, i.

3. "Immigrants' 186mph ride under train," *The Daily Telegraph*, 3 March 2001, i.

4. "Queen Europa" is reproduced from the edition of 1588 (BL Maps 568.h.z.). From Sebastian Munster's Cosmographia, 1588. Reproduced by kind permission of the British Library. I am grateful to Professor Ken Parker for drawing my attention to this remarkable map.

5. Quoted in Shakespeare, *The Winter's Tale*, Variorum Edition, 139.

6. A fine account of gypsies in Elizabethan England is to be found in Gamini Salgado, *The Elizabethan Underworld* (London: Dent, 1977), especially his chapter 7: "Minions of the Moon," 151–62. The publication of Salgado's book—and his teaching— had a profound effect on scholars and writers of my generation.

7. Münster's experience is first recounted in the 1550 edition of *Cosmographia*. The Latin text is reproduced in D. M. M. Bartett, "Münster's *Cosmographia Universalis*," *Journal of the Gypsy Lore Society*, 3 (1952), 83–90. See also Angus Fraser, *The Gypsies* (Oxford: Blackwell, 1992), 64–65.

8. The full text is reproduced in "The History of the Roma Minority in the Czech Republic," http://www.romove.cz/history.html, 1. It seems, however, that there must have been several copies of the original document carried at various times and in varying versions by different groups of Roma.

9. Fraser, 187.

10. Martin Block, *Gypsies: Their Life and Customs* (London: Methuen, 1938), 39. Block, however, takes Váli's discovery very much at face value. A more critical account can be found in Fraser, 1992, 193.

11. Especially his *Masque of the Gypsies Metamorphosed*, presented before James I (James VI of Scotland) in London during August 1621.

12. In his *A History of the Gipsies* (London: 1865), Walter Simson makes out a strong case for Bunyan having been of gypsy stock. See pp. 206, 309, 402, 507–23, 530, 535–36. The case is based on Bunyan's father having been a Bedfordshire tinker. However, though many gypsies have been tinkers, not all tinkers have been gypsies.

13. Fraser, 1992, 157–59, 191, 196, 211, 262.

14. Jeremy Black, *Maps and Politics* (London: Reaktion Books, 1997). Quoted in Richard Horton, "The key to life—or a dead molecule: Unresolved questions about the practical value of the genome," *The Times Literary Supplement*, 9 March 2001, 13–15.

15. Victor Hugo, *Notre Dame de Paris* (Paris, 1831), Book 11, chapter 2, quoting Dante, *Purgatorio*, xii, 89–90, though, oddly from Hugo's point of view, Dante's angel is male.

16. An informative and incisive account of Virchow's career, and of his analogies between physiological and political structures, can be found in Laura Otis, *Membranes: Metaphors of Invasion in Nineteenth-Century Literature, Science, and Politics* (Baltimore and London: John Hopkins University Press, 1999), 8–25.

17. Rudolph Virchow, "Über die Reform der pathologischen und therapeutischen Anschauungen durch die mikroskopischen Untersuchungen." *Archiv für pathologische Anatomie und Physiologie und für klinische Medizin*, 1 (1847). Quoted and translated in Otis, 22.

18. The depth of the book's misogyny can be gauged from its punning Greek epigraph from the poet Palladas. It might be rendered "A woman has two decent positions: in bed and dead."

19. Another source of information and ideas was Pushkin's poem of 1824, *Tsygany* (*The Gypsies*). In 1852 Mérimée made a prose translation of Pushkin's work with a title seemingly influenced by Murger's *Scènes de la Bohème*.

20. Henry Murger, *Scènes de la Bohème* (Paris: Lévy Brothers, 1851), Préface, 1.

21. For a shrewd analysis of Koch's science in relation to his politics, see Otis, 31–36.

22. Quoted in anger by Virchow in "Der Kampf der Zellen und der Bakterien," *Archiv für pathologische Anatomie und Physiologie und für klinische Medizin*, 101 (1885), 1–13. Cited and translated by Otis (23), who, however, renders "chaqu'une d'une vie propre" as "each one (living) its own life."

23. Block (1938), 2.

24. Block (1938), 247.

25. Augustus John's *Woman Sitting* hangs in the portrait section of the newly reorganized Tate Modern in London.

26. For a comprehensive guide to the spread of the cult of bohemianism, see Elizabeth Wilson, *Bohemians: The Glamorous Outcasts* (London and New York: I. B. Tauris, 2000).

27. Mehdi Charef, *Le thé au harem d'Archi Ahmed* (Paris: Mercure de France, 1983). English translation *Tea in the Harem*, trans. Ed Emory (London: Serpent's Tale, 1989), 59.

28. The Coliseum, 15 March 2001.

29. Alan R. Warwick, *The Phoenix Suburb: A South London Social History* (London: The Blue Boar Press in association with the Beulah Group, 1982), 25–32.

30. *Patriotism: The Making and Unmaking of British National Identity*, ed. Raphael Samuel (London: Routledge, 1989). Vol. II (Minorities and Outsiders), xiv.

31. For which see Paul Gilroy, *The Black Atlantic: Modernity and Double Consciousness* (London: Verso, 1993).

2

The Politics of the Perception of Human Movement

Tabish Khair

> Any human movement, whether it springs from an intellectual or even a natural impulse, is impeded in its unfolding by the boundless resistance of the outside world. (Walter Benjamin, *One-Way Street*)

This paper sets out to trace not the trajectories of human movement, but rather the politics of the perception of this movement. In order to do so, one needs to play down the distinction between migration and travel. The concern of this paper is not with the terms themselves, but how their visibility brings to light some of the structures (and strictures) of the world we live in: the world of Capitalism, casting its faint shadow in the fifteenth and sixteenth centuries and with its material body arising from the fetid and fecund bog of colonization in the eighteenth and nineteenth centuries. Of course, travel is not the same as migrancy and, in some contexts, the two ought to be distinguished; one also needs to accommodate the realization that the two are not mutually sealed categories (see Grewal [1996] and Clifford [1997]). I focus below on the politics of the perception of human *movement*, and hence I will use "travel" in a broad sense to incorporate various kinds of spatial movement, ranging from travel (as in the genre of "travel writing" in European literature) to immigration.

When an academic and writer based in a European university looks at the visibility of the narration of human mobility from, say, the fourteenth century to the end of the twentieth century, three different phases are evident: I am talking about the *visibility* of the narration, and neither the narratives themselves nor the actual trajectories of human movement. Perception of human movement prior to the fifteenth century is not too heavily biased in favor of Europe, perhaps because fourth century Chinese pilgrimage accounts, nineth century Arab merchant accounts and fourteenth century Korean or Russian travel texts are all largely the confine of specialist scholars. With the partial exception of Marco Polo (and, to some extent, ibn Battutah, who traveled and wrote more than Marco Polo but is significantly less visible), they do not inform discourses of European centrality as much as accounts by Columbus, Captain Cook, and so forth—all the way down to Richard Burton and Robert Byron—do. As such, this phase—our first phase—will not be discussed in detail in this paper.

RENAISSANCE AND THE COLONIAL PERIODS

The second phase can be seen as beginning sometime in the Renaissance. While early Renaissance accounts indicate both awareness of and blindness to the movements of non-European/semi-European peoples (particularly the "Moors"—a description whose European usage could include Muslims in general—and the "Marranos"), a growing monopoly on accounts of travel, mapping, and discovery is clearly generated by Europeans from the fifteenth–sixteenth centuries to the middle of the twentieth century. From the sixteenth century onward the visibility of travel writing (not defined as a genre) and related texts from outside Europe—and, later, European settlements—suffers particularly in comparison to the burgeoning discourses of European discoveries. One should stress the word *visibility*, as it cannot be safely argued that non-Europeans did not travel enough or even that they did not leave behind travel accounts in various shapes, ranging from prose and poetry[1] to paintings (Liscomb). Extensive areas in Asia and Africa formed complex networks of trade, pilgrimage, and career "routes" after the sixteenth century as well, and such routes were used by Africans and Asians.

However, even astute and important scholars have described the early conquest-colonial centuries along lines that often take for granted a lack of "travel" or "curiosity" on the part of the non-European. As Nabil Matar puts it in the introduction to his brilliant translation of some seventeenth century Arabic travel accounts of the "West,"

> [The opinion that Arabs and Muslims did not travel] has persisted into modern scholarship. In Anthony Pagden's two-volume collection of articles, *Facing Each Other: The World's Perception of Europe and Europe's Perception of the World*, there was not a single entry about the 'perception' *of* or *by* any of the civilisations of Islam. ... Earlier, Bernard Lewis had claimed in his *Islam and the West* (1993) that the Arabs 'showed the same lack of interest [about Europe] as in medieval times'; and in his *The Muslim Discovery of Europe*, he accused Muslims of a total lack of 'curiosity' toward Europeans. (Matar, xiii–xiv)

Matar goes on to document precisely how Lewis's observations are severely faulted.

Europe-related movement—I do not mean the movement of non-Europeans to Europe but the movement of non-Europeans and Europeans along lines and structures of European hegemony—is somewhat more visible in modern scholarship than the movement of Arab and other travelers outside the fold of European colonization. But even when it comes to Europe-related movement, there are large areas of blindness in the hegemonic perception of human mobility during these centuries. The transportation of slaves from Africa to the Americas is one example of human movement that has been largely obscured in favor of the corresponding movement of European settlers to America. Indentured laborers formed another later group, as did sailors: Paul Gilroy notes that "at the end of the eighteenth century a quarter of the British navy was composed of Africans" (Gilroy, 13). The etymology of the word *lascar* reveals the presence of Indian and Asian sailors in the ships of colonization and early capitalism. Robert Fraser has focused on the Gypsies, those "non-European travelers" in Europe whose presence continues to be largely obscured even today. This nexus of occlusion has been continued into the twentieth century and sometimes across "post/colonial" lines: for example, the visibility of Australian soldiers in accounts (fictional or otherwise) of World Wars I and II is far greater than the visibility of Indian soldiers.

Such examples can be multiplied, though even these instances largely leave out the connections that existed outside Europe (or its "bridging" presence). Even much of postcolonial literature, with the exception of work by exceptional writers like Amitav Ghosh, avoids tracing these connections.

In short, even though Asians and Africans continued to "travel" during and after the sixteenth century, their movement appears to grow progressively less visible until, in the nineteenth and early twentieth centuries, all connections come to appear to have been made across the bridge of Europe. It seemed in the 1930s, for example,[2] that the modern world had been made possible solely or largely due to the criss-crossing trajectories of European or European-settler adventurers, sailors, migrants, discoverers, and travelers. Not only did other travelers disappear, even the complexity of other cultures was seriously reduced in these hegemonic accounts.

To avoid stating the obvious, one need offer only a single example: The authors of *The Story of English* (a history that is very open to "new Englishes") write that "[t]he Raj *created* an essentially bilingual society [in India]" (McCrum, MacNeil, and Cran, 360, my emphasis). Against this prevalent ahistorical perception, one is forced to point out that the educated classes of India were bilingual even before the Raj, and the illiterate classes are (mostly) not bilingual even today. There exist in India not only vast regions of monolingualism but also many kinds of bilingualism other than the "Indian"-English bilingualism being touted in Europe and, often, by members of the Indian/cosmopolitan bourgeoisie.[3]

It should be noted in this context that the colonial myth of India's "lack of real history" isolates India from the cluster of relations that have constituted it (both in its parts and as more-than-its-parts) before European colonization—turning India's history with various other peoples and kingdom-states to an emptiness before the "arrival" of the colonial presence as the great connecting link (Khair, 310–14). This erasure of pre- and para-colonial connections is not merely a consequence of the writing of "colonial" histories; it also played a significant part in making colonization possible. It appears today that British dominance in the early years of colonization (1780–1820) was not just a consequence of military, informational, or even economic advantages. The dominance itself grew, to a large extent, from the ability of the British to cut the "practical and honorific"—and, I would add, symbolic—"lines of communication" (Bayly, 58) between the Delhi court and other Indian powers and between Indian powers in general. This was a *conscious* policy—encouraged by Lord Cornwallis and his successors—that broke down the multilateral channels of information between local Indian powers. While this policy "worked" in the political sphere, the colonial myth of India's "lack of history" sought (and seeks) to extend its effects—and that too retrospectively—into the much more complex and resistant fields of culture.

What happened in India can be traced, with regional variations, in other colonized spaces of non-European societies: in all these cases the colonial myth of the "bridge of Europe" became and, in some ways, continues to be central. We have seen that this myth was largely made possible because of the growing invisibility of other lines of connection in hegemonic discourses of the nineteenth and twentieth centuries. It is not overstatement to say that it makes English far more central to Indian transculturality[4] than it actually has been. Similar trajectories can be traced in other colonial histories and discourses as well. The invisibility of non-European movement (migrancy or travel) in the colonial period is part of this general problem.

It is true that the "discovery" of the Americas and Australia added to the self-perception of Europeans as great sailors and discoverers, thus obscuring the achievements of, say, the Arabs and the Chinese. Moreover, by the nineteenth century, in Albert Hourani's words, "the growth of large-scale factory production and changes in methods of communication—the coming of steamships, railways and telegraphs—led to an expansion of European trade" (263)—and hence, probably, documented travel. Though even here the word "probably" should be kept in mind: recent research (Markovits) indicates that Indian merchants continued to operate in a "global world" in the eighteenth and nineteenth centuries as well.

It is also true that various factors, as noted by Giovanni Arrighi among others, ensured that (to quote just one example) Cheng Ho's navy *chose* not to sail around Africa and "discover" Europe a few decades before the Portuguese rounded the Cape (Arrighi, 33–36). There can, again, be a difference between the *survival* of travel accounts in societies with a high use of printing and those in which printing is new, underdeveloped, or unknown. However, even with these qualifications, one is faced with the fact that human mobility came to be seen as a thoroughly European prerogative in the nieteenth and early twentieth centuries in spite of the fact that Asians and Africans did leave behind travel accounts in and after the sixteenth century as well.

One can list quite a few such Asian and African travel accounts. Gul-Badan Begum's (1523–1603) autobiographical account of her brother Humayun's life contains numerous travel narratives. The Bhakti saint and poetess Bahinabai (1628–1700) has given us an interesting account of her journey along River Godavari. Basho's *The Narrow Road to the Deep North* (1689) is undoubtedly one of the masterpieces of world travel writing, where what is often perceived as a "minor genre" merges with both the most concentrated poetry in the Japanese *hoku* tradition and the Zen quest for spiritual enlightenment. Dean Mahomed's account of his days and enterprises in Britain (1759–1851) remains not only the first important text in English by an Indian but also a fascinating travel account (Fisher). On the other hand, Abu Taleb's *Travels in Europe* (1797–1803) proves that English was not necessary even for writing about *Europe*: Abu Taleb wrote his account in (Indo-)Persian and learned English only during his stay in Ireland and England. Then we have later accounts like the Shah of Iran Nasir ad-Din's *Diary of a Journey to Europe* (1873), Emily Said-Ruete's *Memoirs of an Arabian Princess* (1881), and Melek-Hanum's *Six Years in Europe* (1873). There are also somewhat more visible accounts, such as *The Interesting Narrative of Olaudah Equiano*, the most well-known account by a "slave" on the way *out* of Africa.

It should be put on record here that there exist many comparable texts from the earliest periods to the most recent. These include many Chinese, Korean, and Japanese pilgrim accounts and Arab merchant reports in the early centuries (fourth to twelfth centuries), Muslim *hajjnamahs* from all over Asia and Africa (and Spain), travel-based histories and autobiographies in the medieval and early modern periods, and around fourteen extant English-language travel books by Indians in the nineteenth century. There are books like the *World History* of Rashid Al-Din (b. 1247); Hsu Chi-yü's global geography of 1848; and long travel accounts, like 'Abdu'r-Razzâq's *Matla'-I Sa'dain* (1444) or the better-known one by the seventeenth century Ottoman travel writer Evliya Chelebi, whose book was translated into English in the nineteenth century. There are also travel accounts of an anecdotal character, such as the samurai Katsu Kokichi's early nineteenth century autobiography describing his adventures as a youth wandering over much of Japan. There is a largely forgotten treasure trove of shorter travel accounts in prose or poetry—short reports by merchants, diplomats, slaves, and bureaucrats, sometimes running to pamphlet size and sometimes restricted to a couple of pages. There are also Chinese accounts of travel in or visits to the United States in the nineteenth century. Finally, there are letters sent back by embassies as well as personal letters—even more visible ones like those of the major Indian thinker and reformer Raja Rammohan Roy or the famous Urdu poet Asadullah Khan Ghalib—that also need to be collected and (often) translated.

These accounts—and there are hundreds of them, translated and untranslated—range widely in size and literary quality. Texts like Basho's and ibn Battutah's are undoubtedly in different ways literary classics; texts like Dean Mahomed's *Travels* are interesting literary essays (Mahomed's being the first book by an Indian in English and also significant as a sample of cross-generic and cross-cultural influences). Texts like those by Abu Taleb or Said-Reute have some literary merit and more socio-historical value, while other texts, like the shorter slave narratives, are more remarkable as historical accounts than as "literature." Obviously, there is a need to comment on this wealth of texts along "literary" and perhaps even "generic" lines and a need (which I have tried to meet in the introduction to an anthology of Asian and African travel texts under preparation) to provide typologies of travel writing.

While the number of "travel accounts" by Asians and Africans can be multiplied (at least in retrospect), it does not change the fact that by and until the middle of the twentieth century agential human movement came to be seen as a predominantly European characteristic. This was probably connected to the fact that many colonialist discourses tended to deny rational agency to colonized people. In other words, Europeans and their descendants had a monopoly on both history and agency in most accounts of recent centuries. No wonder Europeans and their descendants appeared to have "traveled," "discovered," and "settled"—and, thus, made possible the modern world.

THE POSTCOLONIAL PERIOD

After World War II this story moves us on to the third phase mentioned above. Even as countries became independent, the myth of the centrality of European agency came to be questioned—not only in the colonies (where some natives had always had doubts about it) or by certain European intellectuals, but by many ordinary thinking Europeans. It came to be perceived that non-Europeans had also moved, though the extent of their visibility remains restricted and sometimes even entirely obscured in countries like Denmark. But this was a minor aspect of a greater change. What changed was the character of capitalism, which came to depend less on, in Arrighi's words, the space-of-places and more on the space-of-flows. In simpler words, it became far more profitable to use "free" capital to exploit national markets than to actually colonize and administer regions, a shift also acknowledged by non- and anti-Marxists when they talk of the movement from "industrial society" to "post-industrial (or information) society", or construct similar schemas.

Within the scope of this paper—the exploration of the visibility of different kinds of human mobility—the period from 1945 to the 1970s not only saw the decolonization of most parts of Asia and Africa, but also marked a gradual change in the perception of the directions in which human beings were seen as moving. Suddenly, the travel, settlement, or exploration of Europeans was replaced by the migration of Asians and Africans. The latter perception had a clearly racial logic: white Australians or white Americans, for example, are still seen as posing less of an "immigration problem" in, say, Denmark than colored Pakistanis or Algerians or Australian aborigines (if they had a substantial presence). Today, a single glance at the papers read at conferences on contemporary migrancy reveals that non-Europe has suddenly been made visible as moving into the First World nations of Europe or Europeanized, First World spaces (like the United States, Canada, and Australia).

This academic visibility echoes a greater public rhetoric, even when it sets out to criticize it. Recent instances of this rhetoric in Europe have included the high media visibility of refugee movements from, say, Somalia, as well as incidents like the shipload of immigrants (economic refugees) abandoned off the French coast, the over-publicized "organized smuggling of illegal immigrants" from Africa into Spain, and so forth. In themselves, these mark an imperceptible flow into Europe—for example, by far the greatest burden of Somalian refugees has been borne by neighboring African states—but the Western media paints such incidents as a tidal wave set to swamp Europe.

Similar tendencies can be noticed in the United States, though with a *positive* difference:

> [S]tatistics show that the wealthy countries which build the biggest fortresses around themselves, are far from bearing their share of the [refugee] burden. Asylum-seekers and refugees trying to make their home in Europe and North America account for barely 5 per cent of the total number of the world's refugees and displaced persons. And only 0.2 per cent of that total actually ends up living in the wealthy countries, with more than 95 per cent of them going to North America, which, unlike Europe, has not forgotten how much it owes to immigrants. (Rekacewicz, 8)

Once again, the question is not that of scale. It may be true that more Asians and Africans are moving to Europeanized, First World spaces today, though even this can be questioned from a relational historical perspective.[5] What concerns me here is the fact that the colonial centuries (to use a convenient emblem) involved a near-complete erasure of Asian and African movements globally, while the postcolonial decades have started to focus inordinately on such movement. It can well be argued that just as the first erasure was ideologically significant, the second visibility can be ideologically complicit.

It is also significant that the first perception (involving the erasure of non-European movement) coincided with capitalist exploitation based largely on the control of space-of-places.[6] This not only induced the movement of Europeans but, what is more important in our present context, compelled the self-perception of Europeans as moving almost solely into other spaces (thus providing a justification for the "profits" accruing to their "entrepreneurship"). The second perception (of non-European migrancy in recent decades) has coincided with capitalist exploitation that is increasingly based on the control of space-of-flows, and, as we will see, it provides a similar salve for the capitalist conscience of Euro-Americans.

In some ways, people have never been so tightly penned in by national borders as they are today. Walter Benjamin's keen observation that "never has freedom of movement stood in greater disproportion to the abundance of means of travel" (Benjamin, 59) has been given a new twist in the postwar and postcolonial decades. What is actually very mobile in our world today is capital, and those who own capital or the citizens of countries that "share" most of the international flow of capital. The actual body of the African or Asian "worker" is tightly controlled and seldom allowed to cross national borders, as highlighted by (among others) Amitava Kumar. When this body crosses a national border into the First World, it does so under heightened conditions of the capitalist exploitation of labor: not only are Asian workers underpaid[7] by multinationals in Asia, but Asian and African immigrants are more likely to be underpaid (and have a precarious hold on jobs) in First World countries as well.

On the other hand, Europeans, North Americans, and Australians enjoy much more mobility not only in the First World but also in Asia, Africa, and South America. It is entirely reasonable to speculate that the (exaggerated) threat that "global" terrorism is supposed to pose to "global tourism" is *not* an indication of the curtailment of this freedom to be mobile but an index of this obscenely one-sided freedom of mobility. If this is true, it might well be the case that the criminal and shortsighted targeting of Euro-Americans by some terrorist groups in Asia and Africa is a reaction, among other things, to the greater freedom of movement (and choice of movement) that ordinary Americans and Europeans (and, for that matter, Australians and Japanese) have in comparison to ordinary Asians and Africans.

In short, just as the obscuring of Asian and African accounts of "travel" served the purpose of hiding the actual realities of colonial empire- and society-building—and hence the capital extracted from the exploitation of Afro-Asian space, agency, and labor—the current privileging of Asian/African migrancy often hides the structures of postcolonial high capitalism, as sketched above.

CONCLUDING REMARKS

I have traced and illustrated how Asian and African travel accounts until the mid-twentieth century have been largely obscured,[8] thus leading to a general perception that the contemporary world was made possible largely by the movement of Europeans and their descendants. This elision served the purpose of justifying colonial capitalism, which was based largely on the control of space-of-places. A second point has been the more obvious observation that the neo-colonial (postcolonial, by some accounts) decades have witnessed a heavy rhetoric of immigration (also as "cultural clash," the "refugee problem," multiculturalism, hybridity, etc.) that consciously or unconsciously promotes the perception—often heightened to a feeling of siege by the political right—that Europe and European settler spaces are being (suddenly) inundated with non-Europeans. This perception is erroneous, and should be understood in the context of neo-colonial capitalism, which is based on the control of space-of-flows.

Bringing together these two observations, the paper has suggested that, contrary to the prevalent opinion in certain postcolonialist and radical circles, the present boom in the visibility of the movement of non-Europeans is just as complicit in structures of capitalist exploitation as the preceding invisibility and serves, at least part of the time, a similar purpose of justification and selective vision. If the previous invisibility of non-European movements tended to justify European control of spaces in the name of greater "knowledge" or "entrepreneurship," the current visibility of non-European movements serves to hide the fact that human beings are far less mobile than capital today—perhaps more so, keeping in mind the growing ease and reduced costs of travel, than in the nineteenth century—and that human movements today are both permitted and controlled by capital. Once again, the actual structures and strictures of capitalism that impact on non-European bodies (women, men, and children) are obscured or even made to disappear in the verbiage of words thrown up by the current rhetoric of non-European "diaspora" and "immigration."

NOTES

1. The journey can be almost considered a sub-genre in Chinese Tang Poetry from the seventh and eighth centuries. In India, Kalidasa's nineth century *Meghdootam* (Kalidasa 1989, 135–64) is not only a poem but also the description of a journey. Such examples can be multiplied.

2. Actually, many Europeans and Americans still seem to share aspects of this view.

3. A recent example of this is Rushdie's *The Moor's Last Sigh*.

4. To employ Rustom Bharucha's term.

5. A relational historical perspective would take into account at least (1) the ratio of the individuals moving out to those staying home and (2) the ratio of the distance traveled to the means and ease of transport—in both of the periods under comparison.

6. The difference, of course, is that of degree, for capitalism utilizes both spaces by definition.

7. Underpaid in comparison to their European, Australian, and American counterparts.

8. There are, no doubt, differences between Africa and Asia, and also within them (including differences of gender). However, this paper is concerned with a dominant (but by no means single) global narrative of human movement as ordered and re-ordered across centuries of colonization and neo-colonialism that, in their economic and culturally hegemonic operations, force us to address Asia and Africa together at least in this context. This paper does not claim to be able to step outside the purview of European(ized) discourses altogether, as is reflected in, among other things, its forced but necessary bonding of Asia and Africa.

WORKS CITED

Arrighi, Giovanni. *The Long Twentieth Century: Money, Power and the Origins of Our Times* (1994). London and New York: Verso, 2000.

Bayly, C. A. *Empire and Information: Intelligence Gathering and Social Communication in India 1780–1870*. Cambridge: Cambridge University Press, 1996.

Benjamin, Walter. *One-Way Street*. Trans. Edmund Jephcott and Kingsley Shorter (1979). London: Verso, 2000.

Bharucha, Rustam. *The Politics of Cultural Practice: Thinking through Theatre in an Age of Globalisation*. Delhi: Oxford University Press, 2001.

Clifford, James. *Routes: Travel and Translation in the Late Twentieth Century*. Cambridge, Mass., and London: Harvard University Press, 1997.

Fisher, Michael H. *The First Indian Author in English* (1996). Delhi: Oxford University Press, 2000.

Fraser, Robert. "Mapping the Mind: Borders, Interrogation and Myth." Keynote Address. Writing Europe 2001: Migrant Cartographies Conference. University of Leiden/ University of Amsterdam. March 2001.

Gilroy, Paul. *The Black Atlantic: Modernity and Double Consciousness* (1993). London and New York: Verso, 1999.

Ghosh, Amitav. *In an Antique Land* (1992). London: Granta Books, 1994.

Grewal, Inderpal. *Home and Harem: Nation, Gender, Empire, and the Cultures of Travel*. Durham and London: Duke University Press, 1996.

Grosrichard, Alain. *The Sultan's Court: European Fantasies of the East*. Trans. Liz Heron. London and New York: Verso, 1998.

Hourani, Albert. *A History of the Arab Peoples* (1991). London: Faber and Faber, 1992.

Kalidasa. *The Loom of Time: A Selection of His Plays and Poems*. Ed. and trans. Chandra Rajan. Delhi: Penguin Books, 1989.

Khair, Tabish. *Babu Fictions: Alienation in Contemporary Indian English Novels*. Delhi: Oxford University Press, 2001.

Kumar, Amitava. *Passport Photos.* Berkeley and London: University of California Press, 2000.

Liscomb, Kathlyn Maureen. *Learning from Mount Hua: A Chinese Physician's Illustrated Travel Record and Painting Theory.* Cambridge: Cambridge University Press, 1993.

Markovits, Claude. *The Global World of Indian Merchants 1750–1947: Traders of Sind from Bukhara to Panama.* Cambridge: Cambridge University Press, 2000.

Matar, Nabil. *In the Lands of the Christians.* New York and London: Routledge, 2003.

McCrum, Robert, Robert MacNeil, and William Cran. *The Story of English.* London and Boston: Faber and Faber / BBC Books, 1992.

Rekacewicz, Philippe. "How the Burden of the World's Refugees Falls on the South." *Le Monde Diplomatique (The Guardian Weekly),* London, April 2001.

Rushdie, Salman. *The Moor's Last Sigh.* London: Jonathan Cape, 1995.

Taleb, Abu. *The Travels of Mirza Abu Taleb in Asia, Africa and Europe* (1803). Trans. Charles Stewart. New Delhi: Sona Publications, 1972.

Visram, Rozina. *Indians in Britain.* London: B. T. Batsford, 1987.

3

A Cat in a Kipper Box, or The Confessions of a "Second Generation Immigrant"

Paul Gilroy

The synonymity of European and white troubles me. All across Europe, national identity, belonging, and the imperiled integrity of national states are being articulated with the language and symbols of absolute ethnicity and *racialized* difference. This ought to be the stalest of old news because that combination had been identified long, long ago as an essential element in the workings of a novel, culturalist racism. But once again, the moment of optimum theoretical argument has not coincided with the moment of maximum political salience. We must therefore be prepared to step back twenty years or so in order to establish where the boundaries of our present fall, even if this sort of archaeology risks boring anyone who's been over the same unholy ground a million times before. We owe the dead our patience at the very least.

The old "new racism" remains influential even as it yields to today's emergent genomic and bio-social explanations. It was the characteristic product of a phase of mass migration, and the resulting culturalist tones are still audible in the anthropological subtleties, disavowals, and evasions of the raciological discourse to which it gives voice. This genteel, common sense racism finds it difficult to be overt. The cruder and more belligerent expressions of racial antipathy associated with imperial and colonial domination are still often regarded as unsavory, disreputable, and offensive. Nationalism and patriotism, on the other hand, are seldom judged so harshly. At least when viewed from above, those forms of solidarity are welcomed as desirable features of social and political life. They endow national communities with a necessary strength and confidence. Under their respectable banners, the standard of what counts as acceptable political commentary can become quite different. Arranged reverently around a national flagpole, the mean-spirited people who sounded like nativists, racists, ultra-nationalists, and neo-fascists turn out instead to be plain old patriots.

Defending the simple racial hierarchies invented during the nineteenth century is no longer their principal concern. Instead, a more timely emphasis falls on wider dimensions of cultural difference. These divisions are just as intractable and fundamental as the natural hierarchies they partly replace, but acquire extra moral credibility and additional political authority by being closer to nationalism and more remote from bio-logic of any kind. We're informed not only that divergent cultures can be chronically and permanently incompatible, but also that mistaken attempts to mix or even dwell peaceably together can bring only destruction. From this familiar angle, exposure to otherness always promotes ontological jeopardy. Predictably, these dangers are most acute for those with the most to lose in their tumble off the giddy heights of natural and cultural superiority. I'm sure you all recognize these themes, which have become the staple of European racial nationalisms all the way from Arklöv's Sweden to Jordi Pujol's Catalonia and Alessandra Mussolini's Rome.[1] Post-colonial culture, literature, and art of all kinds can be used to complicate this picture but they cannot provide an antidote to the problems that make it so widely resonant.

The uniformity and ubiquity of these arguments can be explained by the way that nationality gets blurred once "race" becomes a matter of culture. That absence of clarity is strategic. It serves also to suggest that anyone who makes a fuss about racism is getting things out of proportion, engaging in witch hunts, practicing empty moralism, and nurturing the unhelpful fantasies of social purity associated with immature outlooks, loony leftism and, above all, "political correctness." The conceptual and semantic interconnections that have been established between the forms of language that produce race, nation, and culture as interchangeable terms are, in this scheme, irrelevant. Because "race" *ought* to be nothing, it *is* of no consequence whatsoever. Racism either disappears or lingers on as a marginal issue, an essentially pre-political process that should not be addressed by government worthy of the name. To even suggest that it could be productive to approach racism politically threatens a debasement of government and a travesty of justice. There is no problem because racism requires no specific intervention beyond the worn-out rubrics of generic liberalism. Any fool knows that real, grown-up governments cannot legislate the emotions of their populations. Any attempt to do so points them toward totalitarianism.

Tony Blair's Britain has become a very strange place. A government that has consolidated the emotionalization of politics by introducing "Holocaust Day" is the same one that persecutes asylum seekers and lends its dubious prestige to the author of *The Bell Curve* while priding itself on winning back the themes of patriotism and nationalism for the left![2] In that climate it's not surprising that the political morality of "race" confuses almost everybody. However, pragmatics cuts through bewilderment. Being tough on immigrants and refugees pays a double political dividend. It confirms the administration's patriotic credentials and puts high-octane populist fuel in the swollen tank of their corporate managerialism. Those bizarre circumstances are also distinguished by high levels of racially motivated inter-personal violence. One eloquent immigrant voice has made an especially vulgar form of the argument against political anti-racism. Speaking through the corpse of Sir Isaiah Berlin, which functions these days as his ventriloquist's dummy, Michael Ignatieff pronounced upon the issues that were manifested in Britain following the murder of Stephen Lawrence by free-lance racists and his parents' eight-year campaign for basic legal redress. "I see no useful purpose in trying to change the class or racial attitudes of ordinary policemen," he opined in an impatient response to the idiotic souls who sought to bring the issue—not of race but of racism—inside the sphere of social policy. "If racism is in the eye of the beholder," he continued, "we will never be done with it."[3] Ignatieff deploys the disinclination to accord racism the status of a real political problem as a means to communicate the profundity of his increasingly brittle and conservative-sounding opinions. There are no doubt good intentions behind his proclaiming the indivisibility of justice. However, it is obvious that he would never have felt it legitimate to utter these callous criticisms of collectivities based on suffering at the gates of Yad Vashem or Auschwitz. In those places of memory, waving the magic wand of liberal enlightenment at a history of racism that just refuses to obey it would straightaway be seen as a hollow gesture. The very freedom to work out these provocations in the face of the tragedies presented by Britain's recent history of racist murder encapsulates larger flaws in the liberal cause Ignatieff advocates. His intervention was useful precisely because it made clear that, so far as understanding racism is concerned, that lofty liberal project loses all of its buoyancy—exactly as its antecedents did in the era of colonial empires.[4]

The negative reception of Bhiku Parekh's report to the government on the future of multi-ethnic Britain[5] provided a cue for other less-sophisticated voices to pick up these misguided lines of argument. In response, Alan Wolfe and Jytte Klausen scrutinized Europe's problems with ethnic and national identity through the wrong end of their North American telescope. Like Ignatieff they proved incapable of addressing the colonial and imperial histories that had contributed to this confrontation. Like him again, these authors were also reluctant to concede that the history of white supremacist reasoning in law, government, economics, and morality (quite apart from its accumulated force in everyday life) could be factors in the alarming demise of solidarity that they identified in the changing character of Europe's welfare states.

By invoking the story of Alva Myrdal's "patriotic pride" in the establishment of the Swedish welfare state without even mentioning its eugenic fantasies and associated interests in social hygiene, these writers made it obvious that they had even bigger problems than Ignatieff in recognizing the constitutive potency of racism. For them, the precious nationalist solidarity that made welfare states possible and popular could only be menaced and undone by the disruptive "diversity" that immigrants import and enact. Their mission is to steer the left away from its misplaced enthusiasms for diversity and help it find the more controversial will to moralize solidarity proudly once again in terms of national culture. Quite how the left is to remain on the left during and after this re-positioning operation is not at all clear, but that does not matter. Of course, Jörg Haider's calculated protestation that he was only proposing the very same things as Blair's New Labor springs to mind as cautionary evidence against this sort of willful naiveté.

The kindest response to this position is to say that its attempt to locate discussion between the antagonistic poles represented by the options of "solidarity" and "diversity" excludes the distinctive historical processes involved in Europe's post-colonial transition. This facile orientation misses the target when it tacitly assumes a complete lack of cultural, religious, and linguistic continuities as well as an absence of all familiarity between diverse immigrants and their solid hosts. The immigrants appear in this problematic only as the undifferentiated blob of otherness that race-thinking makes them. None of them could be multi-lingual, cosmopolitan, modern, or worldly. They are not civilized. Where this Manichaean delirium holds sway, the postcolonials were not trained in Shakespeare and the classics; steeped in Catholicism, Lutheranism and the Church of England; or educated to recognize the fragile flora of the temperate zone long before they actually reached it. The pre-modern lives they stubbornly refuse to renounce when confronted by the bountiful opportunities of unchecked consumer capitalism are apparently composed entirely—rather like the flesh-only diet of those cannibals in Robinson Crusoe's island kingdom—of religious bigotry, homophobia, polygamy, genital mutilation, and other menacing fundamentalist traits usually figured on and through the bodies of women. The problematic diversity these unwanted guests insert into Europe's political bodies is an effect of their simple, unchanging ways. Complexity, on the other hand, like history and indeed development itself, is the monopoly of those who are in possession of that precious solidarity.

Wolfe and Klausen's grim portrait of multi-cultural Europe is not an accurate assessment of post-war migration. Whether it might illuminate the experience of smaller and more recent groups of refugees and asylum seekers will have to be debated. But they do not leave any space for discussion. Once the idea of immigration has been constructed as a problem with national dimensions, history goes out of the window and we get transported into the frozen realm of mythic time. That domain is ruled by the timeless, iconic constructions of Europe's post-colonial melancholia: criminals, spongers, and their numberless alien offspring. One virtue of Zadie Smith's *White Teeth* (2000) is that it delivers a reminder that we are already three generations or more from the anthropological enigmas of post-colonial arrival.

The would-be policy-makers' memories are faulty in other ways too. They write portentously that it is "easier to feel solidarity with those who broadly share your values and way of life" as if the assimilation of Germany's Jews had been an obstacle rather than an incentive to their murder. If that history offers insights into this moment, it might suggest that much of the time, the anger and hatred that racisms promote are triggered even by the most modest success in those attempts at sharing "values and ways of life" across the leaky barriers of "race." As far as England are concerned, many of its immigrants worshiped the same god even if racism dictated that they were not welcomed in the churches where their hosts knelt to pray and ask forgiveness. This cultural pattern was not just a one-way affair. Many of the anxious En-glish folk who chose to terrorize and intimidate their new neighbors were equally busy indulging themselves with all the pleasures of transgressive intimacy refined during several centuries of global dominance. Sugary tea, after all, was their national drink.

Because Wolfe and Klausen's analysis has been deduced from the abstract, myopically U.S.-centered operation of pitting solidarity against diversity, they cannot explain why the pathological nationalism and xenophobia articulated by so many of Europe's post-modern nationalists and aspirant ethnic cleansers get pronounced with the same hostility along nationalist and racialist lines. This too has been evident in England, where the Germans, Italians, French, and many other European others make their inevitable entrance only through persistent, distorted citations of the 1939–1945 war. Traditionally of course, Britain's wogs begin at Calais. With that racialized cartography in mind, it seems appropriate to ask whether these latest mythic "immigrants" might provide only the most accessible specimens of a non-specific otherness on which more general hatred of difference can be safely discharged.

These are the conditions in which anti-racists are now obliged to judge where acceptable national feeling ends and xenophobic racism commences. This is the moral and political climate in which we need courage to reflect on the history of political nationalism that has been entangled with the idea of race, and to comprehend how Europe's imperial and colonial dominance brought its racisms and nationalisms together in ways that still impact upon present conditions. The hybrid, syncretic cultures prompted by, but not regulated by, post-colonial settlement afford many invitations to join this enterprise in critical history. It encompasses several additional confrontations that remain undetected by the overly innocent liberalism of the writers I have criticized. A more worthwhile liberalism, one prepared to be profaned by its systematic reflections upon its own colonial habits and implications,[6] would be able to confront, first, the distinctive idioms that specify racial, ethnic, and national divisions in subtle patterns as potent as they are inferential; and, secondly, the pragmatic formula that places both racism and anti-racism outside of the political field, leaving them as essentially residual private issues, matters of taste, of preference, and, ultimately, of consumer or lifestyle choice.

Perhaps I can make some aspects of this abstract argument clearer by introducing one more British example that might resonate in other circumstances. For the last three decades or so, the brash motto of true Brit nationalism has been supplied by a curious boast: "two world wars and one world cup, doo dah, doo dah." For the most part, the full, historic force of this fraternalistic and class-bound braggadocio has not been registered in the places where academic analysis of race and its connections with nationalist mentalities is still being invented. Complacent scholarship is culpable here for its failures of imagination and principle and also for the persistent refusal to address the interconnections of nationalism and racism in popular culture. The intellectual commitment to taking these structures of feeling seriously, making them worth understanding and unpacking, involves recognizing the value and dignity of the lives that phrase has helped to lead astray or divert into the arid, empty lands of nationalist fantasy. The words "two world wars and one world cup" can supply a wealth of valuable insights into the morbid culture of a once-imperial nation that has not been able to accept its inevitable loss of prestige in a determinedly post-colonial world. Those words become a means through which to consider the bewildering effects of England's post-colonial melancholia even when they have been intermittently offset by the compensations of the country's rare but nonetheless significant sporting successes. The same phrase can furnish the truly committed investigator with a compressed but priceless history of post-war class relations in what is harder these days to call the United Kingdom. All the latent violence, all the embittered machismo, all the introjected class warfare articulated by defeated victors (mostly men and boys who were baffled and bewildered by a new post-war world that refused to recognize their historic manly qualities) are coded there in an explosive form that defies separation into neatly distinguished elements of racism and nationalism.

Similarly strange raciological poetics have erupted elsewhere on the football terraces.[7] Many of the same assumptions and tropes have also appeared in more respectable locations. They have shaped a special code that applies in circumstances where unmasked expressions of xenophobic hostility would be considered inappropriate, embarrassing, or discordant, precisely because of their stadium provenance. These polite voices start by speaking a fluent anthropological tongue: incommensurable cultural differences, contending civilizations, opposed religions, and untranslatable customs. But

they always end in the idiom of popular racism with the litany of bogus asylum seekers, aggressive beggars, and devious thieves; with danger, dirt, disease, and crime. However culture-minded they strive to be, the momentum
of these thoughts always derives from the oldest impulses of racial antipathy.
Congested urban space stages puzzling confrontations with unblinking alien
alterity and the threatening groups in question turn out to be the very ones
that were already well-known and fixed under the sign of race. Once again,
the hierarchies produced by race-thinking's excursions into political
anatomy are being repeated and endorsed for the test of culture that they
provide. In other words, they draw their power from the specifications of
racial difference that are still latent inside them.

Sadly, the fact that a degree of coyness is evident where impolite expressions about immigrants, strangers, and refugees risk denting the liberal self-
images of the clean polities involved cannot be relied upon as a bulwark
against the resurgence of racial nationalism. Critics and historians of our period must be alert to these difficult connections. If is to be effective, our work
must be ready to confront the complicated discursive figures that have made
tacitly race-coded nationalism an attractive and compelling option both for
confused and anxious European folk and for their increasingly cynical and
manipulative political leaders as both groups face the perils of globalization.[8]
The wider ethical climate in which, for Europe, fervent governmental or
popular racism hark back to the Third Reich must also be taken into account.

Of course, the bio-political commitments that were previously mandated
by old-style racial hierarchy can persist even when the languages of absolute
cultural difference and gene-determinism have taken hold. Their residual
traces combine easily with ethnic absolutism, mechanistic notions of culture,
and deterministic organicism to form a deadly cocktail. It bears repetition
that these operations are not only being conducted by the ultra-right; they
have tempted elements of the social democratic left. Indeed the metaphysics
of "race," nation, and identity fudges those increasingly fluid categories.
When not racism but the legitimate fear of the host community is at last identified as a substantive object of government and statecraft, then it has myste-
riously acquired the power to reconfigure the political field by revealing un-
foreseen connections that operate across the formal divisions of ideology
and party. These important developments are clearly visible through the
prism that histories of racism provide. Thus the critical study of racism contributes a method to the generation of the new cartography we require.

The interpretative puzzles evident in this volatile situation are compounded not only because "race" and nationality are now routinely associated or even because they have regularly hardened and set in the aggressive
patterns of xenophobia, racism, and ethnic absolutism. I want to emphasize
that the unstable ground on which the ramshackle edifice of political anti-
racism was erected—largely (we should remember) by immigrants and their

supporters—has dwindled. This notable contribution to Europe's civic well-being and political health passes unremarked upon by those who babble instead about the conflict between solidarity and diversity. Hasn't anti-racism demanded a more solid and supple democracy? Couldn't there be dynamic, worthwhile solidarity around the noble desire that racism should have no place in political culture? Here anti-racism can move out of its defensive and apologetic postures. Its aims are even now being annexed by corporate interests that are a good deal less squeamish than governments about feeding the popular hunger for a world purged of racial conflicts. Whatever Slavoj Zizek says to the contrary,[9] that market-driven pastiche of multi-culturalism only appears compelling and attractive in the absence of governmental action and political initiatives organized from below. Corporate attempts at manipulating the desire to live lives that are not amenable to race coding have been ham-fisted. The betrayal of utopia is obvious where racial types are reinscribed in the service of commercial reach rather than abolished in the name of human freedom. Meanwhile, the non-racial ideal is at risk of being rendered banal by the spontaneous hetero-cultures at large in the post-colonial metropolis.

As the implications of these large changes begin to dawn, we must also acknowledge that the routinization of cultural plurality does not mean that the work of anti-racism is over. That project must go on because the wholesome, democratic cadences of non-racial nationalism are not being heard either as loudly or as frequently as their academic advocates had anticipated they would be. In many instances, it would appear that the mere presence of new "waves" of immigrants has been enough to silence the cheerleaders of tolerance, negative or positive.

Where the fear and danger that perennial strangers represent become inescapable, the fading authority of Euro-modernity's civic order has been invoked tactically as a disciplinary mechanism of informally race-coded governmental power. The bleached, culture-free norms that have oriented Europe's tattered civic order have been tainted via their association with race. They have been invoked to mute and disregard protests voiced by people whose possession of formal, technical citizenship has not prevented them from being disadvantaged and victimized on the bases of descent, ethnicity, culture, religion, language, birthplace, phenotype, or blood. We are still being told that to take those complaints seriously would be to admit illegitimate and corrosive distinctions into the traditional operations of political cultures that are not disposed to acknowledge differences between their members. As long as this commitment is maintained, defending the fortifications of a homogenous, invariant Commonwealth can then be made into the principal means to illustrate the health and integrity of national democracies.

Faced with this degree of inertia a complex battle ensues. We must be alert to the workings of political racism and able to apprehend "race" as a process of relation, of imaginary kinship and real narration rather than some badge worn on or lodged deep inside the body. Without making any concessions to the reification of "race" or ethnic identity, we must try to find ways to take the divisive, dehumanizing power of race-thinking more seriously than has been done in the past. In other words, we must be prepared to identify raciology as a specific and significant object, to comprehend it as a part of a web of discourse, to see that it has a knowable history, and to appreciate its social implication in the exercise of bio-political powers that have damaged democracy before and can still compromise it. The recurrent interrelation of "race" and nation defines one colonial boundary of European inhumanity.[10] It also touches the living legacy of Europe's enlightenment and the history of the academic humanities that have guided its evolving civilization. Though they may be rightly assertive that humanity *should* not be divided along spurious racial lines, those innocent liberal responses become mistaken where they turn away from the catastrophic political impact of coded racist language and ultra-nationalist organization, dismiss the idea that racialized divisions can be made to matter precisely because of their empty and insubstantial character, and then trivialize the raciologies that produce and sanction them.

We can obtain a vivid glimpse of the unacknowledged power of racial typologies that still haunts these operations when the absurd figure of the "second generation immigrant" makes an inevitable appearance. Acting as the casting director for this pitiful pageant of the "social science" of multi-culture is Jonathan Friedman, another professorial immigrant to Europe from North America, who has recently made a name for himself through his attacks on European political correctness and his robust defense of Swedish nativism. A distinctive brand of decidedly partisan anthropology has made him an opponent of "elitist multi-culturalism" and an academic advocate for fearful, ordinary Swedes who dislike what he calls "enclavized" immigrants and the changes introduced into Scandian "homogeneity" by alien "diversity," which has opened them to accusations of ethnocentrism, xenophobia, and racism.

I disagree with Friedman but I find his protestations to be interesting symptoms. They reveal much about the political choices open to scholars of immigration. The issue that demands our attention here is the overly casual use of that incoherent, deadly phrase "second generation immigrant." I was initially hopeful because in his text those words arrived thoughtfully marked with a footnote that identified them with what he calls "official ethnification," a phrase as ugly as the governmental processes to which it refers. Though he flirts with a critique of that externalizing logic, Friedman does not break it. Indeed he compounds it by wheeling out yet another abomination: this is the grim specter of what he calls "foreign-affiliated persons." This group now apparently makes up 28 percent of the population of the city of Malmö. His scary statistic is glossed in another telling footnote:

"The statistics are always complex, but the breakdown is as follows: foreign citizens, 11 percent, foreign-born citizens, 12 percent, children under 18 with at least one foreign born parent, 4 percent. The total is 70,657 in a total population of 251,408, or 28 percent."[11] Friedman tells us that together with his spouse—a professor of anthropology who has made dubious remarks in support of anti-immigrant organizations—he is waging an important campaign against the unjust, irrational, and unscholarly reactions of their students, the Swedish media, and fellow academics who regard their interventions as harmful misuse of scholarly authority that gave support to anti-democratic and immoral forces. He has chosen to make much of his embattled professional integrity as a genuine scholar whose scientific research eclipses the pitiful failures of his opponents. With that context in mind, I want to pause over the rationality that permits him to produce the terrifying figure of 28 percent and to hold together the resulting compound category "foreign-affiliated people." Surely, for a start, the sub-category of the foreign born must include Swedes born abroad who are not "affiliated" with their birthplaces? In what sense, if any, are refugees and other migrants "affiliated" with the territories from which they have fled or been expelled? Do any attenuated connections they maintain with their places of origin *necessarily* block the possibility of making connections with their new homelands? Friedman's category excludes all these questions *by fiat*. It seems contrived to obscure rather than illuminate, to justify the exclusionary reactions and legitimate the fears of the real Swedes who are in his view rightly concerned about the sacrifice of their welfare society on the altar of immigration. It's hard to avoid the conclusion that for Friedman, immigration is acceptable when he moves to Sweden and sets up home with his foreign affiliated children but not OK when insufficiently flexible and under-civilized Africans and other people from the un-developed world, people who cling to each other and to their own particularity, do it *en masse*. For how many generations are we to remain immigrants—in the words of the late Sir Ronald Bell, "cats born in kipper boxes" struggling to persuade our hosts that we are in fact kippers?

Taking the raciological discourse seriously involves scholarly as well as political tasks. There can be no excuse for the failure to become intimate with the history of Europe's modern invention and projection of humanity in racially divided, antagonistic, and hierarchical encampments. Telling and retelling the story of racism's rational irrationality, of its alchemical articulations of knowledge and power, can contribute significant ethical and political resources to ailing European democracy, particularly where we struggle to make adequate responses to the suffering raciology still creates. A command of that contested history is all the more crucial as the living memory of the Third Reich dies out and ceases to form the constellation under which critical, oppositional, reflexive work on the developing lore that brings the dismal and destructive power of "race" to life can take place. Likewise, the automatic assumption that European history will be told best and most powerfully when it is made to coincide with the fixed borders of its national states will have to be disposed of.

In drawing our new map we must be prepared to make detours away from the geo-body of contemporary Europe into the imperial and colonial zones where the catastrophic power of race-thinking was first institutionalized and its distinctive anthropologies put to the test, above all, in the civilizing storms of colonial war. Making that forgotten history co-extensive with the moral lives of European nations is essential, but a vital anti-racism cannot end with the shame that story produces. We must be able to pass beyond a compensatory acknowledgment of Europe's imperial crimes and the significance of their colonies as places of governmental innovation and experiment. The empires were not simply out there—terminal points for trading activity where race consciousness could grow—in the distant torrid zones of the world at the other end of the colonial chain. They were brought back home long before the migrants arrived since economic, social, and cultural relations were at the core of the colonial systems. That fundamental shift in standpoint makes imperial dynamics much more significant in the constitution of national states than they have been allowed to be before. It sets a number of challenges before historians of the post-colonial present.

The principled opposition to nationalism that was so important to liberal, socialist, and feminist traditions has faded with the Cold War. We have seen that scholastic orthodoxy is keen to re-interpret the xenophobia, nationalism, and ethnic absolutism of today's racists in benign ways. If it is not a grumbling anti-capitalism, then it must be a new anxiety induced by experiences of de-industrialization, downward mobility, and growing inequality that have been prompted by turbo capitalism's merciless destruction of Europe's once-proud welfare states. I have introduced some of the academic voices which have argued that racism should not be an issue as well as those that say culturalist and nationalist racism is after all not racism but rather a veiled protest against the demise of the post-1945 settlement. The either-or nature of these explanations is deeply problematic. Populist racism can be alive in these and other sympathetic or radical responses (e.g., ecology or animal welfare) but its ability to combine with them does not erase the appeal of racial purity or explain the basic attractions of ethnic absolutism, which solves complex problems by renewing certainty in the face of a loss of identity. A more worthwhile approach would seek to understand why it is through the political language of race that these statements of dissent become expressible.

These are the circumstances in which scholastic theory's affirmative nationalists have won their partial victory. It has been achieved only by silence on the idea of race and its relationship to nationalism. I have suggested that

their overly schematic separation of nationalism into discrete civic and ethnic tendencies is impossible to maintain when confronted by the history of
political racism. Faced with strangers who seek entry, today's civic and ethnic nationalisms speak in one hostile voice. If we are to answer this rejection,
we must be extra careful about returning to the migrancy problematic. This
introduces a risk of collusion with the cheap consensus that ties immigration
and social policy to the nebulous discussions of diversity, multi-culturalism,
and "political correctness" that I have criticized. This alarming new orthodoxy stipulates that multi-culturalism is catastrophically bad for Europe, its
national states, and its supra-state system. By multi-culturalism it means social, political, and cultural differentiation along ethnic or racialized lines as
well as the institutional responses to it and the immigration that produced it
in the first place.

This particular interpretative language is neither innocent nor inevitable.
Recent post-colonial conflicts in southern Africa have reminded us that "immigrant" does not sound like "settler," the word that was used to fix the precarious predicament of adventurous Europeans at the other end of the colonial chain. The sharp contrast between these terms helps to show why the
migrant label will always be a cipher of secondariness and marginality if not
of rejection. It is tempting to suggest that the enduring power of that sticky
label and our inability to shrug it off are themselves symptomatic. I want to
end by suggesting you consider the possibility that the figure of the immigrant is part of the very intellectual mechanism that holds us hostage. Its
prominence returns our discourse, against our will, to the idea that immigration and its discontents contain the key to understanding all the bids for
recognition, belonging, and autonomy that have been made recently by non-
white Europeans. This should not mean, of course, that the history of migration is to be abandoned before it has even been produced. But it must be
part of Europe's history rather than its contemporary geography. The post-
colonial migrant needs to be recognized as a historic figure bound to the imperial past. We need to conjure up a future in which we stop being seen as
migrants.

I've tried to show that migrancy becomes unhelpful when it becomes an
explanation in itself for the conflicts and opportunities of this transitional
moment in the life of our polities, economies, and cultural ensembles. As
you might anticipate, I prefer to say that if there must be one single concept,
a solitary unifying idea around which the history of post-colonial settlement
in twentieth-century Europe should revolve, that place should be given not
to migrancy but to racism. The racisms of Europe's colonial and imperial
phase preceded the appearance of migrants inside the European citadel. It
was racism and not diversity that made their arrival into a problem. This is
far more than just a question of perspective. There are significant political interests at stake. Where migrancy supplies the decisive element, the door gets

opened to patterns of explanation that ultimately present immigrants as the authors of their own misfortune. The violence and hostility regularly directed against them by their reluctant hosts are then excused. These responses to difference are seen first as spontaneous and natural and secondly as reactions against the unreasonable expectations placed upon ordinary folk by inappropriately high-minded government and perfidious corporate capital alike.

We can answer this depressed and depressing view with a different analysis. It is premised upon commitment to make modern racism part of the moral landscape through which today's liberals move. It is common for our enemies to remark that blacks suffer from Holocaust envy. Blacks suffer from envy of the ways in which the Holocaust is taken seriously by liberals as part of the moral landscape of the world.

I feel strongly about these matters because I am a European but not an immigrant. Our transitional predicament means we do need a new map but, at this point, to try and orient ourselves through the idea of migrancy seems a big and potentially tricky step. It promotes an unnecessary retreat from the claim to be insiders and would carry us on to ground that our enemies have carved out for us. This is territory on which we become always and only interlopers. At best, our constitutional exteriority to the mysterious inner life of these decaying national states means we are to be "negatively" tolerated rather than admitted with a smile. Our belonging is pending and we are desperately vulnerable while our local affiliation is on trial. We can be rapidly removed to where we really belong by the stroke of a governmental pen or the flash of non-governmental knife. Migrants, let me remind you, are people who are required to occupy an intermediate but juridically second-class position. So far, the best that the left can come up with to challenge that negative diagnosis is a desperate plea that they should be welcomed because they can be the fortuitous answer to Europe's falling fertility rates. That will never be enough. Searching for a more robust and complex position than that, I don't think that migrancy can remain intact at the center of our thinking. To leave it there undisturbed is a vestige of the mid-twentieth century that promotes an implicit agreement to stay in the twilight, to remain on the threshold peering into the cozy but forbidden space of the national hearth, ever mindful of the dubious benefits of being somewhere else. Yes, we do need that new map, but I know that the Europe we are writing, the Europe that we need to bring into being, is not an entity that identifies us with that netherworld, with the migrant lives of my mother's post- and anti-colonial generation, never mind the bolder claims that might be made on the basis of even older intimacies with the mother country than theirs.

This paper is dedicated to the memories of Benjamin Hermansen, Alberto Adriano, Farid Guendoul, and Stephen Lawrence.

NOTES

1. Giles Tremlett, "Immigrants provoke ire in Catalonia," *Guardian*, 1 March 2001. Rory Carroll, "Italy orders anti-fascist snatch squads at Lazio," *Guardian*, 2 February 2000.

2. Jack Straw, the home secretary, shared a platform with Charles Murray at a debate entitled "On the Growing Threat of the Underclass," sponsored by Rupert Murdoch's *Sunday Times* on Tuesday, May 2, 2000. For his combative views on the theme of the left's failure to be sufficiently patriotic and nationalist, see his "Blame the Left, Not the British," *The Observer*, Sunday, October 15, 2000.

3. Michael Ignatieff, "Less Race Please," *Prospect*, April 1999, p. 10.

4. Uday Singh Mehta, *Liberalism and Empire* (Chicago: University of Chicago Press, 1999).

5. Bhiku Parekh, *The Future of Multi-Ethnic Britain: The Parekh Report* (London: Profile Books, 2000).

6. James Tully, *Strange Multiplicity*, (Cambridge: Cambridge University Press, 1995).

7. Think, for example, of the recent racist antics of the Lazio players and fans. Sinisa Mihajlovic abused Arsenal's Patrick Vieira and the Italian case. Alessandro Mussolini has won a place in the hearts of the "irreducibili" and the history of the Lazio club which was originally built up to break the communist culture of AS Roma.

8. At a rally in Paris last May Day, Jean-Marie Le Pen told his dwindling band of followers, "Globalisation and its Trojan horse, a federal Europe, are leading France to its death." *Guardian*, 2 May 2000.

9. Slavoj Zizek, "Multiculturalism or, the Cultural Logic of Multinational Capitalism," *New Left Review* 225, September/October 1997.

10. Ian Hernon, *Massacre and Retribution: Forgotten Wars of the Nineteenth Century*, (London: Sutton Publishing, 1998), and *The Savage Empire: Forgotten Wars of the Nineteenth Century*, (London: Sutton Publishing, 2000).

11. Jonathan Friedman, "Rhinoceros 2," *Current Anthropology* 40, no. 5, December 1999.

4

Virtual Multiculturalism: The Case of Contemporary Britain

Graham Huggan

I am an Englishman born and bred, almost. (Hanif Kureishi, *The Buddha of Suburbia*)

In virtual reality, nothing is real, but we experience it as if it were. So, too, with virtual equality. (Urvashi Vaid, *Virtual Equality: The Mainstreaming of Gay and Lesbian Liberation*)

Has Britain truly come of age as a multicultural society? It certainly appears so, for scarcely a day goes by without our hearing of the delights of living in a culturally diverse country—one in which the arrogance, insularity, and xenophobia traditionally associated with "Little Englanderism" make rare appearances, and racism, while acknowledged as existing in the present, is mostly projected into the past. The reality, of course, is different. During a recent trip I took to Britain, a nail-bomb—apparently motivated by race hatred—was detonated in the streets of Brixton, while the next day, a TV program (of a type that has become legion) attempting to capture the "essence" of English culture identified Englishness stereotypically in terms of charming eccentricity and the suspicion toward strangers—including, almost inevitably, the "foreigner within."

This *plus ça change* motif was particularly noticeable in the run-up to the new millennium, as discourses of novelty/innovation (especially those associated with "revolutionary" technologies) jostled for place alongside discourses of nostalgia (for what is "Englishness" after all?).[1] The term *multiculturalism*, as currently recycled by New Labour, is part of the clash between these two apparently incompatible discourses. On the one hand, multiculturalism belongs to a project of modernization through diversification, the attendant recognition being that Britain's different ethnic communities are all contributing to the making of the future. On the other, multiculturalism continues to have integrationist undertones, for the notion of unity-in-diversity, especially at a time of devolution, has a conservative ring to it, as racial discrimination—even racial violence—are submerged beneath layers of political rhetoric and media spin.

Media spin has also played its part in promoting another idea dear to New Labour—the idea of the *virtual community,* linked by technology across race, class, and gender barriers. In this paper, I want to touch on some aspects of the convergence between multiculturalism and virtuality, including the notion (explored in a rather different context by Arjun Appadurai) of a *trans*national, electronically produced multicultural public sphere. First, though, I want to explore some of the connotations of the term *virtual.* In my dictionary, *virtual* receives the following listings:

—*virtuous (obs.)*
—*having virtue or efficacy (arch.)*
—*in effect, though not in fact; not such in fact but capable of being considered as much for some purposes*

The slipperiness of the term is even more apparent when it is converted into a noun or adverb, with *virtuality* translating into either *essential nature* or *potentiality* and *virtually* wavering between *loosely, almost, nearly,* and *in effect.* In what follows, I want to play with some of these different connotations, recombining them to explore the paradoxes of contemporary multicultural Britain. My examples will be drawn from different media—both printed word and visual image—and will be gathered together in three subcategories, "Multiculturalism and Authority," "Multiculturalism and Assimilation," and "Multiculturalism and Devolution." I shall then offer a brief conclusion placing British virtual multiculturalism within the wider context of mediated perceptions of the (so-called) New Europe. Let me begin, though, with a few clarifications on what multiculturalism might mean in the context of contemporary Britain.

The first and most obvious point is that multiculturalism means different things in different places. In the United States, it is partly a challenge to the assimilationist model of the "melting pot"; in Australia, a counter-discourse to the residual ideology of White Australia; in Canada, a state-sanctioned policy of social equalization based on a recognition of the validity of rival cultural claims. In each of these contexts, multiculturalism is conspicuously *contested,* open to interpretation—and criticism—from both Right and Left. For example, a Rightist critique might point out that multiculturalism exacerbates social division and fragmentation, ignoring the "core" values that define, differentiate, and, not least, defend a particular culture, while a Leftist view might construct multiculturalism as an ideological smokescreen behind which continuing prejudice and intolerance are hidden and inter-racial tensions defused. Both of these criticisms (and several others) have been leveled at multiculturalism in Britain. But what *is* multiculturalism in Britain, and how and when did the debates that currently surround it first appear?

Multiculturalism, as a discourse of cultural pluralism, is generally agreed to have emerged after World War II, a period of economic boom and labor shortage[2] when migrations brought workers from the (former) colonies to take on a variety of usually low-paid jobs. Many of these workers arrived from the Caribbean and South Asia in the 1940s, 1950s, and 1960s, with their arrival generating anxiety among some white Britons as to the changing "racial character" of British society. Afro-Caribbean and South Asian immigrants were—and to some extent still are—regarded as culturally "other," and were/are subjected to varying forms and levels of discrimination, mistreatment, and abuse. A political turning point was the 1966 speech of Roy Jenkins, home secretary in the Wilson government. In his landmark speech, Jenkins advocated *integration* rather than *assimilation*, a distinction later to become crucial to the formation of official multicultural policy in the 1970s. As Jenkins argued, assimilation was, at best, a "flattening process," whereas integration promoted "equal opportunity accompanied by cultural diversity in an atmosphere of mutual tolerance" (Jenkins 1966, 4; Brah 1996, 25). Jenkins's speech might be considered typical of a liberal view of multiculturalism designed to counteract racism in "sympathetic" terms without necessarily acknowledging that it is *institutionally* structured.[3] Structural racism is still a difficult idea for many Britons to accept, as can be seen in mixed reactions to the latest allegations of institutionalized discrimination in the Metropolitan Police Force. In the next section I compare the Indo-British writer Salman Rushdie's multicultural blockbuster *The Satanic Verses* (1988) with media coverage of the Stephen Lawrence inquiry and the subsequent findings of the Macpherson report (1999).

MULTICULTURALISM AND AUTHORITY

Salman Rushdie's *The Satanic Verses* (1988), like his earlier novel *Midnight's Children* (1981), has become something of a touchstone work for British multicultural fiction.[4] Fatwa aside, the novel has exerted considerable influence on the mindset of a whole host of younger writers, one of the most recent examples being Zadie Smith, whose up-to-the-minute multicultural epic *White Teeth* (2000) contains several undisguised references to you-know-who. But just how "multicultural" a novel is *The Satanic Verses*? Certainly it has been praised as such, with seemingly statutory reference to the famous essay in which Rushdie fends off his detractors by claiming that *The Satanic Verses* "celebrates hybridity, impurity, intermingling, the transformation that comes of new and unexpected combinations of human beings, cultures, ideas, politics, movies, songs" (Rushdie 1991, 394). But is this "multicultural-ism"? Rushdie himself appears not to think so. Here, for example, is what he has to say on multiculturalism in another essay:

> [A] whole declension of patronizing terminology can be found in the language in which inter-racial relations have been described inside Britain. At first, we were told, the goal was 'integration'. Now this word rapidly came to mean 'as-similation': a black man could only become integrated when he started behav-ing like a white one. After 'integration' came the concept of 'racial harmony'. Now once again, this seemed virtuous and desirable, but what it meant in prac-tice was that blacks should be persuaded to live peaceably with whites, in spite of all the injustices done to them every day. The call for 'racial harmony' was simply an invitation to shut up and smile while nothing was done about our grievances. And now there's a new catchword: 'multiculturalism'. In our schools, this means little more than teaching the kids a few bongo rhythms, how to tie a sari and so forth. In the police-training program, it means telling cadets that black people are so 'culturally different' that they can't help making trou-ble. Multiculturalism is the latest token gesture towards Britain's blacks, and it ought to be exposed, like 'integration' and 'racial harmony', for the sham it is. (Rushdie 1991, 137)

It might be possible to contend here that Rushdie's novels set up a multi-cultural *aesthetics* that paradoxically opposes multicultural *policy*, in part by making its ulterior motives clear (Huggan & Wachinger forthcoming). I would go further and claim that Rushdie—in *The Satanic Verses* at least—parodies a *virtual* multiculturalism in which commodified images of cultural fusion are filtered through the public sphere. This general point can be clarified by fo-cusing on the controversial topic of police harassment—particularly in view of the Lawrence inquiry, itself something of a touchstone for race relations in late-twentieth-century Britain.

A few words on the inquiry before returning to the treatment of the police in Rushdie's novel. The case of Stephen Lawrence, a young black man stabbed to death by a gang of white youths in south London in April 1993, has attracted an avalanche of media attention over the last half-decade, be-coming "a *cause celebre* exposing the prevalence of racial violence, institu-tionalized racism within the police, and the failure of the justice system at a wider level to seek redress for the victims of racism" (Sivanandan et al. 1999, 65).[5] Although Lawrence's alleged assailants were acquitted—under the most dubious of circumstances—the inquest was to have damaging conse-quences for many of those found to be involved. Not least among these was the implication, later confirmed, of structural racism in the police force—a state of affairs that has since led, not only to the public embarrassment of several senior police (and government) officials, but also to the recommendation of stringent measures to reform Britain's policing and criminal justice system (Macpherson 1999; see also Sivanandan et al. 1999, 66–73).[6]

The Lawrence case has effectively made nonsense of the reconciliatory rhetoric of multiculturalism, appearing to confirm the inequality of Britain's minority citizens before the law. Equally interesting, though, are the ways in which the inquiry has been *covered*. War has been waged about media representation, with sides being taken on the strength of the murder's portrayal and further accusations being leveled at the police for "playing down the significance of racially-motivated crime" (Sivanandan et al. 1999, 70). The publicity surrounding the Lawrence inquiry has revealed the limitations of an officially sanctioned *anti-racist discourse*, designed to assure a skeptical populace that suitable measures against racial crime are being taken while remaining silent about a "substantial body of statistical data demonstrating the over-representation of black people at virtually every stage of the criminal justice system" (Sivanandan et al. 1999, 65–66). At the same time, much of the journalism has arguably itself contributed to this silencing process, first, by refusing to discuss the material effects of its own representational processes and thus underestimating or ignoring the implications of the Lawrence inquiry as a staged "media event," and second, by turning the case into a metonymy for the personal tragedies that unfold from histories of racial assault and murder, thereby drawing attention away from "the wider social, economic and political basis of racism in British society" (Sivanandan et al. 1999, 72).[7]

Back now to Rushdie. In one of the most pungent scenes of *The Satanic Verses*, the putative "illegal immigrant" Saladin Chamcha completes a strange metamorphosis when, having been arrested and beaten, he is whisked off semi-conscious in a police van for further questioning by the authorities. Chamcha appeals in vain to his captors, who cannot help but see him as a devil—for that is what he has become:

> 'My name is Salahuddin Chamchawala, professional name Saladin Chamcha,' the demi-goat gibbered. 'I am a member of Actors' Equity, the Automobile Association and the Garrick Club. My car registration is suchandsuch. Ask the Computer. Please.'
> 'Who're you trying to kid?' inquired one of [the policemen]. 'Look at yourself. You're a fucking Packy billy. Sally-who?—What kind of name is that for an Englishman?' (Rushdie 1988, 163)

The Police National Computer, however, identifies Saladin unerringly as a British citizen—not that this improves his situation, rather it "place[s] him, if anything, in greater danger than before" (Rushdie 1988, 164). Saladin is virtually British, it seems—and therefore not at all. To cover up their error, Saladin's captors spirit him away to the Detention Centre's medical facility, where he joins other pathologically transformed "illegal immigrants," including "businessmen from Nigeria who have grown sturdy tails" and a "group of holidaymakers from Senegal who were doing no more than changing planes when they were turned into slippery snakes" (168). How is this illusion achieved? asks Saladin despairingly of one of his wardmates, "a highly paid model, based in Bombay" (168), who has turned into a fabulous manticore, with the body of a man and a tiger's head. Simple, replies his ferocious-looking companion, "'They describe us,' [he] whispered solemnly. 'That's all. They have the power of description, and we succumb to the pictures they construct'" (168).

The scene satirizes the material effects of a virtual racism played out in images and representations of the abject ethnic body, which mutates to become "in fact" what its detractors have always believed it to be "in effect." Saladin's humanity is denied, just as his citizenship had been confirmed, *by virtual means,* thereby allowing Rushdie to clinch the link between pathologies of racial representation—the demonization of the ethnic Other—and government strategies of surveillance—the protection of the rightful (British) citizen. And it is the discourse of multiculturalism—monstrously twisted, of course—that provides the bridge between them. For throughout *The Satanic Verses,* "diversity" and "difference"—the talismanic properties of the multicultural society—are converted into alibis for marginalization and authoritarian abuse (Huggan & Wachinger forthcoming). In this "multicultural" Britain, mediated images of cultural harmony are grotesquely transformed into their opposites, mutating into the very symbols of what official discourses would deny—racial abuse. There is little to distinguish this virtual multiculturalism from the horrors of institutionalized racism. In the skewed *fictional* world of *The Satanic Verses*—not so far removed, perhaps, from the *real* world in which Stephen Lawrence was murdered—violence is only ever around the corner, for the protectors of the populace may easily turn into its assailants, and "equality," always color-coded, becomes largely an effect of the hyperreal.

MULTICULTURALISM AND ASSIMILATION

The desired goals of multiculturalism, according to Rushdie, are not so different from the coercive ambitions of assimilation: "A black man [can] only become integrated when he start[s] behaving like a white one." This dialectic between difference and sameness (operating, as throughout this paper, under the sign of the virtual) is also played out in current debates surrounding the practice of what sociologists call *transracial adoption.* Transracial adoption, simply defined, is "the adoption of a child of one race by parents of another" (Triseliotis et al. 1997, 160). "In our world, because of unequal distribution of social and economic resources," state three British sociologists, John Triseliotis, Joan Shireman, and Marion Hundleby, transracial adoption "has meant the adoption of black children (or children of 'colour') by white families, there [being] no significant examples of adoption being practiced the other way round" (Triseliotis et al. 1997, 160). Triseliotis, Shireman, and Hundleby go on to outline three basic positions on the practice of transracial adoption:

1. An "internationalist" or "integrationist" view "in which the uniqueness of the individual is prized," irrespective of his or her color, and in which "[t]he emphasis is on fighting racism and recognizing the structural traps in which all disadvantaged groups are caught" (161);
2. A "pragmatic" or "assimilationist" view in which less emphasis is placed on "the social and racial injustices that contribute to [. . .] childcare need" (161), but rather on the likelihood of the adoption being a success;
3. An oppositional view in which transracial adoption is considered both inadvisable and inappropriate, and in which a model of society is preferred "in which each individual is a part of his or her own culture"—a society within which "distinct cultures," while being kept separate, "interact" (161).

Not surprisingly, the authors disagree about which of these views is to be favored. The studies and evidence they allude to is clearly conflicting. On the one hand, they show that "black children adopted transracially do not develop the coping mechanisms to function in a society that is inherently racist" (164); on the other hand, transracially adopted children may develop, and benefit from, a "bicultural orientation" (173). In this section, I briefly draw attention to two *imaginative* explorations of the some of the issues and problems concerning the practice of (transracial) adoption in a conspicuously racist society—Britain's. These works are the Afro-Scottish writer Jacky Kay's poignant narrative poem *The Adoption Papers* (1991) and the English filmmaker Mike Leigh's bittersweet family romance *Secrets & Lies* (1996).

The Adoption Papers weaves between the lives of three women in a Scottish working-class environment—a mixed-race daughter (her father is Nigerian), and her birth and adoptive mothers (both of these are white). The poem movingly explores the competing anxieties surrounding a young girl whose mother has abandoned her and who has been adopted into a society where intolerance regularly spills over into racial abuse. In the following excerpt, the two voices of the girl and her adoptive mother—as so often in the poem—talk past one another:

ADOPTIVE MOTHER:
Maybe that's why I don't like

all this talk about her being black,
I brought her up as my own
as I would any other child
colour matters to the nutters;
but she says my daughter says
it matters to her
[. . .]
DAUGHTER:
I chase his *Sambo Sambo* all the way from the school gate.
A fistful of anorak—What did you call me? Say that again.
Sam-bo. He plays the word like a bouncing ball
but his eyes move fast as ping pong.
I shove him up against the wall,
say that again you wee shite. *Sambo, sambo*, he's crying now
I knee him in the balls. What was that?
My fist is steel; I punch and punch his gut.
Sorry I didn't hear you? His tears drip like wax.
Nothing he heaves *I didn't say nothing*.
I let him go. He is a rat running. He turns
and shouts *Dirty Darkie* I chase him again.
Blonde hairs in my hand. (Kay 1991, 24)

For the adoptive mother—the characters are unnamed—the daughter is "virtually" *white*, having been brought up, like "any other child," as effectively "her own." The daughter knows, however, that for almost everyone she encounters she is unequivocally *black*. Some identity confusion results, as when her teacher asks her to demonstrate some dancing steps in front of her clueless classmates:

> [M]y teacher shouts from the bottom
> of the class Come on, show
> us what you can do I thought
> you people had it in your blood.
> My skin is hot as burning coal
> like that time she said Darkies are like coal
> in front of the whole class—my blood
> what does she mean? (25)

Mostly, however, it is the people around her who betray anxiety and confusion—her adoptive mother, for instance, who is desperate not to lose the child she loves so much to her "real" mother; and the birth mother herself, who fears that the daughter she gave up will always reject her in return. These dilemmas remain unresolved, and the temptation to judge is largely avoided. Meanwhile, by the end of the poem, the daughter, now in her twenties, is more than equipped to make her own decisions. And the main decision she arrives at is to live with the split between her origins and her upbringing, rejecting the clichéd identity tags and hereditary ties that others have attempted to foist upon her ("black-to-all-intents-and-purposes," "no-different-from-any-other," "as-good-as-white," and so forth):

> I have my parents who are not of the same tree
> and you keep trying to make it matter,
> the blood, the tie, the passing down
> generations.
> We all have our contradictions,
> the ones with the mother's nose and father's eyes
> have them;
> the blood does not bind confusion,
> yet I confess to my contradiction
> I want to know my blood. (29)

Kay thus rejects the "ethnic absolutism" (Gilroy 1987) sometimes deployed to disapprove of transracial adoption—the view, for instance, that a "positive black identity" can only be achieved by raising a black child in a black family (see Gilroy 1987, 65; also Samad 1997, 250)—while also questioning the alternative essentialisms implicit in multicultural attempts to recognize and tolerate cultures other than one's own.[8]

Absolutist views are also questioned in Mike Leigh's wryly observed domestic melodrama *Secrets & Lies* (1996), a characteristic blend of suburban comedy-of-manners and gritty documentary realism set in contemporary London. The plot revolves around the attempt of a young black optometrist, Hortense Cumberbatch (sensitively played by Marianne Jean-Baptiste), to track down her white birth mother, Cynthia Purley, from whom the child, illegitimately conceived, had been removed at birth for adoption by black foster parents, both now deceased. In a brilliantly realized scene, Hortense and Cynthia meet for the first time outside the Holborn tube station, and move on from there for a tension-filled confessional exchange in a deserted local café. In the scene—as throughout the movie—Leigh skillfully manipulates racial stereotypes of marginalization and rejection, recoding these in terms of sexual abuse (the abandoned single mother) and, particularly, the anxieties surrounding perceived differences of social class. In a sense, it is the self-assured, dignified Hortense who ends up "adopting" her emotionally fragile birth mother, nursing her slowly back to health and providing the unlikely catalyst that allows her dysfunctional family to resolve their differences and, eventually, to reunite. While the upbeat ending of the film is not immune to the charge of sentimentality, Leigh also uses it to poke fun at the hypocritical pieties of British society as a happy multicultural family. Aware of its own complicity in capturing, but also concealing, domestic upheaval for the camera (Cynthia's put-upon brother Maurice makes his living by staging "intimate" portraits of domestic bliss for the commemorative family album), *Secrets & Lies* presents a series of canny observations of a guilt-ridden, sexually repressed, and occasionally violent society apparently unwilling to come to terms with either the conflicts of the present or the consequences of the past.

MULTICULTURALISM AND DEVOLUTION

Leigh's skepticism toward Britain's capacity to manage its own internal differences turns to caustic satire in Tom Nairn's recent, characteristically uncompromising political memoir *After Britain: New Labour and the Return of Scotland* (2000). *After Britain* is an entertaining, unashamedly partisan book on the transformation of contemporary Britain in the wake of recent devolution processes and the threatened dissolution of what Nairn provocatively calls the "Anglo-British state." As might be expected from a proud Scot, author of the saber-rattling study *The Break-Up of Britain* (1977), Nairn welcomes devolution—a process he adamantly sees in terms not of post-imperial nation-building but rather "the resumption of self-government by [. . .] *already constituted nation[s]*" (Nairn 2000, 13, emphasis mine). Nairn proves more skeptical, though, toward the deeper impact of devolution, arguing that "[w]hile the Republic of Ireland has turned into another country and the UK periphery has been launched on a course of accelerating difference and novelty, the English heartland remains by contrast almost unchanged, [continuing] to behave and feel *as if* Great Britain and its unitary state still existed" (15). Nairn casts similar doubts on the "radical" changes brought about—or, better, promised—by New Labour, which he sees as a government more geared to long-term survival than to revolutionary reform, and whose epoch-making ambitions he likens to the "virtual radicalism" satirised in Robert Musil's novel *Der Mann ohne Eigenschaften* (1952 [1930/32/42])—a novel in which, in Nairn's ironically updated terms, "new-start rhetoric" is supported by "a general mechanics of spin-doctoring, including good-news professors, schmaltzy circus-acts, wondrous uniforms and (had technology then permitted) Power-house Display Modules" (37).

   This "virtual revolution" (73) is complicit, for Nairn, with a commitment to multiculturalism, the ulterior aim of which might be seen to be shoring up an Anglocentric vision of British unity even as it simultaneously gestures toward ethnic and/or regional diversity, and which registers at best the naive "longing for a virtual dissolution of identity [into] a broader [. . .] format within which nations [Nairn surely has in mind Scotland] somehow disperse or painlessly cease to matter" (88). This "multiculturalism-without-tears" has been endorsed by recent, characteristically high-profile New Labour publicity for a properly expansive (i.e., non-chauvinistic) form of patriotism—one by means of which Britain might legitimately be celebrated as "not just a society of many communities, but also a country of nations—with large, contiguous areas of distinct national heritage" (Brown, quoted in Wintour 1999, 12). This is a virtual multiculturalism shorn of regional strife and racial tension—one apparently designed to allow a revitalized, but also sanitized, Great Britain to rediscover a popular sense of its own unique cultural heritage without falling back on the reflex mechanisms of imperial nostalgia and xenophobic national pride. Gordon Brown's sound bite is axiomatic: "Instead of a bland Britain, Britain is buzzing with difference; no longer a state in monochrome, but a nation in living colour" (quoted in Wintour 1999, 12). (Note the media double-speak by which a "society of communities" and a "country of nations" can be effortlessly absorbed by the master trope, "a nation in living colour." Multiculturalism, as Nairn suggests, thus becomes a kind of political safety valve, "captur[ing] the dissolved essence of the nation and remanifest[ing] it as an inherently variegated democracy" [86], but without seriously threatening the constitution or impeding the day-to-day operations of a residually Anglocentric British state.)

While Nairn's argument about the recuperative power of multiculturalism for ideologies of national unity strikes me as being (strategically) overstated, it usefully counteracts the popular view—now increasingly common among social theorists—of a working alliance between multiculturalism and a "*post*national [political] order" (Appadurai 1996) based on connections that transcend the boundaries of the nation-state. Exemplary here is the work of the Indo-American anthropologist Arjun Appadurai, whose book *Modernity at Large: The Cultural Dimensions of Globalization* (1996) is exemplary in that he pays extended tribute to an emergent postnational order—an order underpinned by the increasingly global traffic in goods, ideas, and peoples and by the relation between mass mediation and migration within a wider "diasporic public sphere" (Appadurai 1996, 33).[9] Multiculturalism, in this context, has less to do with the potential to disguise national disunity than with the "incapacity of states to prevent their minority populations from linking themselves to wider constituencies of religious or ethnic affiliation" (33). The implications of Appadurai's highly complex concept of the "diasporic public sphere" for multicultural constituencies beyond the boundaries of the British nation-state could and should be elaborated, but it must suffice here to point out Appadurai's—possibly excessive—confidence in the political efficacy of transnational *virtual communities*, where electronic media provide the opportunity to pursue global movements for cultural autonomy and sustainable justice, many of which Appadurai sees as "rest[ing] on the moral authority of exiles, refugees, and [the] displaced" (33–34). Virtuality, he suggests, affords the chance, not just to experiment with new kinds of identity (Turkle 1996), but also to formulate more flexible paradigms of "imagined community" (Anderson 1983) that have the potential to (re)connect the displaced and (re)empower the dispossessed.[10] The liberating power of the new technologies should not, however, be overestimated. As Ella Shohat and Robert Stam, among others, have argued, "multicultural media activism [may] serve to protect threatened identities or even [to] create new identities"; but disparities continue to exist in *access* to these potentially empowering technologies, while the potential to appropriate them for colonizing uses should never be forgotten (Shohat & Stam 1996, 166–167; see also Shohat & Stam 1995, Fernandez 1999).

For Shohat and Stam, multiculturalism belongs to a wider, self-consciously utopian social project in which global media are seen as providing "a nurturing space where the secret hopes of social life are played out, a laboratory for the safe articulation of identity oppressions and utopias, a space of community fantasies and imagined alliances" (Shohat & Stam 1996, 166–167). Virtual multiculturalisms of this kind, far from being illusory or oppressive, may allow "subjectivities [to] be lived and analyzed as part of a transformative, emancipatory praxis" (166). This is heady stuff, though one cannot help but wonder (as does the skeptical Nairn) what happens when the mantras of postmodern media-theory are loudly chanted by survival-oriented political regimes that pretend to want revolutionary change while contriving, for the most part, to prevent it (Nairn 2000, 70). As Nairn puts it, crushingly: "[W]hat counts most in [Blair's] 'gathering revolution' is clearly the gathering part; execution will come later, as and when opportunity allows (or, quite possibly, fails to allow)" (51). But surely, one must ask, the "newness" of the New Britain (and, by extension, the New Europe) amounts to more than "virtual" change—to more than this?

CONCLUSION: MULTICULTURALISM, RACISM, AND BRITAIN'S PLACE IN THE NEW EUROPE

Certainly, the British sociologist Avtar Brah believes so. In a chapter of the wide-ranging book *Cartographies of Diaspora: Contesting Identities* (1996), Brah asserts that Europeans in the last ten years have lived through a period of profound social, political, and—above all—economic transformation. In 1993, as is well known, the internal borders of the EU states were officially lifted, "with the intent of allowing the free movement of capital, goods, services and certain categories of people" (Brah 1996, 152). While the New Europe that emerged, and within which Britain has taken up an active role, might be primarily understood as a "constellation of economic interests" (152), it is also clear that these economic changes have helped produce a series of—not always beneficial—cultural effects. Brah offers an obvious example of the recrudescence of xenophobia in the New Europe—the resurgence of scarcely buried racist and nationalist sentiments in many countries that current debates on multiculturalism in the European context have made it their business to address. But how effective has multiculturalism been in counteracting racism across Europe? This depends, as ever, on how multiculturalism is conceived of and deployed in dissimilar sets of social and political circumstances.[11] A wide range of examples suggests the difficulties of formulating a coherent set of political strategies capable of addressing the differentiated problems of multiculturalism within the structurally complex "supranational community" of the New Europe (Modood 1997). The question remains moot, in any case, as to whether multicultural policies—however multiply conceived and flexibly implemented—will ever be able to counteract systemic racial discrimination and interethnic violence in any lasting effective way. Certainly in Britain, the recent evidence suggests that multiculturalism is trapped in a state of multiply encoded *virtuality*—"virtual" both in the sense of being part of an unfinished, perhaps unfinishable, social project and in the sense of being apparently condemned to exist—in effect not fact, theory not practice—at the level of the hyperreal.

In this essay I have chosen to emphasize (with perhaps irresponsibly gleeful skepticism) these critical understandings of virtuality. Even so, I hope to have suggested that virtual multiculturalisms are not just the phantasmal creations of the media and public relations industries. Nor, it should be clear, is their solitary function to provide an effective alibi for continuing discriminatory abuse at all levels of the social formation. Virtuality also plays its part, however indirectly, in emancipatory social movements; it affirms the enabling, if by no means unambivalent, role played by different media in processes of collective self-imagining—and collective action. In a purely semantic sense, the "virtuality" of multiculturalism is no longer consonant with its claims to "efficacy" (*virtuality* = *efficacy* = *archaic*) or even "virtue" (*virtual* = *virtuous* = *obsolete*); in practice, it forms the horizon against which multiculturalism can continue to be viewed as evolving "sets of discourse [and] modes of analysis"; as transformatively conceived "political identities"; and, not least, as open-ended "state policy and practices" (Brah 1996, 233).

Virtual multiculturalisms are thus future-oriented, enabling the "emerging recognition that multiculturalism [might] mean a new way of being . . . British—and perhaps also a new way of being European" (Modood 1997, 24). As Tariq Modood also asserts: "What is clear is that multiculturalism will [increasingly] challenge . . . our existing notions of culture, identity, nationality and citizenship across Europe, as peoples and states enter into political dialogues which may mark the crafting of new multicultural citizenships" (24). Multiculturalism, in this last sense, might yet help deliver Britain from its current syndrome of millennial limbo; rescuing it, perhaps, from its own "virtually revolutionary" tendencies: the excited nod to future change—once all things are considered—or the strangled cry that exclaims "almost there!" but, then again, "not quite yet!"

NOTES

1. It is no surprise, of course, to find an active "save-the-English" campaign at the millennium. Popular examples include Aslet, Strong, and, more reflectively, Paxman.

2. For brief historical overviews of multiculturalism in Britain, see Brah 1996, 227–233, and Modood 1999. For more detailed debates on issues relating to ethnic minorities in Britain and the politics of multicultural identity, see Gilroy, Hall, and Rex.

3. For varying positions on structural/institutionalized racism in contemporary Britain, see Balibar, Sivanandan, Solomos, and the essays in Cohen & Bains (eds), particularly Cohen's.

4. For examples of an uncritical acceptance of the novel as a work of multicultural fiction, see King and Marzorati. For a more sophisticated, but also in the main affirmative treatment, see Bhabha; for a more critical view, see Huggan & Wachinger.

5. For more information on the Lawrence inquiry, various websites can be consulted. Particularly useful is the website run by the Institute of Race Relations in London; also the Guardian/Observer website at www.newsunlimited.co.uk/lawrence. The Macpherson report is also available online at www.newsunlimited.co.uk/macpherson.

6. For an up-to-date critique of the collaborative mechanisms used by the government, the media, and the police to orchestrate racialized crime (in Britain and the United States), see Gabriel, chapter 5; for an earlier—also critical—study of the role of the police in controlling interracial violence in Britain, see Hall et al.

7. For an overview of both racist and anti-racist discourses in the British media, see Hartman & Husband.

8. Nor, it might be surmised, is Kay much taken with the "interstitial spaces" (Bhabha) so dear to some postcolonial theorists—the appeals to an enabling hybridity that might magically disrupt the logic of fixed (imposed) cultural identities, working to dissolve monolithic racial/ethnic categories and to outmaneuver narrowly conceived hereditary ties and collective claims. In apparent agreement with Zadie Smith—also an author of mixed race (see previous section)—Kay treats the "hybridity thesis" with as much suspicion as the cultural/biological essentialisms it seeks to replace; the daughter in *The Adoption Papers* is a heroine, in Kay's eyes, because she accepts the contradictions of her upbringing, not because she uses her "virtual" status ("almost the same, but not white" [Bhabha]) to inhabit some notional space "in-between."

9. For variations on this thesis, see the essays in Wilson & Dissanayake (eds); for more critical views, see also Ahmad and Lazarus (esp. chapter 1).

10. For varying views on the possibilities opened up by "cyber-coalitions" and "virtual alliances," see the essays in Crang, Crang, & May (eds) and Leeson (ed). For extreme positions on the liberating power of virtual reality, see Rheingold, who believes that "we are on the brink of having the power of creating any experience we desire" (Rheingold et al. 1991, 386), and Woolley, who reminds us that this power can be abusive and that the hyperreal by no means replaces or invalidates the real.

11. In France, for instance, multicultural lobbyists have positioned themselves against the state's traditionally assimilationist policies, primarily designed to create compliant national citizens equal (in theory) before French law, while in Britain, a de-

bate continues between "liberal" proponents of *multiculturalism* and "radical" advocates of a thoroughgoing *anti-racism* designed to counteract racialized inequalities in a society where "cultural difference" is recognized as being inscribed within conspicuously uneven relations of power (Brah 1996, 230; see also Bharucha 1999, 13–14). The German case is different again, hinging on incipient, if excruciatingly slow-moving, reforms of the laws governing German citizenship and on varying forms of ethnic mobilization, for example, through the formation of "multicultural associations" aimed at strengthening ties between both local and more widely dispersed ethnic communities while contesting the "second-class citizen" status often accorded to minorities within the German state (see Yalcin-Heckmann 1997).

WORKS CITED

Ahmad, Aijaz; 1995. "The Politics of Literary Postcoloniality," *Race & Class*, 36, 3: 1–20.

Anderson, Benedict; 1983. *Imagined Communities*. London: Verso.

Appadurai, Arjun; 1996. *Modernity at Large: The Cultural Dimensions of Globalization*. Minneapolis: University of Minnesota Press.

Aslet, Clive; 1997. *Anyone for England?* London: Little, Brown.

Balibar, Etienne; 1992. *The New Racism*. London: Verso.

Bhabha, Homi; 1994. *The Location of Culture*. London: Routledge.

Bharucha, Rustom; 1999. "Interculturalism and its Discriminations: Shifting the Agendas of the National, the Multicultural and the Global," *Third Text*, 46: 3–20.

Brah, Avtar; 1996. *Cartographies of Diaspora: Contesting Identities*. London: Routledge.

Cohen, P., & H. Bains (eds); 1988. *Multi-Racist Britain*. London: Macmillan Education.

Crang, M., P. Crang, & J. May (eds); 1999. *Virtual Geographies: Bodies, Spaces and Relations*. London: Routledge.

Fernandez, Maria; 1999. "Postcolonial Media Theory," *Third Text*, 47: 11–17.

Gabriel, John; 1998. *Whitewash: Racialized Politics and the Media*. London, Routledge.

Gilroy, Paul; 1987. *There Ain't No Black in the Union Jack*. London, Hutchinson.

Hall, Stuart; 1978. "Racism and Reaction," in *Five Views of Multiracial Britain*. London: Commission for Racial Equality.

Hall, S., C. Critcher, T. Jefferson, J. Clarke, & B. Roberts; 1978. *Policing the Crisis: 'Mugging,' the State, and Law and Order*. London: Macmillan.

Hartman, P., & C. Husband; 1974. *Racism and the Mass Media*. London: Davis-Poynter.

Huggan, Graham, & Tobias Wachinger; forthcoming. "Can Newness Enter the World? Salman Rushdie's *The Satanic Verses* and the Question of Multicultural Aesthetics," in *Imaginary Homelands: Multicultural Perspectives on Rushdie's Fiction*, ed. L. Glage (Trier).

Jenkins, Roy; 1966. Address given on 23 May 1966 to a meeting of the Voluntary Liaison Committees. London (National Council for Civil Liberties).

Kay, Jackie; 1991. *The Adoption Papers*. Newcastle, UK: Bloodaxe.

King, Bruce; 1996. "Thinking About Multiculturalism, Nationalism and Internationalism," in *Nationalism vs. Internationalism: (Inter-)National Dimensions of Literatures in English*, ed. W. Zach & K. Goodwin (Tubingen), 15–21.

Kureishi, Hanif; 1990. *The Buddha of Suburbia.* London.

Lazarus, Neil; 1999. *Nationalism and Cultural Practice in the Postcolonial World.* Cambridge, UK: Cambridge University Press.

Leeson, H. (ed); 1996. *Clicking In: Hot Links to a Digital Culture.* Seattle: Bay Press.

Leigh, Mike; 1996. *Secrets & Lies.* London: Faber.

Macpherson, Sir William; 1999. "The Stephen Lawrence Inquiry: Report of an Inquiry by Sir William Macpherson of Cluny" (CM4262-1/2). London: Stationary Office.

Marzorati, Gerald; 1989. "Fiction's Embattled Infidel," *New York Times Magazine,* 29 January: 100.

Modood, Tariq; 1999. "British Multiculturalism." Online source. www.sscnet.ucla.edu/soc/groups/ccsa/modood.htm.

Modood, Tariq; 1997. "Introduction: The Politics of Multiculturalism in the New Europe," in *The Politics of Multiculturalism in the New Europe,* ed. T. Modood & P. Werbner (London), 1–25.

Modood, T. & P. Werbner (eds); 1997. *The Politics of Multiculturalism in the New Europe.* London: Zed Books.

Nairn, Tom; 2000. *After Britain: New Labour and the Return of Scotland.* London: Granta Books.

Nairn, Tom; 1990 [1977]. *The Break-Up of Britain.* London, NLB.

Paxman, Jeremy; 1998. *The English: A Portrait of a People.* London: Penguin.

Rex, John; 1995. *The Concept of a Multi-Cultural Society.* Occasional Papers in Ethnic Relations No. 3.: Centre for Research in Ethnic Relations, University of Warwick.

Rheingold, Howard; 1993. *The Virtual Community: Homesteading on the Electronic Frontier.* Reading, MA: MIT Press.

Rheingold, Howard, et al.; 1991. *Virtual Reality.* London: Summit Books.

Rushdie, Salman; 1981. *Midnight's Children.* London: Cape.

Rushdie, Salman; 1988. *The Satanic Verses.* New York: Viking.

Rushdie, Salman; 1991. *Imaginary Homelands: Essays 1981–1991.* London: Granta Books.

Samad, Yunas; 1997. "The Plural Guises of Multiculturalism: Conceptualising a Fragmented Paradigm," in *The Politics of Multiculturalism in the New Europe,* ed. T. Modood & P. Werbner (London), 240–260.

Shohat, Ella, & Robert Stam; 1995. *Unthinking Eurocentrism: Multiculturalism and the Media.* London: Routledge.

Shohat, Ella, & Robert Stam; 1996. "From the Imperial Family to the Transnational Imaginary: Media Spectatorship in the Age of Globalization," in *Global/Local: Cultural Production and the Transnational Imaginary,* ed. R. Wilson & W. Dissanayake (Durham, NC), 145–172.

Sivanandan A.; 1976. *Race, Class and the State: The Black Experience in Britain.* London: Institute of Race Relations.

Sivanandan, A., et al.; 1999. "Evidence from the Institute of Race Relations to the Lawrence Inquiry," *Race & Class,* 40, 4: 65–74.

Smith, Zadie; 2000. *White Teeth.* London: Penguin.

Solomos, John; 1993 [1989]. *Race and Racism in Contemporary Britain.* Basingstoke: Macmillan Education.

Strong, Roy; 1990. *Lost Treasures of Britain.* London: Viking.

Triseliotis, John, Joan Shireman, & Marion Hundleby; 1997. *Adoption: Theory, Policy and Practice*. London: Cassell.

Turkle, Sherry; 1996. "Rethinking Identity through Virtual Community," in *Clicking In: Hot Links to a Digital Culture*, ed. H. Leeson (Seattle: Bay Press).

Vaid, Urvashi; 1995. *Virtual Equality: The Mainstreaming of Gay and Lesbian Liberation*. New York: Anchor Books.

Wilson, R., & W. Dissanayake (eds); 1996. *Global/Local: Cultural Production and the Transnational Imaginary*. Durham, NC: Duke University Press.

Wintour, Patrick; 2000. "Labour tries to reclaim the flag," *The Guardian*, 28 March: 12.

Woolley, Benjamin; 1992. *Virtual Worlds: A Journey in Hype and Hyperreality*. Oxford, UK: Blakwell.

Yalcin-Heckmann, Lale; 1997. "The Perils of Ethnic Associational Life in Europe: Turkish Migrants in Germany and France," in *The Politics of Multiculturalism in the New Europe*, ed. T. Modood & P. Werbner (London: Zed Books), 95–110.

5

One Bangle Does Not Jingle: Cultures, Literatures, and Migration in a Globalizing World

Mineke Schipper

We live in an age when all continents are visibly incorporating the same fundamental economic ingredients as well as numerous common cultural features (due to the mass media and electronic culture). Tomlinson (1996: 22–23) cogently defines cultural globalization as "the particular effects which the general social processes of time-space compression and distanciation have on that realm of practices and experience in which people socially construct meaning."

The concept of "globalization" suggests an active process of more or less *anonymous* conquest and unification of the global space. But who is globalizing and who is globalized, and to what effect? At a recent small globalization conference in Tanzania one of the local participants gave his own definition of what it means: globalization is like medicine: if you take too little it does not work; if you take too much, you'll die. And another one put it more violently: globalization is like rape: since nothing can be done against it, we should perhaps just lean back and enjoy it. If this is the situation, will the ongoing global unification process destroy our diversities? Those who fear uniformity worry about whether people's identities are threatened and emphasize the importance of differences. Culture has always been the way members of society create meaning; but existing meanings, especially dominant meanings, also create people and determine behavior of men and women as members of their society through ongoing flows of interactions. Globalization interacts negatively and positively with lived local realities, with people's search for cultural identity as related to their roots as well as their search for integration and assimilation.

A number of human similarities, and possibly some universals, however, are hardly the result of contemporary globalization effects. In other words, in spite of all constructed dichotomies, there are similarities shared by humans, since all peoples belong to humankind. What we have in common has mainly to do with very early common basic human drives such as food, shelter, safety, and procreation. Such primary drives and needs determine behavior and are determined by innate representations. At the level of social structures, institutions, and culture, these primary drives are articulated in order to secure continuity (and to cope with change, if need be) in specific geographical, historical, and socio-cultural contexts. Still, the primary drives and needs, and the anatomy and physiology of the human body, underlie human social, cultural, and linguistic universals. How else would we be able to communicate across cultures at all?

In the context of globalization, one should ask: who is migrating, and what are the underlying reasons for migration? The African writer Sembène Ousmane told me a few years ago: We of my generation may still be so foolish as to stay in the countries of our birth, but, believe me, I know for sure that in my country, Senegal, the whole younger generation desperately wants to leave by all possible means and come to Europe, and they are all trying to prepare their departure in one way or another.

In the twenty-first century the literatures of Europe reflect the effects of migration from the South to the North. It is evident that literature in the West has profited from the immigration of writers and scholars coming from other parts of the world. However, a question rarely asked is what this migration flow of intellectuals and writers and artists means in their respective home countries and cultures. In my opinion, this and related questions should be at the center of the debate on migrant cartographies: which part of the world is culturally enriched and which part is impoverished by the direction most cultural travelers in today's world take?

As a result of migration, new data, new insights, and new knowledge have led to new discussions and ideas, particularly in the human sciences. Research in Africa, for example, has indeed transformed understandings and the disciplines, as emphasized by Bates, Mudimbe, and O'Barr in *Africa and the Disciplines* (1993). This does not mean, however, that the United States, Europe, and Africa have profited equally from these new data and insights.

Biodun Jeyifo (1990: 46) is troubled that in the field of research, the shift has been away from the African continent and the African universities. The agenda of Africanists in the West were little concerned with the bridging of the knowledge gap between Africa and the West in the academic field. Their agenda, in Jeyifo's words, "consists primarily of winning respectability and legitimacy for the discipline of African literary study *in the developed countries*" (44). This shift in location underlines "the problematic continuous production and reproduction of Africa's marginalization from the centers of economic and discursive power" (46). Evidently, the scientific and political implications of contemporary postcolonial relations in the North and in the South are far from similar, as Paulin Hountondji (1990, 1992) states in several publications on the matter. In a commentary with the eloquent title "Scientific Dependence in Africa Today" (1990), he described this dependence history from within. The international labor division has made scientific invention and development the monopoly of the North, while the contribution of the South is restricted to the importation and the application of what others have found. Most students in African universities, according to Hountondji, share "the feeling that, whatever their special fields might be, everything that matters for them is located or taking place elsewhere." Elsewhere, outside Africa that is, methodologies and theories, paradigms for the "really scientific," are invented. Africans have the choice between staying at home—which means accepting the limited local knowledge situation in which researchers feel trapped—and moving to the West. There are almost no possibilities for exchange between African scholars in Africa amongst themselves or with colleagues from other Third World countries. No wonder that an enormous brain drain to the West has taken place, and Hountondji outlines the colonial history of this situation: the theoretical emptiness of colonial science is a side effect of economic domination and forced integration in the world of the capitalist market, a peripherization of the Third World economy (6, 9).

Totally different circumstances are relevant depending on whether a researcher from the North goes to the South or the other way around. The European or American going to the "Third World" is not in search of science but of scientific "raw materials"; in Africa he or she is not in search of paradigms, of theoretical and methodological models, but is in search of new information and facts to enrich his or her own paradigms. The comparison with the proverbial colonial economic greed for African "raw material" is obvious.

It is indeed true, as Bates, Mudimbe, and O'Barr (1993) have stated, that much contemporary knowledge has resulted from Northern scientific investigations in the South. This knowledge has contributed to existing disciplines or has given rise to new ones, such as anthropology. Much of this knowledge went, so to speak, behind Africa's back; it escaped the Third World in general, but it has been enriching indeed for Europe and America. It is knowledge that has systematically been returned from Africa, "repatriated, capitalized, accumulated in the center of the system," in Hountondji's words (1992: 344–346). In this system, Africa seems no more than a detour to be made on the scientific highway leading to the academic insiders' bulwark of knowledge. In the meantime, what is happening to traditional knowledge and skills? In the best case, these continue to exist next to the new knowledge; in the worst, they are wiped out from the collective memory. Here the critical question asked in Kane's novel *L'aventure ambiguë* is crucial: ". . . what you learn, does that compensate for what you forget?" (49).

SIMILARITIES

Those looking for differences will find only differences in their research, and those looking for similarities will certainly find similarities. I'd like to articulate both similarities and differences in this context. On the one hand, it is important to be aware of human similarities, globally speaking, but also as far as Europe itself is concerned: we may tend to aim at differences between the works of travelers coming to Europe and those who "were always there." We tend to forget that as human creatures we certainly have things in common: we are all earthlings; we all have the same body shape; we all are products of genetic, cultural, and societal forces that seem to provoke similar reactions. All peoples breathe, have language, and are sexually active. Anatomical and physiological features have been mostly neglected in anthropological studies, although, as we said earlier, they do underlie social and cultural structures and institutions in society. Culture is transmitted horizontally and vertically between individuals and collectivities, and to a great extent, culture is much less created by individuals than it is imposed upon them (Brown 1991: 40).

We can try to classify certain human phenomena, even when the contents profoundly differ. Examples are cooking, courtship, etiquette, funeral rites, fire making, incest taboos, property rights, numerals, and so forth. In a number of cases, though, there are also universals of content, with universal details, for example, general similarities across the world in the emotions people express during bereavement, such as shortening and easing bereavement by final funeral rites (Levinson and Malone 1980: 297).

People typify the world about them in a variety of words, but there are some basic universal conceptions in the semantic components beneath the cultural varieties in vocabulary, as Goldschmidt (quoted in Brown 1991: 76) argues: "Underlying the diversity of human institutions is a universal set of problems or functions that must be solved or discharged in all societies [and] these functions provide a common framework for the analysis of all societies." As far as the research on the relations between men and women in society is concerned, for example, most comparative studies conclude that "men exercise more power, have more status and enjoy more freedom" (Levinson and Malone 1980: 267).

Some scholars have distinguished universals "of essence" and "of accident." According to Brown, "essence" refers to universals "that could not be eliminated except by unnatural interventions" (e.g., by genetic engineering), "examples of essences being biological features of the species." In his opinion, "much of the debate concerning male and female differences turns around the issue of whether certain of the universal differences are essential or accidental."

Our world is not static; universals may change or disappear, and over time new universals have come into being: the use of plastic containers, phosphorus matches, and manufactured clothing are almost universal by now, and Coca-Cola and McDonald's do not (alas for the romance of anthropology) seem far behind (50). Old universals do not necessarily have eternal life, and numerous new universals, not only material ones, but also ideas, representations, and artistic devices, will spread around the globe in the years ahead, affecting people's earlier perspectives on humanity and the universe. Such new universals spread today, often thanks to globalization.

DIFFERENCES

While the academy may declare all dichotomies dead in today's world, there is undeniably at least one crucial dichotomy that subsists among humans in the contemporary world, although it is not a problematic issue in the European context. Still, what should be far more taken into account in the academy, since it influences research results all the time, is the continuous reality of the enormous information gap and inequality in access to material facilities between the rich and the poor of our world. Globally speaking, there is a huge imbalance in available scholars and available data, in library access, in access to means of communication and information technology, and in the quantitative representation of existing cultural, regional, and gender diversities worldwide.

One human universal is the mechanism of oppositions and hierarchies people have to establish continuously in their perspective on the world. It is important, for example, to be aware of the fact that not only in the West, but in all cultural and social contexts, in all times and places, people constantly develop views of themselves and of those considered to be others; this is how humans think and behave. Juxtaposed to our views of ourselves and of others, there are others' views of themselves and of us—it is as simple as that. However, people's demand for alternative perspectives outside their own center tends not to be particularly intense in the camp of most "selves."

In the last quarter of the 20th century, the academic debate in the humanities has mostly been dominated by emphasis on difference rather than on what people share: difference between "us" and "them," difference in race, class, ethnicity, culture, nation, continent, and so forth. Migration then became a factor of such importance in the Western world of culture and literature, and solutions have been sought to override the emphasis on constructed dichotomies. They were found in "mixture" concepts, such as creolization or hybridity, as the result of mutual influence and migration, with emphasis on the West: travelers from the West going to other parts of the world and travelers from other parts of the world going to the West. Such "solutions" have been invented mainly by scholars located in the West as a result of the multinational Otherness industry that had been developed in this part of the world. Again, the academic attention focused on the relations of the West to the Rest, the old colonial relations of the metropolitan center to its margins.

The centrality of the role of the West in most research has to do with its economic domination of people's destinies, food or famine, war or peace, and migration. Most migrant writers develop after arrival strong connections with their new environment. They have found a much more comfortable place to live than in their countries of origin. This one-way migration of a relatively small intellectual elite will continue as long as the West is economically more prosperous than other parts of the world.

What is happening in migrant literature in Europe in our new century? In Elleke Boehmer's definition, this literature represents a "geographic, cultural and political retreat by writers from the . . . post-colonial world back to the old metropolis," with literatures as one of the results of that retreat (Boehmer 1995: 237).

From the writers' home countries voices can be heard that blame migrant writers and academics for being culturally coquettish: using their cultural background to entertain readers in the West for exotic or economically attractive reasons, without being loyal to the brothers and sisters who stayed at home. On the other hand, writers who stay in their own cultures and focus on the national local context in their work draw little attention from readers and critics in the Western world.

The key question is: what is the difference between writers who have migrated and those who stayed? Did the migrant writers cut off the cultural umbilical cord with their cultures of origin, or has culture become an easily transportable commodity? To what extent do they continue to relate to their original cultures for reasons of loyalty and commitment? And what about the second or third generation, those who were born from migrant parents? Is their position very different? Are they less connected to the country of origin of their parents? Or do they reinvent the cultures of their ancestors to satisfy their own needs or their readers' needs? This has happened, for example, in African-American culture where an Africa has been invented that appears completely alien to Africans in Africa.

Some try to relate by all means to the place where their ancestors lived, for reasons ranging from a passionate search for a lost identity to profitable opportunism. To what extent are their books read in their countries of origin? And if they are read, what is the difference in critical reactions in both parts of the world? Very little is known so far about the varying reception of many of those texts. A case in point is the way the Nigerian writer Ben Okri, living in England, linked his work to that of predecessors in his own transcultural context of origin, such as D. O. Fagunwa and Amos Tutuola, who had transcribed oral Yoruba stories into written texts, in Yoruba and in English, respectively, each in their own personal way. Ben Okri, on the basis of and inspired by oral and writing predecessors of various origins in his own country of birth, and inspired by earlier booming magical realism in Latin America, developed this earlier line of writing in new directions. The most interesting difference between these authors is that Tutuola still respected the old dichotomy between human settlement and forest, whereas Okri made this dichotomy problematic by introducing ghosts and spirits and other characters—belonging to their own separate space in those earlier Yoruba stories—to the "real world" of his fiction. They have become part of the whole scene of life, thanks to the mosaic of esoteric events taking place in the context of "everyday reality." The urban location of his realistic characters in his fictional work thus belongs to a wider intercontinental magical realistic tradition. And Okri makes use of a distancing postmodern irony, which made no sense in the world of Fagunwa and Tutuola. Still, Okri's work would not have been possible without those earlier oral and written West African cultural traditions, and cannot be understood without taking into account his predecessors in his Nigerian background.

In their comments on migrant literature, Western literary critics and academics often take the position that migrant writers are a "special category." In the Netherlands, we have seen this in the Week of the Book 2001, dedicated to "Writing between Cultures," with attention from the media concentrated on those writers who are considered as originating from "other" parts of the world. Although there was indeed attention paid to writers with origins from outside Europe, the message was clearly circular: "they" are different; therefore they have to be dealt with differently—which leads directly to paternalist praise and shoulder patting. One might suspiciously wonder whether this is a way to prevent such writers from "crossing over" to the category of the "real" national or international Western literature canon?

There are also those critics who argue that there should be no such category as migrant writers or migrant literature. They seem to believe in a human universal called "literary quality," a quality that can be found in texts from all cultures and that is not dependent on elements outside the text such as autochthony or allochthony. There are writers and failures, their argument goes: if they are good writers we'll pay attention to them and if they write rubbish we'll ignore them. It is exclusively a matter of quality. Such critics may be harsh in their condemnation of what is in their eyes an obvious lack of quality.

The question then is about what far too often is taken for granted: who decides what quality is? To what extent is the application of the label of quality subconsciously mixed up with the critic's biased perspective on what is considered to be real literature? Those who suggest that they know for sure what quality is may be so myopically concentrated on cultivating and weeding their own little garden that they completely ignore what is growing and blooming in gardens and fields outside the hedge enclosing their own little corner of the world.

My point is that there is much cultural knowledge critics and academics are not "naturally" aware of. We are all condemned to necessarily limited knowledge, despite our globalizing world. We therefore should not only try to be as erudite as possible, but at the same time also cultivate our awareness of the relativity of our own position and perspective.

INTERCULTURAL COOPERATION

In order to define where we want to go, globally speaking, we first of all have to be aware of the restricting legacies of our human socio-cultural past. This certainly holds for research in the field of migrant cartographies. I strongly recommend that those working in departments of European languages and interested in the field of "New Literatures" cooperate intensively with specialists in the fields of the cultures, traditions, and literatures of origin of the migrant writers concerned. Otherwise we may tend to neglect or misinterpret traditions, themes, or devices that seem original and "exotic" to Western eyes, but are in reality nothing new to (or perhaps, on the contrary, totally foreign to) the ancestral traditions of these writers. Lack of knowledge routinely leads to serious lack of insight and very erroneous conclusions.

In a world of globalization and migration, genuine intercultural cooperation is therefore inevitable. We cannot know everything and need to be aware of our limits. This is particularly true for those who are the posterity of a history of colonial expansion and of a Europe that ruled the waves. Humility is a rather underdeveloped quality in the West, as Chinua Achebe warned a long time ago. In spite of human universals and globalization, cultures are not accessible to outsiders without serious study. Why are critics being so sure that they really understand the references to cultural contexts and traditions they have never studied? Migrant writers write in a variety of ways and in this respect they do not differ from other writers. However, they often refer insistently to their cultures of origin. If we wish to do justice to those references, we need solid knowledge regarding those cultural contexts. Postcolonial criticism does not seem to be well equipped to understand the underlying cultural legacies and the specific subtlety of the texts concerned.

We have to acknowledge our profound mutual lack of cultural knowledge before these gaps can be bridged. The approach from a cosmopolitan perspective is one thing. It is practiced, largely, in the Western academy and is mainly limited to texts and criticism in European languages. In this approach the cultural dimensions of the motherlands of origin tend to be neglected, ignored, or exoticized. We should carefully take into account that a history which has brought cultures together is strongly connected to cultural histories with different origins and languages. The contexts and literary (oral as well as written) traditions of those unique histories of origin deserve as much attention as the cultures of destination and the postcolonial perceptions developed in the West. In order to do justice to the new literatures in Europe, more in-depth research is needed to reveal the various real-world cultural contexts that have inspired and contributed to the birth of those new literatures. Neither approach, the cosmopolitan approach from the West or the specialized in-depth approach related to the cultures of origin, can do without the other. Specialized knowledge, and interdisciplinary and intercultural cooperation, are indispensable. As the Fulfulde in West Africa say in their great wisdom: "One bangle does not jingle." This common-sense metaphysics is more than rhetoric; it is applicable to cross-cultural perspectives on new European literatures: the bangles of the cultures and literatures of origin and of destination all contribute to the new ensemble created in a globalizing and globalized Europe in the twenty-first century. The global imbalance in access to data and research (and not only on the subject of migrant cartography) risks the inescapable biasing of research projects and hence results across the humanities. This is one of the reasons to plead for a better exchange and distribution of cultural and scientific knowledge. The various bangles need both to be heard in and to tune to the new intercultural dialogues about the emerging cultural processes and realities of our time and world.

WORKS CITED

Boehmer, Elleke, *Colonial and Postcolonial Literature*, Oxford, UK: Oxford University Press, 1995.

Brown, Donald E., *Human Universals*, New York: McGraw-Hill, 1991.

Hountondji, Paulin. "Scientific Dependence in Africa Today." *Research in African Literatures* 21.3 (1990): 5–15.

Hountondji, Paulin. "Daily Life in Black Africa." In *The Surreptitious Speech: Présence Africaine and the Politics of Otherness 1947–1987*. Ed. V. Y. Mudimbe.

Jeyifo, Biodun. "The Nature of Things: Arrested Decolonization and Critical Theory." *Research in African Literatures* 21.1 (1990): 33–46.

Levinson, David, and Martin J. Malone, *Toward Explaining Human Culture*, New Haven, CT: HRAF Press, 1980.

Tomlinson, J. "Cultural Globalization: Placing and Displacing the West." *The European Journal of Development Research* 8.2 (December 1996): 22–35.

II

WRITING ACROSS THE BORDERS: NEW LITERATURES IN EUROPE

6

Stranger in a Strange Land: Jamal Mahjoub's *The Carrier*

Theo D'haen

In *Imperial Eyes: Travel Writing and Transculturation* (1992), Mary Louise Pratt calls "autoethnographic expressions" those "instances in which colonized subjects undertake to represent themselves in ways that engage with the colonizer's own terms . . . if ethnographic texts are a means by which Europeans represent to themselves their (usually subjugated) others, autoethnographic texts are those the others construct in response to or in dialogue with those metropolitan representations." Pratt stresses that "autoethnography involves partial collaboration with and appropriation of the idioms of the conqueror . . . often . . . the idioms appropriated and transformed are those of travel and exploration writing, merged or infiltrated to varying degrees with indigenous modes" (Pratt 7).

The reasons for privileging travel writing in "autoethnography" are clear. As Pratt observes, "while the imperial metropolis tends to understand itself as determining the periphery (in the emanating flow of the civilizing mission or the cash flow of development, for example), it habitually blinds itself to the ways in which the periphery determines the metropolis—beginning, perhaps, with the latter's obsessive need to present and re-present its peripheries and its others continually to itself . . . travel writing, among other institutions, is heavily organized in the service of that imperative . . . so, one might add, is much of European literary history" (Pratt 6). Where these latter two come together is in those classics of European literature that heavily invest in "writing travel," particularly to the colonies, or to other spaces in the non-European world. In fact, it is not difficult to see that these works owe their canonical status precisely to the conjunction between their own narrative economy and that of their world. Of course classic English-language examples include William Shakespeare's *The Tempest* (1611), Daniel Defoe's *Robinson Crusoe* (1719), Rudyard Kipling's *Kim* (1901), Joseph Conrad's *Heart of Darkness* (1902), and E. M. Forster's *A Passage to India* (1924).

In the form of an Elizabethan drama mixing Italian court-intrigue and magic, *The Tempest* transposes England's growing involvement with the New World onto an imaginary island in the Mediterranean, and in the guise of the "good ruler" Prospero justifies the white man's dispossessing native Caliban from what by right should be his. In one of the first examples of the literary genre traditionally linked to the rise of the middle classes, the novel, *Robinson Crusoe*, as the exclusive first-person narrator of his own tale of island conquest and the self-making of a businessman, speaks into existence both the capitalism and imperialism of the English bourgeoisie. Through its eponymous protagonist, Kipling's third-person narrative *Kim* focalizes Britain's Indian empire with the gaze of the surveyor, the archaeologist, the anthropologist, the military man, and the boy adventurer all rolled into one. In *Heart of Darkness*, Marlow's tale of King Leopold's Congo via modernist *mise-en-abîme* is made to turn on both the British Empire and European civilization from the time of the Romans onward. Finally, in *A Passage to India* the doubts and questions raised by Forster's narrative reflect the impossibility of his white visitors to India to really connect with the land or its people, and the novel ends with an admission of the necessary failure of all such attempts, however well-meant. All these works explicitly capture their periods' and societies' "set" toward Europe's "Others," and implicitly also toward its "Self." As such, they mark the various stages of what over the last few decades we increasingly have come to call "modernity."

For Jürgen Habermas (1990), modernity results from the cross-pollination of the European voyages of discovery, the Renaissance, and the Reformation as of—roughly speaking—1500. Specific to modernity—as different from the Middle Ages—are a reliance on science and scientific method, and a belief in history as the record of progress, leading to a future-oriented way of thinking. With the gradual rise of Europe's military and economic power as evidenced most specifically in Western European, and ultimately English, colonial expansion, it is these same tenets that ever more strongly come to be seen as marking not only the difference between Europe and the rest of the world, but also as legitimating Europe's domination of the world. In *Orientalism* (1978) Edward Said, taking his cue from Michel Foucault, argues that Western scholarship about the Orient significantly contributed toward this legitimizing process. Specifically, it increasingly recast the Orient, and particularly the world of Islam, as devoid of—or as lagging behind in—the features of modernity, and therefore as inferior to the West. In the process, Western scholarship disqualified all non-Western forms of knowledge, reducing them to superstition, myth, legend, and the like. Eventually, the only discourse about the non-Western world to carry any real validity came to be that of the West.

In *Culture and Imperialism* (1993) Said extends the argument to literature, and especially fiction. Because they "are a means by which Europeans represent to themselves their (usually subjugated) others," *The Tempest, Robinson Crusoe, Heart of Darkness, Kim,* and *A Passage to India* can be said to be "ethnographic texts" in the sense meant by Pratt. In fact, the narrative structure of these texts clearly parallels the cultural bias of Western scholarship and specifically Western ethnography, as the scholarly or scientific discipline entrusted with "describing" the West's "Others." In each of these texts, it is only Europeans that "speak": literally so, as character on stage (Prospero in *The Tempest*), as I-narrator (*Robinson Crusoe*), as I-narrator refracted through another I-narrator (Marlow in *Heart of Darkness*), or, like Kim and the various characters in *A Passage to India*, as focalizers in a third-person narrative. Even if in the latter novel focalization can occasionally be said to occur through Indian characters, the overall view at the end remains that of the third-person narrator—unmistakably a "white" man. When Caliban, early on in *The Tempest*, tries to tell his own story, he is immediately silenced by Prospero, who then proceeds to "over-write" Caliban's native "history" with the white man's version—and, needless to say, Prospero carries the day in the play.

For Europe's "Others," then—Caliban, Friday, Conrad's Africans, Kipling's and Forster's Indians—what Simon Gikandi claims in his *Writing in Limbo: Modernism and Caribbean Literature* (1992) undeniably holds true: "entry into the European terrain of the modern has often demanded that the colonized peoples be denied their subjectivity, language, and history" (Gikandi 2), or what he calls "the central categories of European modernity" (Gikandi 4). In their struggle to recover these things, Gikandi argues, "Caribbean writers, in response to their historical marginalization, have evolved a discourse of alterity which is predicated on a deliberate act of self-displacement from the hegemonic culture and its central tenets" (Gikandi 19–20), particularly "the hegemonic European idea of the modern as an affect of Western reason and history" (Gikandi 4). One way to practice such a "deliberate act of self-displacement" is to turn those classics of the West upholding "the hegemonic culture and its central tenets" against themselves, re-writing them from Europe's "Other's" point of view, thus "giving voice" to that "Other." This, I would argue, is the particularly "literary" form that the "partial collaboration with and appropriation of the idiom of the conqueror" Pratt sees as constitutive of "autoethnography" takes in postcolonial fiction. Elsewhere, I have illustrated this point by way of rewritings of *The Tempest, Robinson Crusoe, Jane Eyre, Wuthering Heights,* and *Heart of Darkness* (D'haen 1997, 1998, 2000a, and 2000b). With regard to Islam, I have done so most specifically in relation to *In an Antique Land*

(1992) by the Indian author Amitav Gosh as a rewriting of P. B. Shelley's "Ozymandias" (D'haen 2002).

Here, I would like to concentrate on Jamal Mahjoub's *The Carrier* (1998). This novel autoethnographically represents Europe's "Others" in the guise of both the present-day Hassan, a Danish scholar of Arab origins, and his seventeenth-century subject of research (and perhaps imagination), a Turkish-Moorish traveler called Rashid al-Kenzy. At the same time, by way of Rashid al-Kenzy's voyage to Denmark, and through Hassan's experiences as a "migrant" scholar in the same country, *The Carrier* also "ethnographically" represents to us Europe as seen by its "Others," upending most clichés the West holds with regard to itself as well as to Islam.

In an epilogue to *The Carrier*, the third-person narrator applies the age-old trick of *mise-en-abîme* to drive his message home to the reader. The protagonist—or perhaps better: one of the two protagonists—of the novel for the first time in his life looks through a telescope, an instrument he has been in search of for some time, a search that not only determines his life but also much of the plot of the novel. Here is how it goes:

> With this one eye, gaze out upon the world. Stretching out across the turbulent drumming of restless waves, out over the wax-green ocean towards the simple, perfect brush strokes of the horizon which remains, as ever, out of reach. Towards the very ends of the earth, and beyond. The hollow tubular instrument bringing what is distant near. A gleaming conduit that can reach out, forwards into the distance and the future, and backwards into the past.
>
> The instrument in question is deceptively simple; a brass casing open at either end into which hard droplets of glass are squeezed. The light enters through the glass, bending as it does so—air and glass being so related—and passes, thus transformed, into the long brass tube of time. The rays are collected like so many threads and sewn together again, much like in the telling of a tale. What seems at first sight far thus becomes near. Time is hurled out at the void and the distant extinguished stars. The past reaches out and for a brief, fleeting moment the present is faintly illuminated. (Mahjoub 276)

This is exactly what happens in the novel's tale: a present-day scholar, attached to a Copenhagen museum, is sent out to Jutland to examine some seventeenth-century finds that the local excavators do not know what to do with. The scholar is chosen because he is of Arab origins, as is suggested by his name, "Hassan," and because a brass box found next to a seventeenth-century burial is clearly Arab in origin too. We never learn very much about the background of Hassan, but from clues spread throughout the novel it is clear that he is an immigrant to Denmark, though he has lived there for a long time now, is married to a Danish wife, and is the father of a child. His Danish seems to be perfect, though when pressed as to his origins he becomes nervous and slips occasionally. During the three weeks or so Hassan spends at the excavation site, studying the brass box and its contents, a brief telephone conversation he has with his wife hints at marital troubles. His wife explicitly tells him he has to decide whether he wants to stay with her or leave, presumably with or for some other woman.

The brass box, and its contents—some sodden and badly mauled documents—set Hassan to speculating about the life of the man to whom these artifacts once belonged: Rashid al-Kenzy, a late sixteenth–early seventeenth-century Arab or Turkish traveler to Jutland. It is never quite clear whether the tale of Rashid al-Kenzy, which takes up by far the larger part of the novel, is actually what Hassan reconstructs it to be, or perhaps better: imagines it to be, on the basis of the scant data he has, or whether what we read is the actual, "real" tale of Rashid as told by the same third-person narrator also telling us the story of Hassan. In other words, there is some hesitation as to whether what we have here are two interwoven and interlocking tales told by the same narrator, or whether we are facing a frame-tale construction whereby a third-person narrator tells us the story of Hassan, and Hassan tells us the story of Rashid al-Kenzy. There is a lot to be said for the latter formula, because then we could read what happens to Rashid as a direct projection of Hassan's perception of his own situation. Even if we opt for the less intimate connection between the two stories, though, the reciprocal illumination they provide still holds true.

What is at stake in *The Carrier* is obviously the relationship between East and West, between Christianity, or Europe, and Islam. This is clearest in the story of Rashid al-Kenzy, situated in 1609 and shortly thereafter, that is to say in the beginning of the seventeenth century. This is the time when Europe by all accounts—whether pro-Western as in David Landes's *Wealth and Poverty of Nations* (1998), or anti-Western as in André Gunder Frank's *ReOrient: Global Economy in the Asian Age* (1998)—starts to decisively pull ahead of the rest of the world, and particularly of Islam, in terms of military, economic, and political power, even if throughout the seventeenth century the Ottoman Empire would continue to pose a threat to Europe's southeastern flank. The reasons for Europe's growing hegemony are customarily sought in changes in attitude brought about by the Renaissance and the Reformation, and by advances in science, themselves at least in part enabled by these same changes in attitude. These advances bore fruit first, and perhaps most spectacularly, in the voyages of discovery that opened the world to European domination. Its openness toward progress, then, in the eyes of scholars such as David Landes, explains the success of Europe, and particularly northwestern Europe, under modernity. The rest of the world, in comparison, succumbs because of its religious intolerance and its cultural and scientific inertia.

The Carrier upends this stereotypical view. In general, Islam is shown to be more tolerant than "the West" toward converts, but also toward the descendants of the Jews expelled from the Spanish peninsula, a number of whom are described as living in Algiers, the place where the novel starts and whence Rashid al-Kenzy sets out on his mission to obtain the "Dutch optical instrument" we know as a telescope. This religious tolerance is particularly true of the civil authorities of the then guardian power of Islam's holy places: the Turkish or Ottoman Empire. The Danish authorities, on the other hand, both clerical and civil, show themselves far from tolerant. They, like the Danish commoners of the village where Rashid al-Kenzy eventually ends up in the service of the nobleman Verner Heinesen, associate Islam, and "the Turk" in general, with the devil. This association is not only fueled by the fact that Rashid is not only a Moor in the technical sense of the word, that is, originating from North Africa, having been born in Aleppo in present-day Libya and having lived in Algiers, but also by color, being dark brown, his mother having been a slave girl from Nubia. Here again, that is to say in terms of race, Islam is depicted as far more ecumenical than Christianity. In other words, it is the Ottoman Empire and Islam that are depicted as multicultural *avant la lettre*, whereas Christianity is branded as narrowly puritan in matters religious and racial. Or, put differently again, under seventeenth-century Islam religious zealotry, when it appears, is incidental, whereas under seventeenth-century Christianity it is official policy.

The same thing holds for science and its advances. Early seventeenth-century Denmark is depicted as obscurantist, stifling scientific research such as that conducted by the renowned astronomer Tycho Brahe, eventually forcing him into exile. When Verner Heinesen, an erstwhile pupil of Brahe, after an interval of some years, and using his own considerable fortune, wants to continue Brahe's work, he is effectively prevented from doing so by Danish clerical and civic authorities. Knowledge is branded as of the devil, especially when it goes against the teachings of the established church. Heinesen's efforts receive the definitive deathblow when it becomes known that he harbors a "Turk"—Rashid al-Kenzy. Ironically, Heinesen until that moment has only used Rashid as a source of dumb labor, as an extra hand to help build the observatory that is to house a telescope he has ordered from Holland. It is when trying to prove to the authorities that Rashid is an ignorant sailor, and not the sorcerer he is made out to be by clerical authorities, that Heinesen catches on to the fact that Rashid is as able a scholar and astronomer as himself. In truth, Rashid may well know more than Heinesen, trained as the former is in the best of Islamic science, itself the descendant of the wisdom of the Egyptians, the Persians, the Greeks, the Romans, the Indians, and so on. Rashid, though dumb in the eyes of the Danes because he does not speak their language, is actually a master of most of the languages in which during previous millennia worthwhile knowledge has been accumulated and encoded. The only knowledge he is ignorant of is that garnered in Europe since the onset of modernity, that is to say since roughly 1500. Yet he is very willing to learn. In fact, if there is one thing that distinguishes

Rashid throughout his life it is his insatiable desire for learning, regardless of whether this is of Islamic or any other origin. Moreover, the voyage upon which he sets out—admittedly, under duress, as it is either this or execution in the dungeons of the Dey of Algiers—bears all the signs of the typical European voyage of discovery, the only difference being that the object of "discovery" here is Europe itself. Here again, then, the stereotypical opposition of the West versus the rest breaks down.

At the same time, *The Carrier* does away with some other stereotyping, both Eastern and Western. From the various women that appear in those chapters dealing with Rashid while still in the Ottoman Empire, we receive the impression that under Islam women are deemed incompetent in matters intellectual. At first, Rashid is confirmed in this conviction also with regard to Western women, and in particular by the women he encounters in Denmark. However, just as Heinesen realizes with a start that the "Turk" he has hitherto used as a dumb beast of burden is in fact a trained scholar, so Rashid is shocked to find out Heinesen's sister Sigrid is in fact the better scholar. It is she who reveals to Rashid how European science has evolved since 1500, and how it has found solutions to problems Rashid is already familiar with from his own studies. That such women are not necessarily much appreciated in the West either, though, is proven when the commoners accuse Sigrid of being a witch and of probably carrying the devil's, that is, Rashid's, child. Though the commoners are wrong, and there never develops any such thing as physical love between Sigrid and Rashid, it is clear that in the mind they are indeed attracted to each other. If anything, they are complementary. Significantly, the vocabulary in which Rashid's recognition of this complementarity is couched is that of the cartographer: "she was looking at him, and it was though as in that instant in which she looked up, that he came into being . . . a part of him that had been dead to the world was suddenly located; accurately, precisely charted" (Mahjoub 248). If it is true, as Edward Said maintains in *Orientalism* (1978), that Europe reified the East, and primarily Islam, in a repeated act of scientific dis-location, then Sigrid's look amounts to a righting of this wrong, and hence to a re-location, in the sense of both a recognition of, and a self-recognition by, the Islamic "Other." That the terminology used is both that of the science that contributed more than any other to the successful expansion of Europe, that is, mapping and map-making, and of that by which the very assumptions of the European view of the world itself was being challenged, that is, cosmography, is surely not a coincidence.

Still, there is more to this Platonic, because scholarly, union between Rashid and Sigrid. Their complementarity is also that of East and West in terms of knowledge. The realization of the benefits mutually to be gained from such a union or fusion are consciously contemplated by Rashid, when he tries to link Copernicus's insights to those of a famous Arab astronomer of old. The astronomer in question is a devout Muslim scholar, Copernicus a

notorious unbeliever. To propagate the ideas of either in the world of the
other amounts to sacrilege, yet Rashid "was becoming convinced now that
this was the mission of his lifetime: to reveal" (Mahjoub 243–44). In other
words, whereas he initially set out from Algiers to obtain a telescope to be
put to military use by the armies of the Sultan, and he later is interested in
the same instrument for his own astronomer's purposes, he eventually arrives at the insight that what counts is the reasoning that gave birth to the instrument in the first place. The same thing obtains for Islamic knowledge. To
divorce faith, then, from reason in the East, to infuse reason with poetry in
the West, and to make both see the sense of a synergy, that is Rashid's mission. That is also what he works for in the translations of Eastern treatises—
characteristically again: charts, maps, cosmographical treatises—he under-
takes for Verner Heinesen. And this is what Rashid symbolically signals when
at the death of Heinesen, broken by the forceful imposition of the Christian
faith upon the reason of science when the representatives of the former for-
bid him to continue his researches, he places his own brass box featuring the
layout of the world according to Islam and a help to locate Mecca and Medina for the true believer, in the grave of Heinesen, the Western cosmogra-
pher. Heinesen's abandonment of his endeavors, and his death, already
point to the failure of Rashid's self-imposed mission. Its total failure is obvious when Sigrid perishes in the burning of the Heinesen homestead, after
Heinesen's death, by the commoners, spurred on by the local clergyman.
Rather than the triumph of Western science over the superstitions of Islam,
then, *The Carrier* celebrates an ideal collaboration, and laments an opportunity not grasped, a road not taken.

I earlier cited a passage from the epilogue to *The Carrier* as a *mise-en-
abîme* of the entire novel, insisting upon the connection between past and
present. Whether as parallel tales, then, or with the chronologically earlier
tale a projection by the narrator of the contemporary tale, we obviously
have to read the experiences of the two protagonists as illuminating one
another. It is clear that the experiences of the modern day Hassan in many
ways repeat those of Rashid al-Kenzy, albeit in a much more moderate
form. Both ultimately are strangers in a strange land. Just as Rashid's knowledge is doubted, his race despised, his tongue ridiculed, so also with Hassan, albeit not in the same radical way as with Rashid, but rather swaddled
in the polite obliquities of modern multicultural discourse. The most direct
indication of Hassan's radical and final "Otherness" in the eyes of the common Danes comes one evening, when he returns from a social visit to a col-
league's home. He finds the windows of the little country house he rents
covered with shaving foam and spray paint. A stuffed toy monkey is nailed
to the back door. This scene immediately calls to mind earlier ones in
which Rashid al-Kenzy is compared to a "wretched, tarry beast" (Mahjoub
262), a devil to be shaved, tarred, and feathered, as was apparently the cus-

tom in Protestant countries if we are to go by Nathaniel Hawthorne's well-known story "Young Goodman Brown," or in which he is compared to a monkey. Moreover, we cannot have forgotten that a real monkey belonging to the pilot of the ship in which Rashid reached Denmark was immediately garroted by the Danish commoners. And Rashid himself is described as a monkey by the first Danes that meet him. Curiously, though, this event leads Hassan to finally resolve the dilemma he is apparently in as to his belonging in Denmark:

> He had been away too long, he decided. It was time to leave the past alone and come back to the real world. It was time to go home. Placing the monkey on the table in front of him he sat down. After a time he reached for the telephone and called his wife. (Mahjoub 257)

This is the last we hear from Hassan. The passage is highly ambiguous. What exactly is "home" to Hassan? Is he about to assert his right to belong in Denmark? Does he intend to return to his wife? Or is he about to leave Denmark for another putative, perhaps chronologically prior and ancestral, "home"? Or yet again: is what he means by "home" a state of mind, rather than a geographical location? And if so, where and what is it? Rashid, in the chapters prior to those leading up to Hassan's decision, decides to return, not to any exact place he calls "home," as he has no such thing, but in any case to his own world of Islam, to the Ottoman Empire. He is held back, though, by the relationship that is developing between himself and Sigrid. It is only in the very last chapters, succeeding Hassan's ambiguous resolution to go "home," that everything decisively goes wrong at the Heinesen estate, that Verner and Sigrid perish, and that Rashid tries to make his escape with the telescope and a collection of scientific treatises. In the very last chapter—the epilogue—Rashid quickly is impelled to part with these, as they weigh him down too much. It is not clear whether he then actually does manage to flee, eventually to make his way south again, or whether he dies in the attempt. Is the ambiguity of this ending to be read as an oblique commentary on Hassan's plight too? Is the implication that Hassan would hopelessly fail if he should decide to brave it out in Denmark and claim his place in Danish society? Is it an exhortation for him to leave behind his Western "ballast" and seek illumination elsewhere, in more congenial climes and spheres? Or are the different dilemmas the two protagonists face simply to be taken as contrasting the constraints of former times with the greater liberties and possibilities of the present? I for one should like to think that there is such a thing as a happy ending to Hassan's story, that is, one in which he himself figures as the hero, if not perhaps that he is, or may be—to use a term famously coined by Toni Morrison—"re-memorying." If so, the difference between the fates of the two protagonists might hint at some true progress as to the way East and West, Christianity and Islam, look upon one another. However one looks upon the

ending of *The Carrier*, it seems clear to me that the entire book is a powerful warning as to the terrible consequences of religious bigotry, racial prejudice, and cultural chauvinism: all of these only lead to losses all around,
never to gains.

Taken altogether, *The Carrier* is an example of what I have elsewhere
(D'haen 1994) baptised "counter-postmodernism," that is, a fiction that
avails itself of all the trappings of the postmodern paradigm—the self-
conscious *mise-en-abîme*, the play with time, often via the mixing of
tenses, the possible confusion as to whether there is only one narrator to
the book, or whether we are actually dealing with a staggered system of
narrators—not simply to undermine the certainties of Western civilization
from the inside, but rather to provide a corrective from the margins of that
civilization, or from what Immanuel Wallerstein (1974, 1980, 1989) would
call the periphery of the world system. According to Helen Tiffin, expressing a conviction widely held among practitioners of postcolonialism, relating postmodernism to the postcolonial often comes down to "a way of de-
priving the formerly colonised of 'voice,' of, specifically, any theoretical
authority, and [of] locking postcolonial texts which it does appropriate
firmly within the European episteme" (Tiffin viii). That is also why a post-
colonial critic such as Kwame Anthony Appiah (1991), when dealing with
the question "Is the Post- in Postmodernism the Post- in Postcolonial?" feels
compelled to answer in the negative. And yet, as Tiffin also notes, "there is
a good deal of formal and tropological overlap between 'primary' texts var-
iously categorised as 'post-modern' or 'post-colonial'" (Tiffin vii). "But,"
she continues, "if there is overlap between the two discourses in terms of
'primary' texts . . . there is considerably less in the 'secondary' category
. . . It is thus in the selection and reading of such 'primary' texts, and in the
contexts of discussion in which they are placed, that significant diver-
gences between post-colonialism and post-modernism are most often isolated" (Tiffin vii). Stephen Slemon likewise remarks that Hutcheon's (1988)
poststructuralist and loosely Lyotardian analysis of intertextual parody as a
constitutive principle of postmodernism resembles the postcolonial practice of "rewriting the canonical 'master texts' of Europe," but with the difference that "whereas a post-modernist criticism would want to argue that
literary practices such as these expose the constructedness of *all* textuality,
. . . an *interested* postcolonial critical practice would want to allow for the
positive production of oppositional truth-claims in these texts" (Slemon 5).
Instead of defining the relationship between postmodernism and postcolonialism as antagonistic, I prefer to see it as complementary or "supplemental." In line with what Ashcroft, Griffiths, and Tiffin (1989) suggest, I
see postcolonialism as a "counter-discourse" to the discourse of the imperial or colonialist center. Postcolonial works, then, that share the kind of
"formal and tropological overlap" with postmodernism that Tiffin speaks

of, in my book would figure under the heading of "counter-postmodernism," a term I have elsewhere defined as follows:

> Just as . . . the term "postmodernism" contains within itself both its affiliation with and its rejection of modernism, . . . the term "counter-postmodernism" at the same time signals its genealogical rootedness in both modernism and postmodernism as well as its rejection of or resistance to the conjunction of aesthetics and ethics these two terms imply. Specifically, and in the terminology that Gayatri Spivak (1987 and 1990) and Homi Bhabha (1990), following Jacques Derrida (1976), apply to postcolonial literature in its relation to the literature of the mother country, I would maintain that "counter-postmodernism" functions as "supplement" to postmodernism in its "orthodox" definitions—and perhaps here it is useful to insist that every definition only becomes "orthodox" in comparison with its successor. It "counters" orthodox postmodernism in putting its finger on the latter's complicity with what it purports to subvert or problematize, and thus "rewrites"—in a move favorite to the actual practice of much postcolonial and feminist literature—orthodox postmodernism as one more form of the discourse of modernity, rather than as its transcendence. With the same move, though, counter-postmodernism also "writes" the subjectivity, history, and language of those hitherto suppressed by the discourse of modernity as applied by western bourgeois society. As such, it makes this discourse also accessible to those traditionally excluded or repressed by western modernity. Ironically, by thus marking the end of modernity as the exclusive instrument of hegemonic western man, and the advent of modernity for the hitherto repressed, counter-postmodernism may well be the only truly "post-modern" reading of postmodernism in that it posits the transcendence of "orthodox" modernity, and the attainment of an-"Other" modernity. (D'haen 1994, 61)

Typical of counter-postmodern works is that they refuse to share in the deconstructive attitude with regard to their own culture routinely ascribed to postmodern works issuing from, and commenting upon, the center of the world-system. Instead, they proffer a re-constructive view of their own marginal culture's involvement with the center. In this case, the corrective is provided by two protagonists that stand at the very opposite of what is usually deemed central to Western modernity and postmodernity, respectively: the hated "Turk," anathema to Western Christianity under modernity, and the immigrant Muslim, supposedly the lowest of the low in Western society, at the furthest remove from those layers of Western society supposedly most caught up in postmodernity. Mahjoub carefully, if obliquely, establishes the parallels between Rashid and Hassan. Whereas we do not learn anything of Hassan's professional experience before he came to occupy the position he now holds, it is Rashid who has to perform the hard labor that is usually required of so-called Third World migrant workers in the European Union as well as in the United States, regardless of the real skills or knowledge these migrants may possess. It is only during his final weeks and days at the Heinesen estate that

Rashid comes to exercise the profession that is his and that is also Hassan's: that of a respected scholar. With both, though, the position they hold is tenuous, if more so for Rashid than for Hassan. Yet it is precisely their marginal position that allows Rashid and Hassan to clearly perceive the weaknesses also of Western society, and thus to counter the West's stereotypically negative views of the culture they themselves originate from. Finally, if we are to go by the brief biography *The Carrier* offers us of its author, this is precisely also the position that Mahjoub finds himself in:

> Jamal Mahjoub is a Sudanese/British writer. Born in London, he grew up in the Sudan. Originally trained as a geologist, he has since worked in a variety of jobs. He currently lives in Denmark [Mahjoub meanwhile has left Denmark, and now lives in Barcelona] where he works as a translator and freelance journalist.

Mahjoub, and *The Carrier*, thus go to join the growing body of authors and works forcefully writing the West's "Others" back into the West's cultural memory, not as objects of the Western gaze and discourse, but as subjects in their own right. While not exactly a rewriting of a specific European classic, *The Carrier* does take up two of the genres central to the West's "ethnographying" of its colonial Others, the novel and travel writing, and autoethnographically redeploys them to write into existence these colonial "Others" as "Selves," and thereby also as legitimate shareholders in modernity.

WORKS CITED

Appiah, Kwame Anthony. "Is the Post- in Postmodernism the Post- in Postcolonial?" *Critical Inquiry* 17.2 (Winter 1991): 336–57.

Ashcroft, Bill, Gareth Griffiths, and Helen Tiffin. *The Empire Writes Back: Theory and Practice in Post-Colonial Literatures.* London and New York: Routledge, 1989.

Bhabha, Homi K. "DissemiNation: Time, Narrative, and the Margin of the Modern Nation." *Nation and Narration.* Ed. Homi K. Bhabha. London: Routledge, 1990, 291–322.

Derrida, Jacques. *Of Grammatology.* Trans. G. C. Spivak. Baltimore: Johns Hopkins University Press, 1976.

D'haen, Theo. "'Countering' Postmodernism." *Aesthetics and Contemporary Discourse.* Ed. Herbert Grabes. REAL (Research in English and American Literature) 10. Tübingen: Gunter Narr Verlag, 1994, 49–64.

———. "(Post)Modernity and Caribbean Discourse." *A History of Literature in the Caribbean.* Vol. 3. *Cross-Cultural Studies.* Ed. A. James Arnold. A Comparative History of Literatures in European Languages Sponsored by the International Comparative Literature Association, Vol. 12. Amsterdam and Philadelphia: John Benjamins, 1997, 303–21.

———. "Re-Presenting the Caribbean." *L'exil et l'allégorie dans le roman anglophone contemporain.* Ed. Michel Morel. Paris: Editions Messene, 1998, 103–15.

———. "Caribbean Migrations: Maryse Condé on the Track of Emily Brontë." *Histoire, jeu, science dans l'aire de la littérature, Mélanges offerts à Evert van der Starre.* Ed. Sjef Houppermans, Paul J. Smith, and Madeleine van Strien-Chardonneau. Amsterdam and Atlanta, Ga.: Rodopi, 2000a, 202–14.

———. "Revolutionary Crossings: Caribbean Identities and Caribbean Forms." *Identity and Alterity in Literature.* Vol. 1. 18th–20th c. Ed. Eleni Politou-Marmarinou and Sophia Denissi. Athens: Domos, 2000b, 335–49.

———. "'Writing Travel' under Postcolonialism." *Literatura e Viagens Pós-coloniais.* Ed. Helena Carvalhao Buescu and Manuela Ribeiro Sanches. ACT 6. Lisboa: Ediçoes Colibri / Faculdade de Letras da Universidade de Lisboa, 2002, 33–48.

Frank, André Gunder. *ReOrient: Global Economy in the Asian Age.* Berkeley and Los Angeles: University of California Press, 1998.

Gikandi, Simon. *Writing in Limbo: Modernism and Caribbean Literature.* Ithaca, N.Y.: Cornell University Press, 1992.

Gosh, Amitav. *In an Antique Land.* London: Granta, 1992.

Habermas, Jürgen. "Modernity's Consciousness of Time and Its Need for Self-Reassurance." *The Philosophical Discourse of Modernity.* Cambridge, Mass.: MIT Press, 1990 [1985], 1–22.

Landes, David. *The Wealth and Poverty of Nations.* London: Little, Brown, 1998.

Mahjoub, Jamal. *The Carrier.* London: Phoenix, 1999 [1998].

Pratt, Mary Louise. *Imperial Eyes: Travel Writing and Transculturation.* New York and London: Routledge, 1992.

Said, Edward. *Orientalism.* New York: Vintage, 1979 [1978].

Said, Edward W. *Culture and Imperialism.* London: Chatto en Windus, 1993.

Slemon, Stephen. "Modernism's Last Post." *Past the Last Post: Theorizing Post-Colonialism and Post-Modernism.* Ed. Ian Adam and Helen Tiffin. London: Harvester / Wheatsheaf, 1991, 1–11.

Spivak, Gayatri C. *In Other Worlds: Essays in Cultural Politics.* New York: Methuen, 1987.

Spivak, Gayatri C. *The Post-Colonial Critic: Interviews, Strategies, Dialogues.* Ed. Sarah Harasym. London: Routledge, 1990.

Spivak, Gayatri C. "Can the Subaltern Speak," *Colonial Discourse and Post-Colonial Theory.* Ed. Patrick Williams and Laura Chrisman. London: Harvester / Wheatsheaf, 1993, 66–111; originally in *Marxism and the Interpretation of Culture.* Ed. Cary Nelson and Lawrence Grossberg. Basingstoke: Macmillan, 1988.

Tiffin, Helen. "Introduction." *Past the Last Post: Theorizing Post-Colonialism and Post-Modernism.* Ed. Ian Adam and Helen Tiffin. London: Harvester / Wheatsheaf, 1991, vii–xvi.

Wallerstein, Immanuel. *The Modern World-System.* 3 vols. San Diego: Academic Press, 1974, 1980, 1989.

7

From Guest Worker to Hybrid Immigrant: Changing Themes of German-Turkish Literature

Meyda Yegenoglu

From the very beginning, Turkish migrants in Germany have written about their experiences in their new environment. One of the essential themes in the literature of the first generation was the longing for the homeland left behind and dreams of returning to the space of "origin," which is romanticized and glorified in memory. Contrary to official and popular desire, the social, economic, and political conditions in Germany have led to the permanent settlement of these "guest workers" in their supposedly temporary host country. The literature of the second and third generations echo new conditions under which migrants experience their identity, as former concerns are now replaced with troubles stemming from being German and Turkish at the same time. The characters appear to be hyphenated, moving in and out between two cultures. The language used in the writings of this period also reflects their hybrid identity and the difficulty of identifying a place that can be described as home. This essay aspires to shed light on the different ways in which early and later generation Turkish immigrants are positioned in the German social and political context and how these differences are reflected in their literature. By specifically elucidating how the nostalgia for the homeland tends to be replaced with the issue of hybrid and ambivalent identity in the texts of later generation immigrants, I suggest this shift in concern is indicative of how early and later generation migrants are positioned differently in German society. In examining these differences, I will highlight the relevance of Jacques Derrida's insights into hospitality, Zygmunt Bauman and Georg Simmel's well-known concept of the stranger, and Sartre's very interesting notion of the slimy.

THE LOST HOMELAND

The Turkish and other immigrant workers in Germany have long been referred to and labeled in the popular discourse as *Gasterbeiter* [guest workers], a term that testifies to their temporary status. Although the official term chosen to designate them is not *Gasterbeiter* but *Auslander* [foreigners], what is important about the predominant usage is that they have never been regarded as immigrants.[1] Some other widely used terms are *Fremde* [strangers] and *Fremdarbeiters* [foreign workers]. The negative connotation of the labels that define migrants is not something specific to German society. As Dietrich Thranhardt notes in "Germany: An Undeclared Immigration Country," what is particular about Germany's handling of the issue of immigrants is the emphasis on their *temporary* status as well as on their *foreignness*. The polls conducted in 1980s indicate a fear of being invaded by foreigners, as 62 percent of the population thought that there were way too many foreigners in the country and they should be sent back. Steven Vertovec, in "Berlin Multikulti: Germany, 'Foreigners' and 'World-Openness,'" interpreted the October 1992 poll as demonstrating that the "problem of foreigners" is ranked as the highest issue of public concern. This fear of over-foreignization (*uberfremdung*) is part of a deep collective sense of *heimat*, of being invaded by foreigners. The uniqueness of the German case—in contrast, say, to Britain's response to migrancy, characterized as racialization, or to Holland's, characterized as minorization—is the foreignerization of immigrants ("Germany: An Undeclared Immigration Country"). Czarina Wilpert, in "Migration and Ethnicity in a Non-Immigration Country," underscores the fact that despite the wide range of terms deployed to describe the migrant labor force in Germany, two terms are never used: immigration and ethnic minority. The terms used in describing immigrants are crucial not only because they reflect the ideologies underpinning regulations and laws, but also because they are indicative of the general framework of classification through which borders between proper and improper, order and chaos, friend and enemy, host and guest are drawn, which in sum designate who can be admitted to the domain of friends.

In the 1950s when Germany started recruiting foreign workers, the overriding concern was to recruit labor only for a short term. Accordingly, migration policies were designed to cater to the fluctuating needs of capital for labor. What was desired was flexibility so that when market demands changed, they could dispose of the temporary and mobile labor used in accomplishing the German "economic miracle." During the 1980s increasing anti-foreign sentiment resulted in a new *Auslander* politics, and all kinds of new immigration were circumscribed. In 1983 a law was passed that offered monetary incentives, known as "go-home" premiums, to those workers who agreed to return to their home country. Ruth Mandel, in "Foreigners in the Fatherland: Turkish Immigrant Workers in Germany," notes that this came to be known as "killing passports" among the Turks, as it signaled the end of the possibility of living and working in Germany in the future. The set of laws and regulations were designed not with the aim of conferring rights to foreign workers but to provide an unrestricted flexibility to the state in controlling labor flows when and where the interests of the capital deemed necessary. Since the settlement of foreigners was neither planned nor predicted and desired—after all, guests come and go, and are not expected to stay—all the laws and policies were shaped with the view that workers were there for a temporary period of time. As Stephen Castles notes, regulations did not confer citizenship rights but simply permitted them to stay in Germany "if their personality and the purposes of their stay made them worthy of hospitality" ("The Guests Who Stayed" 522).

The new law of *Auslandergesetz* [Foreign Law] (1965) that replaced the old Nazi regulations did not bring a significant betterment to the temporary and guest status of migrants. Residence permits were not granted as a right of residence but simply as a work permit, explicitly stating that resident permits may be granted insofar as the foreigners' stay did not constitute any harm to the interests of the host society. The *Bund-Laner-Komission* suggested new measures in 1977, and in 1978 some of these were implemented. These provided more security in residence matters or eliminated the deportation threat. Residence and work permits for an unlimited time became a possibility after a five-year stay, on certain conditions: possession of long-term work permits, proof of school attendance of the migrants' children, and having an adequate dwelling ("The Guests Who Stayed" 524). Even in this new regulation residence permits were closely tied to work permits.[2]

It was under the pressures and anxieties of such political, cultural, and social circumstances that early Turkish migrant writings in Germany have flourished. In accordance with the temporary guest status and the persistence of those policies designed to fulfill the expectation of their return, this literature in the main was oriented toward the home country. When attention turned to the host country, it was the *gasterbeiter* experience, the hardships of life in a foreign environment, the loneliness and despair that stemmed from the difficulties of being a foreigner, sanitary conditions, disillusionment about Germany as the promised land of material wealth, poor and unhealthy work conditions, prejudice, and rejection that became the predominant themes in the early writings.[3]

The narratives of homesickness and the dreams of returning to home were one of the means of managing such negative experiences and functioned as a way of coping with the reality of temporariness. It is too simplistic to view the dream of return to and the nostalgic yearning for the home left behind as the inevitable consequence of a deep-seated attachment to mythic territorial roots, as this assumes that "home" has meaning independent of its binary opposite, that is, the non-home. Rather, this nostalgic emphasis on the desire to

return to home needs to be seen within the framework of the temporary status that was accorded to migrants as it contributed to an increasing awareness of a place deemed "home." Following Douglas Porteous's argument in
"Home: The Territorial Core," we can suggest that although home is usually
ascribed to a particular physical space, it rarely consists of this physical
space. It is a psychic space that is identified with a particular physical space.
As mentioned earlier, in early Turkish immigrant writings, the desire for a
place called home is particularly highlighted and serves as a major point of
reference in structuring their psychic reality. The search for a mythical bond
that is solid, fixed, and rooted in the past makes sense in a socio-cultural
context where one is considered nothing more than a guest and is forced to
live and work in a place that has the characteristics of not-home, that is, pro-
visionality, transitoriness, and ephemerality. The formidable opposition between home and non-home needs to be seen as the structuring principle of
the psycho-geographical space of the early-generation Turkish immigrants.
We need to understand the recurrent theme of nostalgic yearning for home
as an upshot of being forced to live in a physical and psychic space that has
the status of non-home. In other words, the yearning for home that is expressed in the writings of early-generation migrants is not necessarily to be
interpreted as a reflection of an inherent desire for a putative origin.[4] Rather,
it is a site defined during confrontation with its opposite, non-home, as the
persistent yearning for a home is indicative of the fact that they are considered guests and therefore are not at home. As Rosemary Marongoly George
suggests in *The Politics of Home: Postcolonial Relocations and Twentieth-
Century Fiction*, "home and nations are defined in instances of confrontation
with what is considered not-home" (4). The theme of longing for home in
these writings can be seen as part of a struggle to achieve legitimacy that is
denied to the guest status. George regards "the themes of loss, painful homelessness and the less-than-whole subject who longs for assimilation into a
national culture" (8) as a characteristic of immigrant fiction in general. But
these themes achieve a more razor-sharp sense in the writings of Turkish immigrants in Germany as the social, cultural, and legal milieu have systematically underlined their presence as impermanent.

GUESTS AND HOSTS

Though their stay has been prolonged, migrants in Germany are nevertheless seen as guests, their presence as temporary. They have never been regarded as settled in or belonging to the precinct of the life-world of the "original" inhabitants. After all, as guests, they are expected to develop only a
provisional attachment even if they come territorially close. Their temporal
remoteness, their strange cultural and social habits, habits of an "ancient

past," are to be kept at a safe distance so spatial nearness will not be turned into psychical closeness. But if they are guests, implying they deserve hospitality, then why are migrants treated with fear and hostility? What kind of a relation prevails between the host and the guest such that the presence of guest workers leads to a reversal of hospitality into hostility? We can question whether hospitality—assumed to be the most elementary character of the host-guest relation involving the welcoming of the other at one's own home—entails an undermining of the sovereign status of the host. Can hospitality, as it entails welcoming, be seen as completely devoid of mastery and ultimate control of one's own space? Does the presence of the guest, who is presumed to be not an enemy and therefore a potential ally, imply that he or she deserves unconditional hospitality? Does this hospitality involve an unconditional welcoming of the other, hence a radical restructuring of the socio-geo-political space so that immigrants (legal or illegal) and exiles of different kinds can feel at home? What kind of relations of mastery and sovereignty between the self and other are surreptitiously replicated when the other is welcomed and offered hospitality while the ownership of a space called home is retained?[5] Can hospitality be offered and the other be welcomed without a radical alteration of the host's mode of belonging to a space deemed to be their own? These questions can be answered in part by drawing out Jacques Derrida's arguments about the nature of hospitality.

In *Adieu to Emmanuel Levinas*, Jacques Derrida directs our attention to the fact that conditional hospitality[6] pulls us into the domain of law and jurisdiction. It is about international agreement and refers to the condition of justice and law decided by nations. As such, it suspends and conditions the immediate, infinite, and unconditional welcoming of the other (87). Most important of all, conditional hospitality is offered at the owner's place, home, nation, state, or city—that is, at a place where one is defined as the master and where unconditional hospitality or unconditional trespassing of the door is not possible. For Derrida, restraining hospitality within the parameters of law weaves it with contradiction, because the other is welcomed on the condition that the host remains the master and thereby retains his or her authority in that place. The *law of hospitality* is the *law of oikonomia*, the law of one's home. Offered as the law of place, legal-juridical hospitality lays down the limits of a place and retains the authority over that place, thus limiting the gift that is offered, retaining the self as *self* in one's own home as the condition of hospitality. In making this the condition of hospitality, it affirms the law of the same and subjects the stranger/foreigner to the law of the host's home. In this way, the foreigner is allowed to enter the host's space under conditions determined by the host. Therefore, conditional welcoming entails a way of constructing a place from which one invites the other and hence lays down the conditions for "appropriating for oneself a place to *welcome* the other, or, worse, *welcoming* the other in order to appropriate for oneself a place and then speak the language of hospitality" (15–16). Therefore the *law of hospitality* is characterized by a limitation. The host affirms the position of a master in his or her own home; in the space and things he or she provides to the stranger/guest, the host assures his or her sovereignty and says: this space belongs to me; we are in my home. Welcome to me. Feel at home but on the condition that you obey the rules of hospitality (14). This gesture affirms one's sovereignty and one's being at one's own home. For this reason, *hospitality as law* limits itself with a threshold (6).

The inherent paradox in the conditional and lawful welcoming of the other as guest can also be productively understood as conforming to "the structure of exception" that Giorgio Agamben discusses in *Homo Sacer: Sovereign Power and Bare Life*. Allow me to quote from another essay of mine, "Liberal Multiculturalism and the Ethics of Hospitality in the Age of Globalization." I once noted the problems involved in liberal multiculturalism in these words:

> All of the laws that regulate the conditions of arrival, presence, and departure of "guest-workers" in Germany reveal that the overriding concern was that of recruitment of a short-term labor force. For this reason, residence permits were conferred only as work permits. Laws explicitly anticipated that the workers will leave Germany when the needs of capital are fulfilled. The fact that the workers' presence was regarded as temporary makes clear that the new regulations were seen as an exception: a parenthesis to be opened and eventually closed. The logic underlying these laws is that the acceptance/welcoming of foreign labor is a conditional one, as the workers' presence, which is expected to be temporary, is deemed to be an exception to the general rule. Tellingly, the term "migrant" is not typically used to name this group. As guests, these workers were accepted as an exception to the general rule of membership in the German polity. Their welcoming is not regulated within the framework of the general rule of law. In accordance with the persistent and widespread sentiment that declares that "Germany is not a land of immigration," the conditional welcoming or the temporary hosting of foreign labor appears at first glance to be set outside the purview of general law. Hence these regulations were nothing but the name of an interim, an exception. Following Agamben, we can ask whether as an exception, the conditional welcoming of workers indicates that they are completely expelled outside the purview of the host society? It is clear that this temporary foreign labor force has been included in the German territory without being turned into proper members of the polity. . . . As guests having temporary abode, they are not properly inside. (7)

One way to understand the paradoxical inclusion of guests in German society is to see them as a *limit figure* that brings into crisis the clear distinction between what is inside and what is outside. In other words, the guest-workers' inclusion is a *paradoxical inclusion*. To restate this in Agamben's words, they are subjected to an "inclusive exclusion" (*Homo Sacer* 21). It is their unexpected and prolonged stay that produced them as ambivalent figures. The writings of later generations can be seen as a by-product of this inclusive exclusion, especially in their themes focusing on difficulties that stem from having an ambivalent identity, being neither properly inside nor outside, belonging neither to German nor to Turkish culture, and finding it impossible to call either country "home."

THERE IS NO HOME

As I suggested above, legal regulations designed to deal with the presence of migrants in Germany were based from the beginning on the expectation that when the needs of the capital were fulfilled, the guest workers would leave. Their temporariness was emphasized to remind both the host society and the migrants that they did not come there to settle. And since then, the hope that they will eventually go away has never fully vanished. The "go-home" premiums that I mentioned earlier can be seen as one instance where this hope took a more tangible form. However, the migrants' sojourn, which was projected to be temporary, never came to an end. Just the opposite: they turned their provisional status into settlement, thus making their "way into the life-world uninvited," to use a phrase from Zygmunt Bauman (*Modernity and Ambivalence* 59). Their uninvited intrusion into the life-world of the original inhabitants, which resulted in their undesired physical closeness, has eventually turned these guests into strangers. As Georg Simmel notes in "The Stranger," a "stranger is not who comes today and goes tomorrow, but rather as the person who comes today and stays tomorrow" (1).[7] Their unallowed but nevertheless realized sharing of the space of the original residents turns them into uninvited guests and implies the violation of the principles upon which the host-guest relations are based. For this reason Bauman suggests that strangers are "always uninvited guests" (*Postmodernity and Its Discontents* 6). The uneasy synthesis of nearness and remoteness that Simmel emphasized is fundamental to the definition of the stranger: the unity of nearness and remoteness implies that "who is close by is far away and strangeness means that he, who also is far, is actually near. It is a specific form of interaction" ("The Stranger" 1). The specificity of this interaction, as Bauman puts it, lies in the fact that they "claim a right to be an object of responsibility" (*Modernity and Ambivalence* 59)—a type of relation only friends are morally entitled to demand. For this reason, it is not simply the crossing of territorial borders that turns migrants into strangers. Rather it was due to transgressing the dividing line between remoteness and nearness, between temporariness and settlement, inside and outside, that migrants became strangers in Germany. Because they trespass over the allowed borders of guest status, migrants engender uncertainty and ambivalence. By refusing to accept the termination of their allowed period of stay and thereby turning their temporary status into an unexpected permanency, they remain "stubbornly and infuriatingly indeterminate," to use a phrase from Bauman (65). It is with this ambiguity, ambivalence, or indeterminacy that the later-generation migrants' writing was mainly preoccupied.

As second and third generations can no longer share the first generation's dream or hope of return they become aware that there is no home to return to. For example, in dealing with the dilemmas of return, Alev Tekinay, in *Daswischen* [In Between], expresses the lack of a familiar space called home in the following way: "the guest from Germany returns to the foreign country," and she talks about how she is torn between homesickness and the new homeland (cited in Suhr, "*Auslanderliteratur*" 101–102). In a similar manner, "home" in Tülin Emircan's "Entfremdung" [Alienation] does not signify a cozy, authentic core or familiar environment, as there is no difference in the degree of familiarity between the foreigner's space or the so-called familiar "homely" space: "better to be a foreigner abroad than a foreigner in one's own country" (cited in Suhr, "*Auslanderliteratur*" 102). In tandem with this, a recurring theme is being split between two cultures yet belonging to neither. In his poem *Doppelman* [Double Man], Zafer Senocak addresses the difficulties of being in two worlds: "I carry two worlds within/but neither one whole/they're constantly bleeding/the border runs/right through my tongue" (cited in Suhr, "*Auslanderliteratur*" 102). Concerns about loss of identity and ways of defining and establishing a non-German self within a dominant context (Simpson) are frequently addressed. Aras Ören's *Manege* [Arena] takes place in Kreuzberg, the so-called "little Istanbul." Despite the fact the protagonist has lived there many years, he cannot escape the feeling of loneliness and hence cannot feel attached to either world. Although he attempts to merge discordant elements of different worlds by bringing together stories from Turkey, memories of his village, dreams, and fantasies with detailed descriptions of his environment, he nevertheless still feels out of place and misses the feeling of belonging to a home, as he asks, "Where is my home?" Germany does not represent home for him, as he regards his room in Leibnizstrasse as "just a room to stay" (cited in Suhr, "*Fremde* in Berlin" 231). Thus for later generations, this longing for a home or the desire for a feeling of belonging does not result in a nostalgic search for, or an idealization of, the home country left behind as a site of security and coherence. In *Deutschlandein, ein turkisches Marchen* [Germany, a Turkish Fairy Tale] Aras Ören expresses this lack of a place that can be called home as follows:

"having found little Istanbuls here, we do not want to go back to Turkey and found little Germanies there, all in one lifetime" (cited in Suhr, *Auslanderliteratur* 86). The idea of belonging to a home country is seen as nothing more than a myth. He says: "My home has always been inside of me, never outside. I carry it around with me. Even though we are fairly distant from one another, we go everywhere together" (cited in Suhr, "*Fremde* in Berlin" 232). As the title of the last part of the trilogy, "A Foreign Place Is a Home Too," announces, he views Germany as a location to earn a living and thus make a home. Consequently, the theme of being a foreigner, despite being born and raised in Germany, appears to be one of the primary means of addressing the ambivalent or indeterminate character of their identity, the stranger position they occupy. The feeling of not belonging to German culture no longer stems from the fact of being temporary. The termination of their guest status does not signify that they are now regarded as settled in or belonging to the precinct of the life-world of the "original" inhabitants and thus accepted as "objects of responsibility," like friends. They do remain foreigners or strangers (though no longer guests) even though they were born and raised there. Or more importantly, Germany cannot be transformed into a home; it remains a host country; it is neither a site of temporary abode nor a home. It is a place where they dwell *strangely*.

The difficulties of expressing themselves in a "strange" or "foreign" language are another means of addressing the dubiousness of their identity. Concerns with language emerge as a way of addressing the question of identity within difference. The loss of self, an unrecoverable past, ambivalence of identity, and the problems of assimilation and alienation from the host country are tackled by means of dealing with questions of language. Emine Sevgi Özdamar's writings are exemplary in this respect, as she addresses the difficulties that stem from living simultaneously between two languages, almost as if she is moving physically between different cultures (cited in Horrocks and Kolinsky, "Migrants or Citizens" xxiii). The unease experienced with the loss of native language is a dramatic way of demonstrating the detachment or alienation from cultural "origins" or home. In an effort to regain this lost origin, Özdamar decides to learn Arabic, the presumed "real" roots that the intense process of Westernization in Turkey has wiped out. This is an attempt to refill a space in her cultural-historical identity left vacant by the elimination of Arabic language and culture and then filled with Western values. Once restored to her roots, she becomes capable of developing a flexible identity without losing herself (cited in Fischer and McGowan, "From *Pappkoffer* to Pluralism" 16). Even the title of one of her texts, *Life is Carvanaserai: has two doors. I came in through one, went out through the other*, expresses being in between two languages, being placed in two cultures, neither of which is deemed hers.

SLIMY FOREIGNERS

By virtue of mixing categories, ambivalent things resist clear separation and thereby defy strict classification. The taken-for-granted classification of certain people as friends and others as enemies is upset by undecidable figures who are neither friends nor enemies, to use Bauman's formulation. Their ambiguity creates discomfort and confuses the easy classification of things and thus implies a sense of danger. What turns certain things into ambivalent and thus threatening elements is not their intrinsic qualities, but their location in the order of things: it is their out-of-placeness that turns certain things into ambivalent and threatening elements. Bauman, in *Postmodernity and Its Discontents,* notes that the deeming of certain things as waste or dirt is a result of classification or order-designing attempts. It is the ordering attempt of the nation-state that turns strangehood into waste in modernity. What is deemed waste are usually mobile things that do not recognize boundaries. Following Bauman's formulation, we can safely say that the migrants' transformation of their guest status into a permanent settlement is what turns them into an ambivalent and threatening instance of otherness, a foreign element that resides in and claims a share in the homely and orderly space of the self.

Migrants' easy crossing of the impermissible borders, thereby rendering them extraneous, signifies their mobile character. In their mobility, they threaten and defy attempts to maintain order. Bauman transposes the meaning of what Jean-Paul Sartre, in *Being and Nothingness: An Essay on Phenomenological Ontology,* calls "slimy" to explicate the mode of being symbolized by the mobile, ambivalent, and thus threatening presence of strangers. In order to describe the essentially ambiguous nature of the slimy, of those things that are characterized by "neither/nor but both" (in our case, neither Turkish nor German but both) qualities, and their relation to the self, Sartre contrasts the qualities of water with that of honey or pitch. It is important to stress the fact that the features of the slimy that Sartre identifies have meaning when the slimy substance's relation to the self is taken into consideration. Indeed, a substance can be deemed slimy in relation to a subject whose presumed mastery and control over the other and his space is under threat.

Although the slimy is like a liquid, its features differ significantly from a liquid's, as its substance is like pitch; thus, it is an aberrant liquid. It is clear from this that, being an ambiguous substance, it both slides and constitutes something one can slide on. Being a substance in between two states, the slimy is continually in a process of becoming. Sartre gives the example of honey: when you watch honey dissolving into itself (the honey sliding off the spoon to the honey contained in the jar), it is possible to notice a visible resistance. It is "like the refusal of the individual who does not want to be annihilated in the whole of being" (608). Its unstable but fixed character discourages its possession. Although water is more fleeting than the slimy, it can nevertheless be possessed as something fleeting. The slimy, however, flees with a heavy flight and cannot be possessed. Although it denies itself as flight it gives the impression that it can almost be possessed and has a solid permanence; it possesses the subject:

> Only at the very moment when I believe that I possess it, behold by a curious reversal, *it* possess me. . . . If an object which I hold in my hands is solid, I can let go when I please; its inertia symbolizes for me my total power; . . . Yet there is the slimy reversing the terms; . . . I open my hands, I want to let go off the slimy and it sticks to me, it draws me, it sucks at me. . . . I am no longer the master in arresting the process of appropriation. . . . In one sense it is like the supreme docility of the possessed, the fidelity of a dog who gives himself even when one does not want him any longer, and in another sense there is underneath this docility a surreptitious appropriation of the possessor by the possessed. (608–609)

It is the reversal of the terms of mastery and control that results in the relegation of certain things to the status of sliminess. It is this peculiar subtle reversal of symbolic direction that can explain the threat the ambivalent strangers or foreigners pose before the subject, as there is the interpreted threat of the undermining of the mastery and control of the subject over its own territory, culture, or home. The guest, the stranger, the foreigner, by coming today and not going tomorrow, violates the conditions of the hospitality. By breaching the temporary status accorded to them, Turkish migrants in Germany defy the limits and terms the host has set and hence pose difficulty for the host to continue to be a master in his or her own house. The host encounters difficulty in maintaining his or her full control of the conditions of hospitality, and experiences difficulty in setting the terms and conditions of the relationship. These terms and conditions are threatened, seemingly appropriated by the guest whose settlement is now permanent, hence claiming and demanding responsibility. It is this reversal that explains why the relation of "conditional" hospitality of the old days changes into a relation of hostility. This might well be one of the factors among the complex network of forces that operate behind the increasing new racism in Germany and elsewhere in Europe.

NOTES

1. Despite the presence of more than two million immigrants, Germany has always officially refused to recognize itself as a multicultural society. The preeminent indicator of this refusal is the official position declaring, "Germany is not a land of immigration."

2. Here I would like to draw attention to the conditionality of granting "permission to stay." I follow Derrida's reading of the aporetic contradiction or the double bind of hospitality, and suggest that this is the principle that structures the nature of the host-guest relations.

3. Güney Dal, Fethi Savasci, Yüksel Pazarkaya, Fakir Baykurt, Dursun Akçam, and Habib Bektas are examples from this early period.

4. Zafer Senocak, a poet, short-story writer, and second-generation Turk who lives in Berlin and studied literature, political science, and philosophy at Munich University, is critical of the fascination of the second generation of Turkish migrants with invoking an image of a lost *heimat*. For him, the desire for *heimat*, like racism and xenophobia, brings intolerance to differences (see *The Literary Representation of Hybrid Identities: The Case of German Turks,* pp. 104–106). It is quite striking that Senocak does not see any difference between the migrants' desire for a place called "home" and the German nationalist image of the pure *heimat*.

5. Concerns of home are understood, in a rather limited way, to belong predominantly to migrants, exiles, and refugees. What I aim to problematize with this series of questions is the converse issue. In the welcoming of migrants, it is the sovereign hosts' concern with their home—*heimat, heimlich*—that becomes the overriding concern.

6. The term "conditional hospitality" (as opposed to unconditional hospitality) is particularly fitting to designate the overwhelmingly restrictive and qualified situation of the *gastarbeiters* in Germany.

7. This is why tourists are not strangers. The host society is sure that they come today and leave tomorrow.

WORKS CITED

Agamben, Giorgio. *Homo Sacer: Sovereign Power and Bare Life.* Trans. Daniel Heller-Roazen. Stanford, CA: Stanford University Press, 1998.

Bauman, Zygmunt. *Modernity and Ambivalence.* Ithaca, NY: Cornell University Press, 1991.

Bauman, Zygmunt. *Postmodernity and Its Discontents.* Cambridge: Blackwell, 1997.

Castles, Stephen. "The Guests Who Stayed—The Debate on 'Foreigners Policy' in the German Federal Republic." *International Migration Review* 19.3 (Fall 1985): 517–534.

Derrida, Jacques. *Adieu to Emmanuel Levinas.* Trans. Pascale-Anne Brault and Michael Naas, Stanford, CA: Stanford University Press, 1999.

Fischer, Sabine, and Moray McGowan. "From *Pappkoffer* to Pluralism." In *Turkish Culture in German Society Today.* Providence, RI, and Oxford: Berghahn, 1996, 1–21.

George, Rosemary Marangoly. *The Politics of Home: Postcolonial Relocations and Twentieth-Century Fiction.* Berkeley and Los Angeles: University of California Press, 1996.

Horrocks, David, and Eva Kolinsky. "Migrants or Citizens: Turks in Germany between Exclusion and Acceptance." In *Turkish Culture in German Society Today.* Providence, RI, and Oxford: Berghahn, 1996, x–xxvii.

Kayaalp, Ebru. *The Literary Representation of Hybrid Identities: The Case of German-Turks.* Unpublished master's thesis, submitted to the Department of Sociology, Middle East Technical University (August 1998).

Mandel, Ruth. "Foreigners in the Fatherland: Turkish Immigrant Workers in Germany." In *The Politics of Immigrant Workers*. Ed. Edamille Guerin-Gonzales and Carl Strikwerda. New York and London: Holmes & Miller, 1998.

Özdamar, Emine Sevgi. *Mother Tongue*. Trans. Craig Thomas. Toronto: Coach House Press, 1994.

Porteous, Douglas J. "Home: The Territorial Core." *Geographical Review* 66.4 (October 1976): 383–390.

Sartre, Jean-Paul. *Being and Nothingness: An Essay on Phenomenological Ontology*. Trans. Hazel Barnes. New York: Philosophical Library, 1956.

Simmel, Georg. "The Stranger." In *The Sociology of Georg Simmel*. Trans. Kurt Wolf. New York: Free Press, 1950, 402–408.

Suhr, Heidrun. "*Auslanderliteratur*: Minority Literature in the Federal Republic of Germany." *New German Critique* 46 (winter 1989): 71–103.

Suhr, Heidrun. "*Fremde* in Berlin: The Outsider's View from Inside." In *Berlin: Culture and Metropolis*. Minneapolis and Oxford: University of Minnesota Press, 1990, 219–242.

Thranhardt, Dietrich. "Germany: An Undeclared Immigration Country." *New Community* 21.1 (January 1995): 19–36.

Vertovec, Steven. "Berlin Multikulti: Germany, 'Foreigners' and 'World-Openness.'" *New Community* 22.3 (July 1996): 381–389.

Yegenoglu, Meyda. "Liberal Multiculturalism and the Ethics of Hospitality in the Age of Globalization." *Postmodern Culture* 13.2 (April 2003): 1–19.

Wilpert, Czarina. "Migration and Ethnicity in a Non-Immigration Country: Foreigners in a United Germany." *New Community* 18.1 (October 1991): 49–62.

8

"Between Foreign and Floating Signs": The Language of Migrant Subjects

Angelika Bammer

It has become fashionable in cultural studies to theorize about contemporary subjectivity in terms of migrancy. In such theories identity is no longer conceptualized in singular but rather in plural terms that more closely correspond to the metaphoric and real unsettledness of people in a global age. From this perspective migrancy is the human condition of our time—of postmodernity.

Postcolonial theory, by bringing postcolonial history to bear on the condition of postmodernity, has historicized the category of the postmodern migrant subject. From the perspective of this history, the instability of postmodern subjects—their physical mobility as well as their intra-psychic mutability—is in part an effect of the displacements brought about by colonial histories and their aftermaths. In the movement back and forth between colonies and metropoles, the meanings of "self" and "other," "us" and "them," changed fundamentally.[1] In the process, the category of "difference" became central to our understanding of relationships that had made us "strangers to ourselves," with identities that were no longer contained within single selves (Kristeva 1991). We had become plural: our lives intertwined, our histories intersecting, our cultures hybrid. The consequence, as Homi Bhabha put it in a decidedly understated way, was "a certain problem of identification" ("Interrogating Identity" 5). And at the heart of this problem was language.

The following essay is a contribution to the ongoing discussion of this problem from the perspective of the postcolonial migrant subject. The position of this subject is marked by multiple discontinuities: homes lost in the making of new homes, bonds untied in the forming of new bonds, languages displaced in acquiring new ones. In this trajectory defined by the poles no-longer and not-yet, the migrant experience is defined by the continual play between loss and gain. My essay explores this dynamic through a reading of two texts that address the contemporary migrant's experience: "Dog Words" ("Les mots canins") by the Moroccan scholar and writer Abdelfattah Kilito, and *Mother Tongue* (*Mutterzunge*) by the Turkish-born writer and filmmaker Emine Sevgi Özdamar. Between them, they represent different versions of the migrant experience through different modalities of migrancy: nomadism and exile. For one, the focus is on the journey, the process of moving on, and the goal is the next destination. For the other, the focus is on the place left behind, and the goal is to return to the point of origin. What both texts have in common is an emphasis on language as key to the migrant's "problem of identification." The protagonists' sense of themselves and their relationships to others—the communities they come from, and those they encounter along the way—is defined through language: whom they speak to, in what language, or whether they choose instead to remain silent. It is in their struggles with language that they experience themselves as migrants and explore the meaning of this experience.

My interpretive point of entry into a discussion of these texts is an essay by Homi Bhabha on the peculiar position of the postcolonial, postmodern migrant subject ("Interrogating Identity").[2] Writing from the perspective of the formerly colonized, still treated as Europe's Others even as Europe has become their home, he depicts them as figures who are commonly disregarded or disavowed. Thus, he notes, when such a figure writes, it is from the impossible position of one who is present but unacknowledged. In this sense, the postcolonial migrant writer is a contradiction in terms: a signifying absence. She is, as Bhabha puts it, "continually positioned in a range of contradictory positions that co-exist" (5). "[P]ositioned in a range of contradictory positions that co-exist," a writer who writes as an Other and thus, by definition, as a non-self challenges the very logic of selfhood. In this sense, Bhabha concludes, the postcolonial migrant writer "changes the very terms of our recognition of the 'person'" (5).

This process of rethinking what it might mean to be a self from the impossible position of a writing Other means rethinking the status of language as an authorizing means toward the end of legitimized selfhood. Language is a profoundly contradictory means that gives and takes in the same gesture. Entry into its symbolic universe empowers, but an entrance fee is charged. Few feel this price more keenly than those asked to leave their otherness at the door. In this sense, the entry into public discourse—the emancipating move of Enlightenment subjects—marks a place of triple loss: of identities that cannot be translated into public discourse terms; of imaginative possibilities curtailed by the symbolic codes of language; and of the psychic shelter to be found in the spaces outside and beyond language.

Bhabha's observations on the contradictions of the postcolonial migrant's condition provide a useful framework for an inquiry into the migrant's ambivalence about language. Bhabha proposes that our inquiry begin with a change in our own location so that instead of looking *at* the migrant we see from her point of view. This change in perspective is precisely what texts like "Dog Words" and *Mother Tongue* effect: they write from the position of the migrant subjects. Seen from this perspective, the migrant subject appears not doubly absent (neither here nor there), but multiply present (both from elsewhere and now here); the scene of her writing is a "double inscription" (Bhabha, "Interrogating Identity"). And, as no one has more powerfully demonstrated than W.E.B. DuBois, a "double inscription" calls for a voice attuned to the spaces in between. Moreover, as DuBois illustrates, central to the creation of such a space is the strategic play with silence. The narratives of "Dog Words" and *Mother Tongue* are marked by multivalent forms of silence: a refusal of the ways in which we are predefined by language, a clearing of space outside of words for reflection and/or feeling; silence even figures as a language of its own that cedes authority of eloquence to the body. The one thing it is not is absence.

In the body of literature informed by a convergence between postmodern cultural practices and a postcolonial historical consciousness that reconfigured European cultural discourse in the course of the 1980s, some of the most aesthetically resonant texts are defined by this play of silence.[3] In texts such as *Dictée* (1982) by the Korean-American and European-trained writer, video, and performance artist Theresa Hak Kyung Cha; *Fantasia: An Algerian Cavalcade* (*L'amour, la fantasia*), published in the same year as "Dog Words," by Kilito's Maghrebian compatriot, Assia Djebar; or *Niederungen* (Lowlands, 1984) by Özdamar's Rumanian-German compatriot Herta Müller, silence is deployed as one of the most powerful tools with which to explore the generative potential of in-betweenness. At the same time, these texts not only *represent* silence, but *perform* it textually as they explore ways of writing that seek a literary form that corresponds to the migrant experience. "Dog Words" and *Mother Tongue* are thus exemplary instances of a new body of European literature. Written from perspectives and in voices based in Europe, but only in part, they mark the limits of the very European subject they reference and rewrite. In the process, they replace the stability of a unitary, self-contained self with a much more fluid and adaptable performance of self in a series of plural positionings. Provisional and contingent, this self-performing self enacts the experience of the migrant subject, moving "between nations and cultures, between foreign and floating signs" (Bhabha, "Interrogating Identity," 5).

"WHAT DOES A BEDOUIN DO . . . ?": A NOMAD'S TALE

Abdelfattah Kilito's "Dog Words," written in 1981 for a conference on bilingualism held at the University of Rabat, is a reflection on the relationship between language and belonging. It is an argument for a concept of belonging not defined by origins or roots that can accommodate foreigners and strangers. At the center of Kilito's parabolic tale is the figure of a lost wanderer. It is night, he is in the desert, and he must return to "human habitation," for there, in the company of his kind, he will find his way and his lost self (xxi). For, as the text establishes from the opening lines on, selfhood is a communal property. We are who we are in the connections we make in the spaces we share with others. And, as the wanderer's tale elaborates, this search for self-in-community is linked to language. Mobility and distance thus create problems, for as we move beyond the boundaries that define our own space communication becomes more difficult. Those we encounter are likely to be different from us: foreigners or strangers. What is more, as Kilito's lost wanderer finds, these differences are myriad and unpredictable.

Nowhere does the wanderer experience this astonishing range of differences more than in the many languages he encounters. However, equally astonishing to him is his discovery of his own multilingual capacity. We are all multilingual, this text proposes. We are, all at once, inarticulate creatures howling in the dark and civilized people discoursing about culture. To underscore this point, the narrator invokes the eminent scholar of classical Arabic culture, Al-Jāḥiz. In order to know ourselves and the world around us, Al-Jāḥiz maintained, we must engage all possible languages: those of the animal world, of human cultures, of the psyche, and of our own physicality. In light of this dizzying multilingualism, the wanderer is confused. What *is* his language? Who *are* his kind? What and as whom should he speak in a given situation and on what basis should he choose? Moreover, the invocation of Al-Jāḥiz, a scholar from ninth-century Baghdad, underscores the historical burden implicit in these choices. For the lost wanderer is simultaneously the Arab of the past ("l'Arabe d'autrefois," as the French original of "Dog Words" puts it), joined across time to an ancient lineage of cultural kin, and the paradigmatic figure of postmodern rootlessness. Which of these Arabs should he be and how could he be just one?

"Dog Words" begins by proposing that the wanderer will recover his lost self by restoring the relationship between self, community, and language. This relationship, however, is a riddle. What is more, it is a riddle that locates him at the very heart of a much larger and complex collective history. For the wanderer's experience of "loss, deprivation, diminution" is arguably one of the most defining experiences of our time, as countless human beings continue to be displaced from their homes, countries, and communities.[4] In that sense, the wanderer's questions about the relationship between identity, belonging, and cultural grounding are questions for us all. The text proposes as much by addressing us directly in the first sentence: "Quick, what does a

bedouin do when he loses his way at night?" (xxi). The wanderer's problem
is all of ours.

What *does* he do? His first move is a startling one, particularly in light of his
desire to "find himself." For he makes himself Other: "He starts barking . . .
[he] pretends to be a dog" (xxii). Hoping that this ploy will help him reach his
goal (the answering barks of other dogs will point him toward human habitation), the wanderer divests himself of speech strategically. As he thus dis-
aggregates himself into functionally different component parts—separating
voice (how he articulates himself) from image (who he appears to be)—the
question of who he *really* is is temporarily suspended. Shedding the false security of a coherent and selfsame self, he engages the risk of otherness deliberately. In so doing, he adopts the very position of a contradictory and *inco*-
herent self that makes the migrant so disturbing to those who need to believe
that identities are inalienable. At the same time, "Dog Words" proposes that
the one most at risk and most disturbed by these shifting identities is the one
occupying the position of Other himself, namely the barking migrant.

"Dog Words" explores the dimensions of this risk. It begins with the migrant's realization that he may have strayed so far from his origins that he is
now lost permanently. The severed connections may be irreparable: "What
if, upon finding his tribe, he did not find his language? . . . What if he were
no longer capable of using the language of his family?" (xxiii). The initially
strategic move to connect with others by acting like an Other—a barking
dog—has initiated a chain of events over which he has lost control: "Trou-
bling symptoms appear . . . he takes a liking to gnawing bones and develops
an intense hatred of cats" (xxiv). To his horror, he is becoming, not just acting like, a dog. Loss, "Dog Words" reminds us, has consequences; it transforms. In some ways, it transforms everything. The wanderer who set out to
find himself is no longer the self he was. And his kin no longer know him.
As he barks instead of speaking, they don't recognize him anymore. In the
process of making himself Other he has become Other to them, too, and
they exclude him from their community. They refuse to let him speak; they
hold his mouth shut. And so, even though his ploy has worked and he has
found them, he is not of them anymore.

But just as it would appear that his loss is permanent, another change occurs. Instead of rejecting him, refusing to accept him unless he rejoins them
on their terms and resumes speaking their old language, the wanderer's kinfolk extend themselves outward to him by adopting his new language. Instead of holding his mouth shut to stop his barking, they start barking themselves. In so doing, they acknowledge that his loss was their loss, too. For he
is not simply "a lost wanderer": he is "their lost child" (xxv). He was not lost
because he had lost his way, but because he had lost his link to them. And
suddenly, a piece of the puzzle linking self, community, and language falls

into place: the migrant and his kin are who they are *to one another*, not in relation to an origin that authenticates them in themselves. Therefore, the various changes that the wanderer undergoes—changes of place, of language, and of behavior ("he takes a liking to gnawing bones and develops an intense hatred of cats")—affect not only him. Amazed and moved as he beholds his newly barking clan, he realizes that "[w]hat happened to him . . . has now happened to his clan" (xxv). They have all been changed: those who left, those who stayed, and those who followed after.

Accordingly, the characters in "Dog Words" display no nostalgia for the things they leave behind: places, languages, or identities. They are wanderers, change is their condition, and under such conditions adaptability is what counts, not some ideal of authenticity. For, as exemplified by their present state—no longer human, because they have become like dogs, but not really having become dogs, either—they inhabit the spaces between no-longer and not-yet. If they ever were truly anything, they've forgotten what it was. Yet from this state of lost origins, contingent identifications, and compromised attachments, new possibilities emerge: new forms of language, new structures of belonging, new modes of creativity. And it is in this freedom from what Gilles Deleuze has called "the codes of settled people" that the nomadic sensibilities of Kilito's migrants reveal their creative potential for transformation.[5]

Nowhere is this potential more evident than in their inventive adaptations. First humans, now dogs, the wanderer and his kinfolk change as is needed as they go. What remains constant is their commitment to maintain connection. This means that wherever and with whomever they are, they must find a common language. Thus, when on their journey they encounter a tribe of people who can neither bark nor speak, they search for new ways to communicate. Their solution is mimicry: they ape the new tribe's ways. And as the tribe apes them back, it becomes apparent that mimicry need not be seen as an act of self-negation. It is also a strategically negotiated act of mutual transformation. It is an attempt to find meaning in what might otherwise have been just loss. As "Dog Words" puts it, "imitation . . . reconfirms our sense of 'ourselves,'" but with a critical difference: for the performance of different selves in response to one another acknowledges alterity and mutuality simultaneously (xxviii). In the process, an understanding of community takes shape that is not based on origins and authenticity, but is constituted here and now, relationally. This provisional and contingent enactment of different selves connected in community is what defines a nomadic sensibility. For, as Teshone Gabriel notes, rather than "glorifying fulfillment in terms of territory or resources" as "settled people" do, nomads "consolidate the community through ritual and performance" (396). This is precisely how "Dog Words" ends. Kilito's wanderer has rejoined his clan, which has taken to acting like the dogs that the wanderer mimicked when he was lost initially. At the same time, they have joined up with a new tribe whose apish behavior they are copying, even as the apes they are copying are in turn copying them. Mimics mimicking mimics, they are all, in the end, joined in the performance of mutually affirming transformations.

Thus, while "Dog Words" begins by acknowledging the multiple losses experienced by the migrant—loss of place, of connection to his community of origin, of the ability to communicate, and of a sense of self—it concludes on a significantly different note, as it affirms the legitimacy of a compromised state and the functional value of inauthenticity. Taking the loss of language as exemplary of cultural losses overall, it proposes that such losses need not be final: to lose one's language does not mean to lose language as such. We can remake it. Whether it is recovered, adapted, or borrowed, or made entirely new, is not what ultimately matters. What does matter, as the migrant and his kinfolk understand, is that they are able to maintain contact with one another over time as well as establish contact with others. As they thus move from speaking to barking to acting like apes, performing the selves that each situation calls for, they model an ability to adapt and compromise that might stand us all in good stead as we negotiate the complexities of postmodern migrancies.

In this light, "Dog Words" returns at the end to the figure of Al-Jāḥiz, who had been invoked at the beginning as a link to the protagonist's cultural past. Upon reconsideration, however, the authority of this ancient source is of questionable value. For the conditions that determined the perspective of an Al-Jāḥiz are no longer ours. As the narrator notes, "the fact of the matter is that Al-Jāḥiz did not need to know any language other than Arabic, for the simple reason that there was, in his time, only one language, namely Arabic. All the rest was mere noise" (xxx). We, however—postmodern migrants in a postcolonial, postmodern age—we live in a time of noise. Like the wanderer in Kilito's parable, we need to be able to move, as needed, from speaking to barking to acting like apes. And also like the wanderer, we need to know when it is time to remain silent and simply listen.

"WORDS [THAT] HAVE NO CHILDHOOD": AN EXILE'S TALE

Emine Sevgi Özdamar's *Mother Tongue*, published in 1990 by the Berlin-based Rotbuch press, takes up similar issues as Kilito's "Dog Words": identity, language, and belonging, and the links between all three. Yet their perspectives on these issues differ considerably. For while migrant subjects are at the center of both texts, Kilito employs the discourse of nomadism and Özdamar the discourse of exile. From the perspective of a nomadic sensibility, "Dog Words" in the end upholds change and displacement as positive. Defining community as a set of contingencies to which we respond situationally, it espouses the ideal of an *adaptive self* that remains open to the new and un-expected. *Mother Tongue*, on the other hand, grounds its ideal of an *authen-tic self* in a notion of cultural rootedness. From this perspective, change and displacement are perceived as threatening, while tradition and attachment to communities of origin are valued.[6] Thus, while "Dog Words" applauds the peripatetic, dis-integrated self that is flexible, adaptive, and inventive, *Mother Tongue* invokes the counter-ideal of the integrated self, securely rooted in the culture that formed it. In short, the very authenticity that "Dog Words" rejects as ultimately maladaptive, *Mother Tongue* seeks out.

Mother Tongue is composed of four separate narratives connected through the actual and imaginary journeys of the characters back and forth between different times and places: Turkey and Germany, the historical present and cultural past. The first two of these segments, "Mother Tongue" and "Grand-father Tongue," are conjoined parts of an extended narrative, the second be-ginning where the first leaves off. It is this story that I will take up here.

"Mother Tongue" starts out much like "Dog Words" in that it begins with a problem of language: the narrator realizes that she has lost her ability to com-municate in her native language, yet does not feel at home yet in her new lan-guage either. Like the narrator-protagonist of "Dog Words," she, too, is a wan-derer, traveling on intercity trains between her native Turkey and current residence in Germany. She does not lose her way.[7] But she has lost her place in language. And she feels this loss viscerally as a body trauma: her tongue, once endlessly adaptable, has become "twisted" (9). She can no longer make herself understood. By the same token, she can no longer understand others. When they speak to her in Turkish, in their shared mother tongue, she trans-lates, in her mind, into German. Remembering a story that a Turkish woman had told her about her son who had been hanged, she can only recollect it as a sequence of strange words "as if she had said the words in German" (11). Her native tongue has become a foreign language. In fact, as she translates everything she experiences or remembers into something else, she loses her sense of reality altogether: she has become foreign to herself. Her body, thoughts, and feelings seem like translations of someone else. In the end, she is virtually paralyzed, unable to communicate, to remember, to act.

Whereas in a similar moment of crisis the protagonist of "Dog Words" had moved forward, the protagonist of "Mother Tongue" decides to turn back. She must go "back to Turkey . . . back to Grandfather . . . back to my mother, back to my mother tongue," she tells herself, as if she could only hope to re-cover the self she seems to have lost if she goes back to where she came from (14–15). Having lost any sense of origins in the multiple translations she has undergone, she believes that only by restoring the severed connection to her roots will she be able to recover her true self. To accomplish this return, she takes up Turkish. But not the Turkish of today that is itself the result of a cultural translation. Rather, she decides to learn the Turkish of the past, the authentic, original Turkish that her grandfather knew before it was modernized and Latin letters replaced the traditional Arabic script. This is where "Mother Tongue" ends and "Grandfather Tongue" begins, when the protagonist starts lessons in Arabic.

If "Mother Tongue" establishes the record of her loss, "Grandfather Tongue" charts her recovery. Her teacher, Ibni Abdullah, lives, like the protagonist, in Berlin. Like her, he has left his native country (identified simply as "Arabia" in the text) to live and work in Germany.[8] His study becomes her home, her own microcosmic Arabia. For Ibni Abdullah—her teacher, lover, and alter ego—also becomes her family and kin. And through this renewed attachment to a familial community, she begins to recover herself. Her recovery, like her loss, begins with language: Ibni Abdullah gives her five letters of the Arabic alphabet. But they are not just letters, they are living things: "Some looked like a bird, others like a heart pierced by an arrow, others like a caravan . . . others like eyes that cannot sleep" (20). And as they become animate and begin talking with one another, they awaken her to herself, a self at once new and deeply familiar.

The text then becomes a dialogue among her disparate parts: she who left Turkey speaks to her who insists she could never leave; she who has forgotten Arabic speaks to her who remembers it. And as she reclaims the ground of language, memories return, too: her father listening to Arabic programs on the radio, the Arabic names of family members. However, the past that returns is not just her personal and familial past, but a past that places her in a larger history. Thus, as the narrator and Ibni Abdullah share the memories that their study of Arabic evoke, they piece together a complex history that links the "Arabia" from which they came with the Europe in which they are living. They remember learning as children about Atatürk and Turkish history; they remember the Arab-Israeli war of their adolescence in which Ibni Abdullah's brothers died; and they remember the student protests in Berlin against the Shah of Iran that marked the political history of their young adulthood.

Most significantly, however, for the narrator-protagonist, restoring the connection to her past restores her sense of meaning and purpose. Moreover, she discovers that this sense has been there all along, merely waiting to be awakened. Summoned now by the call of a familiar language, it emerges in a rush of memories, dreams, and stories. She tells Ibni Abdullah stories that her grandmother had told her; he tells her stories that he heard from his mother. And in this dialogue that connects their exilic present to a shared collective past they tap a primal energy released by their native language: the language of their people, their families, their cultural roots, a language they know without translation. For Özdamar's protagonist this resonant connection to her culture of origin is her lifeline to herself, for in this connection lies her ability to establish relationships, to create, to experience herself as a human being. As she notes toward the end of "Grandfather Tongue," "[i]n a foreign tongue, words have no childhood" (52). Without a childhood, this text implies, without a lived connection to our past, our words—like us who speak them—are always foreign.

Finally, the sense of self that Özdamar's protagonist finds in the return to her roots enables her to encounter foreignness without experiencing it as threatening. One day, when Ibni Abdullah greets her in a traditional German way ("'I wish you a lovely afternoon,' he said"), instead of in the Arabic way that was their custom, she is surprised ("'That is very German,'" she notes). But she accepts it (47). It is then that she realizes how much she has changed. For what had earlier seemed impossible is now easy for her: she can accommodate the foreign, both outside and within herself.

This, then, is the paradox of the narrator's symbolic return home, that only from the security of her connection to home can she face the foreignness of the world. This paradox is revealed at the end of "Grandfather Tongue." For at the end of her narrative, she revisits an incident that had marked her initial crisis of disconnection: a woman had told her the story of a young man who was hanged and she had been unable to understand her. At the end of "Grandfather Tongue" a similar incident occurs, but this time it is resolved differently. She again meets a woman who tells her a story of a young man who was hanged. But this time the narrator is able to hear it all, exactly as it is told to her. The connection between them—the woman talking, the woman listening, and the dead young man—is made on human terms; no translation is needed. Tongues have become untwisted; the possibility of dialogue has been restored. Indeed if, as Edward Said notes, "exile is a solitude experienced outside the group," then her state of exile has ended (359). She has come home. More to the point, she has recovered the sense of herself that enables her to be at home in whatever community she chooses.

The protagonists of both Kilito's and Özdamar's texts experience loss of such scope—loss of a sense of belonging, of community and history, and the familiarity of a mother tongue—that it puts their ability to survive into question. Yet even as they record the shock of finding themselves in "the perilous territory of non-belonging," they turn loss into creativity (Said 359). Kilito's nomadic wanderer finds creative possibilities in the freedom from tradition and fixed forms that he experiences in his encounters with new people, while Özdamar's emigrant finds her voice in the familiarity of her mother tongue and creative energy in the return to her cultural origins.

"BETWEEN FOREIGN AND FLOATING SIGNS"

As they identify the problems and possibilities inherent in migrancy, Kilito and Özdamar map common ground. Where they differ is in their sense of direction. Forward into the indeterminate mix of hybrid identities and communities-in-process, where displaced persons mix and move? Or back to the sources of cultural memories and roots that ground us in the traditions and lineage of a people?

Work in cultural studies locates itself along a spectrum marked by these poles: at one end, identity politics defined by the structural oppositions of "us" and "them"; at the other end, the variegated mix of poststructuralist and deconstructive practices that call such identity positions into question. Within this spectrum of possibilities, Kilito's and Özdamar's texts represent not only different modalities of migrancy, but different perspectives of the contemporary migrant's condition. At the same time, they remind us that the way we think about these things—home, place, self, community, and language—is always also marked by the places from which we think them. Kilito considers the creative potential of displacement from a grounding in his native culture; Özdamar weighs the price of displacement from the position of an immigrant. He writes as a Moroccan in Morocco; she as a Turk in Berlin. In short, they remind us that while exile and nomadism may have become tropes for contemporary experience, trope and experience are not the same.

On the other hand, trope and experience are not unrelated, which takes us back to the notion of migrancy as the human condition of our age and the question of how this condition might remap personhood. Both Özdamar's and Kilito's texts uphold the assumption that language is a constitutive dimension of personhood. Moreover, they seem to accept the Kantian definition of a subject as one who not only speaks in his (or her) own person ("in seiner eigenen Person"), but does so publicly. Indeed, the emancipation that Kant posits as the goal and result of such a process is literally defined as acquiring a mouth with which to speak, or, as the German puts it, becoming "*mündig.*"[9] The philosopher Charles Taylor takes Kant's suggestion and puts it in form of a mandate: we become persons, Taylor argues, only when we take speech into the public realm to speak *for* ourselves *with* others: "I become a person and remain one," he concludes, "only as an interlocutor" (276).

It is here that Kilito and Özdamar, in a slight, but decisive, way, diverge from the Enlightenment-based equation of personhood and public language, for, they propose, the migrant experience undoes the alignments between who we feel to be, who we appear to be, and whom we present ourselves as. Migrants are constitutively marked by in-betweenness. The resulting range of options, bounded by exigencies and driven by a volatile mix of longing, desire, and fear, effect a small, but radical, shift in the notion of the subject defined in Enlightenment terms as proposed by Kant and Taylor. In its place, writers like Kilito and Özdamar put what Homi Bhabha calls a "non-sovereign notion of self," a self for whom otherness is a constitutive dimension ("The

Third Space" 212). From the perspective of such a self, forms of language that might not conventionally figure as authentic, because they include such modalities as mimicry, translation, or even silence, might well need to be incorporated into the full picture of what true human language is.

NOTES

1. For a discussion of the systemic effects of these shifts on the European imaginary, see Jameson.

2. Bhabha begins this essay by positioning himself as "an anglicised postcolonial migrant" (5). The Other of whom he writes is thus a category that includes himself.

3. I am defining "Europe" broadly here, in terms that include texts like Cha's *Dictée,* Kilito's "Dog Words," and the work of Assia Djebar, even though these writers technically figure as American, Moroccan, and Algerian, respectively. However, in each case, their work is profoundly informed by their engagement with and background in European thought and culture, including Cha's studies and work in Paris and Amsterdam, as well as Kilito's and Djebar's scholarly training and publishing in France.

4. This fact and its consequences are the subject of my *Displacements.*

5. Rosi Braidotti's view that "[i]t is the subversion of set conventions that defines the nomadic state, not the literal act of traveling" echoes that of Deleuze (Braidotti, 5).

6. Simone Weil's notion that "[t]o be rooted is perhaps the most important and least recognized need of the human soul" could stand as the preamble to Özdamar's text (quoted in Said, 364).

7. The protagonist's life follows a similar trajectory as the author's. Born in Turkey, Özdamar moved to Germany in 1965 to work in a factory. She moved back to Istanbul to study, then back again to Germany to work. Since 1988 she has lived in Berlin, where she studied Oriental languages and works as an independent artist and writer. *Mother Tongue,* written in German, was her first published work.

8. "Arabia," of course, is not a country, but a non-specific regional designation that connotes a mythic Arab homeland, land of spices and scents.

9. *Mündig* is the adjective derived from the German noun *Mund* (mouth). Emancipation ("Mündigkeit"), in Kant's terms, thus literally means "having (or acquiring) a mouth."

WORKS CITED

Bammer, Angelika. *Displacements: Cultural Identities in Question.* Bloomington: Indiana University Press, 1994.

Bhabha, Homi. "Interrogating Identity." *ICA Documents* 6. London: Institute of Contemporary Arts, 1987. 5–11.

———. "The Third Space." *Identity: Community, Culture, Difference.* Ed. Jonathan Rutherford. London: Lawrence & Wishart, 1990. 207–21.

Braidotti, Rosi. *Nomadic Subjects: Embodiment and Sexual Difference in Contemporary Feminist Theory.* New York: Columbia University Press, 1994.

Cha, Theresa Hak Kyung. *Dictée*. New York: Tanam Press, 1982.

Deleuze, Gilles. "Nomad Thought." Trans. David B. Allison. *The New Nietzsche: Contemporary Styles of Interpretation*. Ed. David B. Allison. New York: Dell, 1977. 142–49.

Djebar, Assia. *Fantasia: An Algerian Cavalcade*. Trans. Dorothy S. Blair. Portsmouth, NH: Heinemann, 1993.

DuBois, W.E.B. *The Souls of Black Folk*. New York: Vintage Books, 1990.

Gabriel, Teshome. "Thoughts on Nomadic Aesthetics and the Black Independent Cinema: Traces of a Journey." *Out There: Marginalization and Contemporary Cultures*. Ed. Russell Ferguson et al. New York: The New Museum of Contemporary Art, 1990. 395–410.

Jameson, Fredric. "Modernism and Imperialism." *Nationalism, Colonialism, and Literature*. Ed. Terry Eagleton et al. Minneapolis: University of Minnesota Press. 43–66.

Kant, Immanuel. "What Is Enlightenment?" Trans. Peter Gay. *The Enlightenment*. Ed. Peter Gay. New York: Simon & Schuster, 1973. 383–90.

Kilito, Abdelfattah. "Dog Words." Trans. Ziad Elmarsafy. *Displacements: Cultural Identities in Question*. Ed. Angelika Bammer. Bloomington: Indiana University Press, 1994. xxi–xxxi.

Kristeva, Julia. *Strangers to Ourselves*. Trans. Leon S. Roudiez. New York: Columbia University Press, 1991.

Müller, Herta. *Niederungen*. Berlin: Rotbuch Verlag, 1984.

Özdamar, Emine Sevgi. *Mother Tongue*. Trans. Craig Thomas. Toronto: Coach House Press, 1994.

Said, Edward. "Reflections on Exile." *Out There: Marginalization and Contemporary Cultures*. Ed. Russell Ferguson et al. New York: The New Museum of Contemporary Art, 1990. 357–66.

Taylor, Charles. "The Person." *The Category of the Person: Anthropology, Philosophy, History*. Ed. Michael Carrithers et al. Cambridge: Cambridge University Press, 1985. 257–81.

9

Roots and Routes: Diaspora, Travel Writing, and Caryl Phillips's Sounding of the Black Atlantic

Lourdes López-Ropero

Certainly, Caryl Phillips is a strong example of the modern diasporic intellectual, in a state of ceaseless wandering. He was born in the small Caribbean island of Saint Kitts in 1958 and moved to England with his parents when he was only three months old. After developing a writing career in England and even keeping concurrent residences in London and Saint Kitts, he is at present a U.S.-based author.

This brief outline of Phillips's trajectory introduces the deterritorialization of this author in the course of his writing career. His recent work *The Atlantic Sound* engages with the far broader theme of migrancy from a diaspora perspective. This paper profiles Phillips as an exemplary writer of the new migrant Europe, reading his travelogue as a mature statement of the author's black identity politics. In this work, Phillips posits a model of identity formation that transcends "ethnic absolutisms," to borrow Paul Gilroy's term (*Black Atlantic* 3), and dissolves his Black-Britishness into a broader black diaspora sensibility. In questioning the essentialist excesses of certain contemporary black diasporic developments, he locates himself in a fluid network between the national and the diaspora perspectives, between the local and the global. I argue that *The Atlantic Sound* amounts to Phillips's *actual* exploration of Gilroy's *intellectual* black Atlantic world, and is itself what Gilroy would consider a black Atlantic project. Gilroy's black Atlantic cartography updates readers on contemporary black nationalisms. My aim is not to provide a detailed analysis of Phillips's travelogue, but to underscore the importance of his intervention in the current debate over the African diaspora.

THE BLACK ATLANTIC POLITICS OF CULTURAL IDENTITY

Purposefully or out of conscious design, through *The Atlantic Sound* Phillips meddles in the current debate over the African diaspora, which, as a co-editor of *African Diaspora: African Origins and New World Identities* suggests, enjoys a growing currency in contemporary black cultural politics (Okpewho, Davies, and Mazrui xi). Discourse about the African diaspora—African-descended people in the Western Atlantic world—is split between two different trends. Afrocentrics such as Molefi Asante highlight the centrality of African origins and the continuity of cultural patterns between Africa and the New World. In this view, the hybridization of black culture in the West is perceived as "acculturization" (Asante 53). Contrarily, anti-essentialists such as Paul Gilroy and Stuart Hall underscore hybridization and the mutability of cultural identity as the defining characteristics of Western blacks. Moderate Afrocentrics such as Isidore Okpewho avoid Asante's stridency but in fact misread Gilroy's anti-essentialism as a "total disavowal of a vestigial history" in the quest for black self-definition (Okpewho, Davies, and Mazrui xx).

The Atlantic Sound is a report of Phillips's journeys across the Atlantic. Phillips crisscrosses the Atlantic in a series of journeys to Liverpool, Ghana, and South Carolina and from the Caribbean island of Grenada to Dover, an important part of his agenda being visits to the black communities living in these places. Interestingly, Phillips charts what Gilroy has heuristically defined as the black Atlantic world, "one single and complex unit" assembling the cultures of people of African descent dispersed in the Western hemisphere (*Black Atlantic* 15), echoing Gilroy's anti-essentialist views. Let us therefore underscore the key point of Gilroy's argument in *The Black Atlantic*.

Gilroy's greatest achievement in *The Black Atlantic* is that he manages to discuss the black diaspora without relying on the paradigm of race. This is a response to the essentialist excesses he perceives in contemporary black cultural studies and politics. Gilroy has serious misgivings about the current compartmentalization of black cultural studies into African American, Caribbean, Black British, or African Studies. Such divisions reproduce the binary oppositions of self/other and black/white that black cultural studies set out to overcome. From his angle of vision, the confinement of, for example, Toni Morrison's *Beloved* to the African American canon is an act of appropriation, of "ethnic absolutism":

> . . . much of the precious intellectual legacy claimed by African American intellectuals as the substance of their particularity is in fact only partly their absolute ethnic property. . . . [T]he idea of the black Atlantic can be used to show that there are other claims to it which can be based on the structure of the African diaspora into the western hemisphere. (15)

In this light, *Beloved* is, above all, a black diaspora project. There is nothing essential or exclusive about *Beloved* for it to be claimed either as an African American or as an Afrocentric work. Gilroy celebrates black Atlantic creativity, the main feature of which is the cross-fertilization taking place between diverse black cultural elements in Western soil. Thus, he cites the song "Keep on Moving" by Funki Dreads, a North London band made up of the children of Caribbean migrants, as an epitome of hybridization. What Gilroy finds remarkable in this song is the fact that it was produced in Britain by people of Caribbean descent and remixed in a Jamaican dub format in the United States by an African American (16).

Gilroy, therefore, aims at dissociating the orthodox fusion of identity and ethnicity. He severs the experiences of New World blacks in the West from the borders and histories of specific nation-states, be they Africa, the United States, Britain, or any other. Labels such as Black British or African American should not be read exclusively as detaching these specific branches from the dense diaspora forest. Instead, he invites critics and academics to apprehend black cultural production as a ground for cross-fertilization and hybridization transcending national boundaries and including what Stuart Hall would call a *European Presence*. One of the tenets of his work and of much of contemporary postcolonial and cultural criticism is that identities should be neither racially nor ethnically constructed, that the seemingly reasonable conflation of national identity and race is misguided.

Two different methodological approaches to cultural identity—essential and fluid—are at stake here. The former considers identity as a stable category, impervious to the flows of history. Its emphasis is on *roots* and, consequently, on the archaeological recovery of a lost past. From this perspective, culture equals folklore, which is understood as a set of cultural artifacts and practices which have been preserved in the face of change and discontinuities. In contrast, the latter approach underscores *routes*. As Hall would put it, "Cultural identities come from somewhere, have histories. But like everything that is historical, they undergo constant transformation" (394). The spotlight is not on what we have been but on what we are becoming.

Obviously, Gilroy adheres to a fluid notion of identity, suitable to describe cultural productions affected by colonization, migration, multicultural policies, and global dynamics. Identity, for the members of the black diaspora, should not be about a return to their roots in an unrecoverable and now just imaginary Africa, but about coming to terms with the routes they have taken in a journey whose first leg was the Middle Passage. The special cultural location of Western blacks implies a constant dialogue with the imaginary homeland of Africa, their actual European homes, and other places such as the Caribbean for blacks of Caribbean descent like Phillips or Gilroy himself. Consequently, Gilroy's black Atlantic is capacious enough to accommodate a European element or presence. It is true that Gilroy's focus is on black identities and cultural production, not existing in isolation, but as an integral part of the West. Stemming from this cultural location is a "double consciousness"—a term Gilroy borrows from W.E.B. DuBois (*Black Atlantic*)—a sense of being both European and black, both British and black. The infamous association of a given national identity with a dominating race has made these two categories seem exclusive. It is responsible for the racism inflicted on Europe's black subjects, which paradoxically Gilroy sees now operating in reverse in black cultural studies.

THE CONSTRUCTION OF BRITISH IDENTITY: FROM POWELL TO THE IRRESISTIBLE RISE OF A MULTI-RACIAL NATION

A crucial thrust of Gilroy's work has been to challenge the racial construction of British identity, whose mutability was put to the test by the arrival of Caribbean colonial migration in the 1950s. These migrants, or to use Gilroy's terminology, "black settlers," were perceived as "an illegitimate intrusion into a vision of authentic British national life that, prior to their arrival, was as stable and peaceful as it was ethnically undifferentiated" (*Black Atlantic* 7). The closure around the idea of British identity as Anglo-Saxon prevented Britain from remembering that blacks had been part of the country's population since the eighteenth century, during the heyday of the slave trade, so that, as Gilroy has argued elsewhere, "an old British script" was being "reworked" with the coming of the *Windrush* generation (qtd. in Trevor Phillips and Mike Phillips 382). Given their colonial bond with Britain, their British passports, their war loyalty, their contribution to alleviating the post-war labor shortage, and their nominal rights of entry and settlement as British subjects, Caribbean immigrants had high expectations about their reception in the mother country. However, these expectations were soon shattered, since colonial migration was constructed from the beginning as a racial problem.

The England that Phillips's generation grew up in was reluctant to accept its increasingly multicultural character. The famous "rivers of blood" speech, made in Birmingham in 1968 by Enoch Powell—a member of the conservative party—became emblematic of England's fears of being taken over by her black subjects: ". . . as I look ahead, I am filled with foreboding. Like the Roman, I seem to see the River Tiber foaming with much blood . . . ," (qtd. in Nairn 256). Powell's speeches received wide media coverage and a great deal of public support. In fact, his line of thought was picked up a decade later by Margaret Thatcher, who in an often-quoted television speech in 1978 expressed the fear that her country might be "swamped by a people of a different culture" (qtd. in Cohen, *Frontiers of Identity* 58). The England of Phillips's upbringing was steeped in racialist discourses. To compound the matter, Phillips's generation, British-born or raised, was not content with merely "being in" the society, but had a strong desire for full acceptance (C. Phillips, "George Lamming Talks to Caryl Phillips" 17). Doubly conscious individuals like Phillips could never feel at home in such a climate. The fact he was born in the Caribbean gave him a sense of mooring that would compensate for the ambivalent status of his generation, children of Caribbean colonial immigrants who had migrated to the "mother country" in the 1950s (Birbalsingh 43–44). Yet Phillips has never managed to feel at home solely on British soil and has sought a more complex web of affiliations.

Phillips concedes that British society has changed radically since the 1950s. In the prologue to *The Atlantic Sound*, featuring Phillips's trip from the Caribbean to England on a banana boat carrying cargo to Dover, the author clearly speaks from a second-generation location. He is able to sympathize with the loneliness and uncertainty of his parents' Atlantic crossing and their subsequent shattered expectations in England, but nonetheless insists on the distinctiveness of his own experience. He is not a colonial going to the mother country with a sense of "hope and expectation" (16), but an accommodated black British citizen arriving in Britain with a sense of propriety. As he approaches the cliffs of Dover, this descendant of Caribbean immigrants appears to be suggesting that, in spite of the endurance of racialist discourses, his generation is inevitably more *of* Europe than his parents'. Contemporary Britain is, however reluctantly, a "postcolonial" society more accustomed to its multicultural makeup (Phillips, *A New World Order* 282). The racial construction of national identity has lost credibility and authority over the decades. The nostalgia for an Anglo-Saxon age of racial purity pervading the Powellite and Thatcherite years has given way to cultural pluralism. In effect, to echo the title of Trevor and Mike Phillips's book, multi-racial Britain has *irresistibly* risen.

In one of the essays of *A New World Order* reporting conversations between Phillips and Jamaican-born and British-raised dub poet Linton Kwesi Johnson, we are encouraged to juxtapose Phillips's views on contemporary postcolonial Britain with Linton's, and to take sides with the former. Whereas Linton misses the radicalism of 1970s black politics and claims that the third generation of black Britons have been co-opted by the establishment—as television anchors, MPs, and the like—losing the radicalism of previous black generations, Phillips argues that such mainstreaming is a measure of success and integration. Naturally, he concedes, the "drive" of an immigrant is different from that of a settled citizen (259). In a coherent gesture, Linton had abandoned Island Records to create his own independent label, being the first reggae artist to do so. Yet rather than celebrating Linton's choice, Phillips underscores the toll his radicalism has taken on his physical strength. After reading this chapter, we are left with a Phillips who appears reconciled with Britain, a much more tolerant nation in the early twenty-first century than the one his parents encountered back in the 1950s.

Given his intercultural positionality, Phillips fits the black intellectual figure Gilroy delineates in *The Black Atlantic*. Here Gilroy celebrates lives with "a rich transnational texture" (19) such as those of Martin Delaney, W.E.B. DuBois, Marcus Garvey, or Richard Wright. Phillips's trajectory dissolves any simple attempts to fix him as consistently ". . . a British writer, a black writer, a black British writer, a West Indian writer, Caribbean writer, a black Caribbean writer . . ." (C. Phillips, "West Indian Writing Abroad" 25). A moving target, Phillips is shown uneasy about the critics' penchant for pigeon-holing him into any of these categories. In the course of his writing career, Phillips has come to apprehend cultural identity in relation to movement and mediation rather than to rootedness. Whereas the rubric "Black British" might have been adequate to describe the Phillips of the 1980s, now the most felicitous label we may apply to him is that of a black diasporic writer of Caribbean descent. Significantly, he has referred to New York City, his present residence, as the place where he "currently spend[s] most of the year" (*A New World Order* 300). Phillips has gradually deterritorialized himself in the course of time.[1]

Despite his conciliatory tone in *A New World Order*, the author is not able to confine his self-definition to Britain as a black Briton. His upbringing in the heyday of British racialism probably blocks him from a full identification with Britain. Hence his need for a decentralized, plural definition of home. In his most recent nonfiction work he is outspoken about his increasing de-territorialization, to the extent that the Atlantic Ocean is avowedly the only place that can stir in him a feeling of belonging. He writes:

> Whenever I stand on the ramparts of Elmina Castle and gaze out at the Atlantic Ocean, I know exactly where I come from. I can look to the north and to the west and see the different directions in which I have subsequently journeyed. And, on a clear day, I can peer into the distance and see where I will ultimately reside. (*A New World Order* 309)

Without any of the official constraints of national boundaries, Phillips's "Atlantic home" is indeed an imaginary and unstable geocultural site. Yet it fits his conception of identity as the routes, here "directions," he has taken over the years. The fact that this Atlantic gazing takes place in Elmina, a city on the west coast of Africa, does not amount to an invocation of roots in an Afrocentric fashion. The African city is simply a strategic vantage point from which Phillips can bring together the different strands woven into his making. West Africa, Europe, and the Americas are the three sites framing the Black Atlantic watery design.

SOUNDING THE ATLANTIC

Gilroy explains that a concern with the Atlantic as a cultural system[2] is not arbitrary but rather "forced on black historiography and intellectual history" by the economic system of plantation slavery (*Black Atlantic* 15). The slave trade is to be held accountable for the dispersal of blacks from the original African homeland, as well as for Europe's modernization and economic growth during the eighteenth and nineteenth centuries. The Atlantic Ocean thus refers us back to the Middle Passage, to Europe's exploitation of African labor. During the infamous slave trade the Atlantic was crisscrossed by ships leaving European ports with goods that were exchanged on the African coasts for human captives, who were then sold into slavery in North American and Caribbean plantations in return for cash or exotic products that would respectively be banked or sold upon returning to Europe.

Far from turning the slave experience into a traumatic event precipitating exile and diaspora in the ancient Jewish sense,[3] Gilroy assigns a historical meaning to slavery, seeing it as both the heart of the history of the African diaspora and as a symptom of the black man's "modernity" (190). Gilroy maintains that while there is no magical African essence holding the African diaspora together, the slavery experience and its aftermath of racial discrimination contributes to sustaining an imagined black community (195). It is an integral part of black history and has therefore to be acknowledged, not silenced. He criticizes the Afrocentric version of African history, which perceives slavery as a site of black victimization and thus urges blacks to erase it. Such approaches not only romanticize African history but rely on a linear idea of time, postulating "a grand narrative of African advancement . . . momentarily interrupted by slavery . . . which made no substantial impact upon African tradition" (190). Moreover, in an ethnically absolutist gesture, it simply inverts the terms of domination, blacks becoming dominant by virtue of culture and whites being allocated a subordinate role. Purged of the slavery experience, the history of the black diaspora would lack historical depth.

The triangular trade is the backcloth to Phillips's chartings in *The Atlantic Sound*. Structured on a series of Atlantic journeys, *The Atlantic Sound* is a travelogue, and is Phillips's second venture into the originally ethnocentric genre of travel writing, after *The European Tribe*. Like its predecessor, it is emblematic of the transcultural black Atlantic creativity Gilroy celebrates. Phillips appropriates travel writing, a quintessentially Western and orientalist genre[4] to render his revision of racial slavery and black identity politics.

Travel writing is no longer an instrument of imperial expansion in the late twentieth century; it has become a powerful vehicle of cultural critique, particularly in the hands of special-interest groups such as postcolonial authors. Barbara Korte maintains that they have infused their travelogues with the preoccupation with history and cultural identity that permeates postcolonial literature. She highlights the prolific contribution to the *postcolonial travelogue* by writers of Caribbean descent such as V. S. Naipaul, Ferdinand Dennis, and Caryl Phillips (155). Conceived as an instrument to increase the author's self-awareness as a black European, *The European Tribe* turned out to be a scathing critique of the widespread racialism of increasingly multicultural 1980s Europe. Similarly, in *The Atlantic Sound*, Phillips's revision of Europe's historical involvement in the slave trade through his trips across the Atlantic provides him with an opportunity to take up his perennial preoccupation with notions of home, belonging, and cultural identity.

In his exploration of Liverpool's entanglement with the economy of slavery, Phillips does not fail to unveil the exploitative trade, but also attempts a new, less impassioned understanding, echoing Gilroy's and Hall's anti-essentialism. In Liverpool, Phillips puzzles over the fact that "history is so physically present, yet so glaringly absent from people's consciousness" (93). Actually, Phillips describes Liverpool's most remarkable buildings as trademarks of the city's past imperial splendor. The author, however, casts a very skeptical look on his guide's radicalized concern with Liverpool's African history. Unlike him, Phillips does not see any purpose in stirring a sense of historical guilt among Liverpudlians. Contrarily, Phillips concedes that the "modern condition" is characterized by a certain obliviousness about the past of the city, coextensive with the course events had taken in the natural flow of history. His guide's militant attitude reflects the anti-essentialism that Phillips upholds throughout the travelogue.

Phillips's spotlight in *The Atlantic Sound* is not on the ordeal and painful consequences of the middle passage, but rather on current trends in black communities. In the African section of the travelogue Phillips is outspoken about his conception of diaspora, which shares more with Gilroy's transcultural black Atlantic formation than with the Afrocentric tradition. Phillips rejects the notion of diaspora that features Africa as the center of the Black Triangle—to borrow Hall's term—and that resorts to Africa as a way to restore an imaginary fullness in the face of historical fragmentation, or to give meaning to black cultural identity. Though Africa is, inevitably, one of the sites of Phillips's Atlantic itinerary, it is not approached romantically as an ancient homeland. In keeping with the author's outlook in his travelogue, Africa affords Phillips an opportunity to underscore the cultural commodification of the diaspora, and the racialism and preposterousness underlying certain diasporic trends themselves. The African city he visits, Elmina, is, in fact, one of the fortified sites of slave-trading activity that have recently become places of pilgrimage and cultural tourism for the most affluent members of the African diaspora.

Phillips's visit takes place during the celebration of Panafest. Whereas the festival uses the idea of Africa to impose an imaginary coherence on the experience of dispersal, Phillips does not underestimate the discontinuities brought about by history. Hence his bewilderment when a performer in a poetry reading unites "Harlem to Ghana, and Ghana to Guyana" (147), emphasizing homogeneity and unity within the black world. What increases Phillips's uneasiness is the spectacularization of identity contained in statements such as the logo *Never forgive, never forget* printed on the revelers' tee-shirts (148). Once more, Gilroy's predicaments, though from a different book this time, resonate in the travelogue. In *Between Camps*, a more recent study of race and black nationalism, Gilroy goes a step beyond *The Black Atlantic,* touching upon the encroachment of fascism in contemporary black nationalism (7). Underlying the paraphernalia of festivals like Panafest is a notion of identity that, as Gilroy would argue, "ceases to be an ongoing process of self-making and social interaction. It becomes instead a thing to be possessed and displayed" (*Between Camps* 103). In this section, Phillips highlights the cultural significance of Elmina in black historiography, even providing readers with background to the exchanges taking place there during the times of the slave trade. Yet he refuses to subscribe to an idea of Africa as essence and of black history as a site of victimization.

Phillips's desire to give an update on current developments in the black diaspora allows him to transcend the watery boundaries of Gilroy's black Atlantic and explore new sites. Thus, in taking issue with contemporary black Zionism, Phillips the traveler transports us to a small town in the Negev desert of Israel, where a community of African Americans have exiled themselves. Watching them move around their village in their daily activities, Phillips regards them as "circus clowns" whose identity is a spectacle and whose community is, to borrow Gilroy's term, an exclusive "national encampment" (*Between Camps* 103). Phillips's report on his stay with these exiles reinforces the idea that, for the descendants of Africans living in Europe or elsewhere, homelands should be myths to be imagined or acknowledged by the collective consciousness of the group, rather than realities to be enacted in a feasible way. As William Saffran argues, rather than a feasible plan, the return drive is an eschatological concept, a myth "used to make life more tolerable by holding out a utopia . . . in contrast to the perceived dystopia of actual life" (94). It is true that blacks have historically identified with the Exodus story as way of articulating their sense of historical identity as a people. In fact, black return movements such as the settlement of Sierra Leone (1787) and the founding of Liberia (1821) are landmarks in black history. Phillips's returnees are nonetheless late twentieth-century exiles who believe themselves to be descendants of the Hebrews dispersed throughout the world. Not surprisingly, cynicism pervades his remarks on these bizarre black Zionists who claim to have found their home in Israel.

While *The Atlantic Sound* has been praised for its vivid portraiture and reportage in the fashion of Jonathan Raban or V. S. Naipaul, it has also been

criticized because of the author's detachment, skepticism, and excessive intellectual engagement. A reviewer complains as follows: "This book is billed as a
personal quest, but I wanted to know more about this Caribbean-born and
England-bred author's own deep feelings for 'home' and how they were affected, or not, by his journey" (Adebayo 26). What I find agreeable in Adebayo's statement is that Phillips's views seem barely if at all altered by his journeys, which seem designed to serve a chosen end. *The European Tribe* only
confirmed the racialism the author blamed Europe for before setting out on his
travels. More recently, in *The Atlantic Sound*, Phillips chooses to dwell on a
series of black individuals and communities lacking a double consciousness,
whose view of cultural identity is flawed, if not strange. Phillips is indeed a
very controlled writer whose works leave very little room for surprises.

All this should not cloud the fact that underlying Adebayo's statement is a
tacit notion of identity as a fixed and stable condition. Phillips's anti-essentialist
view of identity prevents him from meeting the demands of those who expect
him to make a choice regarding where he belongs. As I've argued throughout,
Phillips turns Gilroy's heuristic black Atlantic into a real ocean in which he
sounds his identity politics, finding in the routes that have historically crisscrossed it—patterned on the triangle Europe–West Africa–America—a congenial pattern of self-definition for New World blacks. He not only succeeds in acting out Gilroy's predicament in *The Black Atlantic*, but transcends the Atlantic
boundaries to dwell on other sites of the black diaspora overlooked by Gilroy.
In rejecting both specific ethnic affiliations, such as his Black-Britishness, and
an Afrocentric black diaspora, Phillips locates himself in a complex network between the local and the global. The Atlanticist model of identity that Phillips
puts forward in *The Atlantic Sound* and ratifies in his next piece, *A New World
Order,* is an innovative illustration of the ways in which forms of belonging and
identity have been reinvented by the blacks immersed in Euro-American life.

NOTES

1. Phillips's gradual deterritorialization has had a direct impact on his work.
Whereas his early work is concerned with the hostile reception of Caribbean colonial
immigrants in England and their lives in the mother country, the novels and essays
written in the late 1980s and the 1990s—*Higher Ground* (1989), *Cambridge* (1991),
Crossing the River (1993), and *The Nature of Blood* (1997)—tackle the themes of
racialism and displacement from a cross-cultural perspective.

2. The idea of the Atlantic as a cultural system has a history prior to Gilroy's volume. In fact, Isidore Okpewho cites a number of authors—Robert Farris Thompson,
C. L. R. James, Peter Linebaugh—who have dealt with this issue (Okpewho, Davies,
and Mazrui xxii).

3. See Tölöyan (1991) and Cohen (1997) for the shift of current diaspora scholarship from the Jewish catastrophic tradition.

4. For the complicity of travel writing and imperialism see Said (1991 [1978]), Percy Adams (1983), or Mary Louise Pratt (2000 [1992]).

WORKS CITED

Adams, Percy. *Travel Literature and the Evolution of the Novel*. Lexington: University Press of Kentucky, 1983.

Adebayo, Dilan. "Africa and 'Home.'" *Times* 11 (May 2000): 26.

Asante, Molefi Kete. *The Afrocentric Idea*. Philadelphia: Temple University Press, 1987.

Birbalsingh, Frank. "Interview with Caryl Phillips." *Caribbean Quarterly* 37.4 (1991): 40–46.

Cohen, Robin. *Frontiers of Identity: The British and the Others*. London: Longman, 1994.

———. *Global Diasporas*. Seattle: University of Washington Press, 1997.

Gilroy, Paul. *The Black Atlantic*. London: Verso, 1999.

———. *Between Camps: Nations, Culture and the Allure of Race*. London: Penguin, 2001.

Korte, Barbara. *English Travel Writing from Pilgrimages to Postcolonial Explorations*. Basingstoke: Macmillan, 2000.

Hall, Stuart. "Cultural Identity and Diaspora." *Colonial Discourse and Post-Colonial Theory: A Reader*. Ed. Patrick Williams and Laura Chrisman. New York: Columbia University Press, 1994. 392–403.

Holland, Patrick, and Graham Huggan, eds. *Tourists with Typewriters. Critical Reflections on Contemporary Travel Writing*. Ann Arbor: University of Michigan Press, 1998.

Nairn, Tom. *The Break-Up of Britain*. London: NLB, 1977.

Okpewho, Isidore, Carole Boyce Davies, and Ali A. Mazrui, eds. *African Diaspora: African Origins and New World Identities*. Bloomington: Indiana University Press, 2001.

Phillips, Caryl. "West Indian Writing Abroad: Naipaul and the New Generation." *Caribbean Review of Books* 3 (1992): 16, 19, 24, 25, 27.

———. "George Lamming Talks to Caryl Phillips." *Wasafiri* 26 (1997): 10–17.

———. *The European Tribe*. London: Faber and Faber, 1999.

———. *The Atlantic Sound*. London: Faber and Faber, 2000.

———. *A New World Order*. New York: Vintage, 2002.

Phillips, Trevor, and Mike Phillips, eds. *Windrush: The Irresistible Rise of Multi-Racial Britain*. London: HarperCollins, 1999.

Pratt, Mary Louise. *Imperial Eyes: Travel Writing and Transculturalization*. London: Routledge, 1992.

Saffran, William. "Diasporas in Modern Societies: Myths of Homeland and Return." *Diaspora* 1 (1991): 83–99.

Said, Edward. *Orientalism*. London: Penguin, 1991.

Tölölyan, Khachig. "The Nation-State and Its Others: In Lieu of a Preface." *Diaspora* 1 (1991): 3–7.

10

A Poetics of Home: On Narrative Voice and the Deconstruction of Home in Migrant Literature

Rosemarie Buikema

> Experience which is passed from mouth to mouth is the source from which all storytellers have drawn. And among the writers who have set down the tales, the great ones are those whose written version differs least from the speech of the many nameless storytellers. (Walter Benjamin)

Talking about the specific position of the migrant writer, Salman Rushdie claims that "if literature is in part the business of finding new angles at which to enter reality, then once again our distance, our long geographical perspective, may provide us with such angles" (Rushdie 1991, 15). According to Rosemary Marangoly George's (1996) definition, migrant literature is indeed the contemporary literary writing in which the politics of location and/or dislocation is central to the narrative. More particularly, in line with postmodern transnational thinking, migrant literature has a specific way of thematizing and deconstructing the traditional meaning of the private and the public, the near and the far, the past and the future. Contemporary migrant literature, therefore, is best read as a sub-genre within postmodern writing and postmodern times in which the theme of dislocation and homelessness is articulated in a variety of forms. In order to map out these themes of location and dislocation, however, post-colonial criticism has tended to limit its focus only to the metaphor of the journey and the diaspora. Yet within the diaspora, new connections are made between places, so that the relationship between center and periphery as it exists, for instance, between the colonial power and the former colonies, is changed. In my essay, I illustrate the fruitfulness of thinking about the effects of the diaspora by focusing on the concepts at the other extreme. This broader approach centralizes the poetics of place, metaphorically summarized as the poetics of home.

The approach to the representation of home as both a narratological and a political issue is indebted to feminist studies. From the beginning, the feminist critique not only problematized the opposition between the private and the public through the well-known adage that the personal is political, but also analyzed and commented on the home as a symbol of stability and safety. Biddy Martin and Chandra Talpade Mohanty's "Feminist Politics: What's Home Got to Do with It?" (1986) is an example of the way feminist critics questioned the fixed relationship between the concepts of home, identity, and narrative competence. This is encapsulated in their reading of Minnie Bruce Pratt's autobiographical narrative "Identity: Skin Blood Heart": "not being home is a matter of realizing that home was an illusion of coherence and safety based on the exclusion of specific histories of oppression and resistance, the repression of differences even within oneself" (96). Home, as experienced by Pratt, is tied up with dominant discourses at the cost of marginalized discourses. The concepts of home and identity are thus strongly related to discursive space, to the possibility and the ability to share experiences through storytelling. In that sense it's difficult to distinguish home from community. Pratt no longer belongs to the white heterosexual community of her childhood nor does she share, as the partner of a white Jewish lesbian, the experiences of the people in the black neighborhood where she currently lives. She struggles with herself and the world she was born into, including all the restrictions on and separations between sexualities, classes, and races. Because there's no public story for her private situation yet, both her sense of subjecthood and her ability to feel at home are under scrutiny. Her narrative has a necessarily open end. There's no fixed form. There's still a desire to feel at home but home can no longer be what it was. Here Pratt joins the concern of all minority writers: the desire for a place that doesn't exist, yet which is linked to an attempt to deploy alternative narrative techniques.

Building on the work of Martin and Mohanty, George's provocative claim is that all fiction is homesickness. By this she means that twentieth-century fiction, the great literary works of the human quest, embodies the desire to come home, to be at home, to be recognized and to be protected by boundaries and a sense of sameness. "As postmodern post-colonial subjects however we surprise ourselves with our detachment to the things we were taught to be attached to," George adds (1996, 2000). She demonstrates in her analysis of a corpus of transnational migrant literature that the twentieth-century association between an adequate self and a place or a site to call home is scrutinized by migrant authors, only to be put aside. In these texts identity is linked only hypothetically to a specific geographical space. Migrant literature claims, she concludes, that all homesickness is fiction. She proposes the possibility of distinguishing a genre of migrant literature based on its common theme, in this case the scrutiny of the politics of location. In my contribution to the view of migrant writing as a deconstruction of the concept of home, that is, as the deployment of a particular poetics of home, I intend to expand these prior thematic insights into an analysis of the migrant novel's narratological technique and its language usage.[1]

AWARENESS OF THE WORLD

In order to demonstrate the use of post-colonial narratology for the categorization of migrant literature within the corpus of postmodern literary writing I present an analysis of Moroccan-Dutch Abdelkader Benali's debut novel *Wedding by the Sea*. I have chosen this novel because it deals with the representation of the experience of home in both linguistically and sociologically interesting ways. Abdelkader Benali's background is not that of the average Dutch author; he grew up in a migrant family that had not intended to remain in the Netherlands. His parents came to make money and return home one day with better prospects. This biographical background makes geographical spaces and places, and also languages, somehow serial. The author's use of the Dutch language is unorthodox and also the novel's narrative style is complex and puzzling. Nevertheless it won the author prestigious literary prizes.[2]

My essay is therefore a contribution to a post-colonial narratology that is interested in the cultural contexts and political scope of narrativity. Its objective is the unfolding of the semiotic mechanisms involved in the production of meaning, that is, experience or contact with the surrounding world. My proposal for a specific semiotic approach of the object of post-colonial literary studies is less concerned with the study of a text corpus, and rather more with a discursive practice in which, by definition, we are forced to participate. Post-colonial semioticism should focus on matters where there is something at stake, where a difference is being made. In my view post-colonial studies, before evolving into a sociology of knowledge, should come to grips with the signifying process and by what is set in motion or constituted by it. I think that before actually projecting migrant literature as a field, we should be able to at least suggest what its specific literariness is. Literariness in general manifests itself where there is experience and awareness of the Real through the use of language. Admittedly, this description is somewhat vague. However, in the past few decades literary semioticians have succeeded in developing a theoretical conception of what consciousness is and how it relates to signification. Consciousness or awareness of the Real emanates from difference and divergence. Human beings become aware of the Real at the moment the world does not present itself as expected. The literary or artistic moment then is the imitation of this process; in linguistic terms it "mimes" the unexpected that arouses consciousness and awareness. So, paradoxically, through deviant, diverging linguistic forms we become aware of our deeply conventional, script- and frame-driven ways of dealing with the world. The specific form of human semiosis, and its imitation in and through the artistic, does seem to set the literary and the artistic apart from other social or cultural systems. It also accounts for the simple observation that literature (and art) can be about anything. But whatever it is about at the referent level, its essence is always the production of consciousness or awareness. Literariness then would be a language-driven collision with the Real. The sole concern of post-colonial analysis should be the specific post-colonial awareness of the Real.[3]

As language is the most intricate means of storing experience, the author cannot discard the social and historical reality of language and has to take in, displace, and transform the discourses that make up our social world. This makes contemporary literature, especially narratives polylogous, intertextual, and transformational. Any attempt to restrict intertextuality to an acknowledged literary corpus, which was the preferred solution in traditional academic literary studies, is a destruction of literariness; literature then becomes a game in which only its syntax and semantics matter. Post-colonial postclassical narratology could be the approach that acknowledges the intrinsic transformational quality of language.

My analysis of Abdelkader Benali's novel *Wedding by the Sea* shows that this text itself reflects its content and so creates awareness: this novel cannot be read without recourse to what is already known about the experience of living a life in different cultural contexts, but it also shows that this is not the case at all, and so it transforms our knowledge about the world. The experience mediated by this text deconstructs our expectations. It is this deconstruction that makes the novel both more common, because this migrant's text is actually not about something dramatically different, and more special, because it expresses the deeply human insight that whatever the conditions we live in, we have to cope with them, and no symbolic inversion will change the situation.

WEDDING BY THE SEA

Abdelkader Benali's debut novel, as a young writer, *Wedding by the Sea* went relatively unnoticed when it appeared in 1996. In 1997, to the surprise of many, it was nominated for the prestigious Dutch Libris Prize for Fiction. "A novel scintillating with the desire to narrate. Benali narrates on the dividing line of two cultures, enriching the Dutch language with humorous inventions," runs the eulogy of this "memorable first novel" in the jury's report. In *Wedding by the Sea*, indeed, language becomes the vehicle that brings together two different cultures, the culture of origin and the culture of present-day life, resulting in a bubbling, mercurial, new representation of self. Benali takes his inspiration from Rushdie, whose grotesque language-play succeeds in putting into words the sense of biculturalism as an excess rather than a lack of meaning. In *Imaginary Homelands*, Salman Rushdie makes a similar claim: "Language needs remaking for our own purposes. . . . Having been borne across the world, we are translated men. It is normally supposed that something always gets lost in translation; I cling, obstinately, to the notion that something can also be gained" (Rushdie 1991, 17). Benali uses the Dutch language in an original and florid way, endowing traditional Dutch expressions and maxims with new and fresh meanings by injecting them into unusual contexts. Benali is an example of a new generation of migrant authors, who, unlike many older African American and Caribbean authors, do not feel burdened with the colonial heritage of an imposed standard language that never really becomes their native language.[4]

Nevertheless, reading Benali's novel is not a question of simply applying postmodern and/or post-colonial linguistic insights in order to understand the significance of a text which at first appears breathtakingly grotesque and incoherent. It's not only the way Benali uses the Dutch language, it is also his use of narrative techniques that might have this effect on the reader. One of the most striking narratological characteristics of *Wedding by the Sea* is the narrative voice, which continually problematizes the distinction between extradiegesis and intradiegesis, as well as that between auctorial and actorial narration. That unsettling process is embodied in the use of two central topoi in the text, the taxi and the dollhouse. In the dollhouse, time is at a standstill and events are directed by a master hand, that of tradition and/or that of an authorial voice. In the taxi, where all stories of the region find their proper place, time and place are flexible, and the narrative voice becomes a character in the making of the story.

That story can be summarized in a simple plot: the Dutch-Moroccan family Minar has just arrived in Morocco to marry daughter Rebecca to her uncle Mosa. However, on the wedding day the groom has disappeared. The main character, Lamarat Minar, Rebecca's brother, is to bring Mosa back. Lamarat gets into the taxi of Chalid, the man who is familiar with all the stories of the region and passes them on. It is the stories of this taxi driver that set Lamarat on his uncle's track, and slowly he discovers the underlying, tacit structure of marriage and kinship in Morocco. In the penultimate chapter Lamarat gets off the taxi in the company of his dead-drunk uncle Mosa. His mission has not been accomplished in time, for the assignment given him by his father had been to escort his Uncle Mosa home, so that the wedding could take place properly. This simple plot takes the shape of a sort of road movie; the story unfolds as it is told, and like a TV report the story is told on the spot. While the reader is waiting for Lamarat to find his uncle, he is shown around the region in Chalid's taxi, where the various histories about the inhabitants of Touarirt, the seaside village where the father comes from, are recalled as "true lies." Among them is the story of Lamarat, Mosa, and Re-becca, which the narrator hands over to the reader with the reservation, "I was told this story in some café, by word of mouth; it went from ear to ear, and it is questionable if ever anything like Touarirt existed in the first place" (11). Although the narrator initially seems to be a heterodiegetic narrator pre-senting a story to us, the readers, he appears to have no control over events at all. Lamarat runs his race against the clock in a labyrinth of truth and lies, facts and fiction scarcely held together by a narrative voice. Time and space, truth and lies are all interwoven in *Wedding by the Sea*.

Throughout the novel it becomes clear that the narrator draws from a storehouse of experiences—experiences that are still in the process of being articulated and passed on while he is trying to tell his story to us. This on-going recounting underlines the narratological axiom that memory is the epic resource par excellence and those memories handed down from gen-eration to generation create the chain of tradition. That is why the *Wedding by the Sea* narrator is such a prominent character in the text: precisely be-cause it is he who presents the story to us while it is going off the rails. He definitely is not the authoritative narrator; he does not know where the story will end, nor when and where it actually began. The narrator repeatedly uses comments and asides such as "if the story were to be told correctly" and "if the story ran as it was supposed to" (24), thus referring to the illusion of the consistency of metaphor and logic within the monocultures both of the country of origin and of the country of the future—monisms and traditions founded on stories, on fictions. The narrator functions as the mediator be-tween those two monisms. This running between two aspects of Moroccan culture—the modern and the traditional, the home culture and the hybrid migrant version—reveals the inherently paradoxical position of the narrator who is both in and outside the diegesis, and thus is not able to be a fully re-liable director of the events.

True or not, all of these little histories contained by Chalid's taxi eventu-ally converge in the book's culminating point, and that is the moment when the bride and groom are finally united. The taxi has taken us through the story; in the taxi we have traveled in the stories both about the region and its inhabitants. At the same time the taxi has brought Uncle Mosa to his bride. The unity is brief indeed, for even the traditional love plot is subverted in *Wedding by the Sea*. Nothing is what it seems in *Wedding*, as the narrator well knows, not only at the plot level, but also at the stylistic and metaphor-ical levels. In the perception of the narrator, he thinks of the Moroccan fam-ily and the village in which they live as a dollhouse, that one can only look at, but not act upon. "This tale should be set in a house, really. A house stuffed with puppets from top to bottom. That would be more convenient to me (and to my father): allows one to keep the story simple. Men puppets and women puppets, each with their own color and each with their own strict, well-demarcated symbolism" (34). The house as a symbol of a clear-cut structure, of an authoritative author, of stability and predestination, in fact exists only as a fiction, as make-believe, as a dollhouse. Only in a dollhouse can the repetition of the same take place, can time be stopped and manipulated; only in a dollhouse is there, literally, an oversized hand able to direct what happens, to control meaning, to watch over the inside and the outside, over the strange and the private, to determine how girls are to become women and how boys become men. Paradoxically, the narrator gets entangled in the metaphor of the dollhouse, that is to say, he gets entangled in tradition, in the reference to the illusory character of consistency and closure. He abides within the simile of narration as a structure consisting of building blocks, of materials asking for the direction of the master's hand: "So in lieu of the puppet show we have one youngish young man with a hideous name who hops into a taxi cab—for our purpose a kind of miniature dollhouse— to carry out a mission, a search mission, and with any luck at all this will clear up a lot of things" (34).

The comparison of the taxi with the dollhouse problematizes yet another opposition: departure versus arrival, being home versus being on a journey, tradition versus modernity, tangibility versus contingency. "Go and find your uncle," the father had ordered Lamarat, "bring your uncle back home" (36). And that is tantamount with: restore order, prevent *haram*, avert shame and scandal from our family, ward off the bankruptcy of our culture, our morals and our traditions. Words of similar purport are used by the father in his Dutch home at the dining table. He never tires of repeating that not only has he permanently restored his family to the land of plenty, but he will, equally heroically, lead them back. On such occasions, Lamarat always asks: "how back, back where?" (36). There is no place to return to.

The story inevitably indicates that the big stories have lost their sway and that the old tradition is in decay. In the Netherlands Lamarat's father endeavors to rehabilitate the Moroccan, or at least the Islamic, tradition, when his children show too much interest in "other people's faith": "Ladies and gentlemen, it is darn well time for a darn bit of Islam in this house" (64) are the grotesque words that the author makes the father utter, and in doing so he represents this attempt as ridiculous and superficial, as a transparent displacement of the inability to become new, to become renewed, in a new context. In fact, the father does not succeed in constructing a narrative that complements the new situation, but he tries to cling to an outdated and unsuitable fiction. At the same time, the desire for a home, for stability and immobility, only becomes a real significance when Grandma and Granddad Minar move into the new house that Lamarat's father is having built in Morocco. Although this house begins crumbling while still in its scaffolding, that is not the reason why Grandma "nags about homesickness" (27).

Homesickness, the desire for a home, in Benali's text, is a longing to come home to the magic of stories, a longing for the feeling of community that emerges through the actual telling. The telling, in the sense of dwelling in the same discourse, in the same linguistic house, ceases. It ceases because the craft of narration is strongly dependent on the extent to which the experience may be reported and thus shared.

If anything is lost in postmodern, post-colonial society, it is not so much home as such but the ability to tell a good old story that is true for everybody. The very act of leaving has deconstructed the home as a home bound to old stories and fixed traditions. In Chalid's taxi, we travel through these stories, castles in the air and dollhouses, and discover the mechanisms of inclusion and exclusion concomitant with these discursive structures, the roles meted out to the puppets, the compulsion the stories apply to reality.

The major story from the strongly Islamic and folk tradition–imbued region where Lamarat hails from is, of course, the myth of the hymen. While on his wedding day Uncle Mosa finds it hard to let go of his favorite hooker, Rebecca worries about the success of her first wedding night. According to the region's tradition, it is essential that blood should flow during the deed, and a rocket is let off when "the job is done." Although everybody knows that a blood stain can always be obtained somehow, the myth of the hymen continues to function as an imperative to the bride. In a monologue, Rebecca tells Lamarat that she will follow her mother's advice and enter her wedding night armed with a safety pin and a tiny pair of scissors. When finally Lamarat takes a dead-drunk Mosa to his bride, the guests have already departed and Rebecca is in a graveyard, grieving over the failure of her wedding day. She takes the plastered Mosa in tow, not home, as was her assignment, but to the seaside. The narrator wonders how this derailment of the plot is to be explained, and he once more remarks that logic can only be found in a dollhouse.

The assignment for the narrative's hero had been to restore order, to bring home the prodigal son, and there, by the seaside, Rebecca and Mosa's first night of matrimony eventually unfolds and blood does flow—a lot of it. It is true that to accomplish this, Rebecca has needed her scissors: she cuts off the tip of Mosa's powerless penis, thus forever relegating his activities with other women to the past, to the old tradition. Even though the big stories have evaporated, all that we are left with is story, a mishmash of stories. Although they don't adequately represent our current experiences anymore, we as narrative characters and as living subjects are all constructed in and through those stories and narratives. Consequently, the displacing effect of postmodern, post-colonial times is that these narratives from afar mingle and interpenetrate with those from nearby.

If the wedding feast, which should have been a celebration of machismo, now ends in a celebration of female agency, this also has the effect of subsequently silencing the story. The story ends with a blank page; that much is certain. In the epilogue, the narrator only tells us about the various ways in which the protagonists keep silent to prevent further *haram*.

POST-COLONIAL NARRATOLOGY

My choice to read and analyze the first novel of a young Morrocan-Dutch writer has been inspired by both literary and non-literary motives. The fact that this debut was nominated for the prestigious Dutch Libris award shifted the work immediately from the margins to the center of attention. A lot of work was put into the marketing of the novel as an example of a wholly new niche in Dutch literature—migrant literature. However, the novel's distinctive quality should not be sought in the way it is mediated by literary and societal institutions and circumstances, but in its ability to arouse the senses of the reader and hence become an experience. The novel leaves the reader with a set of impressions of modern pluriform society that include speed, movement, heat, chaos, and disorder, impressions caused not only by the novel's plot—a Dutch Moroccan boy who watches contemporary Moroccan culture and traditions with Western eyes and in turn also views the West, that is, Dutch contemporary culture and traditions, with the eyes of an outsider—but also by the way the story is told, its narrative perspective, its language and its style. Content and form once again prove to be intrinsically bound; the signifying process is realized with a complex set of rhetorical and literary instruments writers and readers have at their disposal or master in the process. A post-colonial narratological analysis of this text means relating to the narrated events, becoming a part of them and experiencing the disorganization resulting from the clash of norms, expectations, and actual behavior of all the parties concerned. It is only after assigning this story a meaning and determining its position in an intertextual nebula that thinking about its mediation can become interesting. As far as I am concerned, the novel's determining characteristic is not the fact that the novel is written by a Dutch-speaking author whose parents happen to come from Morocco, but rather is the not unsuccessful evocation of the at once painful and hilarious process of realizing that there is no place where one belongs, although the politicians, the media, and so forth would have you to believe otherwise. Sharing the narrator's difficulties to get his story on track, witnessing the encounter of a young man with an environment and a culture that should endow him with a feeling a belonging and home, but which only serve to alienate him more—this is what makes this novel worth reading and categorizing. One could call this chaotic freedom the postmodern, post-colonial experience par excellence: in terms of the sociology of knowledge it seems crucial to inquire into the types of discursive play that express transformations within modern society in the conceptions of self and others. As Paul Gilroy has pointed out, global movements have bearings on local cultures, which in turn imbue the global with a shape that leaves the specific local influence visible. Post-colonial narratology should be judged on its sensitivity to and articulation of such transformations; if they perform their task well they might contribute to a less extrinsic and more intricate and finely woven analysis of modern global society.

NOTES

1. I am alluding to David Herman's (1999) analysis of the emergence of a post-classical narratology. Indeed both women's and migrant literature are examples of contemporary writing that is felt by many to make a difference. It has prompted new perspectives in narrative theory summarized by David Herman (1999) as the practice of post-classical narratology. In particular the feminist work of Susan Lanser (1991) is considered to be a significant impulse for changes within classical narrative theory: "Lanser refuses to separate questions about narrative grammar from questions about the contexts in which narratives are designed and interpreted. Her remarks reflect the move toward integration and synthesis that is one of the hallmarks of postclassical narratology" (Herman 1999, 11). In this sense post-classical narratology is an effect of the study of texts and narrative voices that were somehow considered marginal. Post-colonial narratological analysis should be seen as part of that development.

2. The novel has been translated into seven foreign languages, including French, German, and English. It received the French Prix du meilleur premier roman étranger (best foreign novel of the year).

3. I want to thank Elizabeth J. Brouwer for the helpful discussions on the meaning of the literary.

4. For the colonial language paradox, see, among many others, Boyce Davies 1994, Buikema 1999, Gates 1986, Hoving, 1999.

WORKS CITED

Benali, Abdelkader. *Bruiloft aan zee*. Amsterdam: Vassalluci, 1996.
Benali, Abdelkader. *Wedding by the Sea*. London: Phoenix, 1999.
Benjamin, Walter. "The Storyteller." *Walter Benjamin: Selected Writings*. Vol. 3, 1935–1938. Ed. M. W. Jennings. London and Cambridge, Mass.: Belknap, Harvard University Press, 2001.
Boyce Davies, Carole. *Black Women, Writing and Identity: Migrations of the Subject*. London and New York: Routledge, 1994.
Buikema, Rosemarie. "From Literary Criticism to Cultural Studies: Configurations of Gender, Class and Ethnicity in Charlotte Brontë's *Jane Eyre*." *Differences within Sexual Difference*. Ed. Heike Paul. Berlin: Erich Schmidt Verlag, 1999. 40–57.
Gates, Henry Louis, Jr. (ed.). *'Race', Writing, and Difference*. Chicago: University of Chicago Press, 1986.

George, Rosemary Marangoly. *The Politics of Home: Postcolonial Relocations and Twentieth-Century Fiction*. Berkeley: University of California Press, 1996.

Gilroy, Paul. *The Black Atlantic: Modernity and Double Consciousness*. London: Verso, 1993.

Herman, David (ed.). *Narratologies: New Perspectives on Narrative Analysis*. Columbus: Ohio State University Press, 1999.

Hoving, Isabel. *In Praise of New Travelers: Reading Caribbean Migrant Women's Writing*. Stanford, Calif.: Stanford University Press, 2001.

Martin, Biddy, and Chandra Talpade Mohanty. "Feminist Politics: What's Home Got to Do with It?" *Feminist Studies/Critical Studies*. Ed. Teresa de Lauretis. Bloomington: Indiana University Press, 1986. 191–212.

Rushdie, Salman. *Imaginary Homelands*. London: Granta Books, 1991.

11

"The Risks Migrating Words Take": Some Thoughts on the Afrikaans Poetry of Elisabeth Eybers in a Context of Transmigration[1]

Ena Jansen

IN THE GAP

"To explore the idea of poetic discourse as the 'lacerated' space of exile and migration is to venture into the complex temporal and spatial dimension between the memory of 'there' and the time of 'here'. It is to follow a distressful and suffering path streaked by displaced existence; a passage experienced by exiled and migrating peoples who are neither totally removed from their historical antecedents, nor completely assimilated to where they are expected to go. . . . Across an ocean of internal fractures, the space of poetic writing unveils a new territory for the relocation and the reinscription of the scattered fragments of the subject's dissonant and conflictual identities, a territory for the enunciation of a liberating yet painful recuperation of its dispersed self. The poetry of the uprooted subject evokes primary loss, and a world of memory and nostalgia; at the same time, rewriting the dramatic conditions of alterity, reciting the experience of unassimilated lives, also offers a way of survival, a way of seeking another sense of 'home' on the borderline between belonging and exclusion." (Yocum 222)

This is an accurate description of the way poetry written by exiled or migrated poets is usually read: in terms of "unassimilated lives" along borderlines of loss and survival therapy. Another reading strategy is to *not* always read poets who have left their countries of birth expecting in advance that they are constantly tormented by their longing for some elusive homeland. One could, instead, read in search of their active negotiations on the edge, respond in an alternative way to those energetic metaphorical bungee jumpers risking their literary lives in the gap between two or more languages, worlds, and cultures, daringly walking a tightrope spanning two countries. Such a reader's response will be in line with interpretations by contemporary sociologists of the lifestyle of people they call "transmigrants" (Schiller 94–119 and Portes 120–136).[2]

According to these theories transmigrants are not to be pitied. Instead, in a globalizing world it is becoming noticeable that the "assimilation perspective" of migrants where they lose all, or most, of the vestiges of their former cultures once they leave home is often inadequate. This applies not only to "postmodern" migrants but often to those of previous generations as well. The "transnational perspective" is more complex than the "assimilation perspective" and does not automatically assume that migrants give up their natal cultures in favor of an effort to wholly adopt the host country. It observes that so-called transmigrants, through a complex web of interactions, regularly communicate with and visit their families, friends, and neighbors "back home," that they maintain and reproduce social relationships that cross political, cultural, and geographic borders. Many transmigrants are able to lead dual lives in which bilingualism, shuttling between two polar cultures, maintaining homes in two countries, and following dual political, economic, and cultural pursuits are the normative characteristics.[3] Given this, the conventional notion of an immigrant becomes inadequate. Because of the multiple relations and identities that transmigrants actively construct, notions of loss and assimilation become problematic.

Time and again transmigrants from all walks of life stress their need to retain their native language. For those few transmigrants who are writers and wish to continue writing in their mother tongue, whose tools are words, it is to be expected that language will be held in even higher esteem because their work can suffer from not hearing daily the language they write in. In the case of many exiled poets this isolation causes limitation of expression, and the language of those who try to adapt runs the increasing danger of contamination. What is special and different about poets in comparison to non-writing migrant people is of course that they, in and through language, risk misunderstanding when they set out on journeys of articulated identity formation. Furthermore, a transmigrational approach to poetry could prove fruitful in (re-)exploring along these lines the work of many, sometimes famous but more often forgotten, but all too easily typecast, migrant and even exiled poets. By adding the solo voices of poets to the chorus of solicited stories gained by oral history projects, poetry might also prove to be a "useful" contribution to the transnational perspective of and on migrants in general.

Without for a moment underestimating the harsh confrontations of the divided subject with estrangement and otherness, I want to suggest a reading of the Afrikaans poetry that the South African–born poet Elisabeth Eybers has been writing in the Netherlands with the notion of the transmigrant in

mind. Without forgetting the poems she wrote shortly after she arrived in
Amsterdam, which are steeped in longing and loneliness, I want to turn to a
major part of her work in which Eybers actually celebrates the "luxury of
nostalgia" ("weelde van heimwee"), the feeling of being simultaneously "enclosed and capacious" ("ingeslote en vry"; "Stemming"/"Mood," VG 469). In
such poems lines abound like "Each night funnels me back to my origin"
("Elke nag tregter my terug na my geboorteland") and "I seize every chance
to sketch a quick Capeward curve" ("sodra ek kans kry gou 'n Kaapse draai
beskryf"; "Terug"/"Return Ticket," VG 437).

In my quest to position Eybers within the discourse of transmigration and
to advocate a wider application of such a reading strategy, it is important to
do this against the background of the many other South African authors in
positions of exile and migration in Europe and elsewhere. This will, in fact,
add a different perspective to the observation of critics who are convinced
that exile is, "in many respects, the central problem of South African literary
history" (Bunn 34). South African literature, a very diverse and contested site
in which the ideologies of colonialism, language, culture, race, and gender
identity formations all come into play (Gikandi 12–13, 506–511, and
511–518), indeed needs to continue to deal also with the past and present
worldwide dispersions of South African culture. But this can be done in an-
ticipation of heightened creativity, and not necessarily in terms of loss.

PRESENT IN THEIR ABSENCE

The past and present situations of migration of South Africans, which includes the authors, are directly or indirectly a response to the apartheid politics of the country between 1948 and 1990. Before South Africa became a
non-racial democracy in 1994, the "colonial" languages Afrikaans and English and especially their white speakers and authors were privileged, in
contrast to black people and indigenous African languages, which were
never afforded the same status or means of literary production.[4] Most black
writers therefore chose to write in English, and many left South Africa in the
late 1950s when racial discrimination became structurally entrenched. Although the majority of South Africans who fled abroad for political reasons
became proximate exiles, crossing over into neighboring countries such as
Botswana and Zambia, South Africa's literary exiles were atypical of this
broader movement. Most headed for what has been described as "those ven-
erable magnets of the bohemian diaspora": London, Paris, Berlin, Amsterdam, New York, and Chicago. Literary exiles, most notably Dennis Brutus,
played a considerable role in giving the struggle international dimensions,
"by helping import it into the power centres of world politics and the media."
These authors were held in high esteem abroad and also had an impact in

South Africa (Nixon 118). [5] As André Brink, a novelist who stayed in South Africa, has stated: "The absent ones became a part of our consciousness and our conscience, the dark half of our own selves. . . . They continued to be present in their absence; they remained the indispensable supplement to our own existence" (Brink 14).

One of the ANC's specific conditions for at last entering into negotiations with the National Party government was the unconditional return of all exiles, which meant that the era of exile officially ended early in 1990. Some returned, while other "long-term" exiles have "engineered sabbatical homecomings," taking the precaution of temporary leave from their American and European jobs while they "hazard a trial rendezvous with their erstwhile homeland," and others chose to remain abroad, having settled irrevocably or because they could not face the loss of the "familiar sense of deferred responsibility" or "the prospect of imaginative renewal" (Nixon 116). [6] They generally all have strong ties in more than one country and culture and can to some degree be called transmigrants. In recent years they have, in fact, been joined by many other South Africans who, although for completely different reasons, *choose* to live in what is referred to as the New South African Diaspora. For these people there is no political and often no economical or emotional restraint to visiting South Africa from around the globe: from Europe, North America, and especially from England, Australia, and New Zealand. [7]

DOUBLE-EDGED POSITION

In the context of migration studies, which often focuses on large-scale binaries such as black/white, the rest/West, margin/center, poor/rich, and oppressed/oppressors, Elisabeth Eybers is an outsider. Her migrant position is different from that of many other migrants who come to Europe from Africa—mainly because she is white. Like most other colonized African countries South Africa has a complicated history that links it, especially linguistically, to Europe. Quite accurately Eybers describes South Africa as "die brok Europa diep in Afrika" ("that chunk of Europe deep in Africa"; "Diminuendo," UT 110). It is therefore not exactly strange that Eybers chose to migrate to Holland in 1961. A few years before, in 1957, a collection of her Afrikaans poems had already been published in Amsterdam by the influential publisher G. A. van Oorschot, who had fallen in love with her poetry. It was treated to excellent reviews. [8] For an assessment of Eybers's position in Dutch literature it is important to stress that modern Dutch and Afrikaans share a common heritage, but are two distinct languages. [9] Therefore, to be able to communicate successfully in Holland, a modern-day Afrikaans speaker cannot rely on the communal Germanic basis but needs to actively learn Dutch. Afrikaans novels are translated, and the occasional Afrikaans speaker on Dutch television is provided with Dutch subtext. Similarly, Afrikaans poetry, for example, the writing of Breyten Breytenbach, Ingrid Jonker, Antjie Krog, and Wilma Stockenström, also needs to be translated or otherwise provided with extensive glossaries. Elisabeth Eybers is, however, the extraordinary exception to this rule.

She was born in 1915 and her career as a poet continues today. She was the very first woman to publish (in 1936) a volume of poetry in Afrikaans. For this famous debut, aptly called *Belydenis in die skemering* (Confession at Dawn), and her next volume, called *Die stil avontuur* (Quiet Adventure, 1938), Eybers received the first of her many literary prizes. When living in South Africa she published five more volumes of poetry, of which *Die helder halfjaar* (The Vivid Half-year, 1956) was especially highly regarded. In 1961, then recently divorced from one of the wealthiest industrialists in South Africa, she turned her back on her life in Johannesburg and flew to Amsterdam together with her youngest child, a ten-year-old daughter. She was forty-six years old, well educated, someone who was in South Africa a woman of privilege (George 133). She was not, contrary to most other migrant women authors in a cross-cultural perspective, forced to emigrate by political or economically oppressive circumstances (Boyce Davies 10). It was a private, domestic situation that she found intolerable which made her *choose* to resist and to leave a comfortable situation in South Africa. Since living in Amsterdam, her poetry, which she still writes in Afrikaans, is always simultaneously published in Cape Town and in Amsterdam. It receives accolades in both countries, including the most prestigious literary prizes. In *Balans* (Balance, 1962) we find the first poems she wrote in Amsterdam. "Immigrant" (VG 269), "Toeskouer" ("Spectator," VG 273), and "Heimwee" ("Homesickness," VG 275) are some popular examples. Then there is the impressive 1969 volume *Onderdak* (Shelter), containing poems such as "Ontheemde" ("Displaced Person," VG 294) and "Nomadepaar" ("Nomadic Couple," VG 329). Since then there have been another eleven highly acclaimed volumes. All of them contain many poems in which *both* South Africa and the Netherlands are of vital importance. Eybers holds three honorary doctorates. In 2004, at the age of ninety, she still writes poetry and is translating into English a selection of poems from her completed twenty-odd volumes.

Eybers arrived at Schiphol on the same day that South Africa became a republic, 31 May 1960. This was shortly after the prime minister of South Africa, H. F. Verwoerd, had announced with cocky defiance that South Africa would leave the British Commonwealth if the member countries would not endorse his politics of apartheid. In a world still reeling from the aftermath of the Nazi policy toward Jews, Verwoerd found no support for his policy. After South Africa became a republic the path was set for its isolation from political trends elsewhere.[10] Coming to Europe as a white South African so shortly after the much-publicized and shocking events at Sharpeville, with the Soweto uprisings, the death of Steve Biko, and many other tragic events still to follow before Mandela's release in 1990, Eybers often had to bear the brunt of Dutch people's moral high ground. This never happened regarding her position as a poet, but there were numerous situations in which shop assistants, officials, and even new friends self-righteously pointed their finger at her. In "Ontheemde" ("Homelessness," VG 506) she would still, years after arriving in Amsterdam, remark:

> In this strange land, unshielded by a mask . . .
> the people here take everyone to task,
> don't tolerate nor flatter [. . .].

Judging by her many poems about the position of despised outcast, Eybers felt personally "unprivileged" and even discriminated against in confrontations with such straightforward and often rude Dutch individuals. In her ironic poem "Ode aan kontrolleur de Laar" ("Ode to Taxman De Laar," VG 295), she describes understanding and experiencing "what being a child of Ham is like" ("só voel dit dus om Gam se kind te wees"). Some people, encouraging her to assimilate, recommended speech therapy to camouflage her accent and therefore her origin and her past.[11] Eybers, who was very much against apartheid herself, chose, however, not to get rid of her "speech defect," which would have enabled her as a white person to pass for Dutch. She did not want to assimilate in this way. Although she conducts most of her life in Dutch, with a South African accent, she never tried to assimilate by writing in Dutch. That would have meant forfeiting a crucial part of her transnational identity. By continuing to write in Afrikaans, she exploits her double-edged position and becomes much more of interest to two reading publics. In the poem "Voetjie vir voetjie" ("Step by Step," VG 352) she writes:

> You learn migration step by step, you see
> strange and familiar objects, somehow stranded
> on the artificial terrace where you landed
> yet did not settle irrefutably.

It is in this situation of *choosing* to never settle that Eybers in Amsterdam could distance herself from South Africa's state policies. She wrote some explicitly anti-apartheid poems,[12] which occasionally tempted Dutch poetry critics and interviewers to describe her as a political refugee. That would have enabled them to "disarm" her, to gracefully gather her into the fold of their literature, grouped together especially with their two other famous women poets at the time: Vasalis and Ida Gerhardt. In fact, the Dutch would have been much more comfortable had Eybers explicitly claimed that she had "fled" South Africa on the eve of Verwoerd's declaration of independence. Eybers was, of course, absolutely not a lone dissenting voice. The counterhegemonic strain of Afrikaans literature and the tradition of dissi-

dence, which from the early 1960s onward counteracted the Afrikaner nationalist nature of many earlier Afrikaans texts, grew so strong during later
decades that it became the dominant strain in Afrikaans literature rather than
a marginal one (Viljoen 65).

Although Eybers had absolutely no sympathy with the official state policies in South Africa and still often quotes her own father's remark that "only
a Dutchman could have invented such a structured system of apartheid," she
stuck to the truth of the personal circumstances that prompted her to leave
South Africa in 1961: the meandering eye and, to put it as boldly as she herself has done in some remarkably bitter poems, the meandering body of her
husband.[13] She, however, continued to stress her love for South Africa, to
"contain" it "unfailingly" as the other polar extreme, besides Amsterdam, of
her life and her poetry. In the poem "Uitgewekene" ("Displaced Person," UT
22) South Africa is not only in general described as an African country
"where, on the whole / disaster plays an alarming role," but specified as the
place representing her youth, warmth, light, and space, "what I recollect /
and cherish as a sancrosanct debt." The present time in Amsterdam is always
marked by that past whereby the positions now and then, here and there, are
juxtaposed and both maintained, used as anchors for the tightrope she constructs, which she needs and desires to walk. The complex position of the
transmigrant is very clear in such poems. The speaker does not shy away
from exposing the injustices of apartheid and her own past unhappiness in
South Africa, but she also claims other equally vital aspects of it as undeniably present to her. This double-edged and ambivalent relationship to both
South Africa and Holland comes to the fore in her poem "Heimwee"
("Homesickness," VG 275):

> A house is something perched upon a slope
> and bathed in sunlight, every aspect clear,
> it dwindles down to three rooms where you grope
> about. Should house by chance be mentioned here
> where there's no up-down tendency, alas
> no gradual ascension and no sheen
> except the one composed of wire and glass.
> The equalness is reasonable and mean.

This poem was written shortly after Eybers's arrival in Amsterdam. As is the
case with most migrants, the home she had recently abandoned is a complicated space that she cannot allow herself to idealize. In the light of her biography it is therefore very crafty that she constructs her poem about homesickness in such a way that the emphasis is placed on architectural layout
and the specificities of landscape. Although the title "Homesickness" foregrounds an emotional and vulnerable person, the speaker in the main body
of the poem tries to keep a neutral stance by focusing on the word "huis"

("house"). This word then brings her generic, her default South African experience that a house is a sunny and spacious place, on a par with what she
describes as a typical house "here," in Holland. The fact that neither of the
houses she describes is called "home" builds an equivalence between these
two locations, despite the architectural differences between them. This con-
forms to the formulation Rosemary George gives of "location" in opposition
to "home": "Location . . . suggests the variable nature of both 'the home' and
'the self,' for both are negotiated stances whose shapes are entirely ruled by
the site from which they are defined. Locations are positions from which distance and difference are formulated and homes are made snug" (George 2).
George convincingly demonstrates that although "home" is usually represented as fixed, rooted, stable—the very antithesis of uprootedness, "home"
actually moves along several axes. It is in her poetry that Eybers will at last
find a "snug" home, however precarious the risky construction of it might
remain. This she emphasizes by calling her first volume containing only poems written in Amsterdam *Onderdak* (Shelter 1968). Furthermore, the fact
that Eybers would many years later name two anthologies of her poems both
Uit en tuis, meaning "Home and abroad" (quite literally, "away and at
home"), underlines the transmigrant's realization that home is at the same
time everywhere and nowhere.[14] She describes the Amsterdam house she
lives in as a "double-roomed playground."[15]

Many poets in conditions of exile and migrancy, for example German Exil
authors, have suffered badly from not hearing the language they write in on
a daily basis anymore. In the case of Eybers the dangers of reduction and
contamination also clearly exist. However, instead of succumbing to the ancient evil of emigration where language is "refrigerated" and thus "preserved," she is rejuvenated by her new circumstances and by the not completely foreign European tongue with which she is familiar enough to absorb
and manipulate. She turned a possible threat of contamination of her own
language to her own advantage by revitalizing antiquated Dutch words that
have been forgotten in modern Afrikaans, or by using others that refer to
Dutch circumstances not common in South Africa. This fits in perfectly with
theories describing the highly patterned nature of poetic language, the fact
that poems seem to be "encoded" several times and so kept more or less
"strange"—a prerequisite for poetic enjoyment. Readers are thereby held in
the literary system for as long as possible, prevented from an "unseemly rush
from word to world" (Culler 130). Dutch readers know some words and references better, while in other instances Afrikaans readers are more "at
home." Both sets of readers seem to find ample foothold on the slippery
stepping stones into Eybers's world. This is an effect of the fact that Eybers
seems to actually relish the "contrapuntal situation" which Edward Said (171)
described so well in his essay "Reflections on Exile":

Most people are aware of at least two, and this plurality of vision gives rise to an awareness of simultaneous dimensions. . . . [H]abits of life, expression or activity in the new environment inevitably occur against the memory of these things in another environment. Thus both the new and the old environments are vivid, actual, occurring together contrapuntally. . . . Life is led outside habitual order. It is nomadic, decentred, contrapuntal; no sooner does one get accustomed to it than its unsettling force erupts anew.

The situations she describes are often precarious. In "Besoek" ("Visit," VG 304) the speaker describes herself as "out of balance" when she realizes that her "accent still sounds suspicious." She therefore calls herself an "inbetween person" in need of advice from a "bordercase expert." In this poem she describes visiting a psychologist employing metaphors referring to her migrant position. In "an impulse to behave normally," to adapt and to assimilate, she "shows" the psychologist her "private little hell." She then, however, realizes that this "hell," this dangerous and precarious space, is the precondition she needs to remain "sick and healthy enough to be able to create." She realizes that a situation of nonconformity, which would have been a drawback had she willed herself to assimilate, is the poetic impulse she cannot do without. She needs to keep the outsider's position intact, to exploit it in the construction of often ironic and humorous poems, which are, remarkably enough, always coherent and balanced, even "classic."

TRANSMIGRANT STANCE

My suggestion that Eybers's work should not be read only in the more static and binary context of exile or even migrant literature, but rather in the transmigrant discourse, is supported by the fact that Eybers has had so much success constructing a "double-room of her own" in the domains of both South African and of Dutch literature. That she is honored as the "grand dame" of Afrikaans poetry is understandable. That the Dutch make a similar claim is quite amazing since familiarity with the language a poem is written in is usually a prerequisite to understanding and appreciation. Although well-known paradoxes of poetic language include the fact that all poets have their "ideolects," that all poets deviate from the familiar use of language, that all of them leave the all too cosy home of mundane syntax and semantics, that they explore the boundaries and ambiguities of expression, it is amazing that Dutch readers are able to follow Eybers's poetic romp in her "ideolect," which is based on another language, namely Afrikaans, under the "suspension of disbelief" impression that she is "one of them." The Dutch critic Kees Fens described this phenomenon by saying that she "both confirms and denounces her outsider position" in Dutch literature. "That process of strangeness has become familiar to us without forfeiting itself. We have never before recognised our country and ourselves in such incessant descriptions which seem to have been written mirrorwise. Holland has gained a new author and its poetic world has been enlarged" (Fens n.p.).

The fact that Eybers has a niche in the home territories of two sets of readers means that both sets of readers are at different times close or kept at a distance. By the effort that they make to grasp the world and the wordplay of the poet, they become intimately involved and are drawn much closer to the speaker than would have been the case had the language of her poetic world been easily comprehensible right from the start (Jansen 295–297). The enjoyment both sets of readers share is the excited feeling that they're being given a share of the vision and vocabulary of someone in transit, of someone slightly out of breath who has just left or just arrived, who is still searching for words. Her words take risks, risks of not landing safely, of being misunderstood. But then they miraculously always do arrive, enticingly arranged in the traveling-bag of the seasoned transmigrant. For more than forty years now she has been moving across the equator, going backward and forward across the national borders of two different languages, between time present and time past. In spite of or because of dangers, she seems to be forever adventurous and energetic, articulating challenges so many displaced and transmigrant people in comparable but always individually different circumstances experience.

Belonging to two domains provides her with a fluid subject status that has never become unified or autonomous. She has developed a transmigrant stance, often by ironic and self-mocking cultivation, as a preferred vantage point of solitude in which she leads her poetic life in two language locations, unshackled and unbounded by the rules of national literatures and canons based on one language. Although her poetry is welcome in the national homelands of two literatures and she helps to mark a "shifting boundary" (Bhabha 315), her work defies being located on just one margin. She prefers and asserts the mercurial flow of a self that cannot be contained by the very boundaries it prefers to circle. Physically she is completely settled in Amsterdam—the last time she actually went back to South Africa was in 1979. Poetically speaking she regularly dashes off on "a quick Capeward curve," never "settling irrefutably." The transmigrant position has proved to produce a more multifaceted figure than does the equation that delivers an immigrant subject who would forever have been marginal to some mainstream and therefore always condemned to the discourse of assimilation, therefore of shortcoming. Her position as transmigrant proves to be risky and playful; it enables the attentive openness, the vulnerability that is needed in the process of concentration and in the tightening of expression, which to my mind is the crux of poetry writing *and* of poetry reading.

As we see in Eybers's most recent poems about aging, the unsettled and fluid position of the transmigrant is renewed once more: it provides a potent metaphor for her own situation at the age of eighty-eight, and thereby for the position of all of us who are also skirting the border zone of life and death, but who are less articulate, less daring, and less ironic. Eybers continues to unsentimentally interrogate the seductive pleasures of living in more than one place, more than one language, more than one nation, and, ultimately, more than this one earthly life.

NOTES

1. I sincerely thank Elisabeth Eybers, who, for the occasion of this article, did all of the translations of her poems that are quoted here. The abbreviation VG is used to refer to her *Versamelde gedigte* (Collected Poems); UT refers to *Uit en tuis* (Home and Abroad).

2. The words transnationalism and transmigrants are derived from the concept "transculturation," which was coined in the 1940s by Cuban sociologist Fernando Ortiz (1978) in relation to Afro-Cuban culture. It has since been used by ethnographers to describe how subordinated or marginal groups select and invent from materials transmitted to them by a dominant or metropolitan culture. Bill Ashcroft, Gareth Griffiths, and Helen Tiffin (233) remind us that the term "transculturation" refers to "the reciprocal influences of modes of representation and cultural practices of various kinds in colonies and metropoles, and is thus a 'phenomenon of the contact zone,' as Mary Louise Pratt puts it." Dasmariñas (33–42) presents a case study of transmigration and demonstrates the practical use of the concept.

3. Salman Rushdie has been quoted by Hall (8) as calling such people "translated." Reference by Nixon (115). Nixon (114–128) makes a strong case for a reassessment of the role of returning South African exiles who had managed to transform the "affliction" of exile into a cultural resource.

4. South Africa has always been a multilingual region, a fact which was recognized in 1994 by the proclamation of the shared official status of eleven languages, including Afrikaans and English.

5. A. C. Jordan, Nat Nakasa, Vernie February, Bessie Head, Alex la Guma, Arthur Nortje, Lewis Nkosi, Mazisi Kunene, Es'kia Mphahlele, and Mongane Serote were famous black exiled authors. During the second half of the twentieth century many white Afrikaans authors lived abroad voluntarily, mostly in Europe, for shorter or longer sojourns. Amsterdam was home to N. P. van Wyk Louw, Elisabeth Eybers, Abraham H. de Vries, Karel Schoeman, and Marlene van Niekerk. France attracted authors such as Uys Krige, Jan Rabie, André P. Brink, Chris Barnard, and Bartho Smit, while Breyten Breytenbach started his French séjour as a literary expatriate and became a political exile because he fell in love with a woman who was considered "non-white" under the apartheid laws of his fatherland. Krige and Sheila Cussons lived in Spain; Olga Kirsch went to live in Israel; Barend J. Toerien spent several years in North America. Besides sometimes participating at literary events, none of these authors except the "permanent resident" Eybers was given a place in the literary canons of their host countries.

6. Nixon (116) quite rightly writes that homecoming *could* be a priceless prospect for writers who have found themselves "plumbing an ever-shallower pool

of recollections, the initial wrong of banishment having been compounded by that secondary injustice, the evaporation of memory."

7. Writers such as Zoë Wicomb, Dan Jacobson, Lauretta Ngcobo, Christopher Hope, Lindsey Collen, Barbara Trapido, Achmat Dangor, Gillian Slovo, Emma Huismans, Eben Venter, and Marita van der Vyver.

8. In interviews Eybers often mentioned that this collection was important in her decision to go to Holland instead of to England.

9. This language divide is the result of developments that took place 350 years ago. Some linguists such as Edith H. Raidt consider Afrikaans a European language, while others such as Marius F. Valkhoff and Hans den Besten describe it as a creolized, pidgin, or even indigenous African language. The name Afrikaans literally means "of Africa." At different stages Afrikaans has been suppressed and privileged. The formal struggle for its acceptance as a "civilized" language started in 1875. In his exploration of links between nationalism and language Anderson (75) also mentions Afrikaans: "[I]n the latter portion of the nineteenth century, we find Afrikaner nationalism pioneered by Boer pastors and litterateurs, who in the 1870s were successful in making the local Dutch patois into a literary language and naming it something no longer European." This struggle was finally won in 1925 when Afrikaans replaced Dutch as one of the two official languages of the country.

10. Leaving the British Commonwealth was a direct result of the Sharpeville shootings in March 1960, during which sixty-seven black South Africans protesting the pass laws were gunned down by police. And Sharpeville, in a nutshell, says it all about apartheid South Africa.

11. I refer here to the poem "Tongval" ("Accent") published in *Onderdak* (Shelter), 1968.

12. These include two called "Ontheemde" ("Expatriate," VG 294) and "Homeless" (VG 506), and "Regspraak" ("Jurisdiction") about the death of Biko (VG 438).

13. In "Nolens volens" ("Willy-nilly," VG 439) and "Ontheemde" ("Expatriate," VG 294) she is very clear about this.

14. The first *Uit en tuis* was published in South Africa in 1995, when Eybers turned eighty, and the other during the Dutch Book Week of 2001, which had as its theme "Between two cultures." Both were subtitled "Afrikaanse verse uit Amsterdam" (Afrikaans poems from Amsterdam).

15. See "Stemming" ("Mood," VG 469).

WORKS CITED

Ashcroft, Bill, Gareth Griffiths, and Helen Tiffin. *Post-Colonial Studies: The Key Concepts*. London: Routledge. 2000.

Anderson, Benedict. *Imagined Communities: Reflections on the Origin and Spread of Nationalism*. London and New York: Verso. 1991.

Bhabha, Homi K. "DissemiNation: Time, Narrative, and the Margins of the Modern Nation." *Nation and Narration*. Ed. Homi K. Bhabha. London and New York: Routledge. 1990.

Boyce Davies, Carole. *Black Women, Writing and Identity: Migrations of the Subject.* London and New York: Routledge. 1994.

Brink, André. "Preface: A Tough Job." *Exiles: Thirteen South Africans Tell Their Stories.* Ed. Marie-Noëlle Anderson. Athlone: Realities. 2001.

Bunn, David. "'Some Alien Native Land': Arthur Nortje, Literary History, and the Body in Exile." *World Literature Today* 70.1, Winter 1996. 33–44.

Culler, Jonathan. *Structuralist Poetics: Structuralism, Linguistics and the Study of Literature.* London and New York: Routledge and Kegan Paul. 1975.

Dasmariñas, Julio. "Of Religion, Migration and Community: The Filipino Immigrant in New York City." *Diaspora and Memory. Politics of Remembering and/or Forgetting. Constructing Communities.* Amsterdam: ASCA Conference Papers. March 26–28, 2003. 33–41.

Den Besten, Hans. "Khoekhoe Syntax and Its Implications for L2 Acquisition of Dutch and Afrikaans." *Journal of Germanic Linguistics* 14.1, 2002. 3–56.

Eybers, Elisabeth. *Verzamelde gedichten.* Amsterdam: G. A. van Oorschot. 1957.

Eybers, Elisabeth. *Versamelde gedigte.* Amsterdam: Em. Querido's Uitgeverij & Uitgeverij G. A. van Oorschot; Cape Town: Human & Rousseau & Tafelberg. 1990.

Eybers, Elisabeth. *Uit en tuis.* Compiled by Hans Ester and Ena Jansen. Cape Town: Human & Rousseau. 1995.

Eybers, Elisabeth. *Uit en tuis.* Compiled by Ena Jansen. Amsterdam: Singel Pocket. 2001.

Fens, Kees. "Benoemen als een vorm van vervreemden." *de Volkskrant* (18 Feb. 1991): n.p.

Falkhoff, Marius F. *Studies in Portuguese and Creole: With a Special Reference to South Africa.* Johannesburg: Wits University Press. 1966.

George, Rosemary Marangoly. *The Politics of Home: Postcolonial Relocations and Twentieth-century Fiction.* Cambridge: Cambridge University Press. 1996.

Gikandi, Simon (ed.). *Encyclopedia of African Literature.* London and New York: Routledge. 2003.

Hall, Stuart. "Our Mongrel Selves." *New Statesman and Society* (19 June 1992): 6–8.

Jansen, Ena. *Afstand en verbintenis. Elisabeth Eybers in Amsterdam.* Amsterdam: Amsterdam University Press. 1998.

Nixon, Rob. "Refugees and Homecomings: Bessie Head and the End of Exile." *Travellers' Tales: Narratives of Home and Displacement.* Ed. George Robertson et al. London and New York: Routledge. 1994. 114–128.

Portes, A. "Immigration Theory for a New Century: Some Problems and Opportunities." *The Handbook of International Migration.* Ed. Charles Hirschman et al. New York: Russell Sage. 1999. 120–136.

Raidt, Edith H. *Afrikaans en sy Europese verlede.* 3rd revised ed. Cape Town: Nasionale Opvoedkundige Uitgewery. 1991.

Said, Edward. "Reflections on Exile." *Granta: After the Revolution* 13. Cambridge: Granta Publications. Autumn 1984. 157–172.

Schiller, Glick. "Transmigrants and Nation-States: Something Old, Something New in the U.S. Immigration Experience." *The Handbook of International Migration.* Ed. Charles Hirschman et al. New York: Russell Sage. 1999. 94–119.

Van Rooyen, Johann. *The Great New Trek: The Story of South Africa's White Exodus.* Pretoria: Unisa Press. 2000.

Viljoen, Louise. "Postcolonialism and Recent Women's Writing in Afrikaans." *World Literature Today* 70.1, Winter 1996. 63–72.

Yocum, Demetrio. "Some Troubled Homecomings." *The Post-Colonial Question: Common Skies, Divided Horizons.* Ed. Iain Chambers and Lidia Curti. London and New York: Routledge. 1996. 221–227.

III

MIND THE GAP! CULTURAL TRANS/FORMATIONS

12

Street Culture: Dead End or Global Highway?

Alec G. Hargreaves

In 1996, *Newsweek* ran a cover story entitled "In France, the Only Art That Matters Is Street Culture." Photographed on the cover is French rapper MC Solaar. Behind him, almost squeezed out of the frame, is the entrance to that temple of museum culture, the Louvre. In the article Marcus Mabry declares that the Senegalese-born rapper has become "the most widely known French recording artist in the world," personifying "the rise of street culture from France's suburbs [*banlieues*] to the mainstream—as well as its multicultural roots" (*Newsweek* 1996: 42). Also featured are interviews with Mathieu Kassovitz, winner of the 1995 best director award at the Cannes film festival for his stunning portrayal of the *banlieues* in *La Haine*, and with the graffiti artist Megaton, making a handsome living selling his work in upmarket galleries in chic Paris neighborhoods:

> This [say Mabry and co-writer John Leland] is the new cultural energy in France: blunt, assertive, nurtured in hardscrabble housing projects rather than the French academies. It is the culture of the banlieue, a multiethnic mix of Arab, American, Caribbean, African and French idioms that is influencing the way French young people talk and define themselves. . . . The high culture that for centuries has been the nation's pride—the fine arts, literature, classical music, even the couture houses and culinary arts—has stagnated. (*Newsweek* 1996: 38)

A couple of years later, the French cultural critic Jean Baudrillard gave an interview to Roger Célestin in the American journal *Sites*. When asked about the contribution of post-colonial minorities to popular culture in France, Baudrillard replied:

> There isn't any . . . there is no Arab culture, that is, no Muslim culture, that has developed independently. It's not at all the same here [as in the United States]. I don't believe there is any basic culture that they imported or that they re-vived. . . . No, they have really been dispossessed. . . . Of course there are groups . . . in music, perhaps in dance, but I'm not much of an expert on all that, no doubt in terms of music, some groups, some theatrical companies among the younger generations . . . the most recent generation, the one that was born here. But precisely, the generation that was born here is extremely, is entirely assimilated. . . .
>
> One is accepted—there have been many, many elements that have come from outside, in painting for example—but still, one is only accepted when one enters the French cultural zone, when one is assimilated. There is a force that perhaps comes from tradition, I don't really know, but we [the French] are not very receptive to heterogeneity. It has to be transformed, metabolized into French culture. (Baudrillard 1997: 7–8)

The contrast could not be sharper—it is as if *Newsweek* and Baudrillard in-habit different planets. Baudrillard rightly notes that France has a long tra-dition of attracting foreign artists who in many cases have become both permanent residents and integral parts of the French cultural scene. But it is absurd to suggest that they have simply been assimilated into some pre-existing cultural mold. To the contrary, they were attracted to France and helped to keep France at the cutting edge of cultural experimentation partly because the freedom to innovate and resonate appeared greater in France than in their countries of origin. One thinks, for example, of poets such as Apollinaire, painters such as Picasso, and playwrights such as Beckett and Ionesco. If France's new immigrant minorities appear to Bau-drillard especially ill-equipped to contribute anything new to French cul-ture this is no doubt in part because he implicitly equates the core of French culture with highly literate—in every sense of the word—uses of the French language. The few cultural forms in which Baudrillard concedes that second-generation members of minority ethnic groups may be active—music, dance, and theater—all function primarily through sym-bolic codes other than those of the written word. This, of course, is also true of the cultural forms offered to mass audiences through today's elec-tronic media, which are powerful stimulants for artists in the *banlieues* but heartily despised by many intellectuals outside them.

Post-colonial minorities are doubly troublesome from the point of view of France's established intellectual elites because they erode both the familiar hi-erarchy between "high" and "low" culture and the national boundaries within which those elites have been accustomed to setting the cultural agenda. Baudrillard's remarks about cultural assimilation are implicitly posited on assumptions about the power of nationally bounded cultural institutions, which are proving increasingly untenable in the face of the gathering strength of the dynamic that has come to be known as globalization.

When mass communications were still dominated by print media, linguistic and technological constraints generally limited their impact to the same nationally bounded spaces in which state-constructed cultural institutions—the educational systems, for example, through which intellectuals such as Baudrillard built their careers—held sway. Today, the global reach of privately owned audiovisual media based outside France—most obviously, American multinational corporations—constitutes a constantly growing challenge to cultural elites operating within more traditional, nationally bounded frames of reference. At the same time, the settlement of post-colonial minorities has led to the emergence on French soil of a new generation whose cultural references are multi-polar, drawing as freely on American as on French, African, Arab, and other models. The *banlieue* streets in which these new hybrid cultures are being forged, like the electronic media on which they draw, are largely beyond the control of France's traditional intellectual elites.

To speak of these practices as street culture is to speak metonymically, for the streets of the *banlieues* are never more than part of the space within which street culture finds its meaning. This is not simply because the street is a kind of shorthand for the nexus of experiences associated with the *banlieues*. More fundamentally, it is because the cultural practices that have emerged there derive much of their meaning from more distant locations. Cultural spaces are always shaped by three interlinked types of praxis: the appropriation of existing cultural forms, the production of new symbolic practices, and the reception of this work. Certain types of street culture—for example, that of graffiti artists, known in the *banlieues* as *graffeurs* or *taggueurs*—may be produced and consumed wholly on the spot. But the cultural spaces appropriated in their work are invariably wider than the confines of the immediate locality in which it is produced and consumed. Graphically, linguistically, and ideologically, the work of taggers in the French *banlieues*, like that of their peers in similar urban spaces throughout Europe and in other parts of the world, may incorporate elements from the heritage of post-colonial migrants and the countries in which they have settled, but it does so in a *lingua franca* that is global in circulation and that emanates primarily from the United States. This is equally true of other street arts embraced under the umbrella term of hip-hop, which are all in varying degrees inscribed in the Black Atlantic (Gilroy 1993). Although some street arts may be confined initially to a purely local public, they may also be mediated to much wider audiences through the communications industries. To the extent that rappers and other artists tailor their work toward this wider sphere, audience expectations outside the *banlieues* become a constituent element in the meaning of that work, alongside the locale of its production and the symbolic models appropriated in its construction.

Many complex issues are raised by the articulation of these different domains. In this chapter, I focus in particular on links between production and consumption. To what extent have recent forms of street culture in France radiated beyond their place of production, and how are we to explain variations in their diffusion? These are the main questions addressed here. My analysis falls into three main parts. First, I look at those who attempt to use street culture to seal themselves off in micro-localities, refusing access as far as possible to people from outside the *banlieues*. Second, I examine some of the barriers encountered by artists from this milieu when seeking wider audiences, whether nationally or transnationally. Finally, I consider a number of factors that have facilitated wider access of this kind.

SELF-CONTAINMENT

Stigmatized by a large part of the majority ethnic population outside the *banlieues*, practitioners of street culture often have as a prime objective the revalorization of those neighborhoods in the eyes of the local population itself. One of the ways in which they have pursued this objective has been by appropriating symbolic models that, when first adopted at least, appear distinctive and in some ways subversive vis-à-vis nationally dominant cultural forms. While significant segments of France's post-colonial minorities—including the largest among them, those of Maghrebi origin—have no ancestral connections with the Black Atlantic, they have come to identify strongly with that space. Hip-hop, with its African American roots, has been triply attractive: minority ethnic youths in the *banlieues* have been inspired by the cultural assertiveness of blacks in the United States and the challenge that this represents to white-dominated assimilationism, they have found in hip-hop a welcome alternative to established cultural institutions giving primacy to written cultural forms, and their enthusiastic adoption of countless anglicisms has enabled them to escape from and in many ways belittle the cultural protectionism of French elites struggling to resist the advancing tide of American popular culture (Cachin 1996, Cannon 1997). By filling the streets of the *banlieues* with music, lyrics, and graffiti of their own making, they mark this out as *their* territory. Not uncommonly, they seek to heighten this sense of local control by adopting verbal and other forms of behavior designed to positively exclude outsiders. *Verlan* and other types of slang peppered with borrowings from anglophone, Arab, and other cultural spaces are often adopted for this purpose (Seguin and Teillard 1996, Lepoutre 1997, Begag 1997). A similar role is played by ritualized acts of violence such as street battles with the police and the destruction of luxury cars stolen from other neighborhoods, driven to the *banlieues*, and then burned on the streets there like so many hunting trophies. Strasbourg has set the record within France for ritual car burnings of this kind, with 1,375 of them in the year 2000, including 75 on New Year's Eve alone (Fortier 2001). Some seek to use this violence to capture media attention in the hope that centers of power outside the *banlieues* may thereby be persuaded of the need to address the patterns of disadvantage and discrimination from which these localities suffer. Some of the violence is of a more self-sufficient nature, generating gratification inside the *banlieues* at the destruction of status symbols stolen outside. Violence can also take a self-destructive turn, as seen in murders carried out against each other by members of rival gangs engaged in turf wars within the same or neighboring *banlieues* (Body-Gendrot and Le Guennec 1998). These kinds of gang wars are built on micro forms of "cultural insiderism" that in effect invest in gang membership an absolute sense of ethnic difference (cf. Werner Sollers, *Beyond Ethnicity*, quoted in Gilroy 1993: 3). They illustrate very graphically the dangers inherent in some of the more inward-looking locally focused forms of *banlieue* street culture, leading quite literally into dead-ends.

BARRIERS

Exponents of other forms of street culture are often more prepared to engage with the outside world. This is true, for example, of the novelist Azouz Begag and of many other writers from the *banlieues* who, while drawing heavily on oral speech patterns, tailor their work so that it is accessible to the general reading public. The motivations are diverse. Some seek to convey a message to those in authority and to shape public opinion at large concerning the problems confronting the *banlieues*. Others may be more interested in the material benefits that can be reaped by reaching a wider paying public. In other cases, irrespective of any profit motive, the technological and economic realities of the art form in which they work—film, for example—may necessitate sizeable paying audiences or other sources of financial support.

Access to audiences is conditioned by and occurs within a complex web of political, economic, technological, and other factors, in which gatekeepers such as record company executives, publishers, film distributors, academic and media critics, lawmakers, and educationalists can all play significant roles. Their impact may vary considerably between different cultural forms and spaces. Writers from the *banlieues*, for example, have been studied and debated far more extensively in the anglophone world than within the French academic community. Symptomatic of this is the fact that the first book-length studies of post-colonial writers in France were the work of a

British researcher (Hargreaves 1991) and a French academic based in the United States (Laronde 1993). More recently, an anthology of new French writing published in English in London gives pride of place to minority ethnic authors (De Chamberet 1999). As the title of the collection, *XCiTés*, implies, the street culture of the *banlieues* is at the heart of it. When interviewed by *Le Monde* about the anthology, the French publisher Olivier Cohen confessed to being perplexed: "With a few exceptions, it gives the impression that the French novel today consists of Blacks, Beurs, the *banlieues*, drugs and homosexuals. . . . It's like some sort of minorities literature, which is completely wrong, for there is no such thing here [in France], except in a very embryonic state" (*Le Monde* 1999).

At least three sets of factors linked with dominant conceptions of French nationhood appear to have contributed to this blinkered attitude. The first has been the traumatic legacy of decolonization. After the Algerian war of independence (1954–1962), most people in France wanted to forget as far as possible the pain and humiliation in which the colonial enterprise had foundered (Stora 1991). The last thing they expected or wanted was the rise of a permanently settled Maghrebi minority within the former colonial heartland itself. But that is exactly what happened. At both elite and popular levels, it has been difficult for the majority ethnic population to come to terms with the idea of incorporating into its midst a minority group originating in a people that fought an uncompromising war of liberation in order to be independent from France. Significantly, when the writings of post-colonial minorities are studied in French universities, this is generally in departments of francophone or comparative literature, rather than in departments of French. As commonly understood in France, francophone writing is that which is produced in the French language but which does not belong to the national literature of France. In categorizing post-colonial writers from the *banlieues* as francophone rather than French, academics have contributed to public perceptions of these minorities as essentially extraneous to France (Hargreaves 1996).

A second factor contributing to this marginalization lies in the reluctance of many French academics to abandon rigidly defined distinctions between "high" and "low" culture. While literature departments in anglophone countries have increasingly transformed their teaching and research programs, repositioning themselves in the wider field of cultural studies, French universities remain far more wedded to narrowly based literary studies. Popular cultural forms such as film and television are generally shunned by French academics. The writings of post-colonial authors from the *banlieues* are strewn with oral street vernacular from many parts of the world and copious borrowings from the audiovisual media. As such, they appear to many French academics to be a sub-culture in the most negatively connoted sense and by the same token unworthy of scholarly attention (cf. Keil 1991).

Within this optic, street culture appears to be quite literally a contradiction in terms. This kind of thinking is evident, for example, in a recent manifesto signed by scores of leading intellectuals denouncing education ministry plans to give less weight in the school curriculum to literary classics, and more to other types of writing as well as oral forms of communication. The authors of the manifesto, who included such luminaries as Régis Debray, Alain Finkielkraut, and Philippe Sollers, argued that this would be unfair to disadvantaged youngsters, exemplified in their thinking by "Beurs [i.e., second-generation Maghrebis]: what greater proof could we give of our esteem, interest and respect for them than by giving them the chance to share in culture instead of slamming the door in their face and saying 'No literature for you'" (*Le Monde* 2000a). Equating culture with classical forms of literature, the manifesto is similarly dismissive of earlier initiatives by Jack Lang, who as culture minister gave support to taggers and introduced an annual street festival of poetry. "At the end of the day," says the manifesto, "how can poetry be celebrated in the street when it is being killed at school? . . . How can one possibly believe that poetry can be improvised one fine evening in the street by people who have never opened a book?" (*Le Monde* 2000a).

Fear of losing control of the cultural agenda connects up with a third factor contributing to the resistance of French academics in the face of the hybrid cultural practices emanating from the *banlieues*. In shunning the work of post-colonial minorities, many academics probably believe that they are helping to protect the nation from Americanization. In the United States, universities have pursued vigorous policies of affirmative action designed to increase the proportion of minority ethnic teachers and researchers whose presence has helped to strengthen the implementation of a multicultural educational agenda (Bernheimer 1995). With no comparable commitment to greater ethnic diversity, the protectionist reflexes of many French intellectuals have been strengthened by the conviction that multiculturalism is an American import and as such must be categorically rejected.

Other spaces potentially open to artists from the *banlieues* include those in which they have their ancestral origins. For a variety of reasons, Maghrebi minorities in Europe have probably had a weaker impact on cultural dynamics in North Africa than has, say, the Turkish diaspora in Turkey. Governments in both the Maghreb and Turkey have always been free to control the circulation of cultural goods such as books, whether directly (by censorship) or indirectly (by tax or exchange rate policies, for example). During the 1990s constraints of this kind in Algeria were accentuated by the civil war, which led to a massive fall in the circulation of people and goods between France and Algeria, often making it dangerous or impossible for artists from the diaspora in France to perform in Algeria. There was no equivalent of this virtual blockade in relations between Turkey and Germany.

In principle, electronic technologies made it possible to circumvent barriers of this kind, but here too political and economic differences have had a significant impact. While Turkey has licensed a wide range of privately owned television channels, many of which have been open to input from artists in the diaspora (Aksoy 1997), TV broadcasting in the Maghreb remains largely state-controlled and relatively closed to artists outside the national territory (Benantar 1996). Although satellite dishes are now widely available in the Maghreb, giving access to private and publicly owned stations broadcasting from elsewhere, notably France, the relatively marginal presence of minority ethnic performers on French TV (Conseil Supérieur de l'Audiovisuel 2000) again limits their exposure across the Mediterranean.

GATEWAYS

In general, exponents of street culture have achieved their greatest public successes in cultural forms where economics, technology, and politics have combined to effectively bypass traditional elites and state controls. Witness the popular music industry. Privately owned and profit-oriented recording companies and an ever-growing part of the communications media have very different priorities from the public service ethos of older broadcasting organizations and other publicly run cultural institutions such as the national educational system. Mediated by these private companies, French-made rap has become the country's best-selling form of popular music.

The American roots of rap, anathema to much of France's intellectual establishment, are by the same token attractive to young people seeking to establish their independence from older mentors, and this appeal has been strengthened by the contestatory and subversive aspects of rap. Since the early 1980s, with advent of FM and now digital technology, the previously narrow range of general interest French radio stations has been overtaken by a plethora of specialist and themed channels, mainly privately owned, which are able to target youth and other markets far more intensively than in the past. These privately owned stations have no inhibitions about responding to market demand for new musical fashions. Paradoxically and quite unintentionally, efforts by the nation's political elites to impose public controls on these stations gave a major boost to French rap bands. The Pelchat amendment to the 1994 Carignon media law requires commercial radio stations to ensure that at least 40 percent of the songs they broadcast are in French. To encourage creativity, half of the minimum quota has to be allocated to artists still in the early stages of their careers. Multi-ethnic rap bands newly contracted to French recording companies satisfied these criteria to a T, and as a result they gained exceptional levels of exposure on stations such as Skyrock and NRJ, the market leaders among young listeners in France (Davet and

Mortaigne 1996, Hare 1997). In this way, the unintended consequence of a legal instrument designed to protect France from American cultural imports has in practice helped to promote a new fashion in popular music that is heavily impregnated with American, African, and other influences originating outside France, fused together in the streets of the *banlieues*.

The ineffectiveness of the Pelchat amendment and of many similar initiatives designed to curb foreign, especially American, cultural influences vividly illustrates the weakened capacity of the state to set the cultural agenda. Increasingly, public bodies are having to adjust to the new cultural forms that in recent years have emerged and gathered momentum beyond their control. The school curriculum reforms giving greater emphasis to non-literary forms of communication, denounced in the manifesto quoted earlier, are symptomatic of this shift. Even the Académie Française, the epitome of cultural conservatism in France, has shown signs of beginning to catch up. The same academy that has lent its support to the campaign against school curriculum reform—complaining that "schools are no longer compensating for the inferiorities that can arise from culturally starved social backgrounds. . . . [I]t is a counsel of despair to say that schools are now fundamentally incapable of initiating young people of diverse origins into the pleasures of understanding our literary masterpieces" (*Le Monde* 2000b)—has awarded its "grande médaille de la chanson française" (gold medal for contemporary song) to none other than MC Solaar. Meanwhile government ministries and city councils across the country are investing heavily in neighborhood facilities for practitioners of hip-hop, fueling a growing debate about the extent to which autonomous and/or contestatory voices are now being subsumed or neutered within the nation's cultural mainstream (*Mouvements* 2000, *Le Monde* 2000c).

Until recently, post-colonial minorities were relatively marginal figures in French cinema. Today they have a major box office presence with leading production and/or acting roles in movies such as *Taxi 2*, the biggest French money-earner of 2000, and *La Vérité si je mens 2* (2001), the most hyped French release of recent years. Symbolizing this shift, *Taxi 2* transposes the action formula initiated in the first *Taxi* film (1998) from the original locations in the *banlieues* and other parts of Marseilles to the *grands boulevards* of Paris. There are now dozens of new films every year set in France featuring actors of African, Caribbean, and Asian origin. Of course not all of these represent a genuine widening of French cinema to accommodate cultural models reflecting the diverse origins of France's post-colonial minorities. In many mainstream entertainment movies, such as *Taxi 2*, the ethnicity of minority ethnic actors is blurred over or elided altogether. But France's post-colonial minorities are now present in such a wide range of movies—including many in which ethnicity features as a significant social marker—that it is no longer possible to convincingly claim that they are systematically marginalized by the film industry.

While these minorities are now integral features of the French movie scene, they have yet to achieve a comparable degree of exposure in transnational cinema markets. The primary reason for this lies no doubt in the more general weakness of French-made films in a global marketplace dominated by anglophone products. Very few home-grown box office hits within France score a comparable degree of success in non-francophone countries. Language barriers and the resistance of consumers in the huge American market to dubbed or subtitled movies greatly limit the penetration of French-made films. Less constrained by these linguistic barriers, minority ethnic musicians have gained more substantial footholds in transnational markets. Promoted by the global reach of multinational recording companies to whom they are contracted through French subsidiaries and aided by high profile performances in the United States and elsewhere, rappers such as MC Solaar and *raï* artists such as Faudel now enjoy notoriety outside France on a far greater scale than any film director or actor originating in the *banlieues* (Cannon 1997, *Le Monde* 2001).

CONCLUSION

In 1997, the extreme right-wing Front National (FN) took control of Vitrolles, in the *banlieue* of Marseilles. Setting out her policy agenda, the newly elected FN mayor, Catherine Mégret, declared that she was determined to "re-establish cultural order" by attacking "rap culture and everything that goes with it, which isn't ours at all" (*Le Monde* 1997b). Her husband, Bruno Mégret, then number two to Jean-Marie Le Pen in the FN hierarchy, explained: "If we want to send all the Arabs, Africans and Asians back home, it isn't because we hate them, but because their presence is polluting our national identity" (*Le Monde* 1997a). In a variety of open as well as subterranean ways, this kind of thinking has influenced a significant part of the majority ethnic population, including a number of influential cultural gatekeepers. But the popular successes of French rap and *raï* and the increasing visibility of post-colonial minorities in French-made films show that the cultural mainstream is steadily being widened to include new elements reflecting the nation's ethnically diverse population. The attention gained outside France by artists from the *banlieues* illustrates the transnational impact of these minorities. The road from street culture to global highway is in many ways bumpy and uneven, but the traffic moving along it is gaining momentum.

WORKS CITED

Aksoy, A. (1997) "Reaching the Parts State Television Does Not Reach: Multiculturalism in Turkish Television," in Kevin Robins (ed.), *United Nations World Television*

Forum: Programming for People: From Cultural Rights to Cultural Responsibilities (Rome: RAI/EBU), pp. 54–63.

Baudrillard, Jean (1997) "From Popular Culture to Mass Culture: An Interview with Jean Baudrillard by Roger Célestin," in *Sites*, vol. 1, no. 1, Spring, pp. 5–15.

Begag, Azouz (1997) "Traffic de mots en banlieue: du 'nique ta mère' au 'plaît-il?'" in *Migrants-Formation*, no. 108, March, pp. 30–37.

Benantar, Abdennour (1996) "Laissez parler les Algériens," in *La France en question*, no. 1, pp. 181–184.

Bernheimer, Charles (ed.) (1995) *Comparative Literature in the Age of Multiculturalism* (Baltimore and London: Johns Hopkins University Press).

Body-Gendrot, Sophie, and Nicole Le Guennec (1998) *Mission sur les violences urbaines* (Paris: La Documentation française).

Cachin, Olivier (1996) *L'offensive rap* (Paris: Gallimard).

Cannon, Steve (1997) "*Paname City* Rapping: B-boys in the *banlieues* and beyond," in Alec G. Hargreaves and Mark McKinney (eds.), *Post-Colonial Cultures in France* (London and New York: Routledge), pp. 150–166.

Cashmore, Ellis (1997) *The Black Culture Industry* (London and New York: Routledge).

Conseil Supérieur de l'Audiovisuel (2000) "Présence et représentation des minorités visibles à la télévision française: une étude du CSA," in *La Lettre du CSA*, no. 129, June, pp. 12–14.

Davet, Stéphane, and Véronique Mortaigne (1996) "Les réseaux FM protestent contre les quotas de chansons francophones," in *Le Monde*, 10 January.

De Chamberet, Georgia (ed.) (1999) *XCiTés: The Flamingo Book of New French Writing* (London: Flamingo).

Fanon, Frantz (1974) *Les damnés de la terre* (Paris: Maspéro) [1st edition: 1961].

Fortier, Jacques (2001) "Soixante-quinze voitures incendiées à Strasbourg la nuit de la Saint-Sylvestre," in *Le Monde*, 3 January.

Gilroy, Paul (1993) *The Black Atlantic: Modernity and Double Consciousness* (Cambridge, MA: Harvard University Press).

Hare, Geoff (1997) "The Quota of French Language Songs on Radio," in *Modern and Contemporary France*, vol. 5, no. 1, February, pp. 73–75.

Hargreaves, Alec G. (1991) *Voices from the North African Immigrant Community in France: Immigration and Identity in Beur Fiction* (Oxford and New York: Berg) [2nd edition: 1997].

Hargreaves, Alec G. (1996) "French, Francophone or Maghrebian? Maghrebian Writers in France," in Nicki Hitchcott and Laïla Ibnlfassi (eds), *African Francophone Writing: A Critical Introduction* (Oxford and Washington, DC: Berg), pp. 33–43.

Keil, Regina (1991) "Entre le politique et l'esthétique: littérature 'beur' ou littérature 'franco-maghrébine'?" in *Itinéraires et contacts de cultures*, vol. 14, 2nd semester, pp. 159–168.

Laronde, Michel (1993) *Autour du roman beur: immigration et identité* (Paris: L'Harmattan).

Lepoutre, David (1997) *Coeur de banlieue: codes, rites et langages* (Paris: Odile Jacob).

Le Monde (1997a) "M. Mégret voudrait taxer les travailleurs étrangers," 13 February.

Le Monde (1997b) "Le FN à visage découvert," 25 February.

Le Monde (1999) "Comment les Anglais voient notre littérature," 27 August.

Le Monde (2000a) "C'est la littérature qu'on assassine rue de Grenelle," 4 March.

Le Monde (2000b) "L'Académie Française dénonce le 'recul' des études littéraires," 11 April.

Le Monde (2000c) "Les rappeurs redoutent les effets de leur nouvelle reconnaissance," 17–18 September.

Le Monde (2001) "Faudel, du raï communautaire à la chanson fédératrice," 8 February.

Mouvements (2000) "Hip-hop: les pratiques, le marché, la politique," no. 11, September–October.

Newsweek (1996) "Street Culture," 26 February, pp. 36–45.

Seguin, Boris, and Frédéric Teillard (1996) *Les Céfrans parlent aux Français: chronique de la langue des cités* (Paris: Calmann-Lévy).

Stora, Benjamin (1991) *La Gangrène et l'oubli* (Paris: La Découverte).

13

"Migrant Websites," WebArt, and Digital Imagination

Daniela Merolla

One of the most fascinating phenomena of the "technological revolution" of the past ten years is the explosive growth of websites set up by migrant associations and individuals. Both diaspora communities and individual migrants have increasingly used the World Wide Web to overcome spatial and temporal distances in a world that seems to contract under the impact of new technologies and extensive globalization. These websites, which I provisionally call "migrant websites," were initially created as virtual sites of sociopolitical and economic communication for diasporic communities and individuals. Today they have grown into multilingual platforms that host and intertwine verbal genres including short stories, poems, proverbs, and songs within a visual environment involving a confluence of decoration, colors, drawings, vignettes, photos, paintings, fragments of films and videos, and other acoustic and moving elements. This essay seeks to address crucial elements of the digital imagination evident in these dynamic creations by exploring migrant WebArt on the noteworthy websites set up by African migrant associations and individuals located in the Netherlands.[1]

"MIGRANT WEBSITES," WEBART, AND DIGITAL IMAGINATION: AN INTERDISCIPLINARY FIELD OF RESEARCH

A revolutionary slogan of the late 1960s, *l'imagination au pouvoir*, linked imagination with the power of changing the world (or at least the manifestants' world). The 1960s are over, but the power of imagination has taken a central place in studies of group identity. Anthropological, literary, and cultural studies have shown that imaginative expression indeed plays a pivotal role in identity construction as it creates intellectual sites of exchange, new kinds of audiences, and new forms of social and political imaginings.

Artistic expression, itself a product of socio-historical developments, contributes to the formation of a sense of distinctive "our-ness" within the community of writers and among readers and publics who construct and share the language of national creation.[2] A fundamental point is that artistic productions crucially create and open up intellectual spaces where constructions of "us" (and relatedly "you" and "them") as well as of the larger world take form. The migrant writers discussed in this volume constitute an exemplary case in point: they are progressively recognized as influential personalities and their works have come to affect cultural discourses as well as European identity and multiculturalism.

At the beginning of 1990s, in his "Global Ethnoscapes," Appadurai urged social scientists to track "the landscapes of group identity"—formed in relation to displacement and globalization—through the identification processes that are sustained and powerfully enhanced by imaginative productions in different forms and media.[3] He also advocated addressing "classic" literary genres, such as novels and traveling accounts:

> Fiction, like myth, is part of the conceptual repertoire of contemporary societies. Readers of novels and poems can be moved to intense action (as with *The Satanic Verses* of Salman Rushdie), and their authors often contribute to the construction of social and moral maps for their readers. (Appadurai 1991: 202)

> We need to incorporate the complexities of expressive representation (film, novels, travel accounts) into our ethnographies, not only as technical adjuncts, but as primary material with which to construct and interrogate our own representations. (Appadurai 1991: 208)

Since then, a new wave of anthropological research has flourished. Fresh insights have drawn new incisive analyses about the role of mass media (in particular film and television) and "small media" (video and audio cassettes, faxes, mailing lists, etc.) in the invention and maintenance (and relocalization) of group identities.[4] The creation of deterritorialized virtual communities in cyberspace and forms of hegemony and domination linked to hypermedia development have been analyzed as well.[5] Another branch of anthropological research has recently addressed the formation and discourses of community websites defined in linguistic or religious terms. However, studies of such websites have thus far focused only on mailing lists, chat rooms, discussion forums, online news, and online business[6] and have overlooked digital forms of literary and artistic production and communication. When attention was directed to the use of "demotic" media genres,[7] they were seen as expressions of the predominantly oral background of community members and as a function of the speech community formation (Kadende-Kaiser 2000).

So far, as this volume illustrates in the case of migration to Europe, literary and cultural studies have addressed the social and cultural effects of global displacements through the reshaping of individual and collective identities in novels, theater, and songs, and to a lesser extent in films and paintings, as well as their complex relation to national literary canons. Intercultural literary studies thus foreground the linguistic, cultural, gender, and artistic character-istics that create and limit imaginative expression in contexts of displacement and migration. However, when dealing with the Internet, literary studies have been primarily concerned with new literary electronic forms and genre de-velopment issuing from the non-linearity of digital narrative strategies.[8] On-line and offline productions in "migrant websites" (often in languages "other" than European ones) have thus far attracted little attention. Similarly, art and media studies that are exploring the fields of "computer art" and the "art of the World Wide Web" (Bolter and Grusin 2000, Bolter and Gromala 2003, Mal-loy and Bentson 2003, Rush 1999: 168–217 and related bibliography) have fo-cused on the artistic innovation through technology and the reformulation of forms and genres from existent media.[9] The artistic developments related to migration and the Internet have thus far received scant attention.

My approach pays this clearly missing attention to the way digital imagi-nation takes form in the artistic expressions on "migrant websites." Building on the fields explored by anthropological, literary, and cultural studies, I aim to explore digital imagination in the framework of virtual and physical ge-ographies of migration. This requires looking at the interconnections among cultural productions sustained by various media (writing/printing, theater, film, video, music, visual arts, and the Internet) as well as at the identifica-tion processes in verbal and visual art on "migrant websites" that enhance the interaction with local ("offline") communities.

What we find is that migrant websites tend to reinforce *local* group iden-tification by the transnational diffusion of discourses and artistic produc-tions on self-identification (Merolla 2002). The interaction of virtual and lo-cal communities marks the difference between migrant websites and other virtual communities. Studies of the Internet point to the construction of users' communities that are not only disembodied but also isolated from their surroundings. Disembodiment can add to the feeling of freedom and of new possibilities and experiments, but isolation becomes "a paradox of 'connectivity,'" as Willson writes (2000: 646), "[a paradox] of participation with others in a virtual space, [since] the [Internet] technology disconnects the individual from the embodied interactions surrounding her/him."[10] Whether or not this happens for Internet users in general, the situation is different for the users of "migrant websites" who normally are attached to their social environment and participate in the self-identification discourses of their local community. Indeed, "migrant websites" as well as other (linguistically, religiously, or ethnically marked) community websites are increasingly expressing and constructing (the awareness of) a specific collective identity.[11] The artistic production often assumes a central position in such construction of the "us."

On the other hand, transnationalism is enhanced by intensified contacts among migrants in different diasporic locations as well as between the diaspora and the "homeland," and by the deterritorializing effect of new media.[12] The Internet, the World Wide Web, and small media play a significant role in increasing the international communication that is faster and richer than it was possible to imagine just a decade ago. Recording on cassettes and videos is used for general communication when, instead of writing letters, people send cassettes or videos to share private events such as marriages and the like with faraway family members and friends (Dayan 1999). "Migrant websites" amplify the possibility for larger and dispersed groups (who have access to the Web both in the diaspora and in the lands of origin) to enter into contact and exchange information, discourses, and artistic productions beyond immediate national boundaries.

AFRICAN MIGRANT ASSOCIATIONS IN THE NETHERLANDS: WEBSITES AND WEBART

The African migrant associative world in the Netherlands is diverse and fluid. It includes general organizations (migrant, "allochthonous" associations, etc.); religious congregations; national, linguistic, and cultural associations whose goals are the dissemination of socio-cultural information on a certain migrant group; more specific (sub)groups of interest such as women, youth, elders, single parents, restaurateurs, sport, dance and music groupings; and so forth located in a specific region or town.[13] An increasing number of such migrant associations are going online. An inspection of websites such as Catsclem/Migranten (catsclem.nl/migranten) and search engines (such as Google or Excite under a panoply of relevant keywords) offers an idea of the expansion in the number of what I call "migrant websites."[14] The number of associations and relative websites does not directly reflect the demographic growth of a certain community, but this is still a relevant factor. It is thus not surprising that Moroccan associations and websites are particularly numerous when we consider that the Moroccans constitute the third largest migrant community in the Netherlands (after the Turkish and Surinamese communities), and exceed the other African migrant communities taken as a whole.[15]

The situation is, however, far from being stable. New websites appear regularly; others completely disappear or stop being renovated. There are a large number of static sites that serve only to provide the text of the association's statutes and a list of the association's goals. Dynamic websites that have several "pages" and are constantly updated are dramatically increasing in number. Examples of rich and dynamic sites are the Moroccan sites Moroc.nl and Maghrebonline.nl, the Moroccan Berber (Amazigh) sites Tawiza.nl and Amazigh.nl, the Ghanaian site Sankofa.nl, and the Eritrean and Somalian sites Eritrea.nl and Somaliaholland.free.fr.

Most migrant websites are basically information sites modeled on paper bulletins, magazines, and newspapers. At the same time, web design programs play a central role in the visual and content-based structure. We thus find the typical division in vertical and horizontal sections, with the lateral sections containing indexes with hyperlinks to subpages and other websites, while the larger central section of the screen gives the news and main theme (or themes) of the website. Websites of migrant associations located in the Netherlands are typically multilingual. I noted that in the period between 2001 and 2004 basic information and news on migrant sites were progressively offered in Dutch. International languages (such as English, French, and Arabic) still appear, but—depending on the site—they are becoming secondary or they tend to be used in a lateral section of the screen. However, there are also sites on which English and Dutch constitute two separate sections and this seems to indicate a long-term choice. For example, on Somalia Holland Online, the opening section of Somalian information is in English, followed by the Dutch-language section of Netherlands news.[16] Similarly, the Ethiopian site www.ethio.nl is in English with hyperlinks to pages in Dutch and in Amharic.[17]

It is difficult to generalize about the role of mother tongues and community languages in these sites.[18] On some they are present only in the title and header decoration, while in others they are evident in a number of pages. The reasons are clearly context-related: the local Dutch situation of migration should be considered, as well as the socio-political and cultural context in the land of origin. The increase of Amazigh texts on Moroccan Berber websites, for example, is clearly linked to the growing activism of Berber cultural associations in the Netherlands, but also to the long-term quest for recognition of Berber (Tamazight) as the official second language of Morocco and Algeria and to the new possibility of teaching in Tamazight granted in Morocco.

The space allotted to international languages and to community languages and mother-tongues can be considered an indicator of the addressed transnational diasporic community, with the use of community language visually and symbolically loaded with identity construction and affirmation.

On the other hand, the website is rooted in the migrant location of the cultural association thanks to the use of Dutch. Such a process is also reflected in the increasing presence of local Dutch news and opinion polls on current issues being debated in Dutch society at large.

A look at the "migrant websites" shows that the diffusion of visual and verbal artistic genres takes place in the context of an almost standard format. On the homepage one finds news concerning the migrant communities and their lands of origin, and hyperlinks to articles, forums, chat lines, and other interesting sites including other diasporic websites.[19] In addition, one can follow hyperlinks to "literature, culture, and music," "arts and culture," "art, poetry, and songs," and sometimes the more puzzling label "talents," finding pages of written literature, films, songs, oral genres (usually poems and proverbs, but short oral narratives are not absent), and visual arts.

The "literary" pages present book covers and passages from texts already published on paper (often in the mother tongue or in the language of the land of origin); essays about authors or artistic genres or trends; information on current cultural events, meetings, and dancing evenings (in one of the languages used on the site, and often in English or French); and hyperlinks to commercial sites where it is possible to buy the mentioned books or music. Stable or temporary forums allow for timely discussion of contemporary literary matters and publications. The artistic genres produced offline are thus activated and diffused by migrant websites, sometimes with excerpts, descriptions, and comments, sometimes simply as an advertisement, in other cases with short samples that can be listened to and/or viewed. In a number of cases, offline verbal and visual genres interact with a production that finds direct publication on the Web. The sites of Moroccan migrant associations indeed present hyperlinks to "new" productions such as short stories and poems written in Dutch and not (or not yet) published on paper, which is in line with the artistic blossoming of writers and artists issuing from the Moroccan migrant community in the Netherlands.[20] As in the case of offline magazines and newspapers, some of these texts are part of a larger writing project, as is indicated by the form "to be continued" set at the end of the text.[21] On the Moroccan Berber sites, we also find new literary productions in Berber/Tamazight, such as short stories and poems, which reinforce the central concern of such sites, that is, the socio-cultural situation of the Berber language in the Maghreb and the diaspora.[22] In the framework of such virtual spaces even the more "innocent" comic video or love poem, being spoken or written in Berber, assumes an engaged "color." But this seems a development shared by different migrant websites, at least as far as the diffusion of offline production is concerned.

Readers of this volume know that migrant writings in the European languages are extensive. Migrant productions in non-European languages are slowly growing and tentatively mapping novel cultural spaces and identification processes in Europe. These productions are certainly much more limited than the European-language writings in number and diffusion, particularly when migrant writers and groups do not have the support of national agencies and cultural institutions. This happens in the case of immigrants who belong to minorities in their country of origin, or when little national funding is available for cultural initiatives, as in the case of Ghanaian immigrants. The productions in the mother tongues and community languages typically enter circulation as "small media," self-sponsored (and often self-distributed) modest publications (literary texts as well as music, theater, and homemade audio or video cassettes) in local magazines with only a limited distribution. The online creation-diffusion-consumption of literary expression in "migrant websites" offers new spaces of creation and communication for productions in the mother-tongues and community languages. It should be noted that the visual production of African artists in the Netherlands also finds space in museums and exhibitions as well as on institutional websites, since the international and market-directed interests in African arts are well established.[23]

As I said above, most of the literary expression of "migrant websites" is located on subpages, its presence made known by homepage hyperlinks or other embedded subdirectories. Similiarly, these same visual menus display labels that lead to subpages with museum-like expositions of photos, drawings, paintings, and images excerpted from videos, films, concerts, and so forth. But the targeted literary and artistic materials are not only contained in these menus. On the contrary, the ubiquity of artistic productions on the sites is evident. In the sites Sankofa.nl and Tiwiza.nl, for example, attention is drawn to such navigational pointers that are included in a relevant informative text on a central section of the screen. The use of visual elements is very broad and intense, often resembling the newspaper or magazine model with photos of dramatic news, events, places, people, and so forth. These visual and decorative aspects are routinely updated, subtly enhancing their relevance and the impact of the general informational goals of the particular site. Emblems, icons, and photos, as well as words or short expressions in the mother tongue and community language, dominate homepages indicating national or minority group interests, feelings, and identification.

Some of the sites, for example, present an opening page in which an image is briefly offered before the automatic shift to the homepage. Such an initial presentation of the site can rely on symbolic national colors and drawings, visually locating the "homeland" and the migration community in the Netherlands (see Eritrea.nl). It can also propose more intriguing visions, such as the reddish drawing of a young woman's face on Amazigh.nl, an image that seems to rest on the link between beauty, woman, language, and culture, which again implies positionality and self-representation in the socio-political and cultural discourse of and about the Berbers/Imazighen.[24]

We need to ask why the presence of the visual and verbal artistic production is growing on "migrant websites." Miller and Slater (2000) write that for people from Trinidad, being on the Internet with Trinidadian websites is a way to affirm the existence of their island, a manner of being "out there" in the largest (virtual) world. The visitor to websites created by African migrant associations in the Netherlands must note that they appear as showrooms— displaying what the migrant community (or group of interest) is and can offer "out there," and equally "here"; where the offline location is in which the community lives its everyday life; and where the particular association is active. While political, economic, and social questions are problematic and are discussed as such in relation to life in the diaspora and in the country of origin, the concern for the "cultural baggage" in the digital "display" of the self relies on a process of mediation between discourses from within and from without the community. The cultural "baggage" (as well as new artistic developments) is indeed expressed by valued verbal and visual productions— valued within the community for their specific styles and discourses, but also internationally valued when put under the label "arts." WebArt thus becomes an *atout*, a resource that can be exploited in different manners and for different goals, including a rewarding discourse of the self and for pursuing (intercultural) dialogue or discussion from a convenient position. Websites, however, are not just showrooms, since digital imagination is at work presenting specific perspectives and discourses of the self. There remain a host of puzzling issues that invite further careful scrutiny and in-depth analysis: Is there convergence or discrepancy between artistic (and identificational) discourses of singular artefact and their location and interpretation on these migrant websites? If migrant websites are more than "showrooms" for traditional and current literary and visual genres, do they also pioneer in the creation of new forms of virtual art? Are exclusive forms of "our-ness" being constructed through digital cultural productions, or is migrant WebArt (while constructing self-identification locally and transnationally) also able to sustain internal heterogeneity and the development of interculturality—that is, cultural dialogue and cultural interaction within society at large?

NOTES

1. See Daniela Merolla, "Digital Imagination and the 'Landscapes of Group Identities': Berber Diaspora and the Flourishing of Theatre, Video's, and Amazigh-Net," *The Journal of North African Studies*, 7, no. 4 (Winter 2002): 122–131, and my ongoing project on African migration and new artistic developments in the Netherlands (University of Leiden). I would like to thank Ben Arps, Patricia Spyer, and Kitty Zijlmans for their comments on an earlier version of this paper. I also thank the students of the

master course on Digital Imagination and Virtual Migration held at the University of Ca' Foscari, Venice, February 2002, for their reactions and input.

2. Numerous studies have followed the pioneering work of Benedict Anderson, *Imagined Communities* (London and New York, Verso, 1983), in which he emphasized the essential role of print capitalism and the diffusion of narrative genres in the historical processes leading to the creation of national communities.

3. Arjun Appadurai, "Global Ethnoscapes: Notes and Queries for a Transnational Anthropology," in *Recapturing Anthropology*, ed. Richard G. Fox (Santa Fe, NM: School of American Research Press, 1991), 191–210.

4. See Lila Abu-Lughod, "Movie Stars and Islamic Moralism in Egypt," *Social Text* 42 (1995): 53–67; Daniel Dayan, "Media and Diasporas," in *Television and Common Knowledge*, ed. Jostein Gripsrud (London and New York: Routledge, 1999), 18–33; Patricia Spyer, "Photography's Framings and Unframings: A Review Article," *Comparative Studies in Society and History* 43, no. 1 (2001): 181–192; Annabelle Sreberny-Mohammadi and Ali Mohammadi, *Small Media, Big Revolution: Communication, Culture, and the Iranian Revolution* (Minneapolis: University of Minnesota Press, 1994).

5. The Internet is a frequent topic of study in computer science, media and communication, economics and political science, feminist studies, and anthropology. See, for example, Elizabeth Reid, "Virtual Worlds: Culture and Imagination," in *CyberSociety*, ed. Stephen G. Jones (Thousand Oaks, CA: Sage, 1995), 164–183, and Cyberanthropology.org. On hegemony and domination on the Web, see Barney Warf and John Grimes, "Counterhegemonic Discourse and the Internet," *The Geographical Review*, 87, 2 (1997): 259–274.

6. Jon W. Anderson, "The Internet and Islam's New Interpreters," in *New Media in the Muslim World,* ed. Dale F. Eickelman and Jon W. Anderson (Bloomington and Indianapolis: Indiana University Press, 1999), 41–56; Stefania Capone, "Les Dieux sur le Net, l'essor des religions d'origine africaine aux Etats-Unis," *L'Homme*, no. 151 (1999): 47–74; Rose M. Kadende-Kaiser, "Interpreting Language and Cultural Discourse: Internet Communication among Burundians in the Diaspora," *Africa Today* 47, no. 2 (Spring 2000): 121–148; Daniel Miller and Don Slater, *The Internet: An Ethnographic Approach* (Oxford and New York: Bergh, 2000).

7. Such as proverbs, poems, and legends in websites organized by members of diasporas and addressing primarily others from the same lands of origin. Kadende-Kaiser, in "Interpreting Language and Cultural Discourse" (138), uses the definitions "oramedia or folk media."

8. See George P. Landow, *Hypertext 2.0: The Convergence of Contemporary Critical Theory and Technology* (Baltimore: The Johns Hopkins University Press, 1994). An extended bibliography is available in Espen J. Aarseth, *Cybertext: Perspectives on Ergotic Literature* (Baltimore: The Johns Hopkins University Press, 1997).

9. See the concept of "remediation" in Jay David Bolter and Richard Grusin, *Remediation: Understanding New Media* (Cambridge, MA: MIT Press, 2000).

10. Michelle Willson, "Community in the Abstract: A Political and Ethical Dilemma?" in *The Cybercultures Reader,* ed. David Bell and Barbara M. Kennedy (London and New York: Routledge, 2000), 644–657.

11. A recent example is the study of Daniel Miller and Don Slater, in *The Internet*, of "being Trinidadian" on the Internet. They show that in Trinidad "the Internet is being understood and used . . . in relation precisely to those [historical] projects that may be understood as being Trini or representing Trini" (87). While Miller and Slater warn against a simplistic use of culture and understanding of nationalist construction, they insist that this warning not be read as a reason "to deny to a people the integrity of a [ethnic or other] category they apply to themselves and spend much of their lives living in respect of" (87).

12. See Linda Glick Schiller, Nina Basch, and Cristina Blanc-Szanton, *Nations Unbound: Transnational Projects, Post-colonial Predicaments, and De-territorialized Nation-States* (Langhorne, PA: Gordon and Breach, 1994), 6.

13. See Africans in the Netherlands at www.africaserver.nl.

14. These general websites are, however, neither complete nor regularly updated.

15. Statistics show that Moroccans are about 14% of the (non-European) population, labeled as "allochthonous." This category includes those who immigrated to the Netherlands with their children. The other African communities are 9% of this "allochthonous" population. While the nationality of 41% of this subpopulation is not indicated, the other groups are: Somalians, 16%; Cape Verdeans, 11%; Ghanaians, 10%; Egyptians, 9%; South Africans, 8%; and Ethiopians, 5% (Foquz Ethnomarketing 2004, www.foquz.nl; Statistics Netherlands CBS 2004, www.cbs.nl/nl/publicaties/publicaties/algemeen/statistisch-bulletin).

16. At present the Dutch news is updated, unlike the English section.

17. On the other hand, the new Ethiopian website of the Dutch-based association Stichting DIR is largely in Dutch (see www.dirnet.nl).

18. They do not always overlap, as in the case of minority languages (mother tongues) in the lands of origin that may or may not correspond to the national language of the migrant community (community language).

19. News and articles treat politically oriented subjects in a standard way. In forums and especially chat rooms, on the other hand, users ask questions about cultural identity as well as more private questions about living as a migrant or about gender relationships, for example, when and how to marry, what a girl or a boy can and should do and expect from her or his spouse, and so forth.

20. See the introduction and Rosemarie Buikema's paper.

21. See the "unfinished" texts indicated by Bernard Arps and Ignatius Supriyanto, "Javanese on the Internet," *Caraka, The Messenger, A Newsletter for Javanists*, 37–38 (June–December 2002), www.let.leidenuniv.nl/Caraka/37_38/special_report.htm (21 Feb. 2004).

22. Also, the websites of Berber singers and actors are typically introduced with commentary stressing the difficult situation of Berbers in the Maghreb.

23. See, for example, africaserver.nl and the Virtual Museum of Contemporary African Art at www.vmcaa.nl/vm.

24. This was the opening image in 2003, but other illustrations may appear when particularly important or shocking news occurs, for example, a photo of the last terrible earthquake in the Rif, a Berber area in Northern Morocco, was used on 23–24 February 2004.

WORKS CITED

Aarseth, Espen J., *Cybertext: Perspectives on Ergotic Literature*, Baltimore, The Johns Hopkins University Press, 1997.

Abu-Lughod, Lila, "Movie Stars and Islamic Moralism in Egypt," *Social Text*, 42, 1995: 53–67.

Anderson, Benedict, *Imagined Communities: Reflections on the Origin and Spread of Nationalism*, London, Verso, 1983.

Anderson, Jon W., "The Internet and Islam's New Interpreters," in *New Media in the Muslim World*, Dale F. Eickelman and Jon W. Anderson (eds.), Bloomington and Indianapolis, Indiana University Press, 1999, 41–56.

Appadurai, Arjun, "Global Ethnoscapes: Notes and Queries for a Transnational Anthropology," in *Recapturing Anthropology*, Richard G. Fox (ed.), Santa Fe, NM: School of American Research Press, 1991, 191–210.

Arps, Bernard, and Ignatius Supriyanto, "Javanese on the Internet," *Caraka, The Messanger: A Newsletter for Javanists*, 37–38, June–December 2002 www.let.leidenuniv.nl/caraka/37_38/special_report (21 Feb. 2004).

Bolter, Jay David, and Richard Grusin, *Remediation: Understanding New Media*, Cambridge, MA, MIT Press, 2000.

Bolter, Jay David, and Diane Gromala, *Windows and Mirrors: Interaction Design, Digital Art, and the Myth of Transparency*, Cambridge, MA, MIT Press, 2003.

Capone, Stefania, "Les Dieux sur le Net, l'essor des religions d'origine africaine aux Etats-Unis," *L'Homme*, 151, 1999: 47–74.

Dayan, Daniel, "Media and Diasporas," in *Television and Common Knowledge*, Jostein Gripsrud (ed.), London and New York, Routledge, 1999, 18–33.

Glick Schiller, Linda, Nina Basch, and Cristina Blanc-Szanton, *Nations Unbound: Transnational Projects, Post-colonial Predicaments, and De-territorialized Nation-States*, Langhorne, PA, Gordon and Breach, 1994.

Kadende-Kaiser, Rose M., "Interpreting Language and Cultural Discourse: Internet Communication among Burundians in the Diaspora," *Africa Today*, 47, no. 2, Spring 2000: 121–148.

Landow, George P., *Hypertext 2.0: The Convergence of Contemporary Critical Theory and Technology*, Baltimore, The Johns Hopkins University Press, 1994.

Malloy, Judy, and Pat Bentson, *Women, Art and Technology*, Cambridge, MA: MIT Press, 2003.

Merolla, Daniela, "Digital Imagination and the 'Landscapes of Group Identities': Berber Diaspora and the Flourishing of Theatre, Video's, and Amazigh-Net," *The Journal of North African Studies*, 7, no. 4, Winter 2002: 122–131.

Miller, Daniel, and Don Slater, *The Internet: An Ethnographic Approach*, Oxford and New York, Bergh, 2000.

Reid, Elizabeth, "Virtual Worlds: Culture and Imagination," in *CyberSociety*, Stephen G. Jones (ed.), Thousand Oaks, CA, Sage, 1995, 164–183.

Rush, Michael, *New Media in Late Twentieth Century*, London, Thames and Hudson, 1999.

Spyer, Patricia, "Photography's Framings and Unframings: A Review Article," *Comparative Studies in Society and History*, 43, no. 1, 2001: 181–192.

Sreberny-Mohammadi, Annebelle, and Ali Mohammadi, *Small Media, Big Revolution: Communication, Culture, and the Iranian Revolution*, Minneapolis, University of Minnesota Press, 1994.

Warf, Barney, and John Grimes, "Counterhegemonic Discourse and the Internet," *The Geographical Review*, 87, no. 2, 1997: 259–274.

Willson, Michelle, "Community in the Abstract: a Political and Ethical Dilemma?" in David Bell and Barbara M. Kennedy (eds.), *The Cybercultures Reader*, London and New York, Routledge, 2000, 644–657.

14

"London-stylee!": Recent Representations of Postcolonial London

John McLeod

On 25 June 2000 Yasmin Alibhai-Brown published an article in the *New York Times* entitled "A Magic Carpet of Cultures in London" in which she explored with enthusiasm the city's vibrancy and diversity at the millennium. Citing the success of the British television comedy series *Goodness Gracious Me*, written by and featuring a cast of British Asians including the novelist Meera Syal; the art of Steve McQueen; and novels such as Zadie Smith's *White Teeth* (2000), Alibhai-Brown suggested that London's transformation in the 1990s was having an important impact on culture and society at large. Whereas the city had previously possessed "localities seen as immigrant ghettoes," these days "the flux has started to loosen these imagined barriers" (38):

> Notting Hill is now clogged up with the white chattering classes who previously would have headed for Hampstead with its old money and unnatural calm. Brixton, Paddington and Shoreditch, which were once impoverished dumps, are places where dot.com millionaires, artists and designers want to live and play. Brick Lane in the east end, famous for its cruel penury and racial thuggery, now swarms with diners in sharp suits from the City. Multiracial London is coming of age, and it is this that is igniting such energy, buzz and creativity. (Alibhai-Brown 2000: 32)

Alibhai-Brown offered a mapping of the city in which its imagined cartography is reconceptualized and remade as a consequence of multiracial creative energies that are breaking down racialized divides, both concrete and imagined. She acknowledged that "ethnic and social divisions [still] exist" but firmly argued that "evidence of real and irreversible integration is everywhere"

(Alibhai-Brown 2000: 32). It now appeared that at the beginning of a new century London was emerging from its long diasporic history with new possibilities of social and cultural transformation in (and for) a city that had an unhappy record of discrimination and violence.

Alibhai-Brown's remarks beckon accusations of naïveté, if not inaccuracy, in representing contemporary multicultural London so cheerfully. As Bermuda, heroine of Maryse Condé's novel *Histoire de la femme cannibale* (2003), puts it, "quelle ville est plus raciste que Londres? Sa reputation de paradis multiculturel est une invention des intellectuals comme Salman Rushdie qui a d'ailleurs émigré aux Etats-Unis" ["is there a city that is more racist than London? Its reputation as a multicultural paradise is an invention of intellectuals such as Salman Rushdie who, moreover, has emigrated to the United States"] (Condé 2003: 5). Neither does Alibhai-Brown think too deeply about the racialized social and economic divisions in the city that endure when the "white chattering classes" decide to "live and play" in Brixton, Paddington, or Brick Lane. As Harry Goulbourne has argued in his study of ethnicity in postwar Britain, "people of African, Asian and European backgrounds increasingly meet only where they buy and sell commodities," and it is "unlikely that a series of mutually exclusive communities with little more than a vulgar market relationship between them would live together in peace and tranquillity" (Goulbourne 1991: 231, 232). The racist murder of Stephen Lawrence in South London in 1993 is sobering evidence of the continuing problems of "multiracial" London. The five men considered responsible for the killing of a black youth waiting for a bus escaped prosecution due to insufficient evidence. After a considerable outcry about the inadequacy of the police and judicial system's response to the killing a public inquiry led to the 1999 McPherson Report in which the police and other state agencies were found to be institutionally racist (McPherson 1999). In late April 1999, nail bombs were consecutively detonated in Brick Lane, Brixton, and Soho with fatal consequences. Although each was the work of a lone individual rather than a rightwing organization, the choice of each location—significant centers for, respectively, the city's Bengali community, Afro-Caribbeans, and gay and lesbian Londoners—revealed how a well-established stereotyping cartography of London informed acts of urban terror. In her enthusiastic advocacy of a multiracial London "coming of age" Alibhai-Brown seemed blind to the city's deep divisions that, as Stephen Frears's film *Dirty Pretty Things* (2003) would show a few years later, were still very much in evidence.

Or was she? The tenor of Alibhai-Brown's argument is important and must not be too easily dismissed. Her cheerful view of London might be regarded more judiciously as a response to some of the enduring social and political problems of the city that her book *Imagining the New Britain* (2001) evidences. She is perfectly aware that as part of a wider cultural response at (and to) the turn of the century, a number of writers and commentators took a firmly optimistic and deliberately utopian perspective on multiracial London in opposing ongoing social conflicts. In defiance of the durability of racist attitudes, many cultural figures deliberately pointed with enthusiasm to another London—tolerant and diverse, creative and fun—the establishment of which was unstoppable and worthy of celebration. This was not the London "visible but unseen" of Salman Rushdie's *The Satanic Verses* (1988), tucked away in ghettoized neighborhoods and at the mercy of prejudice at the levels of state and street, but a city manifestly changed by its diverse population and no longer determined by institutional and popular racism. Whether this version of London existed was debatable; but as a utopian vision of a city that *should* exist, it was vital. This strategically sanguine response to contemporary London, one which we might call "millennial optimism," is best exemplified by the enthusiastic advocacy in 2000 of Zadie Smith's *White Teeth*. Caryl Phillips was among many in applauding the novel's emphasis on the "helpless heterogeneity" and "dazzlingly complex world of cross-cultural fusion in modern-day London" (Phillips 2001: 283). Despite its modest qualities and regardless of the specifics of its representation of the (often troubled) lives of Londoners, *White Teeth* became the focal point for the promotion of a pointedly utopian vision of London where the city's polycultural admixture suggested a radical and democratizing social blueprint.

A decade ago in his discussion of the cultural dissidence of racially subordinated peoples, Paul Gilroy referred to the "politics of transfiguration" (Gilroy 1993: 37), which are discovered in utopian imaginings of "qualitatively new desires, social relations, and modes of association" (Gilroy 1993: 37). The creative endeavors of such peoples frequently function "[b]y posing the world as it is against the world as the racially subordinated would like it be" (Gilroy 1993: 36). Something of the political utopianism in Alibhai-Brown's lauding of multiracial London and the admiration of *White Teeth* can also be found in postcolonial London writing in recent years, which similarly contests discriminatory discourses with the cheerfully positive advocacy of a London transfigured by its transcultural cartographies.

Two exemplary instances are Fred D'Aguiar's collection of poetry *British Subjects* (1993) and Bernardine Evaristo's novel-in-verse *Lara* (1997). Both writers have particular links to South East London, and their imaginative endeavors are inflected with an urgent politics of transfiguration. This is achieved through innovative modes of representation that establish social consciousness and responsibility through a profoundly antic and playful sensibility. In their different ways D'Aguiar and Evaristo project a utopian vision of London in which the city's perpetually transcultural condition elaborates new desires and modes of association worthy of support.

Although born in London in 1960, Fred D'Aguiar spent his early childhood in his parents' native land of Guyana but returned to London in 1972. He remembers suffering racist abuse at school and grew up with a feeling that

"London did not belong to me, could never belong to me on account of my race, my minority status" (D'Aguiar 2000: 197). As he recalls, during the 1980s "London was spoiled by [Prime Minister Thatcher's] parsimonious government when it came to race policy and running the inner city" (D'Aguiar 2000: 200). Although he supported anti-racist initiatives during young adulthood (he was present at the violence in Southall in 1979, when the anti-racist demonstrator Blair Peach was killed), he turned away from radicalizing notions of race as a means of resistance. He nurtured instead a keen sense of apartness: from Guyana, from London, and from other black Londoners. Several of the poems in *British Subjects* indeed record the unhappy experiences of those living in a "London [which] was spoiled by a definition of Britain that never took my presence into consideration" (D'Aguiar 2000: 200). But at another level, D'Aguiar's poetry attempts to mark and celebrate the changes nurtured in the city in recent years, which bear witness to the remarkable transformative potential of migrants and their descendents in London. London is subjected to imaginative transformation by a poetic persona firmly committed to the transcultural efficacy of the city's vexed contemporaneity. When dealing with sobering issues—police violence, institutionalized racism—D'Aguiar's poems frequently adopt a witty and cheerful attitude that is strategically celebratory.

For example, in "A Gift of a Rose" the speaker records being beaten and verbally abused by two policemen who have taken exception to his "black skin" (D'Aguiar 1993: 11). But the dramatic situation is not at first obvious: D'Aguiar's poem recasts the incident in terms normally associated with affection, namely the giving of flowers. The "red, red roses" the speaker receives are unexpected images of the bruises that he suffers during the beating and that "liberally spread over my face and body" (D'Aguiar 1993: 11). The speaker is told by some that his roses should be photographed and logged as a statistic, while others suggest that the police should receive a similar gift— "a rose for a rose" (D'Aguiar 1993: 11). The roses gradually disappear, but a "rose memory" remains with the speaker, who learns to avoid the police on the street and fancies that "I have a bouquet of my own for them" (D'Aguiar 1993: 11). The effects of the poem are several and instructive to a reading of the collection as a whole. As well as defamiliarizing racist violence through an unanticipated register, the choice of a rose as an image of bruising appropriates a national cliché in order to suggest that the assault on the street has connections to wider issues of state authority and national identity. The speaker is clearly being subjected to a certain exclusionary version of Britain in being assaulted. But most important, perhaps, is the very act of transforming the incident with recourse to the conceit of the rose. D'Aguiar will not allow the ugliness of racist violence to set the tone of his poem nor define its language; instead, the poetic transformation of the incident into a bizarre moment of gift-giving effects an occasion for invention in which the creative agency of the poet is foregrounded. In this self-portraiture, the "bouquet" that the speaker may subsequently offer the police is not an anti-racist beating so much as the poem itself. D'Aguiar's collection prizes new ways of writing that resist the authority of officious representations of social marginality and illegitimacy (in the poem the speaker refuses the advice offered of several ways of responding to the incident).

If "A Gift of a Rose" offers a meaningful and playful cultural response to London's racism, the socially transfigurative possibilities of London's polycultural energies are enthusiastically explored in "Notting Hill," which concerns the annual Notting Hill Carnival held each year in August. It was set up by Claudia Jones in the aftermath of the Notting Hill riots. Newspaper reports of the Carnival even now rarely fail to mention the number of arrests made by the police. In recent years, however, the Carnival has become promoted as a celebratory sign of London's general multicultural and racially harmonious condition that apparently has been achieved. D'Aguiar's poem clearly celebrates the carnival but also regards it as a response to (and not an escape from) wider problems of racial and cultural division. At the Notting Hill Carnival there incubates a potentially radical and inclusive social vision of London that might hold out the possibility of transformation for the nation as a whole.

"Notting Hill" consists of three parts. In the first the speaker celebrates the vivid costumes of those in procession at the carnival while borrowing the calypsonian rhythms of the "steel pan and bass"—"car-ni-val car-ni-val car-ni-val / this is car-ni-val" (D'Aguiar 1993: 39) is a regular refrain. The social significance of the carnival performers is established early. The speaker calls them "freedom fighters in battle dress / the spirit of their banners in their dance" (D'Aguiar 1993: 39). The quest for freedom is also linked to utopian goals in the representation of the carnival as a visionary space, epitomized by the children who sit on shoulders and are "wild-eyed in the wildest of dreams" (D'Aguiar 1993: 39). In the poem's second part those at the carnival "reach for the rainbow / drape it across our streets" (D'Aguiar 1993: 40), suggesting that the rainbow vision and optimism of the carnival can come alive on the otherwise mundane streets of the city. That such an initiative should be generally pursued is stressed by the repetition of the phrase "carnival not once a year" (D'Aguiar 1993: 40). In the third part, the speaker records the singing and dancing on Notting Hill's streets during the carnival. The spectacle is of a community united by a shared delight in the rhythm of the steel drum, which is "part yours and everybody's" (D'Aguiar 1993: 41). Despite being crowded, the street is not a dangerous location. The dance brings together a community that is mutually supportive: "for balance you grab a shoulder or waist; when they jump you take off too" (D'Aguiar 1993: 41). In this "ownerless" space where you "can't see for people" (D'Aguiar 1993: 41) the dancing prompts laughter and room to breathe among the "rattle and thump" (D'Aguiar 1993: 41) of the steel band. In the concluding stanza the speaker denounces the received cartography of the city—"Never mind the street names, they're postal / conveniences" (D'Aguiar 1993: 41)—and suggests that everyone indulges in tasting the sweet honeycomb of life that the carnival makes manifest. The challenge remains to sort out "the sting / from the honey" before the "choreography / comes with ease, grace" (D'Aguiar 1993: 41). "Rock on," declares the elated speaker, "but mind that island in the road!" (D'Aguiar 1993: 41). The island is, literally, a traffic island used to direct and divide transport, yet the image suggests Britain, also a dangerous island impeding yet leading to a cooperative ease of motion. The determined imperative to "rock on" suggests that the island's problems can be overcome by the rainbow vision and exuberant optimism of the carnival, which contains the possibility of a new, socially inclusive vision of life on London's streets. Note that the racial character of the "freedom fighters" is tacit; it is the carnival's cultural resources that can be translated into the occupation and transformation of Notting Hill that welcomes all.

In his determination to "shout about the pain but [not] shut out the bacchanal" (D'Aguiar 1993: 16), D'Aguiar's poetry frequently builds a transfigurative politics committed to reimagining London in terms that contest officious and prejudicial discourses. The "ownerless space" of London becomes the crucible for dissident forms of creativity where cultural initiatives are an invaluable resource for achieving social objectives. The desirability of the carnival's festivity is partly due to the new social relations it reflects, while the "choreography" it creates is equivalent to novel modes of intercultural association that turn the revellers into a rainbow vision of post-racial society. D'Aguiar offers an innovative migratory cartography of London that brings the creative forms of the Caribbean to bear upon the streets of West London in a telling act of spatial creolization.

In turning next to Bernardine Evaristo's *Lara* we discover an analogous articulation of a transcultural urban space made ready for transfiguration and change. Born to an English mother and Nigerian father in South East London in 1959, Evaristo was raised as a Catholic and received her primary education at a local convent before attending Eltham Hill Girls Grammar School. After graduating from drama school she performed in and wrote for theater and traveled extensively—living in Spain and Turkey between 1988 and 1990—before returning to London, where she began to explore other creative forms. In uncovering London's long transcultural history in her novels-in-verse, *Lara* (1997) and *The Emperor's Babe* (2001), Evaristo seeks to reshape a racist city in her work into an utopian (yet never idealized) space of cultural admixture, and as part of a wider transcultural web that connects London to related locations overseas. The social and political future of the British isles rests upon the ability of its conflicted population to reinterpret Britain's past and present in transcultural terms, recognizing and prizing the unruly rhythms of arrival, settlement, and departure that London exemplifies.

Traversing three continents and two centuries, *Lara* is the story of its eponymous heroine's exploration of her family's past. Born in London in 1962 to a Nigerian father and English mother, Lara on her father's side descends from the Igbo of West Africa and the slave populations of Brazil, while on her mother's side she can trace her ancestry back to the Catholic Irish. Growing up in South East London in the 1970s and 1980s, Lara epitomizes many of the trials and tribulations of racialized Londoners. She suffers at the hands of racist white Londoners as well as Nigerian men, respectively keen to construct her identity along the lines of both race and gender. Due to the reticence of her father and the prejudices of her mother's family, her family ancestry remains a mystery during her younger life, and she is forced to cope with the day-to-day tribulations of appearing different to other Londoners without the ancestral resources that, as the novel makes clear, are vital to the redefinition of her self and her city. "Home," she muses as a ten-year-old: "I searched but could not find myself, / not on the screen, billboards, books, magazines, / and first and last not in the mirror, my demon, my love / which faded my brownness into a Bardot likeness" (Evaristo 1997: 69).

When she begins to explore London as a teenager, Lara navigates through a racialized city that offers little hope of her completing her quest to know and realize her identity. Her best friend's boyfriend racially abuses her as a "nig nog" (Evaristo 1997: 68), and the activities of the local National Front bring trepidation and fear. When Lara begins art school in 1981 as a nineteen-year-old she begins to explore Brixton, notable for its "vivacious tableaux of Atlantic faces" (Evaristo 1997: 88). Her relationship with her Nigerian boyfriend Josh enables her to consider the extent to which she might find stable identification as a "Nigerian," but this quickly becomes one of several false anchors. Josh chides Lara for her ignorance of Nigerian ways—her inability to distinguish Jolof rice will make her a "sorry wife" (Evaristo 1997: 90)—and playfully yet insightfully accuses her of spending time with him purely because of his ethnicity: "It's obvious, you hope some of it will rub off on you" (Evaristo 1997: 90). Their relationship soon breaks down when she discovers Josh with another woman in a Portobello pub.

Lara's identification predicament is alleviated only when she begins to reconceptualize herself and her city with recourse to a transcultural consciousness. Throughout the novel the narrator emphasizes London's links with seemingly remote times and places that stress the city's fortunes as a significant center of arrival, departure, and settlement. On a number of occasions London is described in such a way as to compress together its landscape with that of distant lands. For example, the beginning of the 1969 section offers a flamboyant description of dawn over the city: "a silver flash of Thames / emerged from darkness under the insipid eyes / of giraffes which lined the deserted embankments. / Battersea Power station loomed incongrous [*sic*],

Peruvian / temple of energy, magnetising bleary-eyed men / who approached
it" (49). In particular, Lara's family home, Atlantico, beckons the contempla-
tion of London's diasporic legacy, not least in its name, which recalls the Atlantic Ocean that generations of her family have crisscrossed. Like Lara, and
London, the house contains hidden depths:

> Hidden in the moist entrails of Atlantico,
> The basement passage was body-wide, mildewed,
> one medieval wooden door, arched onto the coal hole,
> now populated with a miscellany of saws, shovels,
> sinks, enamel potties, antique telephones and lamps
> which hung on the stone walls like exhibits in a museum. . . .
> black bic biros, a plastic replica of the Eiffel Tower,
> framed wedding photographs and two sullen Yoruba carvings,
> his'n'hers, side by side and grey with dust foundation. (Evaristo 1997: 79)

This peculiar miscellany of relics, juxtaposing the Eiffel Tower with Yoruba
carvings, reveals the interpenetrating histories of Europe and Africa that
meet in London and—indirectly, unpredictably—have produced Lara. Upon
these foundations, through these subterranean passages, Lara comes to explore the transcultural encounters that have made her life possible.

Lara journeys first imaginatively and then in person to Nigeria and Brazil.
In Rio de Janeiro she marvels at "this sexing city" which (recalling D'Aguiar's
carnival) is described as a "rainbow metropolis" (Evaristo 1997: 137). Lara's
view of Rio is by no means idealized or depoliticized: she worries about the
"favela shacks" that are "homes for the disempowered" (Evaristo 1997: 137).
As she travels further, she takes a trip along the Amazon river and docks at a
remote settlement on Palm Sunday where she discovers a hilltop church with
an Indian congregation singing "Catholic hymns hybridized by drums"
(Evaristo 1997: 139). Lara describes this as "one culture being orchestrated by
another" and finds in it a template for social and cultural creativity and
change: "the future means transformation" (Evaristo 1997: 139). She imagines returning to London in the novel's final page ready to regard and recre-
ate the city as a transcultural "rainbow metropolis":

> I savour living in my world, planet of growth, of decay,
> think of my island—the "Great" Tippexed out of it—
> tiny amid massive floating continents, the African one—
> an embryo within me—I will wing back to Nigeria again
> and again, excitedly swoop over a zig-zag of amber lights
> signalling the higgledy energy of Lagos.
>   It is time to leave.
> Back to London, across international time zones,
> I step out of Heathrow and into my future. (Evaristo 1997: 140)

The "higgledy energy" and "zig-zag" patterns of light suggest something of the unpredictable and agreeably untidy journeys to come, where borders marked by international time zones are rendered porous. With the world reclaimed and reconceived in such terms, London is transfigured in the final lines as a place of accommodation, and of both arrival and departure. Lara will return to London to transform it imaginatively, perhaps writing a book like the one in which she appears—which suitably crosses generic boundaries, unpredictably passes the narrative voice between generations, and crisscrosses time and space.

The image of London that ultimately emerges from *Lara* is as complex, hybrid, and indebted to the journeys of myriad peoples as the novel's heroine. Rather than be vanquished by the prejudices and racism of London, Lara negotiates a transcultural sensibility that enables her to recast her self, her city, and the nation(s) beyond in new ways. Such a hopeful, optimistic, and determined vision is predicated upon a politics of transfiguration that contests London's enduring social problems with an alternative perspective, one that prizes the polycultural legacies which constitute the city's historical foundations (as Evaristo further explores in *The Emperor's Babe*). The difficulties of living in contemporary London, or as a part of a Britain with the "Great" relativized and compressed, will remain; but it is the *investment* in a different, transfigured city where cultures orchestrate each other that is of crucial importance. In defiance of those who would deny Londoners like Evaristo and D'Aguiar legitimacy and accommodation in London, both physically and imaginatively, *Lara* refuses to relinquish the possibilities of the "future."

The millennial optimism of D'Aguiar and Evaristo—as well as Alibhai-Brown and others—bears witness to the achievements of Londoners in making the city accommodating for all, not just a select and officious few. At the turn of a new century, these writers and others look to the future with robust confidence and renewed resolve. Their writing creates, in Evaristo's phrase, a "London-stylee!" (Evaristo 1997: 95) that registers transcultural fusions of contemporary London—as in D'Aguiar's transfigurative vision of Notting Hill's freedom fighters reaching for the rainbow on West London's streets to the sounds of calypso and steel drums, or Evaristo's restless fictional style, which crosses generic boundaries of poetry and fiction in an attempt to bear witness to the transcultural cat's cradle of Lara's, and hence London's, identity. These writers' cheerful determination is a sign of the dedication to the perpetual recreation of London in the face of resistance and prejudice, and constitutes its own cultural contribution to the progression of social change. The undaunted investment in both London's polycultural present and its utopian future must not be dismissed as an escape from social and political realities; but neither should we prematurely celebrate the end of unacceptable social relations as a consequence of the writing and popularity of such texts. Rather, recent representations of postcolonial London emphasize the necessary and continuing imaginative engagement with the experiences of prejudice and discrimination while also underlining the uniquely human ways in which cultural creativity offers important resources to the politics and practice of meaningful and lasting change.

WORKS CITED

Alibhai-Brown, Yasmin. 2000. "A Magic Carpet of Cultures in London," *The New York Times*, Sunday 25 June, 30–32.

———. 2001. *Imagining the New Britain*, New York: Routledge.

Condé, Maryse. 2003. *Histoire de la femme cannibale*, Paris: Mercure de France.

D'Aguiar, Fred. 1993. *British Subjects*, Newcastle: Bloodaxe.

———. 2000. "Home Is Always Elsewhere: Individual and Communal Regenerative Capacities of Loss," in *Black British Culture and Society: A Text Reader*, edited by Kwesi Owusu, London and New York: Routledge, 195–206.

Evaristo, Bernardine. 1997. *Lara*, Kent: Angela Royal Publishing.

———. 2001. *The Emperor's Babe*, London: Hamish Hamilton.

Gilroy, Paul. 1993. *The Black Atlantic*, London: Verso.

Goulbourne, Harry. 1991. *Ethnicity and Nationalism in Post-Imperial Britain,* Cambridge: Cambridge University Press.

McPherson, Sir William. 1999. *The Stephen Lawrence Inquiry: Report of an Inquiry by Sir William McPherson of Cluny* (Cm 4262-I), London: The Stationary Office Agencies.

Phillips, Caryl. 2001. *A New World Order: Selected Essays*, London: Secker and Warburg.

Rushdie, Salman. 1988. *The Satanic Verses*, London: Viking.

Smith, Zadie. 2000. *White Teeth*, London: Hamish Hamilton.

15

The Colonial Past in the Postcolonial Present: Cultural Memory, Gender, and Race in Dutch Cinema

Pamela Pattynama

FORGOTTEN PAST

The emergence of memory as a key concern and theoretical concept in Western societies has produced an increased focus on the crises of the twentieth century—two world wars, the Holocaust, and worldwide national liberation movements in former colonized nations.[1] In the process of history-making, the representation of the past in film and television has become a barometer of social and cultural life. While Benedict Anderson (25, 204) has explained how the "old-fashioned novel" provided the technical means for representing and remembering the imagined nation, cinematic spectacle with its immediate and engaging image influences collective memory to a much greater extent than print. Dominated by American mass culture, the international and global film industry has come to play a powerful role in altering and complicating national memory. In postcolonial migrant societies, memory, of course, is often invented in the search of cultural roots or heritage. This so-called "heritage industry" (Sicher 58) feeds on nostalgia to consolidate national, gendered, and racial identities, which often present deterministic and essentialist conceptions of time and human action.

In addressing these processes of memory and identity, this essay focuses on the use of the colonial past in the Dutch film *Oeroeg*. Dutch cinema is inextricably interwoven with the global film industry. Nonetheless, the global often speaks to the local and in a move of so-called "glocalization," Dutch cinema has realized a third market niche position. Beyond the recurring tensions of, on the one hand, popular Hollywood films and, on the other, elite

art house films, it has become a regional mass medium, which has succeeded in engaging a broad local public. Distinguishing itself through the
use of national language and frequent references to World War II or the literary canon, Dutch cinema works through national identification rather than
being pure entertainment or art (Hofstede 131–48). Before focusing on
Oeroeg, I will first take a short historical detour.

Holland lost its former colony the Dutch East Indies in 1949. The loss of its
most treasured colony has become one of the most ambivalent, even traumatic parts of Dutch memory, at both the individual and the public level.
During the postwar reconstruction, the Dutch presence in the East was relegated to a dark corner of national history, ostensibly "forgotten," and the
Dutch East Indies became a well-preserved "family secret," the blind spot in
the national consciousness (Locher Scholten 3–9). As a result, the memories
of Indies migrants who had arrived in Holland after the Japanese occupation
of the colony and the following Indonesian war of independence seemed ir-
reconcilable with the prevailing amnesia in the public domain.[2] Memories of
the German occupation were dominant and left little room for public com-
memoration of other war experiences. The lack of public debate, the silent
assimilation of Indies migrants, and the absence of any critical perspective
on the past that could have highlighted different points of view resulted in
the perpetuation of the prewar idyllic and proud heroic myth of the colonial
period. The exclamation "Daar is wat groots verricht!" ("Those were our
glory days!") is heard to this day.

Many years after decolonization, in the revolutionary climate of the late
1960s, public debate made its faltering entrance. The "family secret" came
out when a call for research into war crimes committed by Dutch forces during Indonesia's war of independence marked a dramatic change in thinking.[3]
In the public recollection, the Dutch East Indies came to signify shame and
guilt about racism, exploitation, and war crimes, and colonial discourses
seemed to be overtaken by postcolonial discourses.[4] On the other hand, in
recent historiography, many Dutch historians still fail to integrate the troubled colonial past into official national history. If it is true that memory is determined in communities, as Maurice Halbwachs argues, the historiographic
amnesia may be the reason why the Indies have no particular place in Dutch
public consciousness.[5] Nonetheless, since the late 1960s, tensions between
divergent interpretations of the past have brought about heated public debates on ethics while dramatic events such as the disruption of commemo-
ration ceremonies, demonstrations demanding Japanese apologies and pay-
backs, and the killing of hostages in hijacked trains articulate highly charged
recollections. Various groups of Indies migrants and veterans who fought in
Indonesia's war of independence each had their own interests and competing memories. They all have tried to reshape national or communal identity
and shift the public commemorative narrative. Those conflicting bodies of
memory are never either unambiguous or univocal. While their image of the

colonial past may either be the simplified result of "memory activism" or simply the product of a nostalgic "heritage industry," the fact is they all actively jostle for a position in Holland's public domain.[6] As a space of contestation and divergent memory, the lost colony returns every so often to haunt the Dutch in artifacts and mass media, as well as in political and cultural events.[7]

It is this act of cultural memory which runs counter to official history that I wish to explore in one of the few Dutch movies about the colonial past.[8] In addressing Holland's colonial past as a major, although contested, element within national memory, *Oeroeg* speaks to the nation. Its cinematic representation of the past works against collective amnesia, but the question remains whose past is involved and what ends are served in this "fetishizing of memory" (Lancy 1–2).

CONTACT ZONES

Hans Hylkema's *Oeroeg* (1993) was released shortly before 1995, fifty years after the ending of World War II, which was commemorated worldwide. *Oeroeg* is based on a novel with the same title written by the well-known Dutch writer Hella S. Haasse. She was born in the Dutch East Indies and wrote her story in 1948, just before the Dutch were forced to turn over their colony to the Indonesians. Using the autobiographical mode, the novel is centered in the consciousness of a white boy, son of a wealthy Dutch plantation owner in the Indies. The narrator's memories concentrate on his friendship with Oeroeg, son of a native servant in his father's house. Located in the colonial context, the boys' friendship transgressed the fixed boundaries between the colonizers and the colonized. The past tense of the book's opening sentence, however, foreshadows the tragic ending of the interracial bond: "Oeroeg was my friend" (Haasse 5). The novel closes by articulating the loss as *total*, when the I-narrator loses not only his friend but his home country and identity as well. Simultaneously it hopefully emphasizes time and its concomitant change: "Have I forever lost my country? Time will teach us" (Haasse 128).

Half a century later, the film takes up the ending of Haasse's novel. Through a timeline in the present, Haasse's I-narrator is "re-presented" in the grown-up protagonist Johan, who returns to the colony after the Japanese capitulation. He is cast as a Dutch army officer, a status that accentuates his position as belonging to the colonizing class. We hear that the army was his only possibility to come back to what he calls "the most beautiful country in the world." Through a second timeline, in flashback mode, the film shows us an idyllic, exotic landscape in which the boy Johan and his dear friend Oeroeg, although living in different worlds, are always together and swear for better and for worse to be blood brothers forever. The grown-up Johan recounts how their friendship came to a standstill when Oeroeg as a young man became involved with Indonesian nationalists, turned against the Dutch colonizers, and rejected his white friend. Johan left for Holland to complete his studies and only returns after the war. Shortly after his arrival, Johan finds his father murdered and suspects that Oeroeg killed him to revenge his own father, who had died in rescuing Johan from drowning. From then on we follow Johan's obsessive yet unsuccessful quest for his old friend. It is not counter-revenge he is after. "No," he tells nurse Rita, one of the other characters, "I just want to know what happened, to him, with us." From the outset Johan's search and his quest for knowledge bring into play the notions of memory and history. To begin with, the visual drama of Johan's arrival in the colony is patterned after the conventional opening of colonial fiction with its constituted set of expectations. The spectator's gaze is thus steered through a Dutch point of view. Like Johan, the viewers nostalgically anticipate an idyllic landscape and are shocked to be confronted with images of the chaos and crisis that emerged after the Japanese collapse. When the Japanese originally invaded the colony in 1942, they encouraged anti-colonialist sentiments. When the war ended in 1945 Indonesian nationalists unilaterally declared Indonesia's independence from the Netherlands. This shattered the Dutch dream of an easy reoccupation of "their" Indies. When the Dutch who had just been released from the war camps failed to restore their colonial authority, unorganized nationalistic groups took advantage of the power vacuum. Violent clashes broke out between hastily shipped-in Dutch forces and nationalistic guerrilla groups, and only in 1949 did the Dutch reluctantly let go of their profitable colony. This background of historical events provides highly dramatic filmic material, which informs the fictional setting of the film. Black and white "public" newsreels are interwoven with the "private," fictional plot of the main characters so that "real" history with its claim of truth acts upon cinematic representation. The film thus not only presents encounters between different races, genders, and nationalities, it also foregrounds the mixing of history and fiction as well as public and private narratives.[9] *Oeroeg*'s story of interracial male bonding is therefore marked by a typical "contact zone" situation.[10] This implicates the film in the process of cultural and public memory-making about the past, just as Dutch literature is involved in this ongoing process. The Dutch East Indies have been a popular subject of Dutch literature since the nineteenth century and continue to appear as the haunting "unsaid, absent text" of national history in best-selling novels to this day (Macherey, Pattynama).

HAUNTING FLASHBACKS

Based on one of the most popular novels about the colonial past, the film *Oeroeg* can be seen as haunting intertext. Adapting literary works to film is, however, not merely a "conscientious visual transliteration of the original"

(McFarlane 7). As narrative elements are selected and rejected in the interests of the film's ideology, adaptation involves a significant reinterpretation, or even deconstruction, of the source text (McFarlane, Orr). Indeed, when compared to its source text, the film *Oeroeg* renders an entirely different effect and meaning. Its use of flashbacks is decisive for such re-presentations. In fact, the images of Johan's adventures in the present timeline dissolve repeatedly into images of the past that present the gist of the novel. Any experienced film viewer will easily understand this narrative device as Johan's subjective memories.

Flashbacks, in shaping narrative junctures between present and past, juxtapose different moments of temporal reference. In re-creating past and present, they re-identify characters (Turin 1). Since in the novel the only point of reference is the white self, traces of colonial discourses can be found, specifically when the I-narrator's colonial gaze "others" the Javanese boy. The flashbacks in the film seem to follow the novel by visualizing the two friends in an anterior unspoiled world. However, newly created memory images and the workings of the timeline in the present destroy this illusion of an idyllic prewar colonial society. Overall, then, this adaptation and its use of alternating timelines essentially amount to the shift from colonial ideology to postcolonial discourses. The film has absorbed many changed attitudes toward the past and its adapted images convey profound changes in perception that have their roots in the activist politics of the late 1960s. At that time, there was a virtual tidal wave of revolutionary black, gay, and women's counter-movements. Within this anti-authoritarian climate, alternative memories emerged that implied ambivalence and doubt and enabled the undermining of dominant nationalist and Christian-humanist discourses (Van Vree). Similarly, a space for critical reflection on the nation with its "forgotten" colonial past opened up.

Released in the 1990s, *Oeroeg* has undoubtedly taken up the critical ideas of the late 1960s, showing the influence of American anti-Vietnam films. As a result, images of Dutch soldiers torturing Indonesian guerilla fighters appear in the cinematic adaptation. The scenes reflect the Dutch nation's shock when, upon receiving reports of war crimes committed by Dutch soldiers, its national self-image temporarily shifted from victim of the Germans to perpetrator in the colony. Another instance of altered memory is the graphic scenes of burned-down native villages surrounded by green jungle. They remind the spectator of the My Lai atrocities that were displayed in the counter-memories of American movies. Likewise, the scene focusing on the "Europeans only" entrance, through which Johan is allowed into the movies while Oeroeg is stopped, brings to mind images of both Nazi "No Jews" signs on doors in the 1930s and "slegs vir blankes" (whites only) benches in South Africa's public space. This tangled imagery in Dutch cultural memory refers to the recent emergence of interest in the Holocaust, and to the collective and vigorous protests of the Dutch in the 1970s against South Africa's appalling apartheid policies, rather than directly to the East Indies. When later on in the film Oeroeg reminds Johan of this event, its meaning is further emphasized. Rather than demonstrating existing colonial apartheid, it seeks to illustrate Johan's easy use of what feminists have called "white privileges" (Frankenberg 1, Morrison).[11]

These three selected re-presentations accentuate the internal contradictions in the seemingly coherent colonial ideology through which the source text is structured. However, despite the shifts in meaning production, differences established through nature/culture dichotomies can still be traced in the film. For example, contrary to Johan's portrayal as a naive child, the assertion of Oeroeg's "already-there" knowledge about the landscape suggests a "natural" and essentialist native identity core. Also, as an adolescent, Oeroeg possesses a seemingly instinctive sexual knowledge, which is lacking in the visualization of naive and clumsy Johan, in spite of the latter's visible wealth and cultural power. These racial-colonial stereotypes are connected to gender.[12] In fact, gender and race are transformed from a "feminine" to a "masculine" domain in the process of adapting. While Haasse's novel is focused on the domestic atmosphere of human relations, the film is framed in the genre of the war film. This discursive "masculinization" is further emphasized by the father-son plot linking the two timelines, as well as by the expression of male desire that energizes Johan's quest. Within this male-identified space, femininity is re-presented in terms of nationality and race. Three female characters, racially different from each other but associated by their names, signify both political agency and traditional views on femininity. Interestingly, their appearances do not merely articulate race and gender; they also mark national difference and interracial contacts.

RE-APPEARANCES

In his efforts to find his vanished friend, Johan encounters Oeroeg's sister Satih, a character not present in the source novel. In sharp contrast to Johan's male, white, and fabricated environment—the military camp—Satih and Johan meet each other in the native's "natural" context of mother-and-baby in the *kampung*, Oeroeg's home village. Johan, in his privileged status as Dutch army officer, occupies the entire *kampung*. Urging Satih to trust him for old times' sake, he attempts to persuade her to betray Oeroeg's hiding place. Although Satih acknowledges "sinjo Johan," she is obviously threatened by his display of military power. Nonetheless, speaking with the "voice of the subaltern," she confronts the intruder with the growing nationalist awareness among Indonesians and tells him that there is no longer one single truth from a privileged perspective: "Your memories may be different from ours!" This refashioned scenario mediates what has been called the "pluralization ethos," in other words, the growing impact of the postmodern narrative turn and feminist, black, and postcolonial views that rejected grand narratives in favor of an increased sensibility to a multivoiced perspective (Plummer 12).

Another instance of postcolonial modification is the reappearance of the Dutch woman Lida in the film. The novel introduced Lida as owner of the boardinghouse where the two boys lived as high school pupils. She is obviously taken with Oeroeg and adopts him as her protégé. Through the eyes of the I-narrator we observe how Lida gradually loses her white energetic self as she gets more and more involved in Oeroeg's nationalistic activities. We find her again at the end of the novel, worn out and untidy. This pathetic portrayal may be linked to the influence of the emerging fear of race-mixing in Europe that paralleled a politics of modernity at the end of the colonial era. Lida's rapid degeneration hints at white anxieties, which were less concerned with interracial sexuality *per se* than with the apprehensions about the decline of the (white) population that would result from staying in the tropics for too long (Stoler 1).

In the film, however, Lida is radically refigured as the boys' old schoolteacher, who after the war reappears as a freedom fighter for the Indonesia Republic. Lida completely disrupts the conventional representation of a typical white woman's cultural positioning as outside the arena of history, politics, and agency. She is rather a politically active, self-assured woman with agency, and her re-presentation may reflect the transformative views on femininity initiated by the second feminist wave of the 1970s. However, since the camera directs spectators to look via Johan's point of view, it comes as a shock to recognize Lida as the woman in charge who keeps the protagonist jailed after he has been captured as a result of the schemes of another treacherous woman. Lida's decision to side with the Indonesians against the Dutch clearly alludes to the postwar controversies about national loyalty and postcolonial ethics among Dutch politicians and citizens alike that flare up every now and then in heated disputes about the colony. Due to Lida's political and feminist agency, she is presented as a narrative opponent instead of a helper in Johan's quest. Through processes of national identification the film associates Lida's political stance with the defector, an abject figure in Dutch debates on World War II.[13]

Another character in the film who, like Satih, is not present in Haasse's novel is Rita. She works as a nurse at the Dutch military hospital. The appearance of mixed-race Rita signifies a perspective that looks further than the conventional opposites of black and white. "Half-caste" Rita is consistent with the usual "attributes" of mixed-race women: seductive beauty and deceitfulness. Hence, in line with her "beautiful" dark eyes tempting romantic Dutch soldiers is her exposure as a thief stealing drugs intended for dying Dutchmen in order to distribute them among Indonesian guerrillas. Even worse is her involvement in a setup for good guy Johan. In these imaginative designs of the

contact zone, Satih gives voice to the native and Lida expands her white position, while colonized "half-caste" Rita echoes the dangers of mixed raciality
that in Western representations is often rendered as a cultural taboo surrounded by ambivalence, mystery, or even repulsion (Sollors).

GUARDIANS OF THE RACE

As many cultural critics have argued, masculinity and femininity, rather
than being fixed identities, are imaginary ethnic identifications, constructed
with and against each other. In the racial-gendered interplay that the movie
displays, Johan's narrative function is in line with feminist descriptions of
the white hero. Adopting "'natural' poses of activity and agency," he is constructed as the "active principle of culture" (Doane 167). The juxtaposition
between female betrayal and his self-righteous quest for knowledge reminds us of traditional Western gender differences in which masculinity
stands for rationality and perseverance, whereas femininity is associated
with irrational and unreliable behavior. More interesting than this obliga-
tory scenario is the construction of national identity through gender and
race. Feminist critics have often accounted for why women play important
symbolic roles in nationalist and racialized narratives: in their bodies they
carry the collective love and honor of the nation. In *Oeroeg*'s visual spectacle, Johan operates as "ethnic agent," while the women mark the boundaries between the groups: they perform as "national guardians of the
race."[14] Evidently, native Satih represents the oppositional other, holding
traditional boundaries in place. In contrast, Lida and Rita, who as (Indo-)
Europeans are considered to belong to the hero's ethnic group, signal betrayal and disloyalty. Instead of following expectations of ethnic "good"
women, they have crossed race boundaries and violated the laws that determine desirable national femininity. In the dramatic design of the film,
they convey the dangers of female race traitors for the hero. Johan, on the
other hand, re-presents the anti-hero and politically correct good guy that
emerged after the 1970s. Not only is his sincerity opposed to female deceitfulness, but he also resists his racist and aggressive fellow Dutch soldiers and longs to overcome political and racial boundaries. Furthermore,
contrary to the assumed resolution of many colonizers to "foreign" the
colony, Johan feels at home in the Indies. Yet his paternalistic comments on
both Lida's and Rita's political involvement, his claim to "know" his birth
country, his dismissal of power structures, his use of white privileges, and
his subsequent wish to remain outside the political arena clearly resonate
two national self-images. First is the self-image of Dutch men who, in comparison with foreigners, prefer to picture themselves as essentially innocent, honest and straightforward, although a bit naïve. Secondly, through

Johan's portrayal of the good anti-hero, the high morals that the Dutch nation has often claimed for itself become operative.[15]

This depiction of Johan as an ex-colonizer in search of understanding and knowledge is ultimately ambivalent and contradictory. Linking masculinity and colonial stereotypes with the national process of memory-making in Holland, the protagonist's portrayal reveals national rather than individual anxieties. The questions underlying Johan's unsuccessful quest are a case in point: "Why have the old harmonious relations changed so rigorously? Why is my blood brother transformed into a murderous enemy?" On the one hand, these questions echo the distress of many Dutch who had no notion of nationalistic sentiments among the Indonesian population and felt themselves forced to migrate to Holland after World War II, and, on the other, they pertain to the unsuccessful public reflection on the Dutch colonial past. Contrary to individuals' memories, Dutch public memory does not encompass a deep engagement with its colonial legacy. Historians have pointed to complicity and shame, which may have precluded a full confrontation.[16] Another view is that the Dutch process may be similar to reasons for postwar Germany's amnesia about its fascist past, namely the need for the creation of national social cohesion and stability (Maier 67, Hoerschelmann 78). A third and, to my mind, the most relevant suggestion is that the Dutch have never felt the need to take responsibility because Indonesia never called upon the Dutch nation to account for its past deeds (Raben 2001). Whatever it may be, indifference or avoidance, the fact is that the Indies—although for many a troubled "present past"—is to a large extent hidden in Dutch public memory.[17] It is thus most significant that *Oeroeg* works toward a "mission impossible." Only at the very end of the film, when he is exchanged for twelve Indonesian prisoners, does Johan meet Oeroeg again. The uneven ratio reveals the deeply colonial context that has determined the rise and demise of their friendship. At the same time, however, the final scene is constructed as a reassuring, happy ending through the return of prior memories. Johan had always thought that Deppoh, Oeroeg's father, had drowned in his effort to save him. He was shocked to hear that Oeroeg had always held him responsible for his father's death. In Oeroeg's memory, Deppoh drowned after he was ordered to recover his master's—Johan's father's—watch from the lake. Later, Johan has taken the watch from the hands of his murdered father and, in their final meeting, passes it on to Oeroeg as a token of their eternal friendship. Contrary to the film's colonial plot, its ending reveals a victorious male father-son bonding surpassing the disconcerting colonial context. Under the pretext of a narrative convention, the happy ending masks Johan's failed quest for understanding and knowledge, in other words, the nation's impotence to master its own past.

The film *Oeroeg* offers us a version of the past, which is a way of talking about Dutch present conflicts and anxieties. It relates colonial history as a story that leaves one with a moral message and a positive feeling. Like all films, *Oeroeg* operates through "mental machinery" (Metz 7) showing the intertwining of individual narratives with the public histories underlying national identities (Sturken 13). Insisting on history as the story of a Dutch man singled out by the camera, the movie "hails" its viewer to take up the imaginary Dutch white male identity it offers through the shaping of cultural memory. Johan's personal problems with the past tends thus to substitute for the historical problem. Hence, by highlighting the personal, the film articulates the avoiding of the more difficult national problems that are also pointed out.

CONCLUSION

Ethnic difference and cultural mixing are the recurrent motives in much contemporary postcolonial fiction. In contemporary Holland, the same themes are the subject of anxious debates, both popular and academic. However, in the current debates about migration, social cohesion, and an increasingly multicultural nation, the Netherlands' own troubled colonial past is rarely even mentioned. My analysis of *Oeroeg* has sought to show how events and ideologies are processed and live on in cultural memory. In adapting the novel *Oeroeg* into a movie, the contemporary concern with memory has come into focus. Taking up the emphasis on temporality with which the novel ends, the movie works through alternating timelines and flashbacks, which emphasize the complicated links between individual memory and public history. *Oeroeg* weaves the shame-and-guilt discourses and subsequent postcolonial awareness into persistent colonial discourses on gender and race. In this double way, the film contributes to the never-ending process of negotiations and contestation that structures public memory on the East Indies. In its articulation of the national incapacity to effectively engage with its colonial past, *Oeroeg* renders the Dutch East Indies as a complicated *lieu de mémoire* (Nora), where memories converge, conflate, conflict, and define relationships between past, present, and future. If narrative fiction has the specific capacity to address sensitive historical questions, *Oeroeg* functions as "experimental space" for counter-memories that do not (yet) find a voice in institutionally anchored discourses such as historiography and politics.[18]

NOTES

1. See Huyssen (21) for the contemporary focus on memory and temporality. See Lancy (1–2) for the commanding role of the media in historicizing processes.

2. For different reasons, many of the people holding Dutch passports immigrated to the Netherlands in five distinct waves of migration after World War II. They were from various ethnic backgrounds and described as "repatriates," even though most of them had never seen the "fatherland" (Willems). See Withuis about the divorce of personal memory from public debate—whether in academic venues or in the media.

3. In his dissertation physiologist J. E. Hueting called for an inquiry into war crimes committed by Dutch soldiers during Indonesia's war of independence (Van Vree; Stam and Manschot).

4. The term "postcolonial" is problematic since it is often used as a monolithic, ahistorical indication of linear progress. For lack of a better term, I will use it here to indicate the effects of colonization on Dutch post-imperial culture. For a discussion of the term, see Ashcroft, Griffiths, and Tiffin, and McClintock 9–17.

5. See Raben 2001 on the absence of the colonial past in a wide range of Dutch historical discourses. For collective memory see Halbwachs.

6. With "memory activism" Raben (2002, 4) describes how memory is used to capture attention in order to serve a political or moral goal.

7. Colonial traits are visible in the way the country is governed, in which the nation proliferates itself within Europe in cultural heritage matters and self-images (Legêne).

8. Two other movies dealing with the East Indies have been released: *Max Have-laar* (Fons Rademakers) in 1973 and *Gordel van Smaragd* (Orlow Seunke) in 1997. In this essay, I'm using Marita Sturken's conceptualization of cultural memory. Sturken (3) is interested in how memory engages with historical narrative in public spheres. According to her, cultural memory is shared outside the avenues of formal historical discourse yet is entangled with cultural products and imbued with cultural meaning.

9. This essay takes gender as a complex and constantly changing system of personal, social, and symbolic relationships through which memories and identities are constructed (Scott).

10. Marie Louise Pratt (6) coined the term "contact zone." See Young for a historical overview of related terms.

11. Sociologist Ruth Frankenberg identifies three aspects of whiteness: location of structural privilege, point of view, and unmarked cultural practices. African American writer Toni Morrison explores whiteness in literary imagination.

12. Historian Frances Gouda (236–54) argues that the "cultural archives" produced by the colonial past are imbued with gender-specific myths and gendered rhetoric that operate in individual and collective constructions of identity.

13. See, for example, the aggressive disputes concerning Poncke Princen's entry into the Netherlands. During Indonesia's war of independence, Princen left the Dutch army and sided with the Indonesian nationalists. After the Dutch left the colony, he remained in Indonesia and obtained Indonesian nationality. When he, forty-five years later, required an entry visa to visit his family in Holland, this was refused and he was branded as a traitor and defector.

14. Although in many ways women are active participants in national and ethnic struggles, in general women are symbols of the nation while men are its agents and act to represent it (Lutz, Phoenix, and Yuval-Davis).

15. Examples of this male self-image can be found abundantly in media reports of recent international actions of Dutch soldiers. At the beginning of the twentieth century the Dutch prided themselves on being an enlightened and "civilized" nation. This was expressed in their non-participation during World War I. As a small nation, the Netherlands had very little political power and tried to manifest itself as a moral heavyweight. With its "moralistic nationalism" Holland took on the role of moral guide in international affairs (Eppink 328).

16. According to Charles Maier, commentators from the right and left alike have suggested that the inability to engage with a shameful past actually contributed to the stability of postwar societies.

17. I am indebted for the notion of "present past" to Andreas Huyssen, who derived it from Reinhart Koselleck.

18. Michel Foucault focuses on counter-memory, which relinquishes existing claims of historiography to truth. Counter-memory offers instead questions about history's role as myth contributing to the consolidation of the nation-state and national citizenship.

WORKS CITED

Anderson, Benedict. *Imagined Communities: Reflections of the Origins and Spread of Nationalism*. London: Verso, 1991.

Ashcroft, Bill, Gareth Griffiths, and Helen Tiffin. *The Empire Writes Back: Theory and Practice in Post-colonial Literatures*. London: Routledge, 1989.

Doane, Mary Ann. "Subjectivity and desire: an(other) way of looking." *Contemporary Film Theory*. Ed. Antony Easthope. London and New York: Longman, 1993. 162–78.

Eppink, Dirk-Jan. "Stille en luide reflexen in de Lage Landen." *Ons Erfdeel* 39.3 (1996): 323–31.

Foucault, Michel. "Nietzsche, Genealogy, History." Trans. Donald F. Bouchard and Sherry Simon. *Language, Counter-Memory, Practice: Selected Essays and Interviews*. Ed. Donald F. Bouchard. Oxford: Basil Blackwell, 1977. 139–65.

Frankenberg, Ruth. *The Social Construction of Whiteness: White Women, Race Matters*. London: Routledge, 1993.

Haasse, Hella S. *Oeroeg*. Amsterdam: Querido, 1979 [1968].

Halbwachs, Maurice, ed. *On Collective Memory*. Chicago: University of Chicago Press, 1992.

Hoerschelmann, Olaf. "Memoria Dextera Est: Film and Public Memory in Postwar Germany." *Cinema Journal* 40.2 (2001): 78–97.

Hofstede, Bart. *Nederlandse cinema wereldwijd. De internationale positie van de Nederlandse film*. Trans. and ed. Anemoon van Hemel. Amsterdam: Boekmanstudies, 2000.

Huyssen, Andreas. "Present Pasts: Media, Politics, Amnesia." *Public Culture* 12.1 (2000): 21–38.

Landy, Marcia, ed. *The Historical Film: History and Memory in Media*. New Brunswick, N.J.: Rutgers University Press, 2000.

Legêne, Susan. *De bagage van Blomhoff en van Breugel. Japan, Java, Tripoli en Suriname in de negentiende-eeuwse cultuur van het imperialisme*. Amsterdam: KIT, 1998.

Lutz, Helma, Ann Phoenix, and Nira Yuval-Davis. "Introduction: Nationalism, Racism and Gender—European Crossfires." *Crossfires: Nationalism, Racism and Gender in Europe*. Ed. Helma Lutz, Ann Phoenix, and Nira Yuval-Davis. London: Pluto Press, 1995. 1–25.

Maier, Charles S. *The Unmasterable Past: History, Holocaust, and German National Identity*. Cambridge, Mass.: Harvard University Press, 1988.

McClintock, Anne. *Imperial Leather. Race, Gender and Sexuality in the Colonial Context*. New York and London: Routledge, 1995.

McFarlane, Brian. *Novel to Film: An Introduction to the Theory of Adaptation*. Oxford: Clarendon Press, 1996.

Metz, Christian. *Psychoanalysis and Film: The Imaginary Signifier*. London: MacMillan, 1982.

Morrison, Toni. *Playing in the Dark: Whiteness and the Literary Imagination*. Cambridge, Mass., and London: Harvard University Press, 1992.

Nora, Pierre. "Between memory and history: Les lieux de mémoire." *Representations* 26 (1989): 7–25.

Orr, Christoffer. "The discourse on adapatation." *Wide Angle* 6.2 (1984): 72.

Pattynama, Pamela. "Secrets and Danger: Interracial Sexuality in Louis Couperus's *The Hidden Force* and Dutch Colonial Culture around 1900." *Domesticating the Empire: Race, Gender, and Family Life in French and Dutch Colonialism*. Ed. Julia Clancy-Smith and Frances Gouda. Charlottesville and London: University Press of Virginia, 1998. 84–107.

Plummer, Ken. *Documents of Life 2: An Invitation to a Critical Humanism*. London: Sage, 2001.

Pratt, Mary Louise. *Imperial Eyes: Travel Writing and Transculturation*. London and New York: Routledge, 1992.

Raben, Remco. "De getuigen en de geschiedenis." *Nederlanders Japanners Indonesiërs. Een opmerkelijke tentoonstelling*. Ed. Stance Rijpma. Zwolle and Amsterdam: Waanders Uitgevers/NIOD, 2002. 18–25.

———. "De wereld van Conimex. De Nederlandse natie, de Indische migrant en het koloniale verleden." Unpublished paper. *Studiedagen Indische Nederlanders VI*. Pasar Malam Besar, Den Haag, 2001.

Scott, Joan. *Gender and the Politics of History*. New York: Columbia University Press, 1988.

Sicher, Efraim. "The Future of the Past: Countermemory and Postmemory in Contemporary American Post-Holocaust Narratives." *History & Memory* 12.2 (2000): 56–91.

Sollors, Werner. *Neither Black Nor White Yet Both: Thematic Explorations of Interracial Literature*. New York and Oxford: Oxford University Press, 1997.

Stam, L., and B. Manschot. "De Hueting-affaire." *Massacommunicatie* 1.1 (1972): 3–16.

Sturken, Marita. *Tangled Memories: The Vietnam War, the AIDS Epidemic, and the Politics of Remembering*. Berkeley: University of California Press, 1997.

Turin, Maureen. *Flashbacks in Film: Memory and History*. New York and London: Routledge, 1989.

Vree, Frank van. "'Onze gemartelde bruid.' De Japanse bezetting van Indonesië in Nederlandse films en documentaires." *Beelden van de Japanse bezetting van Indonesië. Persoonlijke getuigenissen en publieke beeldvorming in Indonesië, Japan en Nederland.* Zwolle and Amsterdam: Waanders Uitgevers/Nederlands Instituut voor oorlogsdocumentatie, 1999. 202–17.

Willems, Wim. *De uittocht uit Indië 1945–1995.* Amsterdam: Bert Bakker, 2001.

Withuis, Jolande. "Het verhaal van de een en het zwijgen van de ander." *Vier wijzen van omzien: hulpverlening voor oorlogsgetroffenen in perspectief.* Ed. Oegstgeest Stichting Centrum '45. Assen: Van Gorcum, 1994. 46–64.

Young, Robert J. C. *Colonial Desire: Hybridity in Theory, Culture and Race.* London and New York: Routledge, 1995.

16

Miss Italia in Black and White: Feminine Beauty and Ethnic Identity in Modern Italy

Stephen Gundle

In 1996 the annual Miss Italia beauty pageant was won by Denny Mendez, a naturalized Italian citizen who was born in the Dominican Republic. In a nationwide telephone poll in which no fewer than nine million Italians took part, Mendez secured her victory over nearly sixty other finalists to become the first ever black winner of the contest. This event was not unmarked by controversy. Mendez's triumph fueled the unseemly polemic that had raged over her candidature. In the run-up to the final, two prominent members of the jury, the German photographer Rob Krieger and the television showgirl Alba Parietti, had questioned whether a woman of color could adequately represent an ideal of Italian beauty. As Parietti put it in *La Repubblica* of 5 September 1996, the victor needed to be "a physical type who incarnates certain traditional characteristics." The thinly veiled implication was that blackness was not among these characteristics. This stand led to an extended debate in the press, to which even the London *Times* contributed with an editorial reminding Italians of the multi-ethnic character of the Roman empire. Although Krieger was forced off the jury and Parietti was obliged to withdraw her comments, the impression remained that some general issue of national self-perception had been raised by their clumsy interventions. Mendez's success certainly signaled a victory for fair play, but it would be naïve to imagine it indicated Italians were fully prepared to consider the growing number of members of ethnic minorities in their midst as being fully Italian. Indeed, in some respects the mass vote for the least "traditional" candidate can be seen as an alibi, exempting Italians from the need to redefine themselves in light of the decline of the country as a mono-ethnic state. It

253

was the easiest and most convenient way for them to assert they were not racist.

Several European countries elected minority beauty queens in the 1990s. Miss Finland 1996 was black, as was Miss France 1999. The Italian case is particularly noteworthy because the Miss Italia contest is very widely followed. In contrast to most West European countries, where such pageants no longer command prime time television coverage, in Italy celebrities, cultural figures, and even politicians comment on the candidates and the pageant receives ample press attention. There are three main reasons for this high profile. First, Italy boasts a long tradition of according a high value to feminine beauty. Poets and artists contributed to a national tradition that sustains the modern idea of Italy as a country with a special relationship with the aesthetic. Second, the Miss Italia contest is well known for having brought to public attention some of the leading postwar film stars. In particular the 1947 contest was won by Lucia Bosè (who would star in two Antonioni films as well as several neorealist works) while Gina Lollobrigida was runner up. The third reason is of more recent origin. In order to win viewers from the private television channels that have become so important since the 1980s, the public broadcaster RAI seeks to squeeze maximum advantage from its monopoly of coverage of such annual rituals as Miss Italia and the San Remo Festival of Italian Song. Coverage of the contest typically spans four or five evenings.

Beyond this general context, an accurate assessment of the earthquake caused by Mendez's candidature and victory requires consideration of other complex issues. Among these are the attitudes of Italians to their colonial past and to the newly multi-cultural status of their country (see Allen and Russo). There is in addition the question of whiteness and ethnicity in Italian identity. How white, in short, are the Italians? What anxieties are triggered by associations between Italy and ethnic darkness? This paper examines these questions in relation to the tradition of feminine beauty covering the whole period between national unification and the present.

THE ITALIAN IDEALIZATION OF FEMININE BEAUTY

Italy has enjoyed a unique reputation as the home of beautiful things, beautiful places, and beautiful people. During the Grand Tour, travelers from northern Europe made pilgrimages to the peninsula to admire its artistic and architectural heritage, enjoy the majesty of its landscapes, and benefit from its temperate climate. Given its role at the center of both ancient civilization and the glories of the Renaissance, an Italian experience became a necessary part of the education of a civilized person. The idea of Italy's special relationship with the aesthetic, as the *bel paese* par excellence, was informed by a poetic tradition stretching back to Dante and Petrarch; knowledge of the paintings of Cimabue, Giotto, and the Renaissance masters; and appreciation of its natural phenomena. Foreigners marveled at ruins, palaces, paintings and sculptures, took pleasure from blue skies and seas, and enjoyed the relaxed lifestyle of the people. Most Italians took pride in their country's extraordinary heritage. They welcomed visitors and basked in Italy's reputation as the birthplace of genius, civilization, and the arts.

While in Germany the concept of beauty typically had masculine connotations, Italians boasted a long tradition of feminine beauty. Not only was Italy considered to be a mother, and a city such as Venice a beautiful lady, but there was a poetic tradition that rested on the idealization of women. "Following the models provided by Petrarch and Boccaccio," Paola Tinagli has written,

> the canon of female beauty became codified by countless descriptions, from Poliziano to Pietro Bembo, from Ariosto to Boiardo. Variations were constructed around a number of features which were constantly repeated: writers praised the attractions of wavy hair gleaming like gold, of white skin similar to snow, marble, alabaster or milk; they admired cheeks which looked like lilies and roses, and eyes that shone like the sun or the stars. Lips are compared to rubies, teeth to pearls, breasts to snow or to apples. (Tinagli 85–86)

This poetic tradition informed the representations of women and female portraits in Italian art of the fifteenth and sixteenth centuries. Both idealized representations, such as Botticelli's Venus and Primavera and Titian's Danae, and the portraits of real women, such as Leonardo's unidentified Mona Lisa or Bronzino's paintings of Eleonora di Toledo and Lucrezia Panciatichi, were contributions to an on-going discourse on beauty.

Feminine beauty formed an important part of the nineteenth-century emphasis on beauty, as the theorists of Italy's cultural supremacy often referred to the poetic and artistic tradition. The inferiority complex that Italy exhibited in relation to more advanced industrial powers combined with a sense of the universality of the Italian contribution to Western culture to produce the belief that Italy had a right, a duty even, to impress itself more forcefully on the contemporary world. At different moments this aspiration informed imperial, political, economic, and cultural ambitions. Thus, far from being constructive and peaceable, the notion of beauty was inherently problematic since it contained within it elitist and potentially anti-democratic values. Its place in Italian national identity always contained an element of ambiguity and instability. In order to counterbalance the inferiority complex that Italians felt toward the great powers, Emilio Gentile has argued, "a greatness complex developed that was based on the myth of the universal primacy of the Italian nation." "The supporters of this primacy appealed, for historical evidence, to the universal civilisations that had sprung up in the peninsula, to Rome and Catholicism, and Humanism and the Renaissance, the two great spiritual movements from which the consciousness of modern man had originated" (Gentile 44). For patriots like Mazzini, it was an article of faith that Italy was God's chosen land and that its ambitions were entirely in line with the universal aspirations of human civilization. In this context, the discourse on beauty was used to mask uncomfortable realities. It bolstered and justified an Italian claim to superiority that clearly could not be grounded in any realistic assessment of the country's economy, civic development, or military strength.

Frequently there were attempts to harness the aesthetic tradition to an appreciation of contemporary Italian women. In particular there was a veritable cult of Queen Margherita, who enjoyed special prominence as the consort of King Umberto. Born in 1851, Margherita was only twenty-eight when her husband inherited the throne, and she was the object of a discourse about her beauty virtually from the moment she appeared on the public stage. During a royal visit to Vienna in 1881 a journalist wrote that "it seemed that she had stepped down from a painting by Titian or Paolo Veronese," while D'Annunzio, catching sight of her at the theater, defined her "a true triumph of beauty. . . . [T]he queen was very beautiful; looking at her yesterday evening I felt as never before the fascination of the eternal regal feminine" (Casalegno 67).

The racist theories of the nineteenth century that sprang from the work of de Gobineau posed a challenge to Italian claims to cultural superiority. In brief, these theories presented the idea that there had originally been a single dominant race in Europe marked by Teutonic characteristics of fair skin, blue eyes, and blonde hair that had become dispersed and diluted through contamination with the races of the East and the South. Insofar as it survived, it was centered in the Scandinavian countries and in Germany, although examples also could be found across a variety of European countries. In this hierarchical view of the world's races, darker hair and skin implied the weaker presence of Germanic elements, and thus a lower ranking of the race. The apparent logic of these ideas, often confused and inconsistent, exercised considerable influence.

For Italians, such notions constituted a double blow. First, they led to claims that Italy's contributions to civilization had been the work of exceptions (Dante, Galileo, Leonardo da Vinci, and so on were seen as displaced Teutons), while the majority of its people were of inferior stock due to Arab, Turkish, and African influences. Second, by positing the blonde male warrior as the archetypal European and relegating women and children to quasi-animal status, they implied that Italy's association with the feminine was compelling evidence of general inferiority. The responses within Italy to this type of interpretation were complex and multifaceted. At one level, there was an attempt to delineate the Nordic qualities of Italians. This found justification in the domination of northerners over the unified Italian state because they generally had lighter skin and hair color than that of Italians of the south. This current drew support from the poetic and artistic tradition that highly valued fairness and attributed it to aristocrats and beautiful young women. Margherita was a natural focus for this type of discourse. Although born and raised in Italy, her mother was Elizabeth of Saxony; she was fair-haired and her appearance matched the traditional poetic image of golden beauty. Comparing her to Dante's Beatrice and Petrarch's Laura, V. De Napoli claims that it was "as though Canova had been resurrected and given life to his works of Venus and Flora, enriched with voices and colors and flowers" (De Napoli 54). The emphasis on Margherita can be connected to a common view in Italy that northerners were more advanced and civilized than the allegedly primitive inhabitants of the south. Such views were popular at a time when the Italian army had to occupy the south to suppress rampant banditry that arose in response to the enforcement of unification (higher taxes, free trade, conscription). In his writings, Alfredo Niceforo, a pupil of the famous criminal psychologist Cesare Lombroso, theorized about the cultural differences between north and south on a racial and psychological basis (Niceforo 1900, 1–27).

Denigratory perspectives on the Italians were tackled less divisively by other exponents of Italian racial science. A crucial role was played by Giuseppe Sergi, a physical anthropologist who, like his northern European counterparts, accepted the hierarchical ordering of races and paid special attention to skull shapes. However, Sergi believed that what he termed "the Mediterranean race" was superior, precisely because its past artistic and cultural achievements were so great. His work is significant because his idea of a Mediterranean race led him to oppose imperial expansion, since he thought militarism incompatible with an artistic vocation. Interestingly, Sergi drew no stark distinction between Italians, Abyssinians, and North Africans, who were all members of the race. In his view, matters such as eye, hair, and skin color were not significant as indicators of racial type. His ideas were taken up by several intellectuals in the early twentieth century, some of whom abandoned the focus on physical characteristics altogether. In 1906 Napoleone Colajanni asserted that it was to miss the point, not to say anti-scientific, to focus on race at the expense of nation. No nation was made up of a single racial type and to understand a people it was more fruitful to look at its history, culture, and mentality rather than cranium sizes and eye color. In terms of civilization, he argued, Greco-Roman primacy within Europe was beyond dispute. These points were reinforced by Niceforo in later writings, who argued that the ancient ascription of blonde qualities to Greek heroes and gods was a poetic device to establish difference and not proof of some intrinsic racial characteristic.

These two positions—belief in the superiority of northern Italians or the physical characteristics associated with them, and assertion of Latin primacy—often combined in ways that did not seem contradictory to those who espoused them. D'Annunzio, for example, conferred on the heroines of his novels the sort of delicate features and alabaster complexions that recalled the poetic figures of Tennyson and the paintings of Alma-Tadema. Yet in his more political phase he championed Latin civilization and sang the praises of the primitive spirit of the Italian people. It is very notable that at no point in the elaboration of responses to the attempt to confine Italians to a low position in the racial hierarchy was dark skin or hair ever celebrated as positive. At best it was left unmentioned or pushed to the margins. In this sense it is not surprising that there was a marked difference between foreign and Italian portrayals of the Italians. For northern European writers and painters, it was natural to highlight the darker, olive complexions of their Italian subjects. Artists rarely found this unattractive, and in English the term "olive skin" is endowed with positive connotations. Italians did not see themselves as exotic and they did not relish references, whether pictorial or otherwise, to swarthiness. In Italian the translation of "olive skin" (*pelle olivastra*) carries a negative connotation, perhaps due to its possible application to Africans as well as Mediterraneans.

The degree of reservation over this can be judged from the fact that even Sergi rejected any affinity between Italians on the one hand and Arabs, Jews, and sub-Saharan Africans on the other. In the early twentieth century, the disadvantages of racial indeterminacy were apparent. In the United States a long battle was fought by Italian Americans to escape location in a racial middle ground between black and white. Italian immigrants were not at first classified as white and indeed they suffered racial abuse in the South as "white niggers" because they worked comfortably among blacks and fraternized and intermarried with them (Frye Jacobson 57). In a context in which the supremacy of the Italian race was being theorized in opposition to the Teutonic idea, some artists embraced the aesthetic appeal of the darker hair of the majority in Italy. But, while dark hair could be embraced, dark skin was not. Increasingly, as aristocratic ideas lost force, the model Italian might have had brown hair, but he or she definitely had a white face. In the complex compound that was Italian identity, this compromise was as much a class matter as a racial one.

FASCISM, RACE, AND COLONIALISM

The desire to render the nation masculine and assertive to the point of bellicosity was manifest in the late nineteenth century. Unwilling to be considered "the least of the great powers," Italy made a bid for colonies. Military disaster at Adowa in 1896 gave Sergi his cue to assert that the Italians were philosophers and artists, not warriors, and should stick to what they knew (Canavan 18). However, other racial scientists were active in promoting nationalism. Scipio Sighele, a collaborator of Niceforo, called for a revival of the warrior instincts that had manifested themselves in Roman imperialism (Canavan 21–29). A sense of racial pride was necessary for the national assertiveness that was required to bury the specter of Adowa. For Sighele, North Africans were not friends or brothers but foes to be vanquished in colonial expeditions such as the Libyan war of 1911. It was in this climate that D'Annunzio sought to connect the tradition of beauty to a power policy. John Woodhouse argues that the poet first mixed praise of the privileged land where Leonardo and Michelangelo had produced their masterpieces with strongly nationalistic tones in 1895. In the introduction to a new journal, *Convito*, he referred both to Italy's great artistic past and to the special virtues of "Latin blood and Latin soil" that justified imperial ambitions (Woodhouse 126). After World War I this theme was taken up by Fascism, an ideology of superiority that provided justification for both internal authoritarianism and external aggression.

Throughout its twenty-year rule, Fascism proudly asserted that it was reviving Italian civilization and fulfilling the promise of the Risorgimento. Italy was depicted as a new country bursting with youthful vigor and energy. Comforting images of Italians as peace-loving and lazy lovers of mandolin music and spaghetti were banished and demeaning external representations tackled through diplomatic channels. Hollywood cinema was a particular target given its various depictions of Italians as effeminate (Rudolph Valentino), charming drunks (*Farewell to Arms*), and criminals (*Scarface, Little Caesar*) not to mention organ-grinders, peanut sellers, and other unedifying occupations. By contrast, Fascism offered the spectacle of its leader, Mussolini, who was held up as the very embodiment of the virile nation. The multiple images of the Duce, which became more systematic and continuous in the 1930s, can be seen in relation to an explicit politics of whiteness. In a pioneering analysis, Richard Dyer has argued that the exhibition of Mussolini's body was a continuation of the cinematic adventures of the muscleman Maciste (Bartolomeo Pagano), who appeared in *Cabiria* and other epics set in places and periods as diverse as seventeenth-century Scotland and central America before taking up the Italian cause in World War I (Dyer 171–75). Read with hindsight, these images can be seen as legitimating Italian aspirations for internal order and external power. "The muscle hero has landscaped his body with muscles and he controls them superbly and sagely," Dyer writes; "the lands of the muscle film are enfeebled or raw bodies requiring discipline. The built white male body and colonial enterprise act as mirrors of each other, and both, even as they display the white man's magnificent corporeality, tell of the spirit within" (Dyer 165).

Dyer argues that the hero's body in peplum films is normally situated somewhere between black and white. He is lighter than natives, to whom his superiority is repeatedly affirmed, but he is darker than other white men. Also, his skin color can vary; it is lighter when battling darker enemies, darker when in contact with white women. "White male heroism is thus constructed as both unmistakably yet not particularistically white," Dyer affirms. "The muscle hero is an everyman: his tan bespeaks his right to intervene anywhere" (Dyer 163). In the interwar years, Fascism tried to establish a similar position for Italy. Latin characteristics were embraced and celebrated, while unequivocal whiteness was established through specific actions, especially in infusing Italians with a new national spirit and embarking on colonial conquest.

The invasion of Ethiopia in 1935 was seen as finally remedying the humiliation of Adowa and putting Italy on an equal footing with France and Britain. Colonialism had no real economic motivation but politically it was vital in establishing a terrain on which Italian superiority could be affirmed. By imposing government and encouraging settlers, Fascists believed, they were fulfilling the civilizing mission that had marked the cause of Italian nationalism. The same techniques of picturesque annexation that had characterized relations with the troublesome south were now employed to incorporate acceptable images of domesticated Ethiopians into the national imagination. While coverage of resistance by tribesmen and atrocities by Italian soldiers, including the use of poison gas on civilians, was minimized, there was a mass diffusion within Italy of accounts of peaceful progress in the battle against backwardness, disease, and chaos. In keeping with the universal practice of characterizing colonized peoples as feminine, particular emphasis was placed on photographic images of Ethiopian women, whose proud nakedness was offered up as a taste of the exotic. Immortalized in the popular song "Faccetta nera," the "bella abissina" was seen as a harmless ornamental appendage to the glories of the Italian state (Ponzanesi 171–72). The "beautiful appearance and noble bearing" of Ethiopian women became a trophy of Italian colonialism (Ben-Ghiat 129).

However, there were constant fears that Italians might become confused with the native population. Fears of blood contamination were such that great efforts were made to maintain racial boundaries. Since the "renowned beauty of the local women, seen as black venuses" had "created the inevitable racial-sexual encounter called 'madamismo'" (Ponzanesi 119), interracial social contacts were regulated and miscegenation became a criminal offence for all Italians from 1937. Men could receive up to five years in prison, but Italian women accused of having sexual relations with African men faced public whippings and being sent to concentration camps. Ben-Ghiat highlights a significant difference with French colonialism in that the Italian colonial authorities—*pace* Sergi—rejected assimilationism in favor of "a politics of difference that would continually remind Africans of their inferior status" (Ben-Ghiat 129). One might add that such a politics was also intended to remind Italians of their superiority. This mentality informed the ban on jazz music in the 1940s. Anxieties over how difference could best be established and maintained led to a series of dispositions designed to ensure that Italian colonists' behavior was at all times in keeping with the superior status they were claiming. The very qualities that Italians have sometimes been seen to share with blacks—earthiness, sensuality, emotional expressiveness, a lack of embarrassment about the body—were to be banished (Gennari 36–48).

During the 1930s a whole new racial social science developed in Italy to accompany the colonial endeavor and inform public policy on demographic and racial issues. This developed further in 1938 when race laws established legal differences of status between Italians and Jews, Albanians, Slavs, and Ethiopians. Although modeled on German legislation, these laws conformed to the long-range desire to eliminate any doubts about Italian racial status and integrity. Debates about the primacy or existence of the Mediterranean race, and the connected question of racial divisions between northern and southern Italians, were subsumed into a more general assertion of the Aryan status of all Italians (Raspanti 75–85). Although there were disagreements among race specialists, the homogeneity of the Italian race became a dogma. Although biological issues were not stressed the way they were in Germany, a belief in cultural-racial purity was widely affirmed. According to Fascism, an Italian race had existed for a thousand years and it was now reasserting itself through a proud sense of identification. "The Italian race exists, it is alive, robust, pure," asserted Carlo Cecchelli; "the Italian race has a mission to achieve in the world and it will achieve it" (Cecchelli 69–70). To some extent, what was being expressed was national pride, but a battery of legislation and discrimination gave Italian identity politics a very sharp racist edge.

BEAUTY AND MODERNIZATION AFTER 1945

With the Liberation in 1945, racial discourses were officially swept aside and former Italian colonies were placed under international jurisdiction. But the legacy of the preceding period was not so easily eradicated The demographic campaign launched by Mussolini in 1927 together with a general attempt to instill racial pride in the Italians had led to cultural battles against modernizing influences. Although the fall of Fascism and the return of democracy softened the edges of this conflict, it continued well into the postwar period. The massive postwar return of American films and assorted pinups and advertisements provided grist to the mill of conservatives (Gundle 1999, 359–78). The hugely popular *La Domenica del Corriere*, a family weekly founded in 1899 as the Sunday supplement of the *Corriere della sera*, ran a campaign in 1945–1946 against the association of beauty with legs, bodies, sex appeal, and glamour. On 18 November 1945 the magazine asserted: "Italy is full of legs:

news-kiosks are covered with them, certain theatres bustle with them, but we don't want to believe that feminine beauty has finished up in the extremities. It shines above all in the face." Italian beauty was seen in the 16 December issue as residing in a graceful face whose "gentle composure of the features" and "thoughtful tranquility of expression" did not require "make-up, swimsuits or ambiguous and studied little smiles accompanied by jazz."

These concerns also influenced Miss Italia, a commercial contest that from the late 1940s became a national institution. Jurors were instructed to select the ideal fiancée for their sons, respectable and modest girls rather than showy, ambitious women. The first winner in 1946 was a Florentine, Rossana Martini, who won because she corresponded to "the type of Italian woman that the greatest artists of our country chose as a model and for which they won a worldwide audience through their masterpieces" (Villani 65). The sponsoring magazine, *Tempo*, which described her as having "brown hair and a virtuous look in her eye," published her photograph surrounded by reproductions of Renaissance portraits.

Feminine beauty was one of the primary vehicles through which Italy reconquered the sympathies of the peoples of countries with which it had been at war. The prominent film stars of the postwar years all came from the beauty contests and they offered a potent reminder of tradition, the sufferings of the Italian people, and the desire of Italians for peace and prosperity. As icons of Italianness, Silvana Mangano, Gina Lollobrigida, and Sophia Loren were in many ways novel figures who mixed natural qualities with "sexy" and "provocative" mannerisms (Gundle 1995, 367–85). It is instructive to note some significant differences between them.

In the 1950s, Lollobrigida was seen as the ideal modern incarnation of Italian beauty. Although she came in second in the Miss Italia competition of 1947, she played the part of the winner in the 1950 film *Miss Italia* and went on in a variety of films to portray several of the great beauties of the past, including Paolina Borghese and Lina Cavalieri. Although she played peasant girls in some of her biggest successes, her image soon became regal. By contrast, Loren began her career in photo-romance magazines playing gypsies. In some early film roles, including *Aida* and *Africa sotto i mari*, she played Africans. Critics of her roles in American films lamented the way she reproduced an old stereotype of the olive-skinned peasant girl dressed in rags. Whereas Lollobrigida was immediately seen as "Italian," her regional origins receding into the background, Loren retained a strong southern connotation. While all these stars were seen abroad as fiery and highly sexed, this sort of image was not widely appreciated in Italy because it was an unwelcome reminder of past representations of Italian primitiveness. Eventually Loren would win widespread recognition as a great screen actress, but in the 1950s her opulent shape and irregular private life were the source of controversy and disapproval.

Lollobrigida and Loren became Italian icons for foreigners, and they enjoyed a high profile in Italy over time. But they encapsulated mainly traditional and southern ideas about Italians. As Italy became a consumer society and modernized, the ideal of feminine beauty changed. The fashion-conscious, slim, blonde woman, who had been stigmatized in the 1930s as a slave of Paris and Hollywood, returned, not as an exotic *femme fatale* but as an embodiment of an ideal of a Western modern consumer lifestyle. Blonde, white, clean, northern, middle class, she became an Americanized ideal figure distant from the reality of many Italian women. But thanks to beauty products, hair dye, hair removal, and so forth, it was possible to approximate the ideal.

Kristin Ross has equated the obsession with cleanliness and whiteness in postwar France with a desire to erase feelings of guilt over colonialism. It is possible to adapt this interpretation to Italy even though the colonial experience, although intense, was brief. There can be little doubt that the economic boom proved a means whereby Italy could finally eliminate those feelings of inferiority that had animated fears of being consigned to the ranks of the poor and uninfluential. In embracing an ideology of sparkling houses and kitchens, it was a literal rather than moral darkness from which Italians were trying to liberate themselves. Since this period witnessed emigration rather than immigration, there was no assessment of past responsibilities.

ETHNIC DIVERSITY AND ITALY TODAY

While countries such as Britain and France witnessed a substantial influx of people from actual or former colonies in the two decades that followed the war, the ethnic profile of Italy changed significantly only in the 1990s. Although immigrants made up only 2.5 percent of the national population, by the end of the decade 10 percent of the population of Milan was made up of immigrants (Foot 169). In schools in the northern regions, approximately 5 percent of pupils were of immigrant families. Once largely a "monocultural and monocolor society," Italy was quickly forced to contend with diversity of religion, culture, and ethnicity (Daly 175). Like Germany, Italy did not grant citizenship to its immigrants, and their existence was not officially recognized. On the one hand, there was a laissez-faire attitude toward the arrival of workers who filled an economic need, especially in low-status manual employment. On the other, government and society were less than welcoming in providing facilities and assistance in terms of housing, health, education, and so on. Virtually all work in these areas was carried out by a Catholic voluntary organization (King and Andall 152).

In the era of globalization, old and new representations of black people appeared in ways that were not always easy to distinguish. The black person as exotic outsider enjoyed a special status in Italian entertainment media.

Black models appeared more frequently in Italian *Vogue* than in other editions of the magazine and were regularly used in advertising and television. But toward black and Eastern European immigrants there was a crescendo of racial discrimination, violence, and abuse. "Since 1989, there has been a veritable catalogue of violent racist attacks and murders in Italy," King and Andall write, "perpetrated especially against Africans, Asians and gypsies, and in some cases clearly orchestrated by the extreme right" (King and Andall 165). They blame the media for the anti-immigrant frenzy but also indicate the role of the Northern League in creating a siege mentality.

Apart from a handful of black sportsmen and women who represented Italy in international competition, Miss Italia 1996 was one of the first occasions on which a black person had claimed the right to stand for Italy. Because of the importance of the tradition of feminine beauty and the symbolism of the Miss Italia competition, this moment was a significant one in which fears and anxieties about identity came dramatically to the surface. The doubts voiced by two prominent jury members about the representativeness of Denny Mendez were echoed in far less civil tones by others. There were reports of her being insulted in the street and, after her victory in the television poll, mothers of other disappointed contestants disputed her right to represent Italy.

How then should the overwhelmingly plebiscite in her favor be interpreted? For Enrico Mentana, a senior television journalist who was also a member of the jury, the vote was a case of "imposed well-meaningness." In an interview published in *La Repubblica* on 9 September 1996, he declared that it was a way "of keeping our consciences clean because everyone was under the potential suspicion of racism simply because we dared to suggest that Denny, despite her great beauty, was not an appropriate representative of Miss Italia." Other commentators confirmed the view that it was a cost-free way of affirming that Italy was modern and open, a fully paid-up member of the global village. In another interpretation, the election of Mendez can be seen as almost identical to an ornamental annexation of a paracolonial type. Although her Dominican origins meant that she had no connection with territories belonging to Italy's former empire, the emphasis on her blackness over all other qualities—including even beauty—inevitably revived memories and unconscious assumptions. Newspapers referred to Mendez quite unthinkingly as a "black Venus" or "the black gazelle," echoing the terminology of the colonial period. From this point of view, her victory was an aesthetic tribute not so much to Italy's tolerance and inclusiveness as to its historical preeminence as a country able to select and evaluate global beauty. The fact that Mendez was Catholic (although not practicing) allowed Italians to situate her in a sort of Italocentric world outlook. By 1996 Italians did not need to assert their whiteness, but feelings of superiority nonetheless require occasional confirmation. In fact the election of

Mendez did not easily meet this need. After her year as Miss Italia, she disappeared from view. But it was not possible to restore the *status quo ante.* Even if some would have preferred that the scandal of her election had never happened, it served to bring to the surface issues that were difficult and problematic. Among these was the question of whether it was possible to be black and Italian in anything other than a legal sense. "I know that I don't represent Italian beauty," Mendez declared in *La Repubblica* of 9 September 1996, "but they have elected me; what was I supposed to do, refuse?" By not refusing, she compelled Italians to take cognizance of the presence in their midst of immigrant communities from North Africa, the Philippines, and Eastern Europe.

WORKS CITED

Allen, Beverley, and Mary Russo. *Revisioning Italy: National Identity and Global Culture.* Minneapolis: University of Minnesota Press, 1997.

Ben-Ghiat, Ruth. *Fascist Modernities: Italy 1922–1945.* Berkeley: University of California Press, 2001.

Canavan, Hilary. "Italian Race Science, Colonialism and Nationalist Rhetoric: Divergent Views of North Africans in the Work of the Italian Psychologists Giuseppe Sergi and Scipio Sighele." Unpublished MA thesis, Royal Holloway—University of London, 2001.

Casalegno, Carlo. *La regina Margherita.* Turin: Einaudi, 1956.

Cecchelli, Carlo. "Origini ed omogeneita' della razza." *Inchiesta sulla razza.* Ed. Paolo Orano. Rome: Pinciana, 1939.

Colajanni, Napoleone. *Latini e anglosassoni (razze inferiori e razze superiori).* Rome and Naples: Rivista Popolare, 1906.

Daly, Faïçal. "Tunisian migrants and their experience of racism in Modena." *Modern Italy.* 4:2 (1999). 173–89.

de Gobineau, Arthur. *Essai sur l'inegalité des races humaines.* Paris: Diderot, 1853.

De Napoli, V. *L'eterna bellezza della Regina Margherita di Savoja.* Naples: Gargiulo, 1886.

Dyer, Richard. *White.* London: Routledge, 1997.

Foot, John. "Immigration and the City: Milan and Mass Immigration, 1958–98." *Modern Italy.* 4:2 (1999). 159–72.

Frye Jacobson, Matthew. *Whiteness of a Different Color: European Immigrants and the Alchemy of Race.* Cambridge, Mass.: Harvard University Press, 1998.

Gennari, John. "Passing for Italian." *Transition.* 6:4 (1996).

Gentile, Emilio. *La grande Italia: ascesa e declino del mito della nazione nel ventesimo secolo.* Milan: Mondadori, 1997.

Gundle, Stephen. "Sophia Loren, Italian Icon." *Historical Journal of Film, Radio and Television.* 15:3 (1995).

Gundle, Stephen. "Feminine Beauty, National Identity and Political Conflict in Postwar Italy, 1945–54." *Contemporary European History.* 8:3 (1999).

King, Russell, and Jacqueline Andall. "The Geography and Economic Sociology of Recent Immigration to Italy." *Modern Italy.* 4:2 (1999). 135–58.

Niceforo, Alfredo. "Italiani del Nord e Italiani del Sud." *La rivista moderna.* 3:2 (1900): 1–27.

Niceforo, Alfredo. *I Germani: storia di un'idea e di una "razza."* Rome: Editrice Società Periodica, 1917.

Ponzanesi, Sandra. *Paradoxes of Postcolonial Culture: Contemporary Women Writers of the Indian and Afro-Italian Diaspora.* Albany: SUNY Press, 2004.

Raspanti, Mauro. "Il mito ariano nella cultura italiana fra Otto e Novecento." *Nel nome della razza: il razzismo nella storia d'Italia 1970–1945.* Ed. Alberto Burgio. Bologna: Il Mulino, 1999.

Ross, Kristin. *Fast Cars, Clean Bodies: Decolonization and the Reordering of French Culture.* Cambridge, Mass.: MIT Press, 1995.

Sergi, Giuseppe. *The Mediterranean Race: A Study of the Origins of European Peoples.* London: 1901, first published 1895.

Tinagli, Paola. *Women in Italian Renaissance Art.* Manchester: Manchester University Press, 1993.

Villani, Dino. *Come sono nate undici Miss Italia.* Milan: Domus, 1957.

Woodhouse, John. *Gabriele D'Annunzio: Defiant Archangel.* Oxford: Oxford University Press, 1998.

17

Outlandish Cinema: Screening the Other in Italy

Sandra Ponzanesi

Cinema is one of Italy's most distinctive modern artistic identities. It has been an integral part of public and private culture, its scope and content varying from minor national productions to internationally acclaimed works and from pure entertainment[1] to orchestrated political propaganda, especially during fascism, when, according to Mussolini, cinema was the strongest weapon (Reich and Garofalo, 2002; Ben-Ghiat, 2001).

While Italian cinema still relies on the reputation of the great masters of the past, such as Roberto Rossellini, Vittorio de Sica, and Luchino Visconti, directors who promoted neorealism as a reaction to the bombastic style of fascism, and later Michelangelo Antonioni and Federico Fellini, the great author-directors of the 1960s, it has relentlessly tried to keep its place within the international film scene.

It is beyond doubt that in the last few decades very few Italian films have achieved similar international visibility, the exceptions being rare (Giuseppe Tornatore's *Cinema Paradiso*, 1988; Gabriele Salvatores's *Mediterraneo*, 1991; Gianni Amelio's *Il Ladro di Bambini*, 1992; Benigni's *La vita é Bella*, 1999; Nanni Moretti's *La Stanza del Figlio*, 2001; Marco Tullio Giordana's *La Meglio Gioventú*, 2003). At a more restricted national level a certain improvement can be observed among new young film directors after the stagnation of the 1980s.[2] This slow resurgence of Italian cinema displays a remarkable focus on emerging novel social and political aspects of Italian life.

My focus here is on the representation of immigration in three films of the Italian cinema of the 1990s: Silvio Soldini's *Un anima Divisa in Due* (1993), which deals with the ancient presence of Roma people in Italy; Michele

Placido's *Pummaró* (1990), which tackles the recent issue of labor immigration from Africa; and Henrique Goldman's *Princesa* (2001), which explores the reality of contemporary sex trafficking involving immigration to Italy. My approach applies and bears on work in textual analysis, film studies, women's studies, and postcolonial theory. The combined aim is to show how a set of unique migrant communities living in Italy handle the fundamental issue of territoriality and how in each case their reception within the host society is critically represented. I do so by developing the concept of "outlandish cinema," explaining its theoretical and stylistic validity, and then applying the concept to the analysis of the three films.

IMMIGRATION AND CINEMA

The arrival of newcomers to Italy, mostly immigrants from the south of the world, has been overblown in the public media (especially television and newspapers) as the new epidemic undermining the supposed normal homogeneity and civility of Italian culture. These media approaches that routinely magnify migrancy have been cast off by Alessandro del Lago, who delineates the actual process through which the Italian system constructs *emergenza immigrazione* (immigration emergency) by representing migrants as a social threat and source of social disorder. In practice the migrant becomes an ideal target for outing the frustrations of a nation that considers itself stable and civil were it not for the "migrant invasion" (Del Lago, 1999).

This hostile reception is due to the fact that, though proceeding at an impressive pace, migration is a relatively new phenomenon in Italy. Of course while migration to Italy is a recent preoccupation, migration from Italy to the world is a long-established tradition that impacted the new Italian nation, especially early in the last century. Donna Gabaccia observes that the formation of the modern Italian nation often seemed to find form more easily outside of Italy than within: "for a country with a long history of sending emigrants abroad, Italy experienced considerable distress in welcoming migrants onto its national territory" (p. 170), and then adds that "a nation accustomed to thinking of its migrants as subject to racist and capitalist oppression abroad suddenly looked into the mirror to see itself as the oppressor" (p. 172). Yet there is something deep to this generalization, most likely the fact that Italy, in contrast to the United Kingdom, France, or Germany, has not developed a clear understanding of how its history of migration has defined its national identity (Gabaccia, 2000).[3]

There are countless images of Italians landing on Ellis Island and a very long list of movies that glorified those images of pioneering destitute peasants, especially from the south of Italy, seeking the American dream. From gangster and mafia movies such as *Once upon a Time in America* (Sergio Leone, 1984) and the *Godfather* (Francis Ford Coppola, 1972, 1974, 1990) to the more nuanced representations of Martin Scorsese (*Who's That Knocking at My Door*, 1969; *Mean Streets*, 1973; and the more recent documentary *Il Mio Viaggio in Italia, My Voyage to Italy*, 1999[4]), Italy has always been represented through a double mythology of rootedness and expatriation. This complex national identification, however, has never shaken the image of the Italian civil society as backward, reluctant to embrace modernity at large or to update its industrial ethos, lifestyle, and mediatic strategies to the rest of Europe (Ginsborg, 2003). This is due to the fact that representations of Italy have always been balanced on a sublime paradox, *il bel suol d'amore* (the beautiful love land), divided not only between home and abroad, colonial memory and its denial, but within itself, north and south, rural and urban, advanced capitalism and state corruption, monumental cultural heritage and unruly postmodern urbanization.

The representation of this predicament has always been central to Italian cinema. However, except for the socially engaged neorealist period and the political cinema of the 1970s,[5] very little attention has been paid to the tumultuous development of post-war Italy in a gripping way. Apart from these two strands, many cinematic productions became either more intimist and episodic or geared toward light comedy (Landy, 2000; Bruno and Nadotti, 1988; Forgacs and Lumley, 1996). By the 1990s, however, several films of political and social relevance began to appear: Daniele Lucchetti's *Il Porta Borse*, 1991 (on state corruption); Marco Risi's *Il Muro di Gomma*, 1991 (on the 1980 Ustica air disaster); Ricky Tognazzi's *La Scorta*, 1993 (on mafia murders of state magistrates in Sicily); and Marco Bellocchio's *Buongiorno Notte*, 2003 (on Moro's murder by the Red Brigade).

Among these new releases are the three films of this analysis. They all concern the representation of immigrants, and have managed to achieve a remarkable visibility, both critical and commercial. In Silvio Soldini's *Un anima Divisa in Due* (1993)[6] the main actor, Fabrizio Bentivoglio, won the Coppa Volpi at the Venice Film Festival as best actor; Michele Placido's *Pummaró* (1990)[7] was presented at Cannes under the rubric "Un cértain régard" in 1990; and Henrique Goldman's *Princesa* (2001),[8] an international co-production, was critically acclaimed at festivals worldwide, including Sundance, Edinburgh, and São Paolo, and at the L.A. Outfest Film Festival, where it won in the category of best foreign film.

Along with these movies there are others that have tackled the issue of immigration, for example, *Terra di Mezzo,* 1997, the directorial debut of Matteo Garrone (best known now for *L'Imbalsamatore,* 2002); the successful *Lamerica,* 1994, by Gianni Amelio; *L'Albero dei destini Sospesi,* 1997, by Rachid Mohamed Benhadj; *Di Cielo in Cielo,* by Roberto Giannarelli, 1997; *L'Appartamento,* 1997, by Francesca Pirani; and *Torino Boys,* 2000, by brothers Marco and Antonio Manetti. Most of these films were produced by and screened on the public Italian television channel RAI and depict the importance of the power of love in overcoming racial prejudices.

The three films chosen here deal with issues of immigration to Italy but from entirely different angles relating to different historical and geo-political fluxes of migration. In these movies Italy as the gateway to Europe is deconstructed through its opposition to the other (nomad, black, transsexual). The other, seen as "outlandish" because still represented though the persistent racialized gaze that developed in colonial times (Kaplan, 1997; Ponzanesi, 2004; Shohat and Stam, 1994), becomes a perturbation and mirror of the unstable nature of Italian identity itself.

OUTLANDISH CINEMA

My coinage of outlandish cinema refers to the double signification of the term, either "of strange and barbarous nature" or "as situated in an unfamiliar spot, remote and non-native." It literally but also metaphorically refers to the deterritorialization that characters impersonate, and to the way they are perceived—as weird and exotic—within the Italian society. I will argue that these representations of the "other" as "outlandish," external, or foreign show that the other is an integral part of Italy's national culture. Outlandish figurations turn the tables on what is civilized, human, and worth fighting for and yet document how an Italy, from the implied marginal position that is backward, insular, and defensive, is simultaneously solidary, transgressive, and evolving.

Outlandish cinema conveys not only the deviation from or subversion of the mainstream cinema, but also the idea of a cinematic tradition that is in search of its lines of flight, embracing the new within the old and searching for possible mediations, transformations, and more egalitarian visions. It is a cinema that reflects on the political power of imagination by making cultural and ethnic clashes central to the diegesis and by searching for new cinematic modes of staging them that steer away from stereotypical portrayals of minority and/or deracinated groups as outsiders and menacing. Outlandish cinema puts forward different narratives and new stylistic modes that confront spectators with their racial and gendered biases by making them uncomfortable with their own assumptions and thereby othering them from their dominant positions. The spectator is asked to affiliate or identify with the outlandish characters against the intolerance of Italian citizenry to which they presumably belong, a process of estrangement that makes the spectator experience an outlandishness of his or her own. These films are intentionally made for a white Italian audience intrigued by the "other" but not yet well equipped for its understanding. Thus, while not devoid of pedagogical or moralistic undertones, they manage to convey an innovative perspective thanks to their skillful combination of expected and surprising, of comforting familiarity and violent estrangement, each is an attempt at culturally translating and representing the other in cinematic forms.

Outlandishness also refers to stylistic questions. The filmmakers experiment with new cinematic registers even though they rely on fairly traditional narrative structures. For example, there is the use of non-professional actors,[9] the use of voice-overs such as in letter reading, the specific use of flashbacks, the way of filming landscapes, and the use of those non-places defined by Marc Augé (1995) as including train stations, bus stops, the metro, and outskirt locations. The emphasis upon architecture is very important since it defines not only the urban landscape, but as well the way the subjects are projected into outer spaces, where alienation and lack of intimacy unsettle the perception of identity. To account for these aesthetic elements within outlandish cinema in its own terms allows us to overcome the too limited and distorting approach to migrancy within cinema as only interesting for its sociological contents. Far too often the sociological content of a film is given attention totally apart from its aesthetic sensibility or merit. The resulting discourse reduces directors to their biographical and political motives, and films to nothing more than plots and themes.

Past glorious films such as *Rocco ed I Suoi Fratelli*, 1960 (Visconti's strong poetic film on migration from south to north, what Verdicchio has called "the denied postcolonial condition within Italy itself"[10]); *Time of the Gypsies*, 1989 (Kusturica's touching movie on nomadic Gypsies moving from the Balkans to Italy[11]); and *Lamerica*, 1994 (Gianni Amelio, on migrant Albanians fleeing to Italy as the land of hopes and dreams), show that it is possible to engage with social issues in an innovative way, both cinematically and culturally.

All three movies concern the reception within contemporary Italian culture of Italian and foreign outlandish figures in the context of shifting new lifestyles. These transitions are caused by the encounter with someone different, coming from unexpected positions (geographical, cultural, ethnic, linguistic, sexual, religious). The main characters are peripatetic souls, migrant, nomadic, and transgender subjects who appropriate the metaphor of traveling. It is constituted as a crossing of languages, boundaries, and identities, experienced as extended moments of alienation in their attempt to pass as normal. Princesa is a hooker on the night boulevards; Pabe is a Gypsy begging in Milan's main city streets; Kwaku constantly redirects his journey north, in search of his brother, whom he will find dead in Germany. However, these so-labeled "foreign" figures are less stranded than the Italian characters they encounter and fall in love with. Their Italian counterparts are drifting, their private lives disordered and badly integrated in a bourgeois society that they find oppressive but are unable to escape: Pietro, in *Un'Anima Divisa in Due*, is divorced, lonely, and unhappy with his job and hardly sees his son anymore. Gianni, in *Princesa*, his marriage on the rocks, is timidly roaming the streets at night in search of prostitutes. Eleonora, in *Pummaró*, also divorced with a child, tries to find meaning in her life by teaching Italian to immigrants, but feels lost in a city that does not approve of her missionary zeal, especially when she falls in love with a black immigrant.

In this way Italian society is portrayed as multifaceted, differentiated within itself on several basic levels. Most obvious is its internal economic split between the more industrial and Europeanized north and the more agrarian and Mediterranean south. There is also the unequal distribution of social status, composed of different class milieus, gender divisions, ethnic minorities already present, the state (especially in its policing role), the Catholic church (in its missionary function), and the schools (where most of these dynamics take place).

SILVIO SOLDINI, *UN'ANIMA DIVISA IN DUE*, 1993

Un'Anima Divisa in Due opens with a subtle Proustian moment. Pietro is returning home by metro, and the playing with a red lipstick triggers his expansive memories. A train of quick flashbacks unfolds in which we see sequential shots of concrete events in his life. We see him arguing with his ex-wife, pretending with his son in an abandoned car to be traveling to the sea, and encountering the Gypsy girl stealing the lipstick. All these images are sealed by Pietro's attack of nose bleeding, a sign of hemorrhaging used to emphasize his being at a loss and adrift. The film, emotionally intense yet formally sober and rigorous, effectively conveys the sense of alienation and oppression experienced by Pietro in a livid and grey Milan.

Pietro awakens through the encounter with Pabe. A movie on the road starts, with Pabe and Pietro driving to Ancona, where a new life can be imagined, away from their respective family ties and social restrictions. They are caught within the impasse of understanding the delicate codes of being a Roma (Pabe does not want to sleep in a hotel room where she feels suffocated; she keeps stealing when the occasion presents itself because for her it is "to find" and not "to steal"; she keeps a knife by her side to protect her reputation while asking Pietro to take her away) and Pietro's need to start afresh. In Ancona a new community of people welcomes them: Salvino, who owns a restaurant and has an instinctive understanding with Pabe, and Abid, a cheerful immigrant guy who helps in the kitchen. The second part of the film convincingly shows a happier phase; Ancona is a brighter place and the seaside conveys the broad horizon of the possible future.

In Ancona Pabe is happy with Pietro and undergoes a metamorphosis. She renames herself Rosi and adopts Pietro's surname Di Leo in order to pass as Italian at the workplace. She throws away her Gypsy clothes and starts wearing young and trendy outfits. Her final adaptation is a short and styled modern haircut like that of a TV presenter. Pietro is delighted that she is so happy with her appearance, as he has himself undergone a bit of a Roma metamorphosis. His hair is long; he has a Gypsy-styled moustache and has learned a few Roma words. He tries to become less of a *gagio*, the Roma nickname for white people. In their reciprocal contamination of language, clothing, and behavior, the characters become more estranged, tolerated but judged by the others as weird outcasts. As Pietro's dream of building up an alternative life for himself and Pabe vanishes, the colors become grey again, and the locations filmed become desolate.

Despite all her efforts at camouflage and disguise, Pabe does not find a compromise between her nomadic background and the so-called civilization she tries to embrace. She is unmasked as a Roma while working as a hotel maid and is wrongly accused of being a thief. The stereotypes about her community brutally catch up with her, and she realizes that her place within Italian society will always be marked with a difference. The outlandishness repeatedly projected onto her by the host society does not allow her to break free and forge an identity that could bridge both worlds and maybe create a new one. Disillusioned and shocked by two Roma women she met on the streets who ask her for money, she leaves Pietro and her "re-made Italian self." She throws off her modern garb and slips into her old clothes before returning to Milan, where the final scene unfolds. She is seen standing in front of an open empty space that we recognize, through a name written on the wall, as her former nomadic camp. All the caravans have gone; her people have moved away, leaving neither traces nor directions. The spectator is left looking through Pabe's eyes—what was once the site of her nomadic community living together is now nothing but a dusty construction site.

The film closes with this allegorical image of alienation, of a failed integration and the impossibility of return to the old world. It is far less than a tangible third space, and more a vacuum that offers neither solutions nor redemption. We are left with this strong and realistic image, wondering about her life in becoming and also wondering about Pietro, who has found in Pabe the strength to carry on. The strong symbolism of the final shot could signify how modernity bulldozes over the strong and ancient ethnic identities of a Roma camp, leaving Pabe and us spectators in search of a new space.

The film shows how in an increasingly multicultural and multiracial society integration and assimilation are inherently ambivalent. On the one hand the host culture's intolerance of the visible culture of the migrant requires almost total annihilation of the migrant identity. On the other hand, the harder the migrants strive for this presumed normality, the more outlandish they appear. The scale seems to weigh unequally against the guests. The Gypsies are the carriers of a very ancient diversity, one that becomes even more unbridgeable than that of the new *extracomunitari*. This current euphemism is a shorthand technically used to designate newcomers who are from outside the EU, but in fact used just to refer to blacks. Probably because of the Gypsies' indisputable resonance as a culturally different group, unwilling to work and settle down, this film's story becomes the magnified emblem of all intolerance among conflicting worldviews and lifestyles that the recent immigration from the Third World has brought to Italy.

MICHELE PLACIDO, *PUMMARÓ*, 1990

This new black immigration is represented in *Pummaró*.[12] Kwaku first travels from Ghana to the south of Italy, then travels from Naples to Rome and further north to Verona, and finally arrives in Frankfurt. At each point his bildungsroman grows as he experiences painful new "beyonds": the exploitation of immigrants by employees without scruples (the illegal tomato picking in Campania) and of prostitutes by squalid figures (Rome), and the sting of xenophobic rejection, shown both in diffident and biased hostility (the ex-metalworker whom Kwaku encounters in a bar in Verona) and overt violence (the aggression Kwaku and Eleonora suffer in Verona).

The love story between Eleonora and Kwaku aims to reveal a possible encounter between different worlds, one that occurs within the presence of a reality of assistance and voluntary work generously engaged toward the *extra-comunitari*. But as in the case of Pietro, the loneliness and disorientation of the immigrants parallels the difficult existential condition of the local people. Even the "professore" in the south who had helped Kwaku to get a passport and escape seems to compensate for the failure and emptiness of his life by helping *extra-comunitari* . Outlandishness portrayed from outside is what actually grips the "autochthonous" characters themselves. Eleonora is a young woman in search of a new course for her life. She is Kwaku's Italian teacher, a voluntary job she does outside her normal schedule as a schoolteacher. She has a broken marriage and has to share custody of her child with her ex-husband, all of which takes place offstage in the film. The disapproving gazes of the people of Verona shake the idyllic love between the two souls, who understand each other through tenderness and cultural interests. The town is depicted as bourgeois and conservative, populated by several migrant communities who come for 24/7 factory and assembly-line work that the locals would reject.

The magic spell between the two is broken when Eleonora hears she cannot get access to her child because her ex-husband does not want the child to have contact with a "black man." The evening scene encapsulates the destruction when Kwaku is reciting some Shakespeare to her, showing at once his education and his being overwhelmed by the life he is leading as a factory worker in an intolerant city. Suddenly youngsters on motorbikes, their faces hidden by masks, encircle the couple, aiming to punish Eleonora for having chosen a black guy, for being a whore and a betrayer of her own community. The two trapped lovers hug each other while the roaring motorbikes gradually create a more and more terrifying atmosphere. With this menacing scene we perceive that whatever those two people had managed to build together against racism and ignorance is now shattered. The two characters are alienated from their surroundings: Eleonora is cast out from her family and neighbors, and Kwaku realizes that though beautiful, his integration through love has only been a momentary bliss.

Kwaku will in fact resume his journey north in search of his brother Giobbe, whom he finds dead in Frankfurt. Together with Nanú, Giobbe's girlfriend, now pregnant, he collects the money left behind by his brother and plans to migrate to Canada, where he can fulfill his dreams of becoming a doctor and of building a new life. Italy has worked for him as a rite of passage, as a transit point on the way from Africa to Canada. Love has been a sweet interlude, and for a moment his connection and integration with Italian society had reached its zenith, but again, as in the other films, society at large gets back at him, and confronts him with a reality that will change far too slowly for him to deal with it in his lifetime. Like Pabe, Kwaku returns to his own path, more confident and experienced, but still marked by a profound sense of outlandishness.

HENRIQUE GOLDMAN, *PRINCESA*, 2001

The outlandishness of *Princesa* adds a new dimension to the previous stories. It is a story of Fernando/a, a would-be-transsexual prostitute, whose agonizing desire to become a woman leads in unexpected directions. Princesa, as she names herself, ends up in a world of prostitution in order to earn enough money for a sex change operation. She leaves her traditional and Catholic life in Brazil, roams the streets of Spain, and eventually ends up in Italy. Here the film opens with her on a train, and when the conductor asks for her documents we realize, like him, that she is not a woman but a man.

In Milan Princesa meets Karin, a middle-aged transvestite who acts as the boss and the mother to a large family of transvestite hookers. Fernanda's beauty quickly makes her a hit with the clients and with Karin, who takes her into her home, where she slowly saves up the money to pay for her operation. Fernanda creates a private corner niche where she collects her own bedroom reliquaries, images of the Madonna and photos of her mother. When struggling she is seen praying in her adopted space, her own Catholic temple.

Fernanda's world changes when she meets Gianni, a reserved, married businessman, and experiences a not entirely successful first encounter. Since he thought she was a woman in the fullest sense, the revelation that she is not leads him to throw her out of his car in disgust. Despite this, he feels the flames of passion rekindled inside him and leaves his wife to start a touching and romantic relationship with her. Life seems to be a fairy tale for Fernanda, with Gianni coming along to rescue her from her life as a street-walker, giving her the one thing she dreams of most, the chance to become a real woman. But life is rarely a fairy tale, and soon she must decide whether her dream is really what she wants. Princesa starts taking hormones in order to undergo the famous operation that will make her body correspond to her desire to be a woman. As a fiancée she is introduced into Gianni's bourgeois entourage, where she starts feeling judged, looked down upon, and enclosed. We see her going shopping every day, feeling lonely at home, almost like an abandoned housewife waiting for her husband to come home. The treatment makes her feel ill and depressed. It is at this low point that Gianni's ex-wife resurfaces and makes it known that she is pregnant with Gianni's child, something that had eluded their marriage until then. Fernanda clearly sees in one shot the woman she will never be, despite all the operations. She will never be able to bear him a child, and never be able to be just a wife.

We see her leaving in pain, abandoning the idea of undergoing a sex operation and returning to the streets, a closing image that in its paradoxical double message shows Fernanda liberated from her obsession, free to roam the streets at night, in charge of her own body and of herself.[13] The outlandishness is here constructed not only around the foreign origin of Princesa, but also around her migration between sexual identities, her need to cross the borders of normality. It is her transgender desire that brings her back to the illicit life on the night streets, a marginal position that is created and cherished by many Italian men in search of the other, both sexually, linguistically, and culturally.

The film scenes are fast and have Fassbinderian tonalities. The street where Princesa plies her trade is a colorful parade of cruising cars, screaming clientele, and working girls glamorously made up like drag queens. Goldman sets these scenes to a throbbing Brazilian beat, which further heightens the unrestrained orgiastic atmosphere. The film tells Princesa's story with admirable simplicity, never indulging in any easy sentimentality or victimization. Consequently, this hardness combines with these other strategies to convey the outlandishness in the movie also at a stylistic level.

First we hear a long voice-over, with Fernanda reading off-screen the letter she writes to her mother. She signs the letters as Fernando and makes up lies to hide her real life from her mother. These voice-overs are in Portuguese, and not translated or subtitled. Many of the dialogues and chats Princesa has with her Brazilian transvestite friends, in particular Charlo, are also in Portuguese. This creates a sense of estrangement and exclusion for the spectator, a feeling of entering a community that keeps secret its own codes of linguistic exchange. Princesa at the beginning of the movie speaks a broken Italian, and although later on she masters the language, she still speaks with an exotic accent.

CONCLUSION

The question of speaking with an accent is strongly put forward in all three movies. Pabe will never give up her peculiar way of phrasing her world, dictated not only by her speaking with an accent but also by the visual references she picks up from her own culture. At the factory, when the girl Lidia with whom she works asks her if she is foreign, Pabe reacts brusquely and tells her she is Italian. When Lidia retorts, "but you have a strange accent," Pabe's mask is given a biographical texture—"it is because I was born in Greece."

The protagonists' accents are strictly directed to express not only their displacement but also their alternative production modes within the hosting society, their different ways of earning a living and of consuming culture and affections. This affects the style, which requires new sets of viewing skills on the part of audiences. This is not dissimilar from Hamid Naficy's injunction, made in his *Accented Cinema* (2001), that new emerging cinematographic genres, such as diasporic cinema in his case and outlandish cinema for the purpose of this essay, require new analytical frameworks to assess output, stylistic variety, cultural diversity, and social impact within global intricacies.

While in each of these three movies the attempt to pass as Italian and conform to the norm of society fails, the films all leave open a space of transformation. Both the characters and the spectators look for alternative forms of integration, away from the assimilation model proposed by the dominant society. The outlandish characters act in the attempt to pass as Italian, but they leave by having changed the autochthonous characters as well. Every one of the strong migrant protagonists is juxtaposed with a weaker Italian counterpart. Pietro, Gianni, and Eleonora are totally at a loss in the world, overwhelmed by feelings of unsettledness and in search of their own identity. Through them the double gaze of racism and intolerance is played out in a positive way, even though their contaminated selves prevent a successful solution.

Fortunately enough all three movies finish in a non-predictable and open-ended way, leaving the spectator puzzled but also stimulated to search for his or her own positioning with respect to the possible developments. It is a territory that is investigated but still left unappropriated, where possible future deviations can be imagined. Outlandishness becomes therefore a moment of transformation, a mobilization of the self through the other.

The major aspects that emerge from this outlandish cinema—hybridization of narrative and cinematic forms, attempts at *passing as* Italian, and the deployment of strategies to cross cultural, social, and linguistic borders—indicate that a shift toward more egalitarian and inclusive forms of representation of the other is taking place. As implied by this essay's title, screening the other is not only about selecting, shielding, or protecting "outlandish figures" within Italian culture, but also about making them visible and audible, exposing and setting them in motion, a representation that finds its place in the reciprocity of estrangement. This double narrative aims at envisioning possible worlds, which so far have only been realized around the shadowy sides of Italian culture.

NOTES

1. The glamorous role of popular stars ranges from Francesca Bertini in the silent period to Alida Valli, Sophia Loren, and Gina Lollobrigida in the 1950s and 1960s, to recent actresses who convey a more diffused form of "divismo" such as Monica Bellucci and Maria Grazia Cucinotta. For an erudite and detailed analysis of the role of female divas in Italian culture, see Stephen Gundle, 1999.

2. See, for example, the films of Gabriele Muccino, *L'ultimo Bacio*, 2000, *Ricordati di me*, 2003; Ferzan Ozpetek, *Il Bagno Turco*, 1997, *Le Fate Ignoranti*, 2000; Mario Martone, *Morte di Un Matematico Napoletano*, 1992, *L'Amore Molesto*, 1995; Roberto Faenza, *La lunga Vita di Marianna Ucria*, 1997, *Prendimi L'Anima*, 2003; Cristina Comencini, *Il più Bel giorno della Mia Vita*, 2001; and Marco Bellocchio, *L'Ora di Religione*, 2001.

3. Donna Gabaccia's *Italy's Many Diasporas* (2000) offers a new account of the different directions taken by Italians in their migratory history. The plural in the title refers less to the global destinations of Italians and more to a dual polymorphism that characterizes the phenomenon: On the one hand, Italians left their country as Venetians, Sicilians, or Neapolitans rather than as "Italians"; on the other hand is the varied character of their dispersion: trade diaspora, cultural diaspora, nationalist diaspora, and mass diaspora.

4. *My Voyage to Italy* is a four-hour documentary on the Italian cinema that influenced Scorsese. By intertwining long fragments of Rossellini, De Sica, and Visconti with his own response and fascination for them, Scorsese has made a captivating film that is more than a lecture on Italian cinema. The title was inspired by Rossellini's film *Viaggio in Italia*, 1953, which starred Ingrid Bergman.

5. See the following films: Bernardo Bertolucci, *Il conformista*, 1970, *Novecento*, 1976; Francesco Rosi, *Il caso Mattei*, 1971, *Cadaveri Eccellenti*, 1974, *Cristo Si é Fermato ed Eboli*, 1979; Pier Paolo Pasolini, *Teorema*, 1968, *Salò o le 120 Giornata di Sodoma*, 1975; Ettore Scola, *C'eravamo Tanto Amati*, 1974, *Una Giornata Particolare*, 1977.

6. Soldini is today an internationally established filmmaker thanks to his recent successes *Brucio nel vento* (Burn in the Wind), 2002, and *Pane e Tulipani*, 1999.

7. *Pummaró* (1990) was Michele Placido's debut as a director. Placido is a well-established actor especially known for his role in the mafia TV series *La Piovra*. He

has also directed other films of serious social engagement (*Un Eroe Borghese*, 1994; *Del Perduto Amore*, 1998; *Un Viaggio Chiamato Amore*, 2002).

8. *Princesa* (2001) was directed by Henrique Goldman and is based on an auto-biographical account by Fernanda Farias de Albuquerque. This was originally written in a hybrid of Portuguese, Sardinian, and street Italian and was straightened into publishable Italian by Maurizio Jannelli, Fernanda's red brigade jail companion in Sardinia.

9. In *Un'anima Divisa in Due* Pabe is played by Mària Bakò, a Roma non-professional actress in her first role. Other neophytes include Thywill K Amenya, as Kwaku in *Pummaró*, and Ingrid de Souza, outstanding in her role as Princesa.

10. See Pasquale Verdicchio, "The Preclusion of Postcolonial Discourse in Southern Italy," in Allen and Russo (eds.), 1997, pp. 191–212.

11. Emir Kusturica's memorable film *Les Temps des Gitans*, 1989, was also partly set in Italy and confirms the historically layered presence of the Gypsy people within Italian culture. As Robert Fraser mentions in his opening essay, it is a long and often denied presence that has shaped the culture of Europe in several unacknowledged ways. Another relevant Italian film, *Prendimi e portami via* (Take Me Away, 2003), by Tonino Zangardi, presented at the Rotterdam Film Festival, deals with the Roma presence in Italy and echoes many of the issues dealt with in *Un'Anima Divisa in Due*, but from the point of view of children. This realistic sociological drama dissects the relations between the inhabitants of a Pasolini-like Italian suburb and a Gypsy camp. The film looks at the teenage love between a Roman boy and a Gypsy girl and at the problematical relationship between the Gypsy community and the local inhabitants. The relationship between the "Gadjo" boy and the Gypsy girl, both rather lonely and unworldly, gives rise to hatred and eventually a savage bloodletting between the two very different groups.

12. The film is inspired by the story of Jerry Maslo, killed in 1989 in Villa Litorno, a small city near Naples. Jerry Maslo was a political refugee from South Africa and a day worker, a tomato picker. He acted for the rights of hundreds of immigrant African workers who were exploited by the feudal agricultural system of southern Italy. His death was never explained, but he became the first case of racist hatred in Italy that attracted national and international media attention.

13. In real life Princesa passes from her naive hope of saving enough money for her sex operation to the increasing squalor and hardship of prostitution and drug addiction. She catches "the disease" and ends up in prison, where she will write her autobiographical account and commit suicide before the film's end.

WORKS CITED

Allen, Beverly, and Mary Russo (eds.), *Revisioning Italy: National Identity and Global Culture*. Minneapolis, University of Minnesota Press, 1997.

Augé, Marc, *Non-Places: Introduction to an Anthropology of Supermodernity*. London, Verso, 1995.

Ben-Ghiat, Ruth, *Fascist Modernities: Italy, 1922–1945*. Berkeley, University of California Press, 2001.

Braidotti, Rosi, *Nomadic Subjects: Embodiment and Sexual Difference in Contemporary Feminist Theory*. New York, Columbia University Press, 1994.

Brinkler-Gabler, Gisela, and Sidonie Smith, *Writing New Identities: Gender, Nation and Immigration in the New Europe*. Minneapolis, University of Minnesota Press, 1997.

Bruno, Giuliana, and Maria Nadotti (eds.), *Off Screen: Women and Film in Italy*. London, Routledge, 1988.

Del Lago, Alessandro, *Non persone. L'esclusione dei migranti in una società globale*. Milano, Feltrinelli, 1999.

Forgacs, David, and Robert Lumley (eds.), *Italian Cultural Studies: An Introduction*. Oxford, Oxford University Press, 1996.

Gabaccia, Donna R., *Italy's Many Diasporas*. London, UCL Press, 2000.

Ginsborg, Paul, *Italy and Its Discontent, 1980–2001: Family, Civil Society, State*. London, Penguin, 2003.

Gundle, Stephen, "Feminine Beauty, National Identity and Political Conflict in Postwar Italy, 1945–54." *Contemporary European History*. 8:3 (1999), 359–78.

Kaplan, Ann E., *Looking for the Other: Feminism, Film and the Imperial Gaze*, New York, Routledge, 1997.

Landy, Marcia, *Italian Film*. Cambridge, Cambridge University Press, 2000.

Naficy, Hamid, *An Accented Cinema: Exilic and Diasporic Filmmaking*. Princeton, N.J., Princeton University Press, 2001.

Ponzanesi, Sandra, *Paradoxes of Postcolonial Culture: Contemporary Women Writers of the Indian and Afro-Italian Diaspora*. Albany, N.Y., SUNY Press, 2004.

Reich, Jacqueline, and Piero Garofalo (eds.), *Re-viewing Fascism: Italian Cinema, 1922–1943*. Bloomington, Indiana University Press, 2002.

Shohat, Ella, and Robert Stam, *Unthinking Eurocentrism: Multiculturalism and the Media*. London, Routledge, 1994.

Index of Terms

adaptation, 156, 243, 251, 272
agency, 72, 74, 184, 233, 244, 245, 246
ambivalence, 16, 144, 145, 243, 246
assimilation/ism, 5, 14, 83, 94, 95, 96,
    98, 99, 111, 140, 145, 190, 198, 207,
    208, 260, 273, 277
asylum seekers, 26, 55, 85

Beur/s, 14, 25, 43, 210, 215
black/blackness, 13, 15, 16, 22–24, 32,
    36, 40–42, 47, 66, 76, 91, 96–101,
    107–8, 119, 163, 165, 175, 186–87,
    236, 238, 201, 207, 208, 210, 215,
    230, 232, 236, 238, 242, 243, 245,
    251, 261–65, 270, 272, 273, 274
body, 13, 56, 59, 60, 62, 67, 112, 114, 134,
    195, 201, 236; colonial body, 74, 261;
    female body, 158, 276; racial body, 87
border/line, 4, 6, 9, 11, 14, 17, 20, 25,
    32, 46, 55, 56, 59, 60, 61, 64, 74, 76,
    89, 104, 121, 138, 144, 146, 167, 199,
    237, 276, 278

canon: literary, 1, 23, 28, 30, 117, 166,
    198, 199, 219, 240, 255; mainstream,
    4; national, 4, 8, 28

cinema, 14, 15, 16, 17, 163, 213, 214,
    240, 250, 259, 267, 268, 269, 270,
    277–80
citizenship, 3, 26, 39, 58, 86, 98, 105,
    107, 139, 250, 263
civilizing/mission, 2, 32, 89, 123, 260
colonial discourse, 14, 135, 175, 240,
    243, 248
community, 21, 29, 30, 38, 42, 59, 85, 94,
    103–5, 108, 149, 154–62, 171, 173,
    178, 184, 201, 209, 215, 218–24, 226,
    228, 230, 233, 272, 273, 275, 276, 279
consumption, 14, 62, 208, 223
cosmopolitan/ism, 2, 3, 8, 28, 69, 82,
    118, 119
Creolization, 31, 115, 234

darkness, 16, 35, 41, 59, 124, 125, 235,
    254, 263
decolonization, 15, 22, 23, 30, 44, 73,
    119, 210, 240, 266
deconstruction, 13, 177, 179, 180, 243
deterritorialization, 4, 174, 270
diaspora, 13, 16, 43, 45, 75, 104, 107,
    174, 177, 201, 211, 224, 225, 266,
    278, 280

memory, 3, 14–16, 26, 41, 59, 63, 81, 88, 113, 131, 134, 137, 182, 197, 200, 201, 232, 239, 240–43, 247–49, 250, 251, 269

metaphor, 3, 15, 25, 41, 59, 60, 62, 65, 177, 182, 183, 197, 199, 271

metropolitan, 1, 2, 6, 7, 8, 10, 21, 22, 95, 116, 123, 199

modernity, 6, 7, 10, 42, 66, 76, 86, 103, 107, 124, 125, 127, 128, 133, 134, 135, 143, 146, 148, 171, 183, 187, 215, 245, 269, 273

multicultural/ism, 5, 15, 16, 17, 23, 26, 29, 34, 42, 75, 92–99, 101–9, 128, 130, 142, 147, 149, 167, 168, 169, 172, 205, 211, 215, 218, 230, 233, 248, 273, 280.

multinational/ism, 7, 11, 74, 92, 115, 207, 214

music, 14, 38, 61, 208, 212–14, 219, 220, 222, 223, 259, 260

myth, 5, 8, 9, 26, 55, 58, 61, 62, 63, 70, 72, 76, 82, 83, 124, 139, 140, 145, 162, 173, 175, 184, 218, 227, 240, 249, 250, 255, 269

nomad/ic, 2, 3, 16, 61, 152, 153, 156, 157, 160, 161, 163, 193, 197, 270, 273, 280

Oriental/ism, 6, 12, 14, 24, 32, 135, 162, 175

Otherness, 4, 7, 8, 10, 80, 82, 83, 115, 119, 130, 146, 152, 155, 161, 190

postmodern/ism, 11, 12, 14, 26, 104, 117, 132, 133, 134, 143, 146, 148, 149, 151, 152, 153, 157, 177, 178, 179, 181, 184, 185, 190, 245, 269

race, 10, 11, 13, 15, 23, 41, 42, 44, 45, 55, 64, 80, 81–87, 89, 90, 92–94, 96, 98, 99, 106, 107, 108, 115, 128, 130, 166, 167, 168, 173, 175, 178, 182, 186, 191, 232, 235, 239, 242, 244, 245, 246, 248, 250, 251, 256, 257, 258, 261, 265, 266

racism, 3, 7, 10, 16, 23, 79–91, 93, 95, 96–99, 104–9, 147, 148, 168, 231, 232, 233, 237, 240, 251, 264, 265, 275, 277

refugee, 9, 26, 28, 29, 30, 73, 75, 77, 81, 82, 85, 88, 103, 148, 194, 201, 279

Renaissance, 9, 56, 68, 124, 127, 254, 255, 262, 266; Harlem Renaissance, 24

representation, 1, 2, 8, 9–11, 15, 17, 21, 42, 97, 98, 112, 123, 148, 178, 179, 181, 199, 218, 237, 238, 239, 241, 242, 245, 246, 251, 255, 259, 262, 263, 267, 269, 270, 278

resistance, 13, 15, 19, 44, 67, 133, 146, 178, 211, 214, 232, 237, 260

sex trafficking, 7, 16, 268

sexuality, 42, 45, 245, 251; interracial, 106, 241, 242, 244, 245, 251, 260; miscegenation, 33, 260; transgender, 17; transracial, 98, 99, 101

silence, 13, 45, 47, 86, 89, 125, 153, 162, 171

sovereignity, 2, 13, 23

stranger, 5, 9, 11, 44, 85, 86, 90, 93, 123, 130, 135, 137, 138, 141, 142, 143–48, 149, 151, 154, 163, 185

Subaltern, 135, 244

Third Space, 6, 7, 162, 273

traffic, 3, 16, 103, 214, 215, 234, 268

transmigration, 14, 191, 189, 190, 191, 199

transnational, 3, 8, 15, 24, 43, 44, 84, 103, 108, 109, 170, 177, 178, 190, 194, 199, 208, 214, 219, 220, 221, 224–27

trauma, 16, 158, 171, 210, 240

travel writing, 9, 13, 67, 68, 71, 72, 123, 134, 135, 165, 171, 175, 251

ultra-nationalism, 10

universalism, 6, 17, 112, 114, 115, 118, 119, 260

Index of Names

285

About the Editors and Contributors

Daniela Merolla is Researcher and Lecturer of African Literatures, Department of African Languages and Cultures at Leiden University. Her work engages anthropological and literary approaches of gender, ethnicity, and narrativity in African literatures and in migrant narrative productions. She is the author of *Gender and Community in the Kabyle Literary Space: Cultural Strategies in the Oral and in the Written* (1996) and coauthor with Mena Lafkioui of *Contes berbères chaouis de l'Aurès* (2002). Her publications include articles on North African literatures, minority languages, migration, and new literary spaces in Dutch literature.

Sandra Ponzanesi is Research Fellow of the Netherlands Organisation for Scientific Research and Assistant Professor of Gender and Postcolonial Studies at Utrecht University, Department of Media and Representation. She has widely published on postcolonial critique, Third World feminist theories, Italian colonialism, and visual culture. She is the author of *Paradoxes of Postcolonial Culture: Contemporary Women Writers of the Indian and Afro-Italian Diaspora* (2004). She has also contributed to the volumes *Thinking Differently: A Reader in European Women's Studies* (2002) and *Italian Cityscapes* (2003).

Angelika Bammer is Associate Professor of Humanities and Comparative Literature at Emory University in Atlanta. Her areas of interest are historical memory, national identity, European modernity, and post-Holocaust culture. Her publications include *Partial Visions: Feminism and Utopianism in the 1970s* (1991) and an edited volume *Displacements: Cultural Identities in*

Question (1994). She guest-edited the special issue *The Question of "Home"* of the cultural studies journal *New Formations* (1992) and has published essays on cultural forms of illness, feminist theory, the politics of memory, and contemporary literature. She is writing a book on the structures of historical memory within European modernity with an emphasis on the constitutive function of forgetting (*Ways of Forgetting*), and another on memory as work in memorial practices (*Memory Work*).

Rosemarie Buikema is Professor of Women's Studies in the Arts at the University of Utrecht. She is the author of *De Loden Venus* (1995), which examines the biographies of famous women written by their daughters, and is coauthor of a handbook on the politics of the representation of gender and race in popular culture, *Effectief Beeldvormen* (1999). She has coedited *Women's Studies and Culture* (1995), a handbook for women's studies in the arts, and two volumes on culture and migration in the Netherlands: *Kunsten in Beweging 1900–1980* (2003) and *Kunsten in Beweging 1980–2000* (2004).

Theo D'haen is Professor of English at Leuven University, Belgium, and at Leyden University, The Netherlands. He has published widely on modern literature in European languages, mainly with respect to (post)modernism, (post)colonialism, and crime writing. His most recent publication is *Contemporary American Crime Writing* (2001, with Hans Bertens). He has served or still serves on the boards of the International Comparative Literature Association, the International American Studies Association, and the International Association for Literary Theory. He is the editor of *Postmodern Studies* and *Textxet: Studies in Comparative Literature* and he serves as advisory editor to a number of scholarly journals in English literature, American studies, and comparative literature.

Robert Fraser is Research Reader in Literature at the Open University, UK. He taught at the Universities of Leeds and London, and at Trinity College, Cambridge, where he was Director of Studies in English. He has an international reputation as a scholar of African literatures and of writing in English, and combines an erudite knowledge of world literatures and history with a sharp questioning of aesthetic parameters. He was Literary Editor of *West Africa* magazine, and for twenty years has been a contributing editor to *Wasafiri: A Journal of Creative Writing and Literary Criticism*. Among his many books are *Ben Okri: Towards the Invisible City* (2002); *The Chameleon Poet: A Life of George Barker* (2002); *Lifting the Sentence: A Poetics of Postcolonial Fiction* (2000); and *Proust and the Victorians: The Lamp of Memory* (Macmillan, 1994).

Paul Gilroy is Professor of Sociology and African American Studies at Yale University. He has been highly influential for the redefinition of European citizenship in its interrelation with black diasporic identity. In his book, *There Ain't no Black in the Union Jack: The Cultural Politics of Race and Nation* (1987) he explores the notion of Britishness, as based on the mutual exclusion between British identity and blackness. In his more recent book *The Black Atlantic: Modernity and Double Consciousness* (1993) he offers the conceptual methaphor of black identity—a ship travelling back and forth between Africa, the Caribbean, North America and Europe, thereby exemplifying the hybrid, diasporic, and transnational character of blackness. His *Between Camps: Nations, Cultures, and the Allure of Race* (2001) is an utopian attempt to move away from the limitations of "race thinking." *Postcolonial Melancholia* (2005) adapts the concept of melancholia from its Freudian origins and applies it not to individual grief but to the social pathology of neoimperialist politics.

Stephen Gundle is Professor in Italian Cultural History at Royal Holloway, University of London. He is the author of *I comunisti italiani tra Hollywood e Mosca: la sfida della cultura di massa 1943–1991* (1995), and its English edition: *Between Hollywood and Moscow: The Italian Communists and the Challenge of Mass Culture, 1943–1991* (2000). He has authored studies and articles on contemporary Italian political parties, cultural change, and intellectual movements. He is coeditor of *The New Italian Republic: From the Fall of the Berlin Wall to Berlusconi* (1995) and is currently completing volumes on cultural consumption in Italy between the 1930s and the 1950s, feminine beauty and Italian national identity, and glamour and consumer culture.

Alec G. Hargreaves, Director of the Winthrop-King Institute for Contemporary French and Francophone Studies at Florida State University, Tallahassee, is a prominent specialist on migrant literatures and cultural formations in Europe. His recent publications include *Immigration and Identity in Beur Fiction* (1991, new edition 1997) and he is coeditor of *Racism, Ethnicity, and Politics in Contemporary Europe* (1995) and *Post-Colonial Cultures in France* (1997).

Graham Huggan is Professor of English and Chair of Commonwealth and Post-colonial Literatures at the University of Leeds, UK. His publications include *Peter Carey* (1996); *The Postcolonial Exotic: Marketing the Margins* (2001); *Tourists With Typewriters: Critical Reflections on Contemporary Travel Writing*, with Patrick Holland (2000); and *Territorial Disputes: Maps and Mapping—Strategies in Contemporary Canadian and Australian Fiction* (1994). He is currently working on a book on Australian literature, postcolonialism, and race; and is cowriting a book with Helen Tiffin on postcolonialism, animals, and the environment.

Ena Jansen is South African and lives and works in Amsterdam. She teaches Dutch literature at the Free University and is Professor of South African literature at the University of Amsterdam. Her publications include a book on Elisabeth Eybers, *Afstand en verbintenis* (1998), as well as articles on women's autobiographical writing, such as travel writing, and Boer War diaries. She has published a few articles on constructions of Eva/Krotoa in South African literature. Her inaugural lecture (2003) is available on the website www.uva.nl/onderzoek.

Tabish Khair is Associate Professor in the Department of English, University of Aarhus, Denmark. His recent books include *Where Parallel Lines Meet* (2000) and *Babu Fictions: Alienation in Contemporary Indian English Novels* (2001). His latest articles have appeared in *New Left Review, Wasafiri, Third Text, P N Review* (UK), *The Hindu, Indian Book Review*, and *Biblio: A Review of Books* (India). He edited a casebook of essays on Amitav Ghosh (2003) and published his second novel, *The Bus Stopped* (2004). He is currently coediting an anthology of Asian and African travel writing from before the twentieth century, *Other Routes* (forthcoming, 2005).

Lourdes López-Ropero is Lecturer at the University of Alicante, Spain. She received her MA in English from the University of Kansas and holds a PhD in English from the University of Santiago de Compostela, Spain. She published a volume titled *The Anglo-Caribbean Migration Novel: Writing from the Diaspora* (2004) and her articles have appeared in *World Literature Written in English, Atlantis*, and *Miscelanea*. These essays discuss the issues of diaspora, Creolization, and genre in the works of Austin Clarke, Fred D'Aguiar, Caryl Phillips, or Paule Marshall. She is now working on Robert Antoni's latest novel, *Carnival.*

John McLeod is Lecturer in English at the University of Leeds, with particular teaching and research interests in postcolonial literature. He is the author of *Beginning Postcolonialism* (2000) and *Postcolonial London: Rewriting the Metropolis* (2004). He has edited two editions of *Kunapipi: Journal of Post-Colonial Literature* (1999, 2003). His essays have appeared in *Moving Worlds, Wasafiri, Interventions*, and the *Journal of Commonwealth Literature*. In October 2001 he was visiting scholar at Barnard College, Columbia University, where he gave the annual Lucyle Hook Lectures. His forthcoming publications include *J. G. Farrell* and (as editor) *The Routledge Companion to Postcolonial Studies.*

Pamela Pattynama is the Endowed Professor for Colonial and Postcolonial Literary and Cultural History at the University of Amsterdam. She is particularly interested in the representation of gender and mixed race in Dutch (post)colonial films and literature. She also works on (self)representations in photography and life narratives of women who lived in the late colonial Indies. She has published widely on gender, identity, representation, and postcolonial memory, including: *Passages* (1992), on narrative and discursive female adolescence; "Assimilation and Masquerade: Self-constructions of Indo-Dutch Women" in *The European Journal of Women's Studies* (2002); "Secrets and Danger: Interracial Sexuality" in Louis Couperus's *The Hidden Force*; and "Dutch Colonial Culture around 1900" in *Domesticating the Empire: Race, Gender, and Family Life in French and Dutch Colonialism* (1998). She is working on a book on cultural memory and representation, specifically of the Dutch East Indies in literature, film, and life narratives.

Mineke Schipper has lectured at several universities in Europe, Africa, and the United States. She is now Professor of Intercultural Literary Studies at the University of Leiden in The Netherlands. Among her books are: *Unheard Words: Women and Literature in Africa, Asia, and Latin America* (1985); *Beyond the Boundaries: African Literature and Literary Theory* (1989); *Imagining Insiders: Africa and the Question of Belonging* (1999); and *Never Marry a Woman with Big Feet: Women in Proverbs from Around the World* (2004). She has also published two novels.

Meyda Yegenoglu is Professor of Sociology in the Department of Sociology at the Middle East Technical University in Ankara, Turkey. She has held visiting appointments at Oberlin College, Rutgers University, New York University, and University of Vienna. She specializes in Orientalism, globalization, postcolonial theory, feminist theory, and migrancy. She is the author of *Colonial Fantasies: Towards a Feminist Reading of Orientalism* (1998). She has published numerous essays in various journals and edited volumes such as *Feminist Postcolonial Theory*; *Postcolonialism, Feminism, and Religious Discourse*; *Nineteenth-Century Literature Criticism*; *New Formations*; and *Inscriptions*. Her recent articles "Liberal Multiculturalism and the Ethics of Hospitality in the Age of Globalization" (in *Postmodern Culture*) and "Cosmopolitanism and Nationalism in a Globalized World" (in *Ethnic and Racial Studies*) are part of her forthcoming book, *Hospitality, Globalization, and Migrancy*.